THE STAMP-SEALS OF ANCIENT CYPRUS

A. T. REYES

Oxford University School of Archaeology
2001

Published by
Oxford University School of Archaeology
Institute of Archaeology
Beaumont Street
Oxford

© A. T. Reyes

ISBN 0 947816 52 6

A CIP record for this book is available from the British Library

The cover photographs are by J. Boardman and R. L. Wilkins

This book is available direct from
Oxbow Books, Park End Place, Oxford, OX1 1HN
(Phone: 01865-241249; Fax: 01865-794449)

and

The David Brown Book Company
PO Box 511, Oakville, CT 06779, USA
(Phone: 860-945-9329; Fax: 860-945-9468)

and

via our website
www.oxbowbooks.com

Printed in Great Britain by
The Short Run Press
Exeter

TABLE OF CONTENTS

PREFACE

In a sense, the writing of this book began over thirty years ago, in the late 1960s, when – as their titles then were – Dr Vassos Karageorghis of the Department of Antiquities in Cyprus invited Mr John Boardman and Mr Robert Wilkins of the University of Oxford to study the seals in the collection of the Cyprus Museum in Nicosia. In April 1967, Mr Boardman flew to Larnaca to examine the objects, and a week later, Mr Wilkins followed to take their photographs. The precise dates for these events none of the principals can now remember, since they took place so long ago: the flights to and from Larnaca were on old British Comet airplanes, and, the model Twiggy had just become something of a global cultural phenomenon when the project was begun. The work, that spring, resulted in an archive consisting of notes, negatives, casts, and contact-prints that was to form the basis for a general study of Cypriot seals, and Mrs Marion Cox prepared drawings for the intended volume in Oxford. In the event, that volume never appeared, although some of the research was incorporated in subsequent books and articles on Greek gems written by John Boardman, who, as Lincoln Professor of Classical Archaeology at Oxford, maintained and regularly updated the materials on Cypriot seals, housing them in the Cast Gallery of the Ashmolean Museum, where they still reside and remain available for consultation.

In the autumn of 1986, I began a doctoral thesis at Oxford on the history and archaeology of Archaic Cyprus under the supervision of Dr P. R. S. Moorey and Professor Boardman. They suggested I make use of the archive of Cypriot seals (a suggestion then received with much relief and not a little gratitude), and in 1989, I submitted to the University a thesis with the title 'An Archaeological Study of the Impact of Foreign Cultures in Cyprus, from the eighth to the sixth centuries B. C., with particular reference to the evidence of stamp-seals'. The historical aspects of that study appeared as a book in 1994, under the mercifully more succinct title, *Archaic Cyprus*. This present volume contains the detailed work on Cypriot stamp-seals, using the material initially gathered and prepared by Professor Boardman and Mr Wilkins and drawn by Mrs Cox, together with additional material gathered and prepared by myself for the thesis, and then revised in the years after its submission.

A work of this sort, spanning – in terms of my own involvement with it – nearly fifteen years, brings with it many debts. Subventions from the British Academy, the British Council, the Dillon Fund of Groton School, the Rhodes Trust, the Social Sciences and Humanities Research Council of Canada, and, at the University of Oxford, the Craven Fund, the Graduate Studies Fund, Merton College, the Meyerstein Fund, and St Hugh's College helped me to meet the costs of travel and research. For allowing me to examine material under their care, I am grateful to the curators of the Ashmolean Museum (Oxford); the Bibliothèque Nationale (Paris); the British Museum (London); the Cyprus Museum (Nicosia) and the different regional museums of the island; the Louvre (Paris); the Medelhavsmuseet (Stockholm); and the Metropolitan Museum of Art (New York). Above all, I am pleased to acknowledge the kindness and consideration of Professor Vassos Karageorghis, Director of Antiquities in Cyprus when I began research, and his successors in that position: Dr M. Loulloupis, Dr A. Papageorghiou, Dr D. Christou, and Dr S. Hadjissavas. I am also pleased to be able to thank Dr Ino Nicolaou, then of the Cyprus Museum, who arranged, one morning, for the removal of the seals-case from its gallery-wall into a backroom, so that I could study the objects displayed inside the case in private and without frightening the tourists.

Some of the revision of this book was carried out during my tenure of the Rhys-Davids Junior Research Fellowship in Archaeology at St Hugh's College, Oxford from 1990 until 1993. For their support, I am grateful to the Fellows of the College, its current Principal, Mr D. Wood, and the previous Principal, the late Miss R. Trickett. Further revision has been carried out intermittently at Groton School, in the course of my duties there as a Classics schoolmaster, and in the periods between terms. The Headmaster, Mr W. M. Polk, kindly granted me a leave of absence for the academic year 1998–1999, when the final corrections and additions to the text were made.

Colleagues in the Classics Department and in the Faculty as a whole have been especially considerate. I am particularly grateful to Mr Warren Myers and Mrs Micheline Myers, who have dispensed much wisdom, advice, and sustenance (of all sorts) at their kitchen-table over the past six years. The detailed archaeological knowledge of Mr L. H. Sackett remains one of the School's most valuable assets, and he patiently answered my questions about the Late Bronze Age in the Aegean. Without the help and assistance of Mr Rogers Scudder as well, it is no exaggeration to say that this project would never have been completed. The Librarian, Mr Michael Tronic, helped resolve certain bibliographic issues. Among pupils who contributed time toward the repair of my computer or the completion of the more mundane tasks associated with research (viz. the gluing and pasting onto card of minute photocopies), I have to thank Mr V. Cassin, Mr B. E. K. Fuller, and Mr H. K. Powers.

In addition to family and friends, for general advice, constructive criticism, conversation on glyptic matters, and logistical support, I am grateful to Mr David Brown of Oxbow Books and Miss Juliet Choppin the typesetter, Dr D. Collon and Dr A. W. Johnston who examined the original thesis, Mrs A. Brown, Professor T. H. Carpenter, Professor J. B. Connelly, Dr J. J. Coulton, Mrs M. Cox, Dr S. Dalley, Dr E. Davis, Mrs M. Doherty, Dr M. Given, Dr E. Herrscher, Professor Dr G. Hölbl, Mrs J. Inskipp, Dr L. Lancaster, Dr G. E. Markoe, Dr P. H. Merrillees, Dr J. Smith, Mrs P. Smith, Dr V. Tatton-Brown, Dr C. Xenophontos, the staff (past and present) of the Ashmolean Library and Griffith Institute in Oxford, especially Mr D. Darwish, Dr J. Jakeman, and Dr J. Taylor, and finally, the members of the Cyprus-American Archaeological Research Institute in Nicosia, in particular, Dr S. Swiny, Director of the Institute for much of the time that I spent doing research on the island, Dr N. Serwint, his successor, Dr R. Merrillees, the current Director, and Miss V. Moustoukki, the ever-efficient Administrator. At Episkopi, Dr D. Buitron-Oliver and Dr A. Oliver allowed me to look at the scarabs and seals from Kourion prior to publication, and I am grateful to them for their generosity on that occasion and later. Dr Judith McKenzie made time to help with the preparation of the plates, a task she first undertook over a decade ago in the previous incarnation of this book as a thesis. I cannot thank her enough. None of the above is responsible for errors that remain.

My greatest debts are to Professor Sir John Boardman, Professor V. Karageorghis, and Mr R. L. Wilkins, who initiated the project, and Dr D. Collon and Dr P. R. S. Moorey, who facilitated its completion. Professor Boardman permitted me to use the material and notes he first brought together, supervised the research, and has saved me from many errors and infelicities, all with kindness and much tact. Professor Karageorghis has taken an interest in my work since I first arrived in Cyprus in 1985 and has read successive versions of the text. Mr Wilkins allowed the use of his negatives and provided many of the prints for the original thesis in 1989; these have been reproduced here. After examining the thesis in early 1990, Dr Collon followed the progress of this volume, and her unparalleled knowledge of the glyptic art of the ancient world has improved the text in every respect. Dr Moorey supervised the original research, read through and made more elegant many drafts of my writing, and has continued to instruct me in the by-roads of archaeology (as well as modern fiction and the literature of the world) over the years. I would like to thank also Professor Martha Sharp-Joukowsky and Mr Artemis Joukowsky for their support, and to the Joukowsky Family Foundation for the generosity which has made this publication possible.

A final note. The study of seals can seem obscure and esoteric even to those with some training in archaeology. I have therefore written this book bearing in mind the needs of readers with less specialised interests, that is, those who, like Lord Emsworth of Blandings Castle in P. G. Wodehouse's *Something Fresh* (1915), may imagine a scarab to be 'a kind of fish'. For such readers, diagrams of common shapes and a glossary of technical terms and words which may cause a certain confusion have been added at the back, and I trust that the more forbearing style in which the text has been written will not detract from the enjoyment or patience of those with more expertise in the subject.

A. T. R.

Oxford
St. Bartholomew's Day, August 1999

Maps

MAP 1: CYPRUS

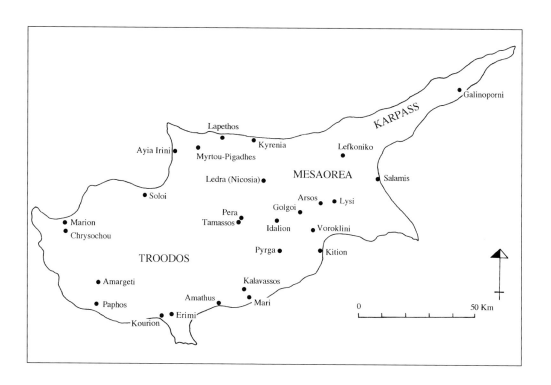

MAP 2: THE EASTERN MEDITERRANEAN

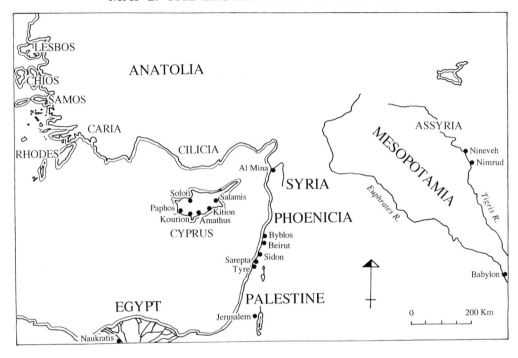

MAP 3: THE MEDITERRANEAN

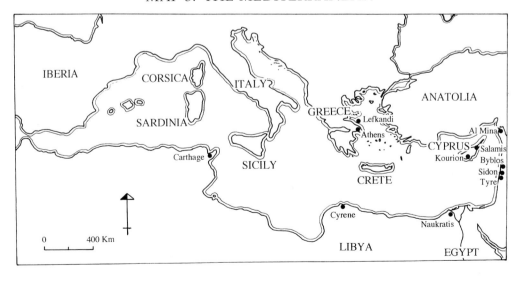

ABBREVIATIONS

Abbreviations correspond to those in *L'Année philologique*, with the following used in addition:

Beazley, *ABV*	J. D. Beazley, *Attic Black-Figured Vase Painting* (Oxford, 1956).
Boardman, *AGGems*	J. Boardman, *Archaic Greek Gems* (London, 1968).
Boardman, 'Encore'	J. Boardman, 'The Lyre-Player Group of Seals: An Encore' *AA* (1990), 1–17.
Boardman, *GGFR*	J. Boardman, *Greek Gems and Finger Rings* (London, 1970).
Boardman, *IGems*	J. Boardman, *Island Gems* (London, 1963).
Boardman, 'Seals and Amulets'	J. Boardman, 'Cypriot, Phoenician, and Greek Seals and Amulets' in V. Karageorghis *et al.*, eds., *La Nécropole d'Amathonte, Tombes 110–385*, vol. 5 (Nicosia, 1991), 159–62.
Boardman and Buchner, 'Lyre-Player'	G. Buchner and J. Boardman, 'Seals from Ischia and the Lyre-Player Group' *JdAI* 81 (1966), 1–62.
Boardman and Vollenweider, *Ashmolean Gems*	J. Boardman and M.-L. Vollenweider. *Catalogue of the Engraved Gems and Finger Rings in the Ashmolean Museum* (Oxford, 1978).
Bordreuil, *Sceaux ouest-sémitiques*	P. Bordreuil, *Catalogue des sceaux ouest-sémitiques inscrits* (Paris, 1986).
Brandt, *AGDS* 1	E. Brandt, *Antike Gemmen in deutschen Sammlungen*, vol. 1 (Munich, 1968).
Buchanan and Moorey, *Ashmolean* 3	B. Buchanan and P. R. S. Moorey, *Catalogue of Ancient Near Eastern Seals in the Ashmolean Museum*, vol. 3 (Oxford, 1988).
CAH	*Cambridge Ancient History*, new ed. (Cambridge, 1970–).

Cesnola, *Atlas*

L. P. di Cesnola, *A Descriptive Atlas of the Cesnola Collection of Cypriote Antiquities in the Metropolitan Museum of Art, New York* (Boston, 1885).

Charles, 'Pyrga'

R.-P. Charles, 'Les Scarabées égyptiens et égyptisants de Pyrga, district de Larnaca (Chypre)' *ASAE* 58 (1964), 1–34.

Clerc, 'Aegyptiaca'

G. Clerc, 'Aegyptiaca' in V. Karageorghis *et al.*, eds., *La Nécropole d'Amathonte, Tombes 110–385*, vol. 5 (Nicosia, 1991), 159–62.

Clerc, *Kition 2*

G. Clerc *et al.*, *Fouilles de Kition*, vol. 2 (Nicosia, 1976).

de Clercq

M. de Clercq, *Catalogue méthodique et raisonné: Antiquités assyriennes*, vol. 2 (Paris, 1903).

Collon, *BM Cat 3*

D. Collon, *Catalogue of the Western Asiatic Seals in the British Museum: Cylinder Seals 3: Isin-Larsa and Old Babylonian Periods* (London, 1986).

CMS

Corpus der minoischen und mykenischen Siegel (1964–).

Culican, 'Cubical Seals'

W. Culican, 'Syrian and Cypriot Cubical Seals' *Levant* 9 (1977), 162–7.

Culican, 'Iconography'

W. Culican, 'The Iconography of Some Phoenician Seals and Seal Impressions' *AJBA* 1 (1968), 50–103.

Culican, *Opera*

W. Culican, *Opera Selecta* (Göteborg, 1986).

Delaporte, *Catalogue*

L. Delaporte, *Catalogue des cylindres orientaux, cachets et pierres gravées du Musée du Louvre*, vol. 1–2 (Paris, 1920–1923).

Forgeau, *Amathonte 3*

A. Forgeau, 'Scarabées, scaraboïdes, et cônes' in R. Laffineur, ed., *Amathonte*, vol. 3 (Paris, 1986), 135–76.

Galling, 'Beschriftete Bildsiegel'

K. Galling, 'Beschriftete Bildsiegel des ersten Jahrtausends v. Chr. vornehmlich aus Syrien und Palastina' *ZDPV* 64 (1941), 121–202.

Gubel, 'Cubical Stamps'

E. Gubel, '"Syro-Cypriote" Cubical Stamps: The Phoenician Connection' *Studia Phoenicia*, vol. 5 (Leiden, 1987), 195–224.

Karageorghis, *Salamis* 2	V. Karageorghis, *Excavations in the Necropolis of Salamis*, vol. 2 (London, 1970).
Kenna, *BM Cypriote Seals*	V. E. G. Kenna, *Catalogue of the Cypriote Seals of the Bronze Age in the British Museum* (Göteborg, 1971).
LIMC	*Lexicon Iconographicum Mythologiae Classicae* (Zürich, 1981–)
Markoe, *Bowls*	G. Markoe, *Phoenician Bronze and Silver Bowls from Cyprus and the Mediterranean* (Berkeley, 1985).
Marshall, *BM Jewellery*	F. H. Marshall, *Catalogue of the Jewellery, Greek, Etruscan, and Roman in the Department of Antiquities, British Museum* (London, 1911).
Masson, *ICS*	O. Masson, *Les Inscriptions chypriotes syllabiques* (Paris, 1983).
Murray *et al.*, *Excavations*	A. S. Murray, A. H. Smith, and H. B. Walters, *Excavations in Cyprus* (London, 1900).
Myres, *HCC*	J. L. Myres, *Handbook of the Cesnola Collection of Antiquities from Cyprus* (New York, 1914).
Myres and Ohnefalsch-Richter, *CCM*	J. L. Myres and M. Ohnefalsch-Richter, *A Catalogue of the Cyprus Museum* (Oxford, 1899).
Ohnefalsch-Richter, *KBH*	M. Ohnefalsch-Richter, *Kypros, the Bible and Homer* (London, 1893).
Pauvert	E. Babelon, *Collection Pauvert de la Chapelle* (Paris, 1899).
Richter, *Engraved Gems*	G. M. A. Richter, *Engraved Gems of the Greeks and Etruscans* (London, 1968).
Rowe, *Scarabs*	A. Rowe, *A Catalogue of Egyptian Scarabs* (Cairo, 1936).
SCE	E. Gjerstad *et al.*, *The Swedish Cyprus Expedition*, vol. 1–4 (Stockholm, 1934–72).
Southesk	Carnegie, Helen, ed. *Catalogue of the Collection of Antique Gems Formed by James Ninth Earl of Southesk K. T.* (London, 1908).
Vollenweider, *Geneva* 1	M.-L. Vollenweider, *Musée d'art et d' histoire de Genève: Catalogue raisonné des sceaux, cylindres, intailles, et camées*, vol. 1 (Geneva, 1967).

Vollenweider, *Geneva* 3

M.-L. Vollenweider, *Musée d'art et d' histoire de Genève: Catalogue raisonné des sceaux, cylindres, intailles, et camées*, vol. 3 (Mainz, 1983).

Walters, *BM Gems*

H. B. Walters, *Catalogue of the Engraved Gems and Cameos, Greek, Etruscan, and Roman, in the British Museum* (London, 1926).

Young and Young, *Terracotta Figurines*

J. H. Young and S. H. Young, *The Terracotta Figurines from Kourion* (Philadelphia, 1953).

Zazoff, *AGDS* 3

P. Zazoff, ed., *Antike Gemmen in deutschen Sammlungen*, vol. 3 (Wiesbaden, 1970).

Zwierlein-Diehl, *AGDS* 2

E. Zwierlein-Diehl, *Antike Gemmen in deutschen Sammlungen*, vol. 2 (Munich, 1969).

In catalogue entries, unless otherwise stated, the following designations apply:

Berlin	Staatliche Museen Preussischer Kulturbesitz, Antikenabteilung
Boston	Museum of Fine Art
Geneva	Musée d'art et d'histoire
Larnaka	Larnaka Regional Museum
Limassol	Limassol Regional Museum
London	The British Museum
New York	The Metropolitan Museum of Art
Nicosia	The Cyprus Museum
Oxford	The Ashmolean Museum
Stockholm	The Medelhavsmuseet.

CHRONOLOGICAL TABLES

A: Absolute dates for the different archaeological periods of Cyprus. The dates are intended simply as a general guide. In the text, the term 'Archaic' is used interchangeably with the term 'Cypro-Archaic'. All dates are B. C.

Late Cypriot Bronze Age	I	1600–1450
	II	1450–1200
	III	1200–1050
Cypro-Geometric Period	I	1050–950
	II	950–850
	III	850–750
Cypro-Archaic Period	I	750–600
	II	600–475
Cypro-Classical Period	I	475–400
	II	400–325

B: Historical events within the Cypro-Archaic period.

c. 707	Cypriot kings send gifts in tribute to Sargon II.
?	Luli, a Sidonian king, stops a revolt in Kition.
701	Luli escapes to Cyprus, fleeing the Assyrian king Sennacherib.
673/2	Esarhaddon, king of Assyria, receives building materials from ten kings of Cyprus.
667	The same ten kings march with Ashurbanipal, king of Assyria, against the Nubian king Taharqa.
612	The fall of Nineveh, capital of the Assyrian Empire.
c. ?574–70	Naval engagement involving Cyprus, Phoenicia, and the Egyptian Pharaoh Apries.
c. ?570	Amasis blockades (?) Cyprus; establishment of treaty (?) relationship between Cyprus and Amasis.
568/7	Amasis defeats Nebuchadrezzar II and Apries with Cypriot help.
c. 525	Cyprus enters the Persian Empire.

INTRODUCTION

In a play produced in the fifth century B. C., the tragic poet Archaios of Eretria described a prize to be awarded at a contest:[1]

> An honour worth its weight in silver they shall give into his hands: a Cypriot gem and Egyptian ointments.

The value of the gem was probably determined by the stone from which it had been cut, rather than by its specifically Cypriot origin. As Theophrastos and Pliny, both experts in natural history, explain, Cyprus was an important source for gemstones.[2] Pliny also tells the story of a certain Ismenias, a Theban gem-collector and flautist of the fourth-century B. C., who was willing to pay six gold pieces for a gem, perhaps a green quartz, from Cyprus, cut with the figure of the nymph Amymone. He eventually acquired the stone for four gold pieces, still no doubt a great sum, but was disappointed that he could not boast about having acquired the piece at the higher price.[3] Thus, although the island's own gem-cutters may not have been unique in the Mediterranean for their expertise, there is every likelihood that glyptic craftsmanship was an important part of the local Cypriot economy, given the presence of appropriate natural resources.

Glyptics had already had a long history in Cyprus by the time Theophrastos and Pliny and even Archaios wrote. From at least the fourteenth century B. C., the island had produced seals in significant quantities in a variety of shapes and styles. This early history has been well documented, to the extent that, when one thinks of Cypriot seals today, one thinks primarily of the cylinders from the Late Bronze Age. (Fig. 1) That is a tribute to the very fine and perceptive work of the late Professor Edith Porada whose system for classifying the different styles cut on cylinder-seals has remained fundamental to the study of the island's glyptic past for over fifty years.[4] Her stylistic groups have been the foundation for all subsequent work on Cypriot cylinders (although modifications have been suggested over the years), and she went on to show the wider significance of this body of material for an understanding of artistic, administrative, religious, and funerary practices in the eastern Mediterranean, both past and present.[5]

In contrast, the stamp-seals of Cyprus, the immediate precursors of the gems to which the Greek and Roman authors allude, have been neglected as materials for study, dismissed almost as if they were, to borrow the poet Paul Celan's famous

Fig. 1. (2:1) Late Bronze Age cylinder-seal of haematite (fourteenth century B. C.) from Amathus Tomb 276, showing a bird-headed figure (T. 276/307). H. 0.018 m. The tomb dates to the end of the CAII period, however, showing that the seal somehow 'survived' after manufacture, into much later historical times.

phrase, no more than 'pebbles and scree'. But they too deserve attention for what they reveal about society at the end of the Late Bronze Age when they first appear and the subsequent Iron Age when they proliferated and moved into common use within the island. That is the purpose of this volume.

It begins by surveying briefly the history of the Cypriot stamp-seal in the Late Bronze Age and the Geometric period. Particular attention is then paid to the seventh and sixth centuries B. C., when glyptics especially flourished in Cyprus. At the Archaic sanctuary at Ayia Irini in the north-west, the Swedish Cyprus Expedition recovered over three hundred seals, the largest cache of glyptic material recovered from the island for any period.

As an initial basis for a chronology, this study takes the meagre evidence of stamp-seals recovered from controlled excavations. Certain seals are then grouped together for consideration, on the basis of what appear to be significant criteria: essentially either the shape of the object or else the styles in which the devices have been cut. When a stamp-seal may be considered within different groups, cross-referencing has been provided. As a whole, then, this volume is a general guide to a bewildering mass of material that has accrued over the years as a result of both antiquarian interest and scientific research and yet has been, for the most part, neglected or undervalued.[6]

EARLIER STUDIES

Cypriot stamp-seals were studied in the past largely for what they revealed about Greek or Near Eastern gems, rather than as part of a craft indigenous to the island and its society.[7] For the Cypriot Late Bronze Age, the pioneering works are those by Myres and Kenna, since Furtwängler's earlier classic study of ancient gems had treated Cypriot seals of the Late Bronze Age in only a peripheral way.[8] Because the ideas of Myres and Kenna had been formulated and developed when Cyprus was viewed largely as an adjunct of the Hellenic world, both men resolutely maintained the dominance of Greek elements in Cypriot stamp-seals, but recognised the possibility of interaction between Aegean, Near Eastern, and local traditions.[9] Others have followed the lead taken by Myres and Kenna, although the individual nature of the seals has, more recently, come to be better appreciated.[10]

When discussing the island's Archaic and Classical seals, older works tended to describe them as 'Graeco-Phoenician' or 'Orientalising', both terms indicative of the tendency to see these as either Hellenic or Near Eastern, rather than as objects specifically Cypriot.[11] Myres was the first to attempt a brief systematic study of the development of stamp-seals in the Iron Age, basing his work on material from the Cesnola Collection.[12] But as he himself realised, the problematic nature of the collection rendered his tentatively-advanced conclusions suspect.[13] Earlier, Furtwängler had touched briefly upon the beginnings of Cypro-Archaic glyptic, but was more interested in establishing the artistic primacy and development of purely Greek gems, viewing (not incorrectly) Cypriot stamp-seals as a separate artistic phenomenon.[14] The publication of Boardman's *Archaic Greek Gems* in 1968 and *Greek Gems and Finger-Rings* in 1970 defined more precisely the individual character of certain Cypriot stamp-seals, especially those cut from hardstones, and illuminated more clearly their relationship to Greek glyptic.

METHODS AND LIMITS

So large a body of material as the Archaic stamp-seals of Cyprus initially brings with it a corresponding sense of confusion. But certain distinctions may still be drawn within this body in order to produce an immediate sense of order. There are, for example, seals that have inscriptions additional to their devices, and those that are completely uninscribed. Some may have contexts that are votive, others non-votive. But one of the most crucial distinctions to be drawn is the one based on differences of material.

The significance of the glyptic materials and the questions that they raise are discussed in detail in Chapter 4, but a few preliminary comments are necessary here. The stamp-seals of Cyprus are cut from either hardstones, such as quartzes, or else from softer stones, generally referred to as serpentine or steatite. A significant number are fashioned from glazed materials or glass or frit.[15] There are also metal finger-rings that are used as seals.

Seals made from the harder materials and found on the island usually have devices cut in either a purely Phoenician or Greek, often East Greek, style. It is indeed likely that certain stamp-seals with devices cut in these styles were manufactured on Cyprus itself, whether by East Greek or Phoenician immigrants or else by craftsmen trained in either geographical area. But because there is generally no clear way of distinguishing a stamp-seal imported *via* East Greece or Phoenicia from one produced on the island in the same style, it seems best to concentrate on those seals identifiable as 'Cypriot' in a narrow sense.

These are the serpentine seals. They are roughly fifty percent more numerous than the hardstone seals, an indication that they are local products, rather than imports.

Often, their devices have no proper analogues or correlates to Greek or Phoenician styles, and although certain motifs may derive ultimately from Egyptian hieroglyphs, they are so far removed from these that there is no question of confusing one with the other. On the other hand, certain comparisons may be drawn between seal devices on serpentine seals and motifs that appear on other local media, in order to confirm their indigenous nature.

Furthermore, serpentines are rarely found together with hardstone seals in the same findspot, and they are largely uninscribed. These observations suggest that hardstones and serpentines represent, to a certain extent, separate archaeological phenomena. Since many hardstone materials do not occur naturally in Cyprus and have to be imported, whether already cut or in order to be cut, it is easy to assume that hardstone seals represent ancient life on a 'higher', more 'international' plane, whether they were originally owned by Cypriots, East Greeks, Phoenicians, or any of the many travellers in the Levant. Serpentines, however, represent local life at a more immediate level.

I have therefore concentrated on the serpentine seals as they are most likely to shed light on ancient Cypriot society as a whole. Metal finger-rings or those seals, mostly scarabs, made of glazed materials, glass, or blue frit, have not been ignored, but these have already been the subjects of general studies. I have, however, when appropriate, used this body of material to elaborate on the picture that emerges from the serpentine stamp-seals.[16]

Frit scarabs or scarabs of faience and other glazed materials have been excavated in significant numbers from Amathus, Ayia Irini, and Kourion and are found alongside the serpentine seals in tombs and sanctuary-sites. Indeed, when found side-by-side, these seals usually outnumber the serpentine or hardstone examples. But the faience and frit examples generally differ from the serpentines in that their devices represent either actual Egyptian hieroglyphs, or else seem closely derivative of these, whether they are imported from the Levant or cut locally.[17] On the other hand, the serpentine devices are, for the most part, so far removed from actual hieroglyphs, that there is no question of confusing the two. The faience and frit seals, furthermore, travel around the Mediterranean and Levant to an extent that cannot be demonstrated for the serpentines.[18] This suggests that it is not inappropriate, then, to treat the serpentine stamp-seals as a separate subject of enquiry, while still using patterns evident among these other types of stamps as a way of setting in relief significant cultural trends that emerge from the analysis. Similarly, I have also used the evidence of hardstone Cypriot stamp-seals as warranted.

ORGANISATION

Seals that are closely related, whether by the distinctiveness of their shapes or the styles of their devices, have been listed together, since *prima facie* it seems likely they were cut by different seal-cutters aware of each other's work or perhaps even by the same hand. Seals identified as belonging to particular groups are not listed comprehensively. The examples are representative only, and I have tried to list, for the most part, those seals whose provenances may be taken as reasonably secure and for which I have first-hand knowledge.

Brief introductions explain the criteria that determine the composition of a particular group. Within each group, stamp-seals are classified according to their provenances, as a way of establishing, if possible, styles peculiar to an area. I have tried to indicate whether the seal has been acquired through controlled excavation or antiquarian activity, but the distinction is not always clear. In the notorious case of the Kourion Treasure, it is now evident that, whatever the truth behind the tale of its acquisition by Cesnola at the end of the nineteenth century, the seals and other objects comprising the find came from that area, or at least from nearby Amathus.[19]

Each entry begins with the relevant museum accession number (when this information is available), followed by brief notes on the shape, colour, material, and known dimensions of the object. A brief description of the device follows, together with the principal bibliographic information. Devices are described as seen in impression. If no specific material is named, the seal may be understood to be 'serpentine'. When no bibliography appears, the seal is, to the best of my knowledge, unpublished. As much as is practicable has been illustrated, either by a photograph, a line-drawing, or both. Reproductions are at a scale of two to one, or, in the cases of the larger seals, one to one.

CHRONOLOGY

The necropolis at Amathus and the Iron Age sanctuary at Ayia Irini are the two sites that provide significant archaeological and chronological data for the glyptics of the Cypro-Archaic period. The sanctuary-site of Ayia Irini, overlooking Morphou Bay, was excavated by the Swedish Cyprus Expedition in November 1929. Finds recovered from clandestine excavations at a nearby necropolis were reported in 1962,[20] and an Italian team conducted further work on the necropolis from 1970 to 1974.[21]

At Ayia Irini, Gjerstad assigned the Cypro-Archaic finds from the Iron Age sanctuary to four successive periods (periods 3–6), chronologically defined as follows:[22]

> Period 3 = 'middle of CGIII...to about the middle of CA I' (*c.* 800–675 B.C.);
> Period 4 = 'middle of CAI to the beginning of CAII' (*c.* 675–600 B.C.);[23]
> Period 5 = 'the beginning of CAII to about the middle of that epoch' (*c.* 600–525 B.C.);
> Period 6 = 'the later part of CAII' (*c.* 525–500 B.C.).

But after considering the evidence provided by the German excavations at Samos, Lewe proposed a different scheme:[24]

> Period 4 = '650/640 – 600/590 v. Chr.';
> Period 5 = '600/590 – 550/540 v. Chr.';
> Period 6 = '2. Hälfte des 6. Jahrhundert v. Chr.'.

As a notional guide, Lewe's dates are probably not far wrong, as more recent excavations at Samos have suggested.[25] Her dates have been adopted here, with period 3 corresponding roughly to the first half of the seventh century.

The sanctuaries and necropoleis of Amathus have been under continual excavation by French and Cypriot teams since 1975.[26] The tombs have produced a significant number of stamp-seals. The dates given here for the tombs of the Amathus necropolis follow those summarised by Tytgat.[27]

As a whole, then, this study is intended to give some idea of a craft that, in Cyprus, achieved a certain prominence. Stamp-seals are often overlooked as evidence for the Cypriot past, in the face of the vast quantities of sculpture and pottery more readily recovered from excavations and more firmly established chronologically. But they have their own stories to tell, and it is worth looking at the ways in which they complement, expand, and even contradict what is known from other types of historical and archaeological sources. The next chapter considers the evidence for the origins of the stamp-seals on Cyprus and traces their history prior to the Archaic period.

1

BEGINNINGS AND BORROWINGS

As a result of his pioneering work on early Cypriot stamp-seals, the Revd V. E. G. Kenna concluded that the manufacture of stamp-seals on Cyprus had begun in the Early or Middle Bronze Age. At the beginning of the Late Bronze Age, however, that tradition was supplanted by the adoption of the Near Eastern cylinder-seal, and at the end of the second millennium, the local stamp-seal tradition reasserted itself.[28] Kenna never identified fully the range of seals on which he based his conclusions, but he compiled for *SCE* a list of Late Bronze Age cylinders and stamps, often giving without argument an assessment of the influences on a particular motif.[29] From this list, it is clear that his chronology for stamp-seals depended primarily on stylistic analysis, because there were – and still are – few properly excavated seals with contexts unequivocally dated to the Bronze Age or Early Iron Age. More than two decades since the publication of Kenna's last article on the subject, it is worth considering the extent to which his views still remain valid in light of recent excavations.

EARLY STAMP–SEALS?

At first sight, recent finds seem to add weight to Kenna's thesis. Dikaios had already suggested that fourth-millennium 'conical stones' and 'engraved pebbles' from the Neolithic settlement of Khirokitia were, in fact, seals, and Peltenburg identified three possible stamp-seals of the third millennium B. C. from settlements at Lemba and Mosphilia in Paphos.[30] Flourentzos has also excavated a single object of green serpentine, possibly a stamp-seal, from a Middle Bronze Age tomb at Alassa in the Limassol district.[31] But as the excavators of all these seals candidly admitted, these are crudely carved objects, with devices for the most part lacking proper stylistic analogues, and so an element of doubt must remain over their identifications as seals.[32]

At Mosphilia, the supposed seal, cut with a cross-hatched design, was recovered from a complex with a large number of cones and storage vessels (Fig. 2). Interpreted as an administrative site – a rudimentary sort of counting house – the main structure may well provide the first evidence for seal-use in Cyprus, perhaps an attempt to convey in stone what had been more often rendered in wood.[33] But there can be no certainty. Thus, even if the objects from Lemba, Mosphilia, Khirokitia, or Alassa are seals, it seems best to accept them as isolated phenomena, rather than as a part of a

Fig. 2. (2:1) A possible seal from Mosphilia, near Papnos, maae oj limesrone ana wirn a cross-hatched design (KM 597). H. 0.023 m.

more general trend within the island. There are also on Cyprus, before the Late Cypriot period, neither sealings on clay nor examples of seals stamped on pottery, such as have been found on the neighbouring mainland where they, in addition to the seals themselves, provide evidence of glyptic usage.

In essentials, then, it remains true that, when the ancient Cypriots needed to develop a system of sealing at the beginning of the Late Bronze Age, they adopted – at least in form, if not in precise function – the Near Eastern cylinder, probably because there was no firmly established local glyptic tradition at the time. On the basis of current evidence, then, Catling's laconic assessment of Cypriot glyptic history prior to the Late Bronze Age still remains accurate, although published nearly thirty years ago:

> 'Seal usage was unknown in Cyprus before the Late Cypriot period, a revealing symptom of her underdeveloped and isolated state'.[34]

Kenna also identified a number of objects that are certainly seals as typical of the Early and Middle Bronze Ages. But none of these are necessarily as early as he supposed. Many now have better Late Bronze Age parallels for their shapes and styles than were available when he wrote, and, on the basis of their excavated contexts, others may well belong to later periods.[35]

THE CYPRIOT CYLINDER

This early use of cylinder-seals in Cyprus coincided with an intensification of interaction between Cyprus and the Near East. In the late third and early second millennia B.C., there is nothing to indicate that long-distance trade involving the island was anything but negligible.[36] The emergence of a local glyptic tradition, therefore, was very likely linked to the island's increased participation in the trading networks of the Late Bronze Age, when seals were needed to identify, authorise, and guarantee consignments and transactions. But the absence of a significant number of sealing impressions in the Near Eastern manner from Cyprus itself, either on clay bullae or on clay tablets, strongly suggests that cylinder seals were also used in some manner differently on the island than on the mainland, where such materials are well attested.

The Cypriot cylinder-seals span the entire Late Bronze Age, the majority, as with the later stamp-seals, made of serpentines ranging in colour from black to a pale green and crudely cut with designs showing human figures, bucrania, ox-hide ingots, dotted circles and other motifs. Some of the darker stones have been identified scientifically as chloritite.[37] Serpentine is probably indicative of local manufacture, with raw materials derived from sources in and around the Troodos mountains serving as a major source of material.[38] Of harder stones, rock crystal and haematite are attested from the early LCIII period.[39] They may well have been carved locally, but many of these hardstones would have had to be imported into the different localities of the island in raw form.

CYPRIOT STAMP-SEALS

The earliest certain examples of local Late Bronze Age stamp-seals with datable archaeological contexts are a rectangular stamp of grey serpentine from Apliki in north-west Cyprus; a black serpentine scarab from Yeroskipou, near Paphos; and three conoid seals from Kalavassos-Ayios-Dhimitrios near Limassol.[40] All of these may be assigned on the basis of associated finds to the LCIIC period (c. 1325–1225 B.C.). The chronological consistency demonstrates that it is at this time, along the south-west coast of the island, that stamp-seals first become common within Cyprus. Found as they are in a settlement (Apliki), a necropolis (Yeroskipou), and what appear to be administrative and industrial areas (Kalavassos-Ayios-Dhimitrios), these seals support the proposition that the adoption of the stamp in preference to the cylinder affected essentially non-religious practices, perhaps those having more to do with adminis-trative procedure or personal and economic necessity.[41] As with the cylinders, the use of serpentine is probably indicative of local manufacture.

Scarabs with Egyptian or Egyptianising designs made of glazed materials are contemporary in date and most notably found at Enkomi and Kition. Objects similar to these may well have inspired the cutting of the Yeroskipou scarab, the device of which imitates Egyptian hieroglyphs. (Fig. 3) It seems reasonable to suppose that the

Fig. 3 (2:1) Black serpentine scarab from Yeroskipou, Paphos with a hieroglyphic device. L. 0.017 m. W. 0.012 m. H. 0.007 m.

Fig. 4. (2:1) Bone scarab from Toumba tou Skourou, with a lion on the device. L. 0.013 m. W. 0.010 m.

adoption of the scarab-shape into the local glyptic repertoire was stimulated, at least in part, by the use and appearance of Egyptian and Egyptianising scarabs from the Levant, a number of which were excavated alongside the serpentine seals from Kition and Enkomi.[42]

Only a solitary bone scarab from a tomb in Toumba tou Skourou (north-west Cyprus), dated by the excavator to between the LCIB and LCIIA periods (*c.* 1560–1480), presents a chronological anomaly.[43] (Fig. 4) It is not easily dismissed as an import:

'It is more usual for Hyksos scarabs to be cut in steatite or faience; perhaps, again, this is local Cypriote bone-work by someone familiar with Hyksos styles.'[44]

The manufacture of Egyptian or Canaanite scarabs in bone is rare,[45] and there was a tradition of bone-work in Late Bronze Age Cyprus.[46] But because bone scarabs are not unattested in Syria and Palestine, it is preferable to see the scarab from Toumba tou Skourou as an import, given the greater amount of archaeological evidence from elsewhere around the island in the later LCIIC period.[47]

THE CONOID

Of seal-shapes attested in Cyprus during the Late Bronze Age, the conoid is the most prolific and the most enigmatic. Archaeologically, it appears around the time spanning the end of the LCIIC period and the beginning of LCIIIA (*c.* 1300–1200 B. C.). In discussing the origins of the type, Schaeffer cited similarly shaped seals from Palestine and argued that the appearance of the conoid resulted from the presence of Sea Peoples at the end of the Late Bronze Age.[48] But a connection between Sea Peoples and conoids is not self-evident, since it need not be the case that an influx of a population into a particular area will result in new cultural phenomena. A warrior identified as a 'Philistine' appears on a well-known conoid from Enkomi, but the distinctive feathered head-dress is not a conclusive indication of origin.[49] (Fig. 5) Since conoids are not certainly attested in the Aegean, Anatolia, the Near East, or Egypt prior to their appearance in Cyprus, the shape probably represents local innovation, rather than foreign intrusion; and if that is the case, then later Near Eastern examples may reflect the influence of Cyprus, rather than the reverse.[50]

Fig. 5. (2:1) 'Philistine' warrior on a conoid seal of serpentine from Enkomi. L.0.016 m. W. 0.011 m. H. 0.013 m.

The inspiration behind the conoid shape can no longer be securely identified. Porada suggested the sizes of the oval bases were influenced by the shapes of local finger rings, and she also noted the similarity of the shape to local stone anchors.[51] The conoid may therefore have been considered an appropriate amulet on a sea-voyage, but this is no more than hypothesis.

a. (2:1) Rectangular stamp of black serpentine with a loop-handle from Ayia Irini, with a bucranium, a disc, and small animals (?) on the device (Stockholm A. I. 1119). L. 0.019 m. W. 0.018 m. H. 0.010 m. The loop originally had a central hole, but the handle was subsequently repaired by drilling two holes on either side. The seal is from period 4 of the sanctuary, but probably dates to the Late Bronze Age.

b. (2:1) Tabloid seal of black serpentine from Ayia Irini, showing a male figure, a bucranium, and dotted circles (Stockholm A. I. 2661). L. 0.012 m. W. 0.010 m. H. 0.005 m. The seal is from period 6 of the sanctuary, but was probably manufactured in the Late Bronze Age.

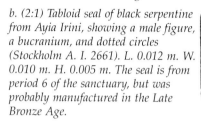

c. (2:1) Rectangular stamp with a loop handle of mottled green serpentine from Erimi, near Limassol (Nicosia 1935. v-22. 5). L. 0.013 m. W. 0.011 m. H. 0.013 m. The device shows a stylised heraldic bird within a linear border.

Fig. 6. Some Late Bronze Age Stamp-seals.

The fashion for conoids presumably followed as a result of its functional appeal. Stylistic similarities, discussed below, between devices found on cylinder-seals and conoids, as well as the subsequent predominance of the latter over the former, suggest that the conoid took over from the cylinder those functions for which a stamp was more convenient and better suited than a curved shape. The adoption of conoids and other stamp-seal shapes, such as the scarab, the rectangular stamp, or the tabloid, in preference to cylinders, was a conscious one on the part of the local population.[52] (Fig. 6a–c)

OTHER SHAPES

The popularity of the conoid should not obscure the range of shapes attested in Cyprus at the end of the Late Bronze Age. Cypriots made both practical and aesthetically pleasing seals, as well as awkward and proportionately less-pleasing ones: variety and experiment are characteristic of the time, not uniformity and conservatism. It may not be accidental that rectangular stamps whose handles are curved along the top resemble, in profile, the conoid seals.[53] If deliberate, the

Fig. 7. (2:1) Serpentine ovoid showing an animal with two figures above (Oxford 1891.643). L. 0.027 m. H. 0.014 m.

resemblance may have resulted from an attempt by local cutters to marry the 'narrative' qualities of the cylinder-seal to the new conoid shape, avoiding the more 'static' qualities of an oval frame.[54]

Distinctive Egyptian or Canaanite shapes imitated locally include scarabs, head-seals, and tabloids.[55] Levantine influence is possibly seen also in a tall, flat-topped cone from Enkomi which resembles second millennium seals from Tell Halaf and Byblos.[56] Like the seal from Enkomi, the examples from Tell Halaf and Byblos use geometric designs as motifs, but the Cypriot example lacks a stringhole and is made of black serpentine.

Buchanan assigned a 'circular ovoid' of black serpentine to Late Bronze Age Cyprus, but his criteria are not obvious.[57] (Fig. 7) The seal device appears unique in Cypriot glyptic, and although the shape finds parallels from Syria and Palestine, it cannot be closely dated. In contrast, a lentoid from Enkomi probably owes something to Mycenaean glyptic for its iconography and shape.[58] Late Bronze Age pyramidal seals have also been reported from the island, but these seem rare.[59]

USING STAMP-SEALS

No texts survive to elucidate the uses of Cypriot stamp-seals in the Late Bronze Age. If the device on a stone disc found at Hala Sultan Tekke is correctly identified and understood as the Hittite ideogram for 'scribe', an administrative purpose is suggested, but this need not be taken as primary evidence for Cypriot usage.[60] (Fig. 8) Indecipherable Cypro-Minoan signs inscribed on certain seals may also indicate administrative or commercial use,[61] but on analogy with later Cypro-Archaic stamp-seals, the inscriptions are more likely indications of ownership.

Fig. 8. (2:1) Disc seal from Hala Sultan Tekke. D. 0.012-0.014 m. H. 0.006 m.

The stamp-seals from Enkomi were found in areas largely given over to residential or industrial use. One example was found in a room that contained copper slag.[62] Another was recovered from a room that may have had a ritual function, positioned as it was adjacent to the room from which the bronze statuette of the Horned God was recovered, but this area too seems to have been part of a metallurgical complex over which the divinity simply presided.[63] Stamp-seals from the acropolis at Idalion and from the necropolis of Bamboula at Kourion equally suggest purposes that are more personal and administrative than religious and devotional.[64] Seals from a sanctuary at Ayios Iakovos indicate some votive usage, however.[65]

Metal settings and stringholes show that the seals were carried and displayed, some perhaps serving as charms and amulets.[66] Pendants worn by the bronze Ingot Goddess and similar statuettes may be taken to be seals, but their appearances are too non-descript to judge.[67] A conoid from Idalion is made of lead and may have functioned as a weight, as well as a seal.[68]

Current evidence suggests that, in the Late Bronze Age, Cypriots wrote on clay, following the Mesopotamian pattern, although no locally sealed clay tablet is yet known from the island. When the cylinder, ideal for this medium, was adopted from the Near East in the second quarter of the second millennium, cylinder-seals were rolled around the shoulders of pottery vessels, presumably as decoration.[69] In the Levant, stamps when used as seals, rather than as amulets or charms or ornamental devices, served to endorse clay sealings on papyrus or skin rolls, or clay tags fixed on bales and other consignments of goods, and stamp-seals were also impressed onto jar handles. None of this is as yet evident in Late Bronze Age Cyprus to any significant degree, however.[70] Still, on present evidence, Cypriot seal-usage wrould seem to be consonant with usage elsewhere in the Near East, Egypt, and the Aegean, where sealings suggest the particular importance of seals as administrative tools for accounting, filing, storing, and authenticating, with subsidiary use as talismans and votives.[71]

LOCAL TRADITION AND FOREIGN INFLUENCE

Kenna argued that the devices of the Cypriot conoids reflected Aegean influence not only in their subjects, but also in their styles.[72] This conclusion underestimates the extent to which local or Near Eastern motifs were used as devices. Certain common motifs – archers, date-palms, heraldic eagles, or processional scenes, for example – derive from the iconographic tradition of cylinder-seals largely, as noted above, of Near Eastern inspiration. Furthermore, many motifs on conoids and other stamp-seals are too summary for comparisons to be made with contemporary artistic traditions and are best considered local, without any conclusions being drawn about Aegean or Near Eastern inspiration. Certain bird-motifs may indicate Cretan influence, but others are without Aegean parallels.[73] Of monsters and composite creatures illustrated, a sphinx shown on a black serpentine scarab from Kition is not Mycenaean in style, although the demon on a Berlin conoid is the well-known Minoan genius

Fig. 9. (2:1) Serpentine conoid showing a Minoan genius, a pitcher in front (FG53). L. 0.024 m. W. 0.019 m. H. 0.019 m.

who had already appeared on Cypriot cylinders and bronze vessels.[74] (Fig. 9) The Cypriot griffin has also been seen as a peculiar amalgam of Syrian or North Syrian elements, only influenced to a secondary degree by Aegean art.[75]

Some Aegean influence cannot be denied, and certainly, Minoan and Mycenaean seals imported into Cyprus potentially served as sources of inspiration.[76] Kenna argued that individual animal studies, scenes showing animal attacks, and depictions of warriors best exemplified the Aegean tradition. Such influence on depictions of lions, bulls, deer, and other animals is clear, but the issue is not always straightforward.[77] Seals from Enkomi and elsewhere showing crudely cut, unidentifiable quadrupeds are stylistically distinguished from their more realistic and natural counterparts in the Aegean tradition. (Fig. 10a–g)

In other seals, objects intrude to suggest clearly non-Aegean inspiration. A bird occasionally perches on the back of a quadruped,[78] a motif that may be traced back to the fourth millennium in the Near East.[79] (Fig. 11) In addition, the warrior seals which Kenna thought representative of a Mycenaean tradition are not a homogeneous group, and their ultimate origins remain unclear.[80]

Fig. 10. Animals on Late Bronze Age Seals (a–b)

a. (2:1) Deer on a device from a conoid found at Idalion (acropolis sanctuary, Idalion 885). L. 0.017 m. The seal is from a context dating to the LCIII period.

b. Crudely cut quadrupeds on serpentine conoid seals from Enkomi. Dimensions (from left to right): L. 0.014 m. W. 0.010 m. H. 0.013 m.; L. 0.016 m. W. 0.011 m. H. 0.013 m.; L. 0.018 m. W. 0.013 m. H. 0.016 m.; L. 0.016 m. W. 0.012 m. H. 0.011 m.

c. (2:1) Crude quadruped on a conoid seal (Oxford 1891. 642). L. 0.019 m. W. 0.017 m. H. 0.018 m.

d. (2:1) A stag, on a conoid seal (Oxford 1968. 1521). L. 0.018 m. W. 0.015 m. H. 0.015 m.

e. (2:1) An animal attack (?), on a conoid seal (Oxford 1891. 625). L. 0.016 m. W. 0.012 m. H. 0.016 m.

f. (2:1) A bucranium with an animal nibbling a tree, on a conoid seal (Oxford 1889. 276). L. 0.015 m. W. 0.012 m. H. 0.014 m.

g. (2:1) A bull (?) beside a tree. The seal-shape is lentoid, a shape typical of the Greek world in the Late Bronze Age, although the device itself is carved in the local idiom. L. 0.015 m. W. 0.014 m. H. 0.007 m.

Fig. 11. (2:1) A bird perched on the back of a quadruped, used as a device on a conoid. L. 0.017 m. W. 0.014 m. H. 0.016 m.

Fig. 10. Animals on Late Bronze Age Seals (c–g)

SHARED STYLES

The small size of a seal means that, as an object, it is readily transported. Seals, both cylinders and stamps, thus become particularly sensitive indicators of contact, however defined, between different areas of Cyprus and the Mediterranean. Stamp-seals from different sites may thus be grouped together and compared as a way of identifying areas in contact with each other during the Late Cypriot period. To describe these groupings as 'workshops' may perhaps go beyond current evidence, but no doubt within Cyprus, there were specialist craftsmen in particular areas with their own distinctive seal-cutting styles.[81]

Fig. 12. (2:1) The Egyptianising linear style on a serpentine tabloid seal, unprovenanced (Geneva 20453). L. 0.027 m. W. 0.012 m. H. 0.007 m.

The Egyptianising Linear Style

Schaeffer was the first to identify a group with devices cut in what has been called the 'Egyptianising Linear Style'. (Fig. 12) It favours, as subjects, archers or figures in procession wearing long, striated robes.[82] Over fifteen examples of cylinders have survived at Enkomi, and the style was also extensively used for the devices of stamp-seals. Comparable cylinder-seals have been found at Kourion, Idalion, Hala Sultan Tekke, and the Levant, while examples of stamp-seals in this style are known from Enkomi, Kourion, and Idalion.[83]

Date-Palms

Stamp-seals and cylinders also share the motif of a particular type of date-palm, consisting of fronds curving outward or inward on either side of a stem made up of circles, with leaves emanating like an aura from the top.[84] (Fig. 13a–e) Often, the cylinders will show the date-palm flanked by two griffins. Ohnefalsch-Richter recorded two tabloid seals with this type of date-palm as probably coming from the Salamis area and noted similarities to cylinders with the same provenance.[85] Another black serpentine tabloid from Amathus shows a similar date-palm on one side with a running goat on the other.[86] Known provenances for this group of seals seem mostly confined to the south and central regions, although an example of a cylinder is known from Myrtou-Pigadhes in the north.[87] In the south, provenances include Kourion, Amathus, Arpera (Larnaka region), Ayia Paraskevi (near Idalion) and Khafkalia (near Idalion).[88]

Fig. 13. Date-palms on serpentine tabloid seals of the Late Bronze Age (a–b)

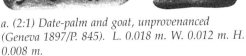

a. (2:1) Date-palm and goat, unprovenanced (Geneva 1897/P. 845). L. 0.018 m. W. 0.012 m. H. 0.008 m.

b. (2:1) Date-palm and striding figure, unprovenanced (Oxford 1968. 1288). L. 0.019 m. W. 0.012 m. H. 0.008 m.

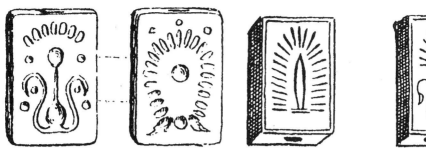

c. (2:1) Date-palm and floral design (where-abouts uncertain). L. 'five-eighths and one-half inches'.

d. (2:1) Date-palm and floral design (where-abouts uncertain). L. 'five-eighths inches'.

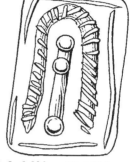

e. Date-palm and goat (Nicosia E. 50). L. 0.020 m. W. 0.015 m.

Fig. 13. *Date-palms on serpentine tabloid seals of the Late Bronze Age (c–e)*

The Aegeanising Style

The third of the styles shared between stamp-seals and later Cypriot cylinder-seals is one dependent on Aegean prototypes and consisting largely of naturalistic animal studies.[89] (Fig. 14a–c) Seals using this animal-style include examples from Enkomi, Idalion, Kourion, and Ayios Dhimitrios (Limassol area).[90]

These are the most readily distinguished connections. Other, more tentative, ones may also be noted. Enkomi produced a series of rectangular stamps with handles comparable to one found in Karamallos, near Apliki in north-west Cyprus.[91] A Late Cypriot rectangular stamp-seal from Kition resembles in shape two examples from Enkomi.[92] A bird with an upraised wing used as the device of another rectangular stamp-seal from Enkomi may be compared to the bird-motif on a grey serpentine conoid from Bamboula at Kourion.[93] The heraldic eagle on a conoid seal and, more impressively, on a rectangular stamp from Enkomi, appears on cylinder-seals found in Nicosia, Kourion, and Amathus.[94]

What stylistic evidence there is, then, suggests contacts in the Late Bronze Age between the east around Enkomi and the central inland region around Idalion and further along the south coast until Kourion. The north especially seems isolated, at

a. (2:1) A grazing bull, branches above on a serpentine conoid seal (Geneva 20440). L. 0.020 m. W.015 m. H. 0.014 m.

b. (2:1) A feline (?) animal on a serpentine conoid seal (Geneva 1897/P.854). L. 0015 m. W. 0.012 m. H. 0.012 m.

c. (not to scale) Deer resting (Idalion 643). The device is from a serpentine conoid from the Archaic levels of the acropolis sanctuary. H. 0.014 m.

Fig. 14. Animals Showing Aegean Influence.

least in glyptic terms. There is also no strong evidence linking the eastern half of Cyprus and the farthest western points of the island.

EXTERNAL RELATIONS

Connections with areas outside Cyprus may be noted briefly. A quadruped on a broken conoid of greenish stone, probably Cypriot and found at Perati in Greece, may be compared to certain of the cruder Enkomi quadrupeds.[95] An example of a seal in the Egyptianising linear style is known from Tell el-Ajjul in Gaza.[96] A cylinder-seal from Gezer has the same date-palm motif common to several Cypriot tabloids, and a conoid of dark-green serpentine, from Syria, shows a man carrying a sword, with a Cypro-Minoan sign in the field.[97] A Cypriot cylinder-seal is reported from Lachish in ancient Palestine.[98] Iconographic parallels between the stamp-seal motifs from Enkomi and the art of Ugarit underscore the well-known economic partnership between the two areas.[99]

The presence of a small number of Anatolian seals within Cyprus may also indicate some influence from Hittite lands, where a tradition of stamp-seals had long prevailed. (Fig. 15) A gold tripod-seal from Tamassos, a disc excavated at Hala Sultan Tekke, and a stalk-handled serpentine stamp-seal from Maa are undoubtedly imports and part of an Anatolian or, perhaps, North Syrian stamp-seal tradition.[100] Similarly, the appearance, at the end of the second millennium, of a small but not insignificant number of rectangular stamp-seals with handles, usually of serpentine, may have resulted from the direct influence of Anatolia or northern Syria, since there is documentary evidence for a close political relationship between Cyprus and the Hittite empire at this time.[101]

Taken as a whole, the glyptic tradition of Cyprus suggests a late entry into the economic expansion characteristic of the Mediterranean in the Late Bronze Age. With the advent of the conoid, far easier to use for Cypriot purposes than the more

Fig. 15. (2:1) Anatolian circular stamp with a stalk-like handle, probably silver, provenance unknown (Larnaka, Pierides Museum 1973). D. 0.009 m. H. 0.020 m.

cumbersome cylinder, it may be hypothesised that the island became more fully integrated into the network of contacts extending from Asia Minor and the Levant into the Aegean and beyond. But only certain parts of the island seem to be especially active participants: the east around Enkomi, and the southern areas around Amathus and Kourion. The end of the Late Bronze Age, however, brought disruptions to this network. The following chapter considers what the evidence of the stamp-seals reveals about this collapse and the subsequent state of the island in Cypro-Geometric times.

2

INTO THE IRON AGE

If it is correct to say that the Late Bronze Age glyptic tradition of Cyprus was fostered by greater interaction with its neighbours, then one should expect some sort of decline in the production and use of seals in the Cypro-Geometric period, a time of social change and breakdown in the Mediterranean and the Near East. Even if the island, as a whole, fared less badly than other areas, it should still be clear, *ex hypothesi*, from the stamp-seals that administrative and commercial exchange are not primary concerns for the local kingdoms at this time. This chapter examines the range of glyptic materials attested for the early Iron Age in Cyprus and considers whether or not such evidence reflects any changes. It also asks what may be learnt about Cypriot society in this notoriously obscure time in its history.

CHANGE AND CONTINUITY

By the end of the second millennium, the stamp-seal had – for whatever reasons – superseded the cylinder in use in Cyprus. The glyptic history of the island, as with all other areas in the eastern Mediterranean, now becomes particularly difficult to trace. A certain amount of continuity is indicated by the presence of conoids, flat-topped cones, pyramids and tabloids in Cypro-Geometric contexts, but these may well have been manufactured in the Late Bronze Age and not specifically used as seals in the subsequent Iron Age.[102] (Fig. 16a–b for examples)

They are all found in tombs, suggesting use as personal objects. Some Late Bronze Age cylinders may have been kept as personal possessions, but it is doubtful, on current evidence, that they were of significant administrative or even votive use in the Cypro-Geometric period.[103] There are no sealings and no examples recovered from sanctu-aries. On the whole, the glyptic remains do not reflect the local prosperity evident elsewhere in the material record, and excavations at the Cypro-Geometric settlements and cemeteries of Paphos and Salamis did not recover seals approaching those of the Late Bronze Age in quality.[104]

a. (2:1) Conoid seal with device showing a figure on either side of a tree, from Tomb 67 (CGI/II context). D. 0.016 m. H. 0.016 m. The material is said to be 'diorite'.

b. (2:1) Tabloid serpentine seal with devices showing a striding figure and a bull, from Tomb 85 (CGIA context). L. 0.015 m. W. 0.013 m. H. 0.065 m.

Fig. 16. Seals from Cypro-Geometric Paphos.

Blue Frit Conoids

One group of conoids made of blue frit and using Egyptianising motifs may be assigned with confidence to a glyptic centre active at this time. (Fig. 17a–h) Often, a conoid in this group will have a line incised above the base and favour, as a device, a quadruped confronting a human figure wearing a tall, conical helmet. Roughly half of the approximately two dozen known examples were recovered from a necropolis at Amathus, where this group of seals may have been at home. Other examples are known from tombs at Lapethos and Paphos and settlements in Sarepta and Tyre on the Phoenician coast. These indicate a certain amount of contact between kingdoms in the western half of the island and Phoenicia.[105] Their contexts suggest personal and private use, and although blue frit, often associated archaeologically with luxury goods, is a material not without a certain value in the ancient world, it is not likely that these seals played a significant part in the workings of the local economy, in the way that the earlier cylinders and stamp-seals had in the Late Bronze Age.[106]

a. (2:1) Conoid from a settlement at Sarepta, with device showing a man and a quadruped (Sarepta 3046 II-K.20, late LCIII-early CGII context). Approx. H. 0.016 m. Approx. D. 0.017 m.

  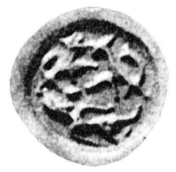

b. (2:1) Conoid with device showing two quadrupeds and a male figure from Amathus, tomb 486 (CGIII-CAI context). H. 0.014 m. D. 0.017 m.

c. (2:1) Conoid with device showing quadruped and male figure from Amathus, tomb 523 (CGI-CAI context); gold band around base. H. 0.014 m. D. 0.015 m.

 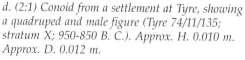 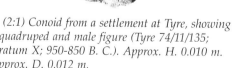 

d. (2:1) Conoid from a settlement at Tyre, showing a quadruped and male figure (Tyre 74/11/135; stratum X; 950-850 B. C.). Approx. H. 0.010 m. Approx. D. 0.012 m.

e. (2:1) Conoid of uncertain provenance with device showing quadruped and male figure (Geneva 1897/P.858). H. 0.016 m. D. 0.015 m.

Fig. 17. Some Blue Frit Conoids (a–e)

f. (2:1) Conoid reportedly from Ayios Dhimitrianos, showing two opposing quadrupeds on either side of a line (Nicosia 1948. x-26. 1). Approx. H. 0.016 m. Approx. D. 0.018 m.

g. (2:1) Conoid of uncertain provenance, showing a scorpion on either side of an animal (Nicosia E. 27). Approx. H. 0.016 m. Approx. D. 0.016 m.

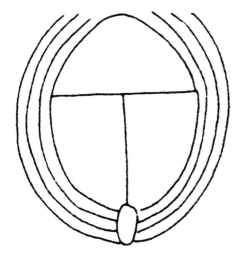

h. (2:1) Roughly conoid seal from Amathus, tomb 222 (British excavations), of green frit, but probably representing the same output as the other blue frit conoids. The device shows an animal with a branch (?) above. The markings on the top of the cone may have been intended to represent the parts of a scarab (London 1894. 11-1. 378). L. 0.022 m. W. 0.018 m. H. 0.013 m.

Fig. 17. Some Blue Frit Conoids (f–h)

Limestone Stamp-Seals

As in Greece, stamp-seals may also have been manufactured out of perishable materials such as wood.[107] There is some evidence too for seals made of limestone at this time. In the Cypro-Archaic period, limestone is unusual, and it therefore seems likely that seals made of this material are chronologically early. Two conical limestone seals with flat tops and crude devices were found in tomb 1 at Salamis dated to the eleventh century, and these may be related to a LCIIB limestone conical seal from Kition and other limestone conoids known from the end of the Late Cypriot period.[108]

a. (2:1) Limestone conical seal with a flat top from tomb 1 (eleventh century context). The device at the base shows a figure standing on a quadruped (Salamis 1346). L. 0.016 m. H. 0.019 m.

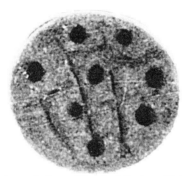

b. (2:1) Limestone conical seal with eight drill-holes irregularly positioned at the base (Salamis 5292, uncertain context, but found with pottery dating to the eleventh century). L. 0.023 m. W. 0.022 m. H. 0.021 m.

Fig. 18. Cypro-Geometric Seals from Salamis.

(Fig. 18a-b) The manufacture of limestone seals may have spanned the end of the Late Bronze Age and the Cypro-Geometric period. A pyramidal stamp-seal from Kition and a tabloid from Kyrenia may also belong here chronologically.[109] (Fig. 19a-b) Two unprovenanced limestone seals from Cyprus, one now in Nicosia, the other in Berlin, may also be noted. (Fig. 20a–b) A limestone scarab said to be from Kazaphani may represent one of the latest of the series within the Cypro-Geometric period, since its motifs and their division into separate registers suggests the influence of Iron Age Phoenicia.[110] (Fig. 21)

The presence of blue frit conoids in Tyre and Sarepta necessarily raises the possibility that the use of seals in Cyprus during the Cypro-Geometric period is, in some measure, related to the Phoenician westward expansion at this time. It is now known that the Bronze-Age trading networks of the Mycenaeans and Canaanites were very quickly

a. Pyramidal stamp-seal from Kition with zigzag patterns on the side and base (Nicosia 1939. x-3. 1). L. 0.031 m. W. 0.025 m. H. 0.040 m.

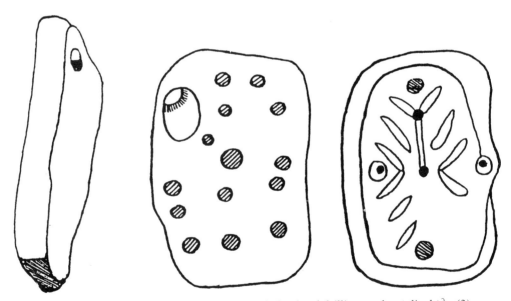

b. Tabloid from Kyrenia (Lamboussa area), with irregularly placed drillings and a stylised tree (?) (Nicosia 1934. v-14. 2). L. 0.080 m. W. 0.041 m. H. 0.015 m.

Fig. 19. More Limestone Seals

a. (2:1) Conical seal with flat top. The device at the top shows a cross with a short line in one quadrant. At the bottom is a central line with two short lines and two drillings in either half (Nicosia 1948. ii-20. 3). L. 0.025 m. H. 0.032 m.

b. Conical seal with a flat top. The device at the top shows a quadruped. The base shows two quadrupeds (Berlin FG 67). L. 0.030 m. W. 0.025 m.

Fig. 20. Unprovenanced Limestone Seals.

taken up by Euboians and Phoenicians in the Iron Age, certainly by the eleventh century B. C, and it is precisely in those areas in which the blue frit conoids are found that Phoenician activity is first detected in Cyprus.[111] The western and northern parts of the island now emerge as glyptic entities in contact with the Near East, notably the area around Tyre, with sites closer to Enkomi no longer much in evidence. The same quadruped trampling a human figure, so often used as a device for the blue frit conoids, is also found at Lefkandi in Euboia on a faience head-seal, a shape particularly associated in the Archaic period with Kourion and Amathus. Thus, there are hints and intimations that Cypro-Geometric glyptic activity in Cyprus may be associated with Iron Age trade between the Levant and the Aegean, much as earlier activity had been associated with Bronze-Age economics and administration.

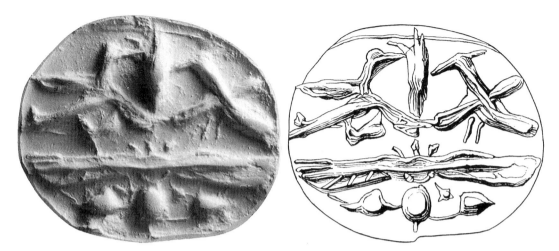

Fig. 21. (2:1) Limestone scarab from Kazaphani (Mines area), near Kyrenia, a square with a cross-formation incised on the back (Nicosia 1937. 1-22. 6). The device is in two registers, divided by a winged disc (?). The top register shows two birds facing each other, a plant in between. The bottom shows three drillings. L. 0.035 m.

With the advent of the Cypro-Archaic period, there is a marked expanse in the use of stamp-seals. There is also a break with the Cypro-Geometric tradition and the tradition of the Late Cypriot period, since there are no certain examples of Cypro-Archaic conoids or cylinders, although examples of what are probably Late Bronze Age survivors have been found in contexts that date to later times.[112] As an archaeological phenomenon, this expansion requires explanation. The following chapters examine this problem in detail by examining the Cypriot stamp-seals of the Archaic period as an archaeological phenomenon.

3
A USER'S GUIDE

The question 'What is a Cypriot stamp-seal' assumes some knowledge of what a stamp-seal is. To begin with, it assumes an object usually no more than three centimeters long with a design cut in intaglio on at least one face or facet. It assumes also that these designs identified their respective owners and rendered the seals identifiable to others, perhaps not everyone, who saw the devices. In addition to these assumptions, certain deductions may be made concerning seal-usage on Cyprus from the appearances and find-spots of the seals themselves. This chapter considers what may be reasonably inferred from the material to hand, since no literary references specifically mention Cypriot seal-use in the Archaic period.

INSCRIPTION-SEALS

Seals in the Levant are commonly used to identify ownership or establish authority by virtue of devices that are simply inscriptions naming the owners.[113] Often, the names denoted by the inscriptions are carved retrograde on the actual seal, indicating that they were meant to be read in impression. With some exceptions, those few Cypriot seals that have inscriptions also have figural devices and are cut from hardstones. This general association between harder stones and inscriptions suggests the importance of these seals as items denoting a certain status, prestige, or authority. The same was true for the earlier cylinder-seals at Mari, for example, and for the later stamp-seals at Persepolis.[114] But there are also a small number of Cypriot serpentine seals in the Levantine fashion, with only a name inscribed as a seal-device cut in the customary serpentine stone. These may be called inscription-seals, and it is fair to conclude that, following the custom in the Near East, the names on these seals identify their owners. Statues showing votaries carrying more than one seal suggest that several seals could have identified a single owner.[115]

The Cypriot seals that simply have inscriptions as devices are listed below. None has a specific provenance within the island, but the use of the Cypro-syllabic script clearly implies a Cypriot milieu or, at the very least, the possibility of having the device read by someone familiar with the Cypro-syllabic script. Precise chronological criteria are lacking, but in view of the dating of similar seals from the Levant, the Cypriot examples are probably Archaic in date.[116] A silver finger-ring from Marion with a leaf-shaped bezel designed to be used as a seal simply has an inscription as a device and was recovered from a tomb that could be closely dated to the late Cypro-Archaic or early Cypro-Classical period.[117] (Fig. 22) It confirms to an extent the chronology suggested here for the unprovenanced inscription-seals and suggests an area within the island where such seals might have been in use. A second unprovenanced silver ring, with a double bezel and a two-line Cypro-syllabic inscription, also has affinities to this group of seals.[118] (Fig. 23) The double-bezel ring has its origins in Phoenicia.[119]

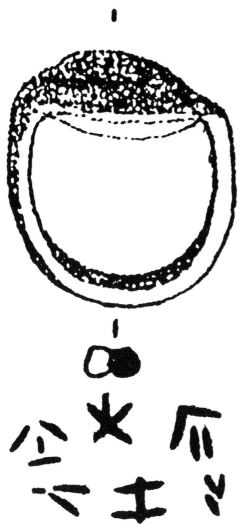

Fig. 23. (2:1) Silver ring of uncertain provenance, with a double bezel (Nicosia 1934. i-15. 1). The inscription is in two lines, with a bird at the extremity of the lower line: (1) a-ri-si-to-ka-ro-ti; (2) se (? Ἀρισταγόρα(ς)). L. 0.016 m. W. 0.011 m.

Fig. 24. Cat. 1. (2:1) Impression.

Fig. 25. Cat. 2. (2:1) Impression, drawing.

Fig. 22. (2:1) Silver ring with leaf-shaped bezel from Koilada Tomb 125, Marion, CAII-CCI context). Inscription in two registers: (1) ka-i-re; (2) [ ]-pa-[ ]. D. 0.022 m.

Fig. 26. Cat. 3. (2:1).

1. (Fig. 24) Oxford 1970. 519; scarab; green; summary beetle; carinated, gabled spine; legs not shown; L. 0.019 m. W. 0.015 m. H. 0.010 m.
   Boustrophedon (?) Cypro-syllabic inscription: pa-si-ti-mo-se (Πασίτιμος); linear border (Boardman and Vollenweider, Ashmolean Gems, 15, no. 72; Masson, ICS, 421, no. 367c; A. Brown and H. Catling, 'Additions in the Cypriot Collection in the Ashmolean Museum, Oxford, 1963–77' OpAth 13 (1980), 131, no. 107; fig. 92).
   The name is also that of a king.[120]

2. (Fig. 25) Nicosia D. 6; scarab; green; L. 0.018 m.
   Three line Cypro-syllabic inscription: (1) te-mi-si; (2) ni-o-pa; (3) pu-ki-se (?); other signs obscure; linear border (Masson, ICS, 347 and 421, no. 358).

3. (Fig. 26) Paris, Louvre AM 1187; scaraboid; grey ('marbre'); L. 0.015 m.
   Two line Cypro-syllabic inscription: (1) ti-mo-ke; (2) re-te-o-pe (Masson, ICS, 349, no. 361). (Τιμοκ/ρέτεος)

Inscribed seals suggest the common use of safeguarding property or authenticating particular transactions. Cypriots, like Greeks, usually limited their seal-inscriptions to a single name in the genitive without indication of rank or function, in contrast to the inscribed stamp-seals of Phoenicia and her neighbours and the cylinder-seals of Mesopotamia.[121] It has not been possible, therefore, to identify the seals of rulers and state officials, merchants, tradesmen, or other individuals. All of this may indicate a different administrative procedure on Cyprus than on the Near Eastern mainland.

SEALINGS AND SEAL-IMPRESSIONS

Indicative as well of administrative or economic use are the few ancient sealings and seal-impressions that have been found in Cyprus. It is possible that the general lack of sealings may be explained by the Cypriot habit of using a writing medium different from the clay tablets of Mesopotamia. But if this medium were papyrus or parchment, we should expect more sealings from this time, as in Syria and Palestine.

The method of using clay roundels to seal documents is known to have been used by Achaemenid officials during the Persian period. Such sealings are usually stylistically identifiable as Achaemenid, but local Phoenician ones are also known. Phoenician sealings have also been found in Palestinian sites in periods dating to Assyrian times, and an impression of a Lyre-Player seal in Tarsus suggests the practice was common in North Syria, where the group was at home.[122] There is no evidence for multiple-sealing systems, such as are known from Crete and Anatolia.[123]

At an Archaic sanctuary-site in Kition, excavators recovered two sealings of baked clay, one with papyrus markings at the back. Both impressions show devices cut in purely Phoenician styles and probably made by seals cut from hardstones.[124] (Fig. 27a-b) It is possible then that certain administrators and owners at Kition employed seals with Phoenician motifs, or else local administrators could have been in correspondence with people on the mainland, who employed seals with Phoenician motifs. Thus, although the contexts of neither sealing could be defined specifically, the two indicate some local commercial, administrative, or archival use. Since, however, these sealings

a. (2:1) Baked clay bulla showing Isis suckling the child Horus, from the courtyard of the Phoenician temple at Kition (Kition 516, disturbed context). L. 0.015 m. W. 0.011 m. H. 0. 006 m. b. (2:1) Baked clay sealing with a small hole and papyrus markings at the back (Kition 1072, site II, bothros 1, CAII context). The image shows a seated lion surrounded by a papyrus brake. L. 0.015 m. W. 0.014 m. H. 0.004 m.

Fig. 27. Sealings from Kition.

show typically Phoenician devices and were excavated at a Phoenician sanctuary in a Phoenician colony, they need not be taken as primary evidence for specifically Cypriot usage.

Recent excavations have recovered examples of other sealings dated to later times and related perhaps to seal-usage in the Archaic period. A number of late fourth or early third century B. C. clay sealings recovered from the palace-site at Amathus was very likely part of an archive comprising documents made of papyrus or parchment.[125] These indicate that this method of sealing documents was practised not only in Kition, but also at Amathus, and a published impression from the latter site, probably made by a hardstone seal, shows a *Kore*-figure.

At Paphos were found, as part of the debris belonging to a public administrative building, a cache of 11,334 clay sealings, some inscribed with Cypro-syllabic signs, in a context securely dated between the second half of the second century and the end of the first century B. C.[126] They tend to show divinities such as Athena, Zeus, Aphrodite, Bes, and Isis, and they all have papyrus markings on their backs. Some are archaising in style, and perhaps a dozen sealings, none inscribed, may even be authentically Archaic. If so, then there are indications here too of administrative and archival usage.

Also from Paphos is a set of clay loomweights, perhaps Cypro-Classical in date, each with a gem-impression. The loomweights (if that is what they are) were found in the remains of what appeared to be a a weaver's quarter and a metal-working area.[127] The practice of stamping such objects is unknown in Egypt but well-attested in the Near East and Aegean at all periods.[128] The impressions may represent some method of industrial organisation and may have been intended to signify ownership, origins of manufacture, or even ultimate destination. There is no reason to suppose that a similar use of gems would not have prevailed in earlier times. These impressions may be associated with 298, found in an industrial area at Kition.

VOTIVE PRACTICES

Dedications in tombs and sanctuaries point to the amuletic and votive functions of the gems.[129] From the way in which the seals at Ayia Irini were found on the ground, the excavators reasonably suggested that they had been 'hung up on the hurdle-fence of the temenos enclosure and on the wooden posts of the shelter along the temenos wall'.[130] Seals from Kition must have originated from within the precincts of the sanctuary as well, although the excavators recovered them from *bothroi*.[131] A rock-crystal scarab from Kourion, still with its metal setting, was found near the semi-circular altar of the precinct.[132] Scarabs from Pyrga, near Kition, although recovered as a hoard, very probably derived from a nearby sanctuary whose location remains undetermined as yet.[133]

These dedicatory practices represent a certain shift from those of the Late Bronze Age. At that time, there is limited evidence for votive use in sanctuaries.[134] The proliferation of glyptic dedications around altars and in temple-precincts seems characteristic of the Cypro-Archaic period.

PERSONAL ADORNMENT

The stringholes drilled through most stamp-seals and the metal-settings belonging to certain examples show that seals were threaded and suspended and carried around one's person as amulets or talismans or simply as personal jewellery. Limestone and terracotta votive sculptures of the Archaic and Classical periods represent votaries with stamp-seals worn singly or in pairs. A few statues carry more than two seals.

The carefully-carved pendants on the seventh-century sculpture from Arsos show that a length of cord was passed through the metal-settings and hung about the neck or around the waist.[135] Other votaries wore their seals diagonally across their chests like bandoliers.[136] Whether all of the seals represented on a single statue are to be construed as having been used – in whatever sense – by one individual is not known. Some may have been gifts. One thinks perhaps of Wemmick in Dickens's *Great Expectations*, and the 'several rings and seals hung at his watch-chain', carried as mementoes of old clients, looking 'as if he were quite laden with remembrances of departed friends'.[137]

In Cyprus, in general, only scarabs and scaraboids cut from hardstones have been found with elaborate metal settings, another indication of the prestige accruing to these materials.[138] Some faience scarabs may also have metal settings, but serpentine seals, in contrast, are usually found without them.[139] Cubical seal 450 and head-pendant 532 were found with metal wire passed through their stringholes, and these give some indication of the way in which serpentine scarabs and scaraboids were carried. Materials more perishable than metal wire may also have been used. A serpentine tabloid seal from Paphos from a Hellenistic tomb has been recovered with a silver pendentive setting, but the excavators report that the mounting of the seal is secondary, attached to the tabloid when it was re-cut and re-used.[140]

The gems of the Cesnola Collection in New York provide the best preserved examples of the metal settings for hardstone seals. Settings are usually of gold, silver, or bronze. Hoop, ring mount, and pendant attachment are not always of the same metal. There are four types commonly found:[141]

(a) The least elaborate uses a thin metal band as a hoop; wire is then twisted around one end of the band, passed through the stringhole, and twisted around the other end (e.g., 277).[142]

(b) Occasionally, the ring is mounted in a box setting decorated with filigree along the sides. The ends of the hoop are then inserted into attachments at the sides of the mount (e. g., 393 for the box setting).[143]

(c) A more common setting uses a crescent-shaped metal hoop slightly thickened at the centre. The ends are inserted into swivel attachments at the side of a plain metal mount,[144] although occasionally, the ends may be inserted directly into the stringhole of the gem (e. g., 225, 226, 227, 228, 229, 242, 292, 294, 300, 304, 354).[145]

(d) Finally, the gem may be set in a plain mount and attached to a heavy metal hoop, bowed at the centre and with a distinct pendant attachment soldered on (248, 289).[146]

These Cypriot settings differ from the contemporary ones in Anatolia and the Punic world, but are closely related to types known from Phoenicia.[147]

Head-seals and Head-Pendants

Head-pendants, that is, serpentine beads cut in the shape of a head, reflect another way in which one particular type of seal, the Cypriot head-seal might have been worn as jewellery. A head-seal resembles a scarab in size, but instead of having a back carved with the markings of a beetle, it is carved in the shape of a head.

Examples of head-pendants with tomb-contexts dating to the late CAI period are known from Amathus and imitate, in local idiom, faience pendants known from Phoenicia.[148] The head-pendants from Amathus are peculiar to the area, showing a roughly triangular face with the hair deeply furrowed and a long, pointed beard, usually covered with cross-hatching.[149] (Fig. 28a–c) A stringhole appears above the ears. There are similar heads

a. (2:1) Serpentine pendant from tomb 550 at Amathus (T. 550/70). H. 0.022 m.
b. (2:1) Ivory pendant from tomb 542 at Amathus. H. 0.031 m.

Fig. 28. Head-Pendants from Amathus. (a–b)

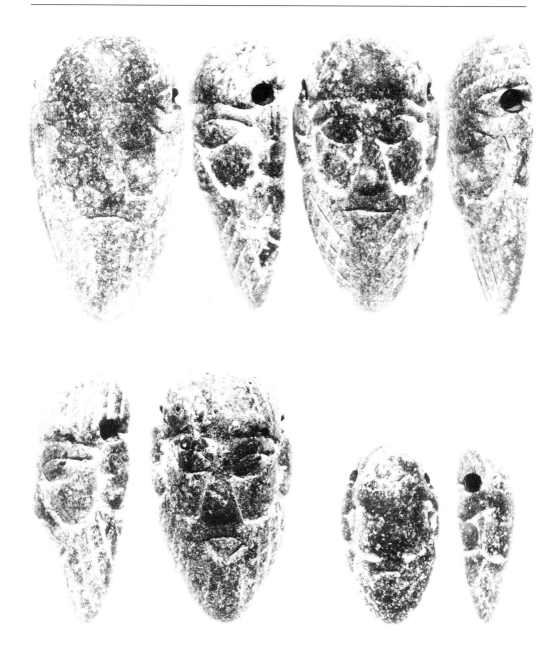

Fig. 28. Head-Pendants from Amathus. c. (2:1) Serpentine head-pendants possibly belonging to one necklace, from Tomb 297 (T. 297/810.4-7; CAII context). Dimensions (from top row, left to right): L. 0.038 m. W. 0.021 m. H. 0.010 m.; L. 0.037 m. W. 0.020 m. H. 0.010 m.; L. 0.034 m. W. 0.020 m. H. 0.010 m.; L. 0.024 m. W. 0.014 m. H. 0.007 m.

made of terracotta from the same area.[150] At Amathus, a series of four such head-pendants in diminishing size was recovered from a CAII tomb, 'apparently part of a necklace with shells and a faience *uzat*-eye'.[151] Since head-pendants and head-seals are clearly related archaeological phenomena, it is likely that head-seals were strung and worn in a similar way.

Stamp-seals in the shape of heads are well-known from the Near East and Aegean.[152] Some are clearly negroid in their features.[153] The shape derives from similar seals of glazed materials long manufactured in Egypt and the Levant.[154] A black serpentine example with a Late Bronze Age context is known from Enkomi, and it is apparent that the type became current again in Cyprus during the Archaic period, if it ever fell away entirely from use.[155] Evidence for continuity has not been found, but a head-seal of faience is known from a tomb at Lefkandi in Euboia with a Cypro-Geometric context.[156] All examples of head-seals are of serpentine, but head-pendants were also manufactured in ivory.[157]

In Cyprus, head-pendants and head-seals are especially at home in the area around Amathus and Kourion, where the largest number of examples have been recovered. It is therefore tempting to associate the example found at Lefkandi, significantly with the device common among the Cypro-Geometric blue frit conoids of a quadruped trampling a human figure with contact from this particular area of Cyprus.[158] Consequently, the head-seal and head-pendant attested at Pyrga (7) and Idalion (532) also suggest contact with this area.[159] Head-pendants from Ayia Irini (530, 531) and Salamis (534) seem to represent a different tradition and need not suggest contact.

The Cypriot head-seals are listed below.[160] Two types of heads are especially characteristic, aside from the Amathus-head discussed above. These are a round face, with cross-hatching for the hair, and the negroid head. Motifs used are common to other serpentine seals, but the often fine workmanship of the carved heads stands in contrast to the summariness of the devices. This suggests that some motifs are secondary additions, perhaps with the devices cut after the initial acquisition of the blank seal. The heads of 5, 9, and 10 are very similar and may belong together.[161]

Amathus

4. (Fig. 29) Nicosia (Amathus 242/76; tomb; late CAI – early CAII); black; hair indicated by dotted circles; pointed chin; negroid features; L. 0.013 m. W. 0.010 m.
    Winged uraeus (?) (V. Karageorghis, *Blacks in Ancient Cypriot Art* (Houston, 1988), 19, no. 11; Clerc, 'Aegyptiaca', 25).

5. (Fig. 30) Nicosia (Amathus 236/60; tomb; CAII-CCI); black; head with single line across the crown; hair indicated by squares radiating ouward from crown; negroid features; L. 0.013 m. W. 0.013 m.
    Quadruped (V. Karageorghis, *Blacks in Ancient Cypriot Art* (Houston, 1988), 18–9, no. 10; Clerc, 'Aegyptiaca', 19–20).

Kourion

The head is shown with large eyes and broad eyebrows; hair is indicated by cross-hatching.

Fig. 29. Cat. 4. (2:1) Seal, original, impression.

Fig. 30. Cat. 5. (2:1) Seal, original, impression.

Fig. 31. Cat. 6. (2:1) Seal, original.

6. (Fig. 31) New York 74. 51. 4393; black; head with large eyes and broad eyebrows; hair indicated by cross-hatching; L. 0.018 m.
Horse-Group motif (V. Karageorghis, *Blacks in Ancient Cypriot Art* (Houston, 1988), 17, no. 7).

In the Iron-Age Levant, a group of head-seals was current using as a device the 'Horse-Group' motif, showing a galloping horse with animals and other filling motifs above and below.[162] (Fig. 32a–b)

Pyrga
7. Larnaka (once Nicosia 1960. xi-21. 26); black; cross-hatching to represent hair; L. 0.010 m. Striding griffin wearing aprown shown by cross-hatching in front; line overhead (? intended as disc); linear border.

Provenances unknown
8. (Fig. 33) Oxford 1891. 624; black; hair indicated by dotted circles; pointed chin; negroid features; stringhole through ears; finely carved; L. 0.013 m. W. 0.011 m. H. 0.009 m.
    Deer, with head turned back, attacked by lion from behind; lion's paw on back back of deer; hatched border (Buchanan and Moorey, *Ashmolean* 3, 83, no. 568; pl. 18).

9. (Fig. 34) London 311 (1899. 11–10. 1); black; L. 0.013 m. W. 0.012 m.
    Bird in heraldic pose; object on either side (V. Karageorghis, *Blacks in Ancient Cypriot Art* (Houston, 1988), 39–40, no. 31).

Fig. 32. Levantine Head-Seals with Horse-Group Devices.

a. (2:1) Seal purchased in Beirut of black serpentine (Oxford 1914. 59). L. 0.017 m. W. 0.013 m. H. 011 m.

b. (2:1) Black serpentine seal of uncertain provenance (Geneva 20449). L. 0.017 m. H. 0.014 m.

Fig. 33. Cat. 8. (2:1) Seal, impression

Fig. 34. Cat. 9. (2:1) Seal, original.

Fig. 35. Cat. 10. (2:1) Seal, impression.

Fig. 36. Cat. 11. (2:1) Seal, original.

10. (Fig. 35) Geneva 20451; dark green; L. 0.014 m. W. 0.011 m.
   Winged griffin; hatched border (Vollenweider, *Geneva* 3, 116 , no. 158).

11. (Fig. 36) Paris, Bibl. Nat. (once de Clercq 2577); black; head similar to 5, 9, and 10, but lacking the single line across the crown; stringhole through the temples; shallow drilling into the forehead; L. 0.012 m. W. 0.011 m. H. 0.010 m.
   Two rampant quadruped back to back (?); disc with hatched area above; linear border (V. Karageorghis, *Cypriot Art* (Houston, 1988), 18, no. 9).

12. Nicosia D. 62; grey; cross-hatching to represent the hair; L. 0.016 m.
   Standing two-winged deity in long, striated robe and wearing tall headdress, carrying stick (? sceptre); object with rounded top in front.

Taken as a whole, the evidence for glyptic usage in Archaic Cyprus reflects a variety of uses. They could be used to identify ownership whether by an individual or by a group of individuals. But as important as these 'public' purposes are the 'personal' ones, in which seals are used as votives, charms, amulets, and jewellery. Since serpentine seals and hardstone seals are generally not found together in the same findspot, they may well have been used in somewhat different ways. The latter may have been reserved for the more administrative tasks, as the sealings suggest.

To use these seals in these ways depends to a large extent on the portability of these artifacts. They represent property that can be carried. The seals are therefore ideal vectors for the transmission of iconographic motifs as they travel from place to place with their owners, and to a certain extent they must have been viewed as objects worthy of possession precisely because they were odd, unusual, and produced with a modicum of skill (and a certain near-sightedness). They may even have promoted literacy by introducing the notion, in certain parts of the ancient world to which they travelled, that names and words may be written down. Such hypotheses are difficult to ascertain from the archaeology, since material evidence is often not sensitive enough to define the nature of cultural influence precisely, but these scenarios are plausible ones. Mr Wemmick's attitude toward seals and rings may again be cited as a final word:

> 'Oh yes,' he returned, 'these are all gifts of that kind. One brings another, you see; that's the way of it. I always take'em. They're curiosities. And they're property. They may not be worth much, but, after all, they're property and portable. It don't signify to you with your brilliant look-out, but as to myself, my guiding-star always is, Get hold of portable property.'[163]

4

MATERIALS AND MANUFACTURE

The distinction between serpentine seals and those made from harder stones now deserves closer attention.[164] The majority of seals are of the soft stone conventionally called 'serpentine', but is actually chloritite or a variety of serpentine, and the best attested harder stones in the Cypro-Archaic period are cornelian and chalcedony. In this latter respect, the island follows the pattern recognised elsewhere in the Near East and the Aegean.[165] But because few stones have been identified scientifically or can be accurately identified by eye, conclusions concerning materials should be drawn with caution. Nevertheless, it is still worth defining Cypriot seals in terms of their materials. From where were the raw materials acquired, and to what degree could the island provide for harder stones from its own resources?

SCIENCE AND AUTOPSY

The study of Cypriot glyptic materials has not yet reached the stage at which one may speak confidently from the results of testing *via* the electron microscope, chemical analyses, or geological appraisal.[166] The terminology for the different stones is fraught with ambiguities, and older archaeological literature favoured a system of nomenclature peculiar to itself, but uninformative to specialists in rocks and minerals.[167] Recent work has attempted to correlate different systems of reference across the Near East and the Mediterranean, but that enterprise is still nascent.

Certain assumptions may be made about Cypriot seals, however, on the basis of practices attested at other sites in the Near East and confirmed by scientific experiment, as a supplement to information gleaned purely by autopsy. It may be assumed, for example, that the manufacture of Cypriot seals followed the Near Eastern practice of using metal cutting tools, such as gravers, gouges, and drills.[168] The drill especially would have been used for the cutting of the more elaborate devices.[169] The products were then smoothened with powdered abrasives.

PICROLITE (?)

Since the majority of Cypriot seals are made of serpentines, it is likely that these are products fashioned on the island. The archaeological term 'serpentine' has been retained here for convenience, embedded as it is in glyptic literature. Some Cypriot cylinder-seals of the Late Bronze Age have been tested and been determined to be made of chloritite.[170] It is possible that, when scientifically tested, some of the so-called serpentine seals of Cyprus will be found to have been manufactured of the same material. Chloritite, however, has to be imported into the island and the raw material would have been worked locally. It is likely too that, more precisely, certain 'serpentine' stamp-seals are, in fact, made from the stone known locally as 'picrolite', a type of soft stone that is smooth, easily cut, and, more importantly, readily available. In colour, it ranges from a light green to a bluish or even darker colour. This is precisely the range of colours attested for the serpentine seals.

The use of picrolite would not be surprising or unexpected. As a material, it had been used in the manufacture of Cypriot votives and pendants since well before the Bronze Age.[171] Because suitable sources in the Troodos Mountains are apparently arduous to reach, it is likely that the raw material was collected after having been transported downstream by water-courses.[172] In the north of Cyprus, the Karyotis river flows downstream from the Troodos range and emerges some twenty kilometres to the south-west of Ayia Irini. It may have provided a concentration of picrolite suitable for use by local seal-cutters. The only other river that drains the Troodos Massif, carrying picrolite pebbles, appears to be the Kouris river which runs to the south, accessible to Paphos, Kourion, and Amathus. These are the areas – Ayia Irini to the north and, in the south, the areas around Paphos, Kourion, and Amathus – that were important centres for the production of serpentine seals.

That there was a trade in picrolite in Chalcolithic times and the Bronze Age has now been established with reasonable certainty.[173] The raw materials themselves were transported into different parts of Cyprus from areas along the Kouris and Karyotis rivers. There is every reason to suspect that this trade persisted in the Archaic period.

As in Syria and Palestine, the devices of the vast majority of serpentine seals suggest production for use within the immediate vicinity. Cyprus seems to follow the general pattern in the Near East.[174] Of areas in Cyprus with a large number of seals attested, it is notable that no serpentine seals are thus far known from Marion. Conversely, only serpentine seals are known from Pyrga, near Kition.

THEOPHRASTUS AND PLINY

If the serpentines represent local products, must the harder stones necessarily be imported? Without the aid of a comprehensive and modern geological survey of the entire island, the sources of the finely-cut and brightly-coloured hardstone seals are difficult to establish. In ancient times, Theophrastos and Pliny surveyed the gem-stones for which the island was renowned, mentioning the following:[175] 'adamas' (?; NH 37. 15. 58);[176] agate (achates; NH 37. 54. 141); amethyst (amethystus; NH 37. 40.

121); azurite (? *cyanus*; *NH* 37. 38. 119; κύανος; *de Lap.* 8. 55);[177] bloodstone or dark green chalcedony (*heliotropium*; *NH* 37. 60. 165);[178] chalcedony (*iaspis*; *NH* 37. 37. 115; ἴασπις; *de Lap.* 6. 35; 4. 25–7);[179] opal (? *paederos*; *NH* 37. 32. 84; 37. 41. 130); plasma (? *smaragdus*; *NH* 37. 3. 6; 37. 17. 66; 37. 19. 75; *de Lap.* 4. 25–7; 6. 35);[180] 'copper smaragdus' (*chalcosmaragdus*; *NH* 37. 19. 74); and rock crystal (*crystallum*; *NH* 47. 9. 24).

Theophrastos and Pliny are writing at times far removed from the Archaic and early Classical periods, but there is a measure of agreement between their literary testimony and the archaeological remains. Agate and rock crystal are attested among the gems. There is some agate on Cyprus, although not of a particularly fine quality. Rock crystal, called by Pliny 'the most costly product of the earth's surface' is known from 'nearby Paphos' (often in veins in serpentinite, but not in sizes suitable for seal manufacture) and thus far, the only rock crystal seals with recorded Cypriot provenances are from that area and neighbouring Kourion.[181] The inscription of 408 seems to have been part of the original design, suggesting local manufacture.[182] Other rock crystal seals from Cyprus but without exact provenance (30, 365, and 370) may well have been manufactured in this area. There are also amethyst and plasma seals, but, contrary to Pliny, there seem to be no local sources for that stone.[183] Cypriot seals of plasma are known only form the Kourion and Amathus areas (228, 277, 300, 306, 345, and 356).

There are porous, unsuitable haematite deposits in the island, and haematite had been used for cylinder-seals in the Late Bronze Age.[184] But the stone itself probably came from Anatolia or North Syria, where the use of haematite as a glyptic material had a more extensive tradition.[185] Haematite jewellery is also known from Egypt.[186] Onyx is not found in Cyprus, and the best known sources are Egypt, particularly from the period of the Twenty-Second Dynasty, and Arabia; it was rarely used in Western Asiatic jewellery, 'possibly reflecting the lack of local sources.'[187] Suitable brown jasper (silicified umber) is known from sources in the Troodos mountains.

No other conclusions can be drawn concerning the sources of the green and red quartzes or jaspers. Not enough is known, and some materials are insecurely identified. Chalcedony and cornelian are the most common quartz materials known in Cyprus, a phenomenon also true of the Near East in general. Of the quartzes, chalcedony is known in the Troodos, along the foothills. There are no local sources for cornelian or sard, which would have had to be imported.[188] But some Cypriot jaspers, ranging in colour from green to red or yellow, may superficially resemble cornelian, and it is not impossible that some of the so-called cornelian stones are, in fact, of this material.[189]

Lapis lazuli and marble do not occur naturally in Cyprus, and their ultimate sources may be disputed. These materials, whether from Egypt or Western Asia, had to be imported.[190] Lapis lazuli may even have had to be carried from as far away as Afghanistan.

Since a certain number of the stamp-seals from Cyprus are manufactured from materials that had to be imported, it is very likely that the transport of these harder stones at least in raw form into the island was mediated *via* Phoenician traders known to be active throughout the Near East.[191] A famous passage from the book of Ezekiel describes Phoenician trade in the sixth century and refers to the import of precious stones, notably chalcedony and malachite, from Edom.[192] The prophet Ezekiel also records that the king of Tyre was renowned for his gem stones, including 'cornelian, topaz and jasper, chrysolite, beryl and onyx, sapphire (? lapis lazuli), carbuncle, and emerald.'[193] These are, significantly, the sealstones largely attested from the island.

5
Devices and Designs

The seals now need to be defined in terms of general appearance, to understand more clearly what makes a Cypriot seal characteristically Cypriot. There are two aspects to this problem. The first is the issue of design: what shape is most common? The second concerns device: what styles are most typically used by local seal-cutters? Both questions are considered in turn.

SCARABS AND SCARABOIDS

The earliest and most common shapes are the scarab and scaraboid, with the former outnumbering the latter, and both surpassing all others to a significant degree. Widely disseminated throughout the island, scarabs and scaraboids usually appear together whenever a large enough sample of Cypriot glyptic survives. The scarab- and scaraboid-shapes account for nearly seventy-five percent of all Cypro-Archaic seals, with roughly two-and-a-half times as many scarabs as there are scaraboids.

Scarab shapes may be divided into two categories on the basis of their materials. Scarabs made of harder stones are, as one might expect, given the expensiveness of the materials and the difficulties in obtaining them, well cut, usually with somewhat lumpy profiles. The beetle-legs are carefully shown, with some striations at the front. With the exception of the scarabs from the Kourion and Amathus areas, proper depictions of winglets are rare, the gem-cutters preferring an oblique line or a V-shape to indicate winglets, or else not representing them at all. The back very often has a carinated spine, or else a distinct ridge.[194] Serpentine scarabs are less carefully cut, with legs summarily indicated or not indicated at all, but replaced with a double groove, as so often on scarabs made from glazed materials. Prothorax and elytra are usually distinguished by single lines.

Exceptional are the serpentine scarabs from Ayia Irini, many of which which tend to have carefully modelled, lumpy heads; backs are summary, but, like the hardstone scarabs, occasionally prefer a double line to distinguish the prothorax from the elytra. The spines are usually without carination, but serpentine scarabs with devices in Phoenician style sometimes have ridge backs or lightly carinated spines in imitation of the Phoenician models made from hardstones. If Boardman is correct in observing that carination is a short-lived phenomenon in Phoenician scarabs from the mainland, then the argument that the Greek scarab shape, often carinated, resulted from the influence of the specifically Cypriot scarab is strengthened.[195]

There are two types of scaraboids. The more common is a faceted scaraboid, its back clearly distinguished from sides that taper toward the bottom. The type occurs among both hardstones and serpentines. Less common is the scaraboid with a back that simply curves into the sides, without any clear delineation between the two.

STYLE

When devices are executed in only summary fashion, it is difficult to write categorically about styles that are typically Cypriot. But there is one particular group of stamp-seals that may be taken as a starting point in this regard. This is a group whose devices show a figure cut in what has been called a 'Sub-Geometric style'.[196]

Sub-Geometric Warriors

The devices of this group all have figures with pointed chins and spiked helmets, as well as limbs, joints, bodies, and extremities articulated by gouges and blobs and drillings. Serpentine examples from Amathus, Kourion, and Ayia Irini demonstrate that the sequence had begun by the middle of the CAI period (c. mid-eighth century B. C.), and the type persists through the CAII period. The type is, in a way, reminiscent of Cypro-Archaic terracottas, also with pointed chins and tall helmets.[197] Terracotta sculpture represents ancient art at its most popular level, a medium of mass-production distinguished from objects in limestone or marble or metal in its relative cheapness. The warriors on the seals may be taken as glyptic analogues to these figures, and since many examples were recovered from the sanctuary at Ayia Irini, better known for the life-size and half-life-size anthropomorphic terracottas discovered set up around the altar, these devices may, like those statues and statuettes, be described as typically Cypriot – a material record of life at a general, rather than at an exclusive, level.[198] This 'generality' is equally suggested by the widespread appearance of the Sub-Geometric type throughout the island, attested as it is in the north-west at Ayia Irini, in the east, along the Karpass, and in the south, at Amathus and Kourion. Two-thirds of seals with such a warrior are cut from serpentines, the rest from hardstones, suggesting that the use of these devices spanned different levels of society.

The figures are seen in a variety of activities: fighting lions, riding horses, driving chariots. The last motif is particularly popular, and appears on many CA stamp-seals. This chariot-device was also used in Syria and Palestine, where examples are known from the Late Bronze Age and subsequent periods. The inspiration for the series may ultimately derive from the Egyptian motif of the Pharaoh riding his chariot.[199] An example is known on a faience scarab from Late Bronze Age Kition,[200] and a chariot is probably the intended device on a black serpentine scarab of the Late Cypriot period from Maroni.[201] The representation of a warrior-type riding a horseback, as seen on 18 and 19, may perhaps be taken as a variant on the popular motif of the chariot-scene, which naturally lends itself to the depiction of warriors.

There is a certain Cypro-Phoenician flavour to some of these seals, since many of the motifs in which the warriors are seen may be parallelled by depictions on the well-known series of Phoenician bowls recovered from the island. Chariot representations, for example, occur on these bowls, aside from being seen on Cypriot vases and sculpture.[202] Markoe suggests that the scene may have been influenced by North Syrian and Neo-Assyrian art, but its origins are otherwise obscure, and the motif was widespread in the Near East.[203] As a glyptic motif, the chariot-device may have eventually come to influence the Greek Island Gems.[204] Gubel has attempted to distinguish between a western Mediterranean glyptic series showing chariots and an eastern Cypro-Phoenician one.[205] The motif of the warrior fighting a lion, as on 20, 21, 25, 30, 31, and 32, is equally well-attested in Cypriot and Phoenician iconography of the Archaic period, as are warrior files.[206]

Amathus
13. (Fig. 37) Limassol; Amathus T. 237/72 (tomb; mid-CAI-early CAII);[207] scarab; black; L. 0.016 m. W. 0.011 m. H. 0.007 m.
Warrior wearing high-crested helmet in the running-kneeling position popular in the Archaic period.[208] Both arms are raised; one hand represented by a drilling; cross-hatched exergue; no linear border (Boardman, 'Seals and Amulets', 161–2, pl. 4).

Ayia Irini
14. (Fig. 38) Nicosia A. I. 1148 (period 4); scaraboid; grey and white mottled stone; L. 0.013 m. H. 0.007 m. W. 0.010 m.
Chariot mounted by three men wearing spiked helmets; three reins and a single whip visible; linear border (SCE 2, 713, no. 1148; pl. 244, no. 8).

15. (Fig. 39) Nicosia A. I. 2539 (period 4); scaraboid; grey; L. 0.017 m.
Chariot carrying three warriors wearing spiked helmets; chariot drawn by one horse; seven-spoked wheel; bodies of warriors shown by drillwork; linear border (SCE 2, 768, no. 2539).

16. (Fig. 40) Stockholm A. I. 2662 (period 5); scarab; black; large beetle; lumpy profile; L. 0.017 m. W. 0.012 m. H. 0.011 m.
Two warriors in a chariot drawn by a single horse; bodies of men shown by drillings (SCE 2, 771, no. 2662).

17. Nicosia A. I. 2726, now missing (period 5); scarab; black; L. 0.018 m.
Chariot mounted by two men; one horse visible (SCE 2, 772, no. 2726).

18. (Fig. 41) Stockholm A. I. 2526 (period 5); scarab; black jasper (?); body damaged; striations on front legs; extant L. 0.011 m. W. 0.012 m.
Warrior riding horse; body of warrior and horse shown with drillings (SCE 2, 767, no. 2526).

19. (Fig. 42) Stockholm A. I. 2749 (period 4); scaraboid; pale green; flat back; L. 0.012 m. W. 0.009 m. H. 0.004 m.
Warrior on horse with bristling mane; bodies of horse and warrior shown by drillings; warrior wearing crested helmet and with one arm raised; linear border (SCE 2, 773, no. 2749).

Fig. 37. Cat. 13. (2:1) Seal, original, impression.

Fig. 38. Cat. 14.
(2:1) Impression.

Fig. 39. Cat. 15.
(2:1) Original.

Fig. 40. Cat. 16.
(2:1) Original.

Fig. 41. Cat. 18.
(2:1) Original.

Fig. 42. Cat. 19.
(2:1) Original.

Fig. 43. Cat. 20.
(2:1) Original.

Fig. 44. Cat. 21.
(2:1).

Fig. 47. Cat. 24.
(2:1) Original.

Fig. 45. Cat. 22. (2:1) Impression, drawing.

Fig. 46. Cat. 23. (2:1).

20. (Fig. 43) Stockholm A. I. 2445 (uncertain context); scarab; green jasper; L. 0.016 m. W. 0.012 m. H. 0.008 m.

Helmeted warrior grabs rampant lion by muzzle and prepares to strike it with his sword; lion with curving tail, lolling tongue, and one leg on knee of warrior; eyes, tongue, and feet of lion represented by drillings, as are body and head of warrior; linear border (*SCE* 2, 764–5, no. 2445).

21. (Fig. 44) Nicosia A. I. 2592 (period 5); scaraboid, almost square in shape; light-brown; L. 0.014 m. W. 0.013 m. H 0.010 m.

Crude device: warrior grasps lion (?) by the paw and prepares to slay it with a sword (?); ground line (*SCE* 2, 769, no. 2592; pl. 248, no. 13).

22. (Fig. 45) Nicosia A. I. 1014 (period 5); scarab; dark-grey; L. 0.011 m. W. 0.010 m. H. 0.007 m.

Warrior wearing crested helmet in running-kneeling position; both arms raised; sword in one hand; other hand represented by a drilling; cross-hatched exergue; linear border (*SCE* 2, 704, no. 1014).

Seal 23, now lost, may belong:

23. (Fig. 46) A. I. 2680, now missing (period 4); scarab; grey; simple back; L. 0.013 m.

Figure wearing tall conical helmet; arm raised (?); object held in other arm (? bow); linear border; hatched exergue (*SCE* 2, 771, no. 2680; pl. 249, no. 21).

Cf. also 325 for a figure in the smiting pose, which had originated in Egypt and was eventually adopted into the Near Eastern and Cypriot iconographic repertoire.[209] .

24. (Fig. 47) Stockholm A. I. 2626 (period 4); scaraboid; pale grey-green; L. 0.009 m. W. 0.007 m. H. 0.004 m.

Helmeted warrior, one arm raised, making love to second warrior bent over; both bodies shown by drillwork; bird perched on head of second figure; linear border (*SCE* 2, 770, no. 2626).

For the motif, cf. 524. The use of a perched bird as a filling motif is often seen on Near Eastern seals; cf. 201 and 202.

Galinoporni (Karpass area)

25. (Fig. 48) Nicosia D. 1 (once Peristianes); scarab; chalcedony; L. 0.022 m.

Warrior, wearing pointed helmet, grasps roaring lion by the paw and prepares to stab the animal with his sword; linear border; Cypro-syllabic inscription: *pa-u-wo* (Φαύω) (Masson, *ICS*, 328, no. 328; H. W. Catling, 'The Seal of Pasitimos' *Kadmos* 11 (1972), 63, no. 7; fig. 2). Cf. the cutting of 20.

Fig. 48. Cat. 25. (2:1) Impression, drawing.

Idalion

26. (Fig. 49) Whereabouts uncertain; Idalion 1434 (sanctuary; periods 5–6); scarab; black; double curving line dividing prothorax from elytra; L. 0.020 m.
    Chariot carrying two men and led by two horses; four-spoked wheel; driver holds a whip (*SCE* 2, 56, no. 2434; pl. 286, no. 8).

Kition

27. (Fig. 50) Nicosia 1937. x-11. 1; scarab; grey; ridge back; L. 0.015 m.
    Figure on horseback confronted by a second figure standing and carrying a spear (?); object behind horseman (P. Dikaios, 'Principal Acquisitions of the Cyprus Museum, 1937–1939' *RDAC* 1937–9 (1951), 202).

Kourion

28. (Fig. 51) New York N. E. 74. 51. 4399 (Kourion Treasure); scarab; black; two short notches at the front for the head; plain back; L. 0.014 m. W. 0.011 m. H. 0.008 m.
    Three striding warriors, each carrying a spear and a round shield with central boss and wearing a high-crested helmet (Myres, *HCC*, 447–8, no. 4399).

Provenance unknown[210]

29. (Fig. 52) Private collection (found in eastern Cyprus); scarab; black; back damaged; L. 0.020 m. W. 0.015 m. H. 0.012 m.
    The principal parts of the figures are represented by drillings: three men, wearing helmets, ride a chariot drawn by one (?) horse; man crouching in front and facing chariot; another man behind chariot; dog (?) shown beneath horse; linear border (A. Furumark, 'A Scarab from Cyprus', *OpAth* 1 (1953), 47–65; P. Zazoff, *Die antiken Gemmen* (Munich, 1983), 71; Taf. 14.3).
    Furumark argued for a Late Bronze Age date, but recognised that the lumpy beetle approximated the Cypro-Archaic scarab-shape. On the basis of the popularity of Mycenaean chariots as a decorative motif on Late Cypriot vases, however, he assigned the seal to the LCIII period, although chariot representations also occur in Cypro-Archaic vase painting and sculpture.[211]

30. (Fig. 53) Nicosia D. 3; scarab; rock crystal; double curving line separating elytra from prothorax; L. 0.018 m. W. 0.015 m. H. 0.011 m.
    Warrior grasps lion by paw; linear border.

31. (Fig. 54) Hague RCC Inv. No. 1979; scarab; green jasper; L. 0.014 m. W. 0.012 m. H. 0.006 m.
    Chariot with eight-spoked wheel drawn by a horse and carrying two men in high helmets; plain exergue; linear border; Cypro-syllabic inscription with uncertain reading: (?) *zo-mo-ni* (M. Maaskant-Kleibrink, *Catalogue of the Engraved Gems in the Royal Coin Cabinet, The Hague* (The Hague, 1978), 74, no. 6).

32. (Fig. 55) Stockholm MM 1956. 93 (once Pierides); scarab; chalcedony; L. 0.018 m. W. 0.014 m. H. 0.008 m.
    Warrior grasps rampant lion by the paw and prepares to stab it with a sword; ground line (H. H. von der Osten, 'Altorientalische Siegelsteine' *Med. Bull.* 1 (1961), 35, no. 27).

33. (Fig. 56) Geneva 1897/ P. 31; scarab; dark grey; L. 0.012 m. W. 0.010 m. H. 0.006 m.
    Man in running-kneeling position, wearing high-crested helmet; face and hands represented by drillings; cross-hatched exergue; linear border (Vollenweider, *Geneva* 1, 138, no. 185).

Fig. 49. Cat. 26. (2:1) Impression, drawing.

Fig. 50. Cat. 27. (2:1) Impression, drawing.　　　　Fig. 51. Cat. 28. (2:1) Impresssion.

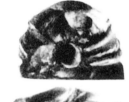

Fig. 52. Cat. 29. (2:1) Seal, original.　　　　Fig. 53. Cat. 30. (2:1).

Fig. 54. Cat. 31.
(2:1) Original.　　Fig. 55. Cat. 32. (2:1) Seal, impression.　　Fig. 56. Cat. 33.
(2:1) Original.

The following may be attributed confidently to Cypriot manufacture:

34. (Fig. 57) Geneva 20422 (once Kenna); scarab; dark grey; legs not cut; L. 0.018 m. W. 0.014 m. H. 0.010 m.
Warrior in running-kneeling position wearing a high-crested helmet; both arms raised, one carrying a spear; hand represented by a drilling; branch in back; crude linear border; cross-hatched exergue (Vollenweider, *Geneva* 3, 125, no. 169).

35. (Fig. 58) Nicosia 1941. i-15. 2; scaraboid; green; top broken; L. 0.016 m.
Four standing figures, each carrying a shield with central boss in front; heads represented by drillings.

36. (Fig. 59) Oxford 1891. 623; scarab; green jasper; chipped; L. 0.016 m. W. 0.012 m. H. 0.009 m.
Figure in front of bull; disc and crescent above; ground line; linear border (Buchanan and Moorey, *Ashmolean* 3, 82, no. 562; pl. 18).

37. (Fig. 60) Oxford 1891. 632; scarab; dark grey; grooved sides instead of legs; L. 0.018 m. W. 0.014 m. H. 0.008 m.
Two standing figures wearing high helmets; one on either side of a stylised tree; drilling above; hands represented as drillings; cross-hatched exergue; linear border (Buchanan and Moorey, *Ashmolean* 3, 81, no. 541; pl. 17).

38. (Fig. 61) Berlin FG 76; scarab; dark grey; legs net carved; deep groove at side; L. 0.019 m. W. 0.015 m. H. 0.009 m.
Two figures side by side; drillings for hands; both wear high crested helmets; cross-hatched exergue; linear border (Zwierlein-Diehl, *AGDS* 2, 61, no. 120).

39. (Fig. 62) Geneva 1897/P. 829; scarab; black; L. 0.014 m. W. 0.010 m. H. 0.006 m.
Seated warrior wearing a pointed helmet with the top bent forward; hands not shown; head shown by a drilling; linear border (Vollenweider, *Geneva* 1, 139, no. 186).

40. (Fig. 63) London 1949. 11–16. 1; scarab; green jasper; large beetle; carinated spine; striated legs; head carefully cut; lumpy profile; double curving line to separate prothorax from elytra; short notches for winglets; L. 0.020 m. W. 0.015 m. H. 0.012 m.
Warrior attacking a griffin; disc above head of griffin; figures standing on curving line; linear border; Cypro-syllabic inscription: *pu-to-ke-re-o-ne* (Πυθοκρέων) (Masson, *ICS*, 345–6, no. 355).
The griffin, with a disc above its head and slightly curved wings, is based on the Phoenician type.

41. (Fig. 64) Private collection; seal in the shape of a lion with open jaws; black; L. 0.017 m. W. 0.016 m. H. 0.012 m.
Horse-drawn chariot carrying two men; horse galloping over a fallen man; branch in field above horse (J. Boardman, *Intaglios and Rings* (London, 1975), 112, no. 211).
For similarly-shaped lion seals from Cyprus, cf. Amathus tomb 5. 11 (CAII context) of blue faience and 192 of lapis lazul

42. (Fig. 65) Larnaka (Pierides 1972); cubical seal; black; L.(base) 0.013 m. (top) 0.010 m. W. (base) 0.015 m., (top) 0.012 m. H. 0.015 m.
(a) (base) Warrior figure on either side of a tree; ladder exergue; (b) crudely cut quadruped; star above (A. T. Reyes, 'Stamp-Seals in the Pierides Collection, Larnaca' *RDAC* (1991), 123, no. 12).

Fig. 57. Cat. 34. (2:1) Impression.

Fig. 58. Cat. 35. (2:1).

Fig. 59. Cat. 36. (2:1) Impression.

Fig. 60. Cat. 37. (2:1) Seal, impression.

Fig. 61. Cat. 38.
(2:1) Original.

Fig. 62. Cat. 39.
(2:1) Original.

Fig. 63. Cat. 40. (2:1) Original.

Fig. 64. Cat. 41. (2:1) Seal, impression.

Fig. 65. Cat. 42. (2:1) Impression, drawing.

43. (Fig. 66) Larnaka (Pierides 1968); disc (? reworked scarab-shape); black; two grooves around middle; L. 0.017 m. W. 0.016 m. H. 0.006 m.
(a) Stick-like quadruped; object above; linear border; (b) two seated warrior-like figures facing each other; tree in between (A. T. Reyes, 'Stamp-Seals in the Pierides Collection, Larnaca' *RDAC* (1991), 123, no. 11).
For the motif of (b), see below on figures with branches.

44. (Fig. 67) Larnaka (Pierides 1956); scarab; grey-green; tall beetle, lumpy head; L. 0.018 m. W. 0.015 m. H. 0.010 m.
Warrior figure seated on high-backed chair and approached by standing figure with pointed chin (? arm raised) (A. T. Reyes, 'Stamp-Seals in the Pierides Collection, Larnaca, *RDAC* (1991), 123, no. 10).
For the motif, see below, on worshippers.

45. (Fig. 68) Cambridge; Fitzwilliam Museum GR. GL. 37; scarab; green glass; L. 0.018 m. W. 0.014 m. H. 0.009 m.
File of warriors (M. Henig, *Classical Gems* (Cambridge, 1994), 23, no. 39).

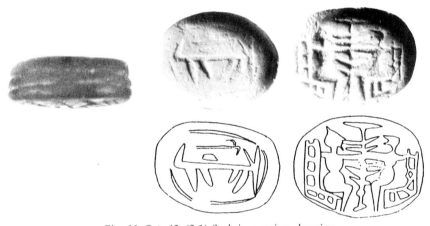

Fig. 66. Cat. 43. (2:1) Seal, impression, drawing.

Fig. 67. Cat. 44. (2:1) Seal, impression, drawing.

Fig. 68. Cat. 45. (2:1) Seal, impression.

The lumpy profiles of the Ayia Irini serpentine scarabs may have been influenced by the shapes of the green-jasper beetles, well known in Ayia Irini (20, 103, 104, 105, 106, 107, and 108) and discussed further below. It is noteworthy also that the pinched tail characteristic of green-jasper scarabs appears in some Ayia Irini beetles as well (173 and 493), and there are examples of the Sub-Geometric Warrior Series (20, 36) in green jasper. Characteristic of Cypriot work also are the zigzag exergue and the use of either a flying bird (e.g., 154, 366, 458) or a perched bird or a winged disc (e.g., 24, 201, 202) to fill a space. The use of drillings in the field (e.g., 168) may also be characteristically Cypriot, since these seem rare on Phoenician glyptic.

It is apparent from the above examples that the Sub-Geometric type is found on a wide variety of stamp-seal shapes, in addition to scarabs and scaraboids. This variety in shape helps substantiate the identification of the Sub-Geometric type as the *koine*-device within the island. But certain Sub-Geometric devices are more closely allied than others. It is likely that, at least 14, 15, 16, 19, 20, and 24, all from Ayia Irini, were cut by the same hand or by related hands. These are very closely related to 25 from Galinoporni in the Karpass region, indicating contact between these two areas.

Chariot Devices

The popularity of the chariot among devices that employ the Sub-Geometric figure indicates that, as a motif, the chariot-ride may also be taken as 'emblematic', in a sense, of the repertoire of Cypro-Archaic glyptic, in much the same way that chariot groups in terracotta are typical of the time as well.[212] Further examples of this motif are listed below. They are clearly related to the Sub-Geometric examples, although the warrior figure in these examples is either more crudely executed or somewhat less stylised in appearance.[213]

Amathus

46. (Fig. 69) London 322 (British excavations, 1894; tomb 242; CA);[214] scarab; black; oblique lines to indicate winglets; L. 0.017 m. W. 0.014 m. H. 0.010 m.
    Chariot carrying two men; one horse; eight-spoked (?) wheel; bird apparently perched on reins; linear border; body of bird and horse hatched (Walters, *BM Gems*, 40, no. 322; P. Zazoff, *Die antiken Gemmen* (Munich, 1983), Taf. 14, no. 5).
    The seal was found with 214.

Lapethos
47. (Fig. 70) Nicosia D. 17 (once Konstantinides); scarab; black; dimensions unavailable.
    Three registers; linear border: (a) (top) two opposing chariots, each drawn by one horse; one chariot with three people, the other with two (?); (b) (middle) recumbent lion facing another animal; object in field; (c) zigzag pattern (M. G. Amadasi, *L'Iconografia del Carro da Guerra in Siria e Palestina* (Rome, 1965), 84, fig. 25.1; Ohnefalsch-Richter, *KBH*, 456, pl. 152, fig. 17).
    For a similar Phoenician seal, cf. Delaporte, *Catalogue* 2, pl. 104, no. 1148.

Provenance unknown[215]
48. (Fig. 71) Oxford 1891. 630; scarab; dark grey; back damaged; L. 0.015 m. W. 0.012 m. H. 0.008 m.
    Chariot with two riders; hatched area above horse; drillings for heads (Buchanan and Moorey, *Ashmolean* 3, 81, no. 539; pl. 17).

49. (Fig. 72) Nicosia D. 28; scarab; grey; legs not cut; L. 0.018 m.
    Two men on a chariot; heads shown by drillings.

50. (Fig. 73) Nicosia 1956. vii-27. 3; scaraboid; green; L. 0.016 m.
    Chariot carrying two men, drawn by a horse; wheel shown as a dot within a circle.

51. (Fig. 74) Berlin FG 71; scaraboid; flat-topped; white stone; L. 0.016 m. W. 0.014 m. H. 0.009 m.
    Horse-drawn chariot carrying three men; wheel shown by a dot within a circle.

The following may be an abbreviated version of the motif:
52. Princeton 40. 382 (once Mather); scaraboid; black; slightly chipped; L. 0.020 m. W. 0.016 m.
    Male figure with upraised hands carrying whip (?) and riding horse; hatching on neck and body of horse; dog (?) beneath horse; branch in front (B. A. Forbes, 'Catalogue of Engraved Gems in the Art Museum, Princeton University', Ph.D. thesis (Berkeley, 1978), 218–9, no. 194; pl. 53).

Boardman has attributed the next seal to Cyprus on the basis of its material and device:
53. (Fig. 75) London 480 (1865. 7–12. 90; seal in the shape of two conjoined heads, one bearded, the other not; pale green; L. 0.014 m. W. 0.011 m. H. 0.007 m.
    Biga; one rider; one horse visible; seven legs shown; hatched border (Boardman, *AGGems*, 162, no. 591).
    The use of conjoined heads as a motif was popular in the Cypro-Archaic period.[216]

Note also the following:
54. (Fig. 76) Berlin FG 125; scarab; 'faience'; L. 0.015 m. W. 0.012 m. H. 0.008 m.
    Chariot with eight-spoked wheel; one rider brandishing whip over single horse; harched border (Zwierlein-Diehl, *AGDS* 2, 50–1, no. 85).

Fig. 69. Cat. 46. (2:1) Original.

Fig. 70. Cat. 47.

Fig. 71. Cat. 48. (2:1) Impression.

Fig. 72. Cat. 49. (2:1).

Fig. 73. Cat. 50. (2:1).

Fig. 74. Cat. 51. (2:1) Original.

Fig. 75. Cat. 53. (2:1) Seal, impression.

Fig. 76. Cat. 54. (2:1) Impression.

The Pyrga-Style

One other group of seals may be considered here as typically Cypriot, but with devices that tend to show animals, rather than human-figures. When human-figures are shown, they can, as with seal 69, resemble the Sub-Geometric warriors. But they appear in a style that makes less use of the drill. In general, the devices are cut in a very angular way, with drillings reserved for the field. Human figures and animals are linear, but not rigidly so, with bodies and limbs incised and V-shaped in section. There is occasional drillwork at the extremities. Branches often appear as filling motifs. Exergues are uncommon; linear borders are standard. The scarab shapes tend to be simple. Legs are usually not well defined, with the prothorax and elytra simply shown by short, summary incisions at the back. Winglets are not shown.

This group of seals is named after a site near Larnaka, where a hoard of scarabs and scaraboids was found, the majority cut in this distinctive style.[217] Since the hoard could not be precisely dated, seal 65 from Ayia Irini is of particular importance as a chronological peg. Its archaeological context shows that the style flourished in the last quarter of the sixth century.[218]

The Pyrga group also favoured cubical stamps. These are large seals in the shape of a cube with devices cut on all sides, and usually with a small handle. That these were not made in isolation from the scarabs is demonstrated by the scarab atop the handle of 69. Cubical seals are, as a whole, discussed in Chapter 11. With respect to these seals, however, it is important to note that even on these over-size seals, the Pyrga-style represents something local. Culican thought that the cutting on certain cubical seals from Pyrga had been influenced by Greek styles, but the affinities to the Sub-Geometric warriors demonstrate that seals in the Pyrga-style represent Cypriot, rather than Hellenic, art.[219]

Below, the seals from Pyrga itself are listed first. Seals from different sites that may be attributed to this group then follow.[220]

Pyrga

55. (Fig. 77) Larnaka (once Nicosia 1960. xi-21. 6); scarab; black; legs not cut; L. 0.016 m. W. 0.012 m. H. 0.008 m.
    Striding horse; bristling mane; branch in front; branch above; linear border (Charles, 'Pyrga', 24–5, no. 6).

56. (Fig. 78) Larnaka (once Nicosia 1960. xi-21. 4); scarab; black; details of back indicated by short, summary incisions; L. 0.020 m. W. 0.016 m. H. 0.010 m.
    Striding goat; circle with dot in the middle beneath animal; branch above; linear border (Charles, 'Pyrga', 23–4, no. 4).

57. (Fig. 79) Larnaka (once Nicosia 1960. xi-21. 5); scarab; black; deep incisions to indicate different parts of the back; legs not cut; L. 0.017 m. W. 0.012 m. H. 0.010 m.
    Insect (?) crawling up a branch (?); top of branch is knobbed (Charles, 'Pyrga', 24, no. 5). The same hand probably cut side (d) of 64.

58. (Fig. 80) Larnaka (once Nicosia 1960. xi-21. 11); scarab; black; crude, summary lines at back; L. 0.014 m. W. 0.010 m. H. 0.008 m.
    Seated lion; head turned back; branch above back; linear border; plain exergue (Charles, 'Pyrga', 29, no. 11, incorrectly described as a winged griffin).

59. Larnaka (once Nicosia 1960. xi-21. 14); scarab; black; L. 0.022 m. W. 0.017 m. H. 0.012 m.
    Human figure (?) confronting lion; tail curves forward; objects in field; linear border (Charles, 'Pyrga', 31–2, no. 14)

60. (Fig. 81) Larnaka (once Nicosia 1960. xi-21. 8); scarab; black; horizontal line to indicate prothorax; no legs; two grooves around sides; L. 0.018 m. W. 0.014 m. H. 0.010 m.
    Figure wearing long dress, seated on ladder-backed chair, holding blossom to nose (?); object (? branch) in front; linear border (Charles, 'Pyrga', 25–6, no. 8, incorrectly drawn).

61. (Fig. 82) Larnaka (once Nicosia 1960. xi-21. 9); scarab; black; L. 0.013 m. W. 0.011 m. H. 0.009 m.
    Three registers, each divided by two parallel lines; linear border: (a) (top) two drillings; (b)

(middle) three drillings; (c) (bottom) three drillings (Charles, 'Pyrga', 28, no. 9).
The device imitates Phoenician seals in its use of three registers, each separated by two lines.

Fig. 77. Cat. 55. (2:1) Impression, drawing.

Fig. 78. Cat. 56. (2:1) Impression, drawing.

Fig. 79. Cat. 57. (2:1) Impression, drawing.

Fig. 80. Cat. 58. (2:1) Impression, drawing.

Fig. 81. Cat. 60. (2:1) Impression, drawing.

Fig. 82. Cat. 61. (2:1) Impression, drawing.

62. (Fig. 83) Larnaka (once Nicosia 1960. xi-21. 1); black; cubical stamp with handle; H. 0.030 m.
(a) Winged griffin with knobbed tail; linear border; (b) seated human figure holding branch; linear border; (c) striding horse; serpent (?) above; line in front with drilling above; drilling below; linear border; (d) recumbent lion with knobbed tail; two drillings in field; linear border; (e) (base) striding bull; three branches above back; branch in front; linear border (Gubel, 'Cubical Stamps', 198, fig. 2).

63. (Fig. 84) Larnaka (once Nicosia 1960. xi-21. 2); grey; cubical stamp with handle; H. 0.025 m.
(a) Recumbent ibex; drilling in field; linear border; (b) winged griffin; disc above head; linear border; (c) striding lion with curved, knobbed tail; drillings in field; linear border; (d) lattice pattern; drill holes in between lattices; lintear border; (e) stylised date-palm; linear border (Gubel, 'Cubical Stamps', 199, fig. 3).

64. (Fig. 85) Larnaka (once Nicosia 1960. xi-21. 3); grey; cubical stamp with rectangular handle spanning width of cube; bevelling beneath handle; L. 0.021 m. W. 0.013 m. H. 0.031 m.
(a) (top of handle) Eight drillings arranged in a rough square; rough linear border; (b) goat following bird; linear border; (c) bird; three drillings in field; linear border; (d) animal with long tail crawling up tree; (e) branch; crude linear border; (f) (bottom) winged quadruped; head turned back; linear border.
The same hand probably cut 57.

Ayia Irini
65. (Fig. 86) Nicosia A. I. 2719 (period 6); scarab; dark-grey; L. 0.018 m. W. 0.013 m. H. 0.008 m.
Seated figure holding branch in extended arm and wearing a crested helmet (?); top of branch with curved leaf-shaped object; drilling above; linear border; zigzag exergue (*SCE* 2, 779, no. 2719; pl. 250, no. 6).
The zigzag exergue is typically Cypriot, though unusual for Pyrga seals.[221]

Kition
66. (Fig. 87) Nicosia D. 25; scarab; black; legs not cut; L. 0.014 m.
Striding horse; branch and flower in front.
The same hand may have cut 55.

Pera (near Tamassos)
67. (Fig. 88) Nicosia D. 31; scarab; black; double groove above base; L. 0.014 m.
Standing, winged griffin; disc above head; linear border.
Cf. side (b) of 63 for the wings and side (c) for the body type.

Salamis (?)
The following is now lost, but was probably found in the area around Salamis. It is clear from preserved drawings that the seal was in the Pyrga-style.
68. (Fig. 89) Whereabouts unknown; probably black or grey; cubical stamp with handle; 'one-inch high'.
(a) Seated figure with conical helmet holding a branch; (b) quadruped; branch above back; (c) standing human figure grasping branch; (d) quadruped; branch above back; (e) (base) quadruped; branch above back; object in front (Gubel, 'Cubical Stamps', fig. 5).

Fig. 83. Cat. 62. Impression, drawing.

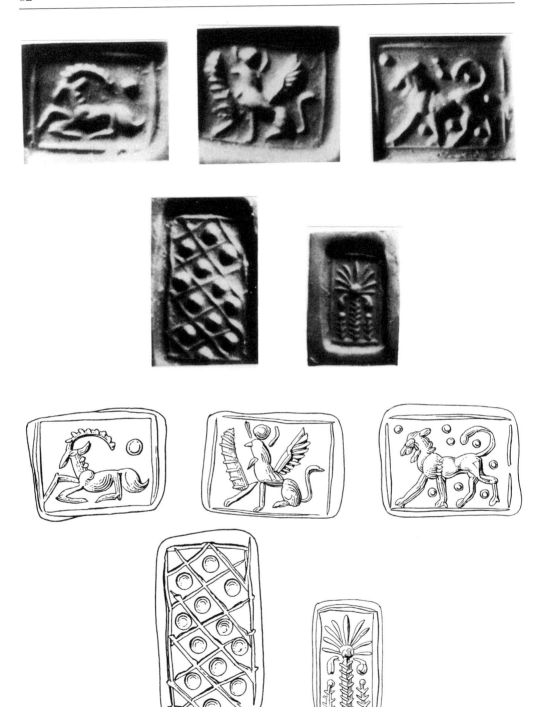

Fig. 84. Cat. 63. Impression, drawing.

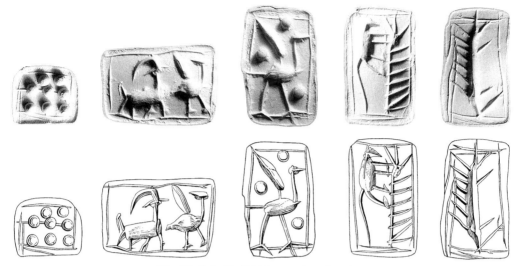

Fig. 85. Cat. 64. (1:1) Impression, drawing.

Fig. 85. Cat. 64. (1:1) drawing.

Fig. 86. Cat. 65. (2:1) Impression, drawing.

Fig. 87. Cat. 66. (2:1) Impression, drawing.

Fig. 88. Cat. 67. (2:1) Impression, drawing.

Fig. 89. Cat. 68. (1:1).

Provenances unknown[222]

69. (Fig. 90) New York 1874–1876. 74. 51. 4385; black; cubical stamp with handle; scarab (simple back; oblique lines to indicate winglets; legs not cut) carved atop protruding handle (0.016 m. high, rectangular in section); L. 0.022 m. W. 0.016 m. H. 0.027 m.

(a) Seated human figure holding branch; linear border; (b) striding warrior wearing high-crested helmet and in smiting position; branch on either side; linear border; (c) lion (?) with tail curved forward; branch in front; drilling (?) above; linear border; (d) scorpion; bird underneath; linear border; (e) (base) recumbent ibex; two branches above back; linear border (Culican, 'Cubical Seals', 165–6; Gubel, 'Cubical Stamps', 200, fig. 4).

70. (Fig. 91) Geneva 20456 (once Kenna); cubical stamp without handle (similar to a tabloid); black; L. 0.012 m. W. 0.014 m.

(a) Rider brandishing whip on horse; horse with flowing limbs and bristling mane; branch in front; linear border; (b) striding lion (?); knobbed tail; bristling mane; drilling in field; branch in front; unfinished hatched border behind (?); linear border (Vollenweider, *Geneva* 3, 129–30, no. 175).

71. (Fig. 92) Geneva 20455 (once Kenna); cubical stamp without handle (similar to a tabloid); black; L. 0.015 m. W. 0.012 m.

(a) Striding lion with knobbed tail; (b) recumbent bull; drilling in front; two branches above back (Vollenweider, *Geneva* 3, 133, no. 177).

72. (Fig. 93) Larnaka (Pierides 1972); scarab; black; L. 0.013 m. W. 0.012 m. H. 0.009 m.

Seated figure wearing tall headdress (?); arm extended holding sceptre with triangular top and hatching along stem; traces of linear border (A. T. Reyes, 'Stamp-Seals in the Pierides Collection, Larnaka' *RDAC* (1991), 124, no. 13).

Fig. 90. Cat. 69. (1:1) Seal, impression.

Fig. 91. Cat. 70. (2:1) Impression.

Fig. 92. Cat. 71. (2:1) Impression.

Fig. 93. Cat. 72. (2:1) Seal, impression, drawing.

Unlike the Sub-Geometric style, the Pyrga-style may be closely linked with a particular area of Cyprus, since the cutting of the devices is so distinctive. It is therefore possible to argue for contact between the different regions in which seals in this style are attested. Kition and Pera are geographically close to Pyrga, but it is noteworthy that there is contact with Ayia Irini and Salamis, sites that are further afield. There is no evidence for contact with the south and west of the island.

Cypriot seals have now been defined in terms of their purpose and their appearance. The typical Cypriot stamp-seal will be either a scarab or a scaraboid, with a device that often shows human figures cut in an apparently Sub-Geometric style, or else animals carved in a very angular way. The following chapter considers what external factors influenced local glyptics. In this way, it will then be possible to consider the reasons for the proliferation of stamp-seals in the Archaic period after the relative dearth of material in Cypro-Geometric times.

6

NEIGHBOURING INFLUENCES
AND INFLUENCING NEIGHBOURS

The earliest of the serpentine stamp-seals within the archaeological sequence from Ayia Irini is a single grey scarab assigned to period 3 of the sanctuary. There are four short, oblique lines on either side of the back to indicate winglets, a groove around the base, and the beetle-legs have been left uncarved. The device shows a galloping horse with an unidentifiable animal above and below, inside a linear border.[223] (Fig. 94) The seal belongs to the 'Horse-Group', well-known in the Levant and isolated by Buchanan, with devices that are all variants on the motif of the galloping horse.[224] Examples of head-seals with Horse-Group motifs are also attested in Cyprus.[225] The Levantine examples all fall within the Early Iron Age, and since period 3 at Ayia Irini commences *c.* 800 B. C., there is no conflict with the chronological data from elsewhere.

Fig. 94. (2:1) Grey serpentine scarab with 'Horse-Group' device from the sanctuary at Ayia Irini (Stockholm A. I. 2760; period 3; mid-CGIII to mid-CAI context). L. 0.015 m. W. 0.012 m. H. 0.007 m.

The Horse-Group seal from Ayia Irini may well be an import into the island, rather than a local product. In either case, its presence at the sanctuary early in the Cypro-Archaic period hints at the importance of the Levant in elucidating the phenomenon of Cypriot stamp-seals at this time. As a geographical term, the word 'Levant' is general and almost vague, referring to the stretch of land from North Syria, through Palestine, passing into Egypt. This chapter considers the influence that specific areas in the Levant may have played in developing the stamp-seal tradition of Cyprus. If it is correct to suggest that the glyptic tradition of the Late Bronze Age resulted from increased interaction with the Near East, it is worth investigating the extent to which the same may be said of the Cypro-Archaic period.

Increased contact with the Hellenic world seems, on present evidence, a less likely source of inspiration and influence. A seal said to be from Soloi and now in Vienna may suggest otherwise, since it belongs to the well-known group of Greek Island

Fig. 95. (2:1) Island gem of
mottled, light-green serpentine
from Soloi (Vienna ix. 1977). The
device shows a man sitting down
and holding a flower (?). L. 0.014
m. W. 0.011 m. H. 0.006 m.

gems produced primarily in Melos.[226] (Fig. 95) The style of this seal falls within Boardman's Class B for Island Gems, dating to the mid-seventh century, and thus, the beginnings of Cypro-Archaic glyptic are roughly contemporary with this seal.[227] It is possible that the pale green colour common among Cypriot seals was intended to recall Island Gems, but the latter favour amygdaloid and lentoid shapes, rare in the Cypriot repertoire, and the drill seems to have been employed more extensively on Cypriot seals.[228]

It is important to consider, as a way of solving the problem of what outside areas affected Cypriot seal-production, those groups of seals that appear in a certain quantity within the island early in the Archaic period and are, for the most part, imports. Two groups of seals meet these criteria. The first is the famous group of Lyre-Player seals, very homogeneous in the style of its devices, probably cut in North Syria or Cilicia and flourishing by the middle of the eighth century. The second is a less-homogeneous group, but equally well-known: gems manufactured in what appears to be green jasper.

LYRE-PLAYERS

Archaeological evidence from Ischia in Italy and elsewhere have established the chronology of the Lyre-Player seals securely.[229] Although they are only attested in Ayia Irini from period 4 of the sanctuary, it is likely that the examples from the sanctuary are earlier in date than that period would suggest. In Cyprus, only Ayia Irini has produced examples of these seals, but they appear in quantity there. Porada thought that some Lyre-Player seals from Cyprus were actually local copies and this may have been the case with 82.[230] The examples from Ayia Irini are listed below.

73. (Fig. 96) Stockholm A.I. 1318 (period 4); scaraboid; red stone; L. 0.015 m. W. 0.012 m. H. 0.005 m.
Striding winged sphinx; disc above head; palmette above; blob under body (Buchner and Boardman, 'Lyre-Player', 36, no.132).

74. (Fig. 97) Nicosia A.I. 2123 (period 4); scarab; light blue; large, lumpy beetle; L. 0.018 m. W. 0.015 m. H. 0.010 m.
Seated lyre-player facing woman with tambourine; altar (?) in between objects in field; linear border; ladder exergue (Buchner and Boardman, 'Lyre-Player', 27, fig. 36, no. 125; 35, no. 125; Boardman, 'Encore', 7, fig.12).

75. (Fig. 98) Nicosia A. I. 2180 (period 5); scaraboid; black; L. 0.021 m. W. 0.016 m. H. 0.010 m.
Lyre-Player and sphinx; hatched exergue (Buchner and Boardman, 'Lyre-Player', 35, no. 126).

76. (Fig. 99) Nicosia A. I. 2181 (period 5); scarab; blue; L. 0.017 m. W. 0.013 m. H. 0.009 m.
Striding winged griffin , wearing apron; palmette above; hatched exergue; linear border (Buchner and Boardman, 'Lyre-Player', 36, no. 130).

77. (Fig. 100) Nicosia A. I. 2262 (period 5); scaraboid; cream-coloured stone; low back; L. 0.010 m. W. 0.007 m. H. 0.005 m.
File of three birds; linear border (Buchner and Boardman, 'Lyre-Player', 36, no.129).

78. (Fig. 101) Nicosia A. I. 2517 (period 6); scaraboid; pale grey; low back; L. 0.011 m. W. 0.009 m. H. 0.005 m.
Palm tree flanked by two birds; heads turned away; linear border (Buchner and Boardman, 'Lyre-Player', 35, no. 127).

79. (Fig. 102) Stockholm A. I. 2561 (period 4); scaraboid; red stone; cross-hatching on back; L. 0.014 m. W. 0.013 m. H. 0.008 m.
Two birds facing each other; ankh above each; hatched area above; chevron in between birds; linear border (Buchner and Boardman, 'Lyre-Player', 36, no. 128).

Fig. 96. Cat. 73. (2:1) Original, impression.

Fig. 97. Cat. 74. (2:1).

Fig. 98. Cat 75. (2:1) Impression, drawing.

Fig. 99. Cat. 76. (2:1) Impression, drawing.

Fig. 100. Cat. 77. (2:1).

Fig. 101. Cat. 78. (2:1).

Fig. 102. Cat. 79. (2:1) Original.

Fig. 103. Cat. 80. (2:1) Original.   Fig. 104. Cat. 81. (2:1)   Fig. 105. Cat. 82. (2:1).
Original, impression.

80. (Fig. 103) Stockholm A. I. 2567 (period 4); scaraboid; light blue; L. 0.018 m. W. 0.014 m. H. 0.009 m.

Heraldic bird; stylised disc and crescent above; triangular hatched area on either side (Boardman, 'Encore', 14–5, fig. 22).

81. (Fig. 104) Stockholm A. I. 2573 (period 4); scaraboid; red stone; L. 0.012 m. W. 0.010 m. H. 0.006 m.

Striding winged griffin with apron; palmette above head; plain exergue; linear border (Buchner and Boardman, 'Lyre-Player', 36, no. 131).

The following may be included here, since the tree shown in its device is close to the one in 78 and may be imitative of it.

82. (Fig. 105) Nicosia A. I. 2216 (listed in SCE 2 as no. 2300; context therefore uncertain); scaraboid; dark-blue; low back; L. 0.015 m. W. 0.013 m. H. 0.004 m.

Man wearing a tall, conical headdress and with one arm raised approaches stylised tree; ape-like figure on other side of tree; linear border (SCE 2, 753, no. 2300; pl. 246, no. 23).

The ape is presumably based on representations of the Egyptian ape-god Thot. For a Phoenician seal showing both a crouching ape and a striding figure in Egyptianising costume, cf. Bordreuil, *Sceaux ouest-sémitiques*, 34, no. 23 (white agate with a Phoenician inscription).

As a whole, then, the Lyre-Player seals suggest contact with the North Syrian coast and the influence of the Syrian tradition in encouraging the development of Cypriot glyptics in the Archaic period. A black serpentine seal from Amathus from a CAII tomb with a winged horse as a device and cut in an ovoid shape known from the Syrian coast reinforces this conclusion.[231] Also reported from Cyprus, but without precise provenances, are two seals in the shape of studs, one of the most distinctive shapes in the Syrian seal repertoire.[232] (Fig. 106 for the device of one such seal) Cubical seals from Cyprus, notable for their large size relative to other seals, are discussed below, but they are relevant here in that their origins may lie in the Hittite tradition of hammer seals.[233] In the early first millennium, the type was also well-known in North Syria.[234] Only one possibly Phoenician cubical stamp is reported, although the

Fig. 106. (2:1) Stud-seal of grey serpentine with irregularly-shaped branches (?) (Nicosia E. 34). L. 0.019 m. H. 0.013 m.

shape may have been current in that part of the Levant as well, and unprovenanced examples are known with devices in a 'Syro-Phoenician' style.[235]

Isolated examples of seals found in Cyprus also suggest interaction between the island's glyptic tradition and a North Syrian or Anatolian one. Those seal-shapes reported from Cyprus with possible North Syrian or Anatolian antecedents have been listed below. Amathus, Kourion and the Karpass area are the only regions attested.

Fig. 107. Cat. 83. (2:1).

Fig. 108. Cat. 84. (2:1).

CONOIDS WITH KNOBBED HANDLES

These seals are essentially conoids, but with a distinct knob or looping handle at the top; cf. L. Jakob-Rost, *Die Stempelsiegel im Vorderasiatischen Museum* (Berlin, 1975), 104, no. 104 (Syrian); R. M. Boehmer and H. G. Güterbock, *Glyptik aus dem Stadtgebiet von Bogazköy* (Berlin, 1987), Abb. 65–6. But because the conoid is the one shape that, on archaeological evidence, is local and seems to have continued in use during the Cypro-Geometric period, the knobbed conoids may possibly claim descent from this shape, if they are not, in fact, spurious additions to the Cypriot glyptic corpus.

Kourion

83. (Fig. 107) Nicosia 1947. vii-18. 6; mottled dark green; L. 0.011 m. W. 0.011 m. H. 0.012 m.
Anchor-like pattern.

Provenances unknown

84. (Fig. 108) Nicosia 1947. x-17. 1; grey-green; L. 0.018 m. H. 0.021 m.
Three crude standing figures.

85. (Fig. 109) Nicosia E. 58; pale green; L. 0.010 m. H. 0.016 m.
Heraldic bird; drilling on each of four corners of roughly rectangular base.

86. (Fig. 110) Nicosia E. 75; pale green; L. 0.013 m. H. 0.016 m.
Carefully cut crouching lion with curving tail.

87. (Fig. 111) Larnaka (Pierides 1962); green faience; L. 0.014 m. H. 0.011 m.
Circle with lines radiating outward (A. T. Reyes, 'Stamp-Seals in the Pierides Collection' *RDAC* (1991), 126, no. 22).

Fig. 109. Cat. 85. (2:1).

Fig. 110. Cat. 86. (2:1).

Fig. 111. Cat. 87. (2:1)
Seal, impression.

DISCS

For the shape, cf. H. H. von der Osten, *Altorientalische Siegelsteine der Sammlung Hans Silvius von Aulock* (Uppsala, 1957), 48–9, no.46; id., *The Alishar Hüyük* 2 (Chicago, 1937), 417, no. e. 625; d. 1847 (post-Hittite Phrygian period); id., *The Alishar Hüyük* 3 (Chicago, 1937), 92, no. e. 357 (second half of the first millennium).

Provenances unknown
43, 125, 188, 541.

FOOT-LIKE SEAL

On the foot as a seal-shape, note D. G. Hogarth, *Hittite Seals* (Oxford, 1920), 17 (a 'freak form') and 43, no. 274. But the seal below need not have been intended to represent a foot.

Kourion
88. (Fig. 112) New York N. E. 74. 51. 4386; four-sided upright with protrusion on one side, giving the appearance of a foot; black; stringholes through protrusion and upright; L. 0.009 m. W. 0.006 m. H. 0.026 m.; protrusion: L. 0.015 m. W. 0.06 m. H. 0.004 m.
   Each side with two registers: (a) seated stick-like figure above; sun below; (b) standing stick-like figure above; curving line below; (c) seated stick-like figure above; square (?) below; (d) standing stick-like human figure above; two curving lines below; (e) (top) summary scratches; (f) (foot) scratches (Myres, *HCC*, 446, no. 4386).

PYRAMIDS

The shape may derive from the Anatolian or North Syrian tradition of Iron Age stamp-seals, but a similarly-shaped seal of black serpentine with a star-like pattern used as its device was recovered from Late Bronze Age Enkomi.[236] Compare also the cubical seals below (433, 434, 436, 437, 438, 443, 449, 457, 459, and 461) with pyramidal shapes, often with devices cut on several faces.

Amathus[237]
89. (Fig. 113) Limassol; Amathus T. 556/31 (CAI context); 'picrolite grise'; dimensions unreported.
   Linear design on two faces (V. Karageorghis, 'Chronique des fouilles et découvertes archéologique à Chypre' *BCH* 113 (1989), 811, 814; fig. 85).

See also 434.

(?) Karpass region[238]
90. (Fig. 114) Paris, Louvre MNB 379 (A. 1170); brown; stringhole through top; irregular

Fig. 112. Cat. 88. (1:1) Impression.

Fig. 113. Cat. 89. (not to scale) Original.

Fig. 114. Cat. 90. (1:1)
Original, impression.

Fig. 115. Cat. 91. (2:1).

Fig. 116. Cat. 92. (2:1)
Impression, drawing.

scratches on sides; L. 0.016 m. W. 0.015 m. H. 0.028 m.
Two intersecting lines; drilling in each quadrant (Delaporte, *Catalogue* 2, 210; p. 106, no. 1a).

Kourion
Note also 443. The pale green colour of the following suggest local manufacture:
91. (Fig. 115) Nicosia 1954. ix–17. 2; pale green; L. 0.013 m. W. 0.010 m. H. 0.023 m.
    Quadruped.

92. (Fig. 116) Nicosia E. 63 (1933. iii–18. 3); pale green; L. 0.011 m. W. 0.009 m. H. 0.020 m.
    Schematic face: two drillings for eyes; vertical line for nose and outline of head.

The following seal may also be noted here, although of a somewhat different shape; cf. H. H. von der Osten, *Altorientalische Siegelsteine der Sammlung Hans Silvius von Aulock* (Uppsala, 1957), 54–5, no. 30; R. M. Boehmer and H. G. Güterbock, *Glyptik aus dem Stadtgebiet von Bogazköy* (Berlin, 1987), 35–6, dating the type between the end of the eighth and seventh centuries. Delaporte, *Catalogue* 1, pl. 54, no. 34a (D. 140a) with a device derived from the Neo-Babylonian tradition shows that the shape was current at least into the sixth century.

Myrtou-Pigadhes
93. (Fig. 117) Myrtou-Pigadhes 405 (surface find); 'white steatite'; looping handle; grooves around body; L. 0.010 m. W. 0.008 m. H. 0.019 m.

Described as 'cursory animal above three joined dots'. (J. DuPlat Taylor, *Myrtou-Pigadhes* (Oxford, 1957), 94, no. 405).

Provenances unknown
See also 449, 457, 459, 461.

94. (Fig. 118) Nicosia E. 43; grey; L. 0.011 m. H. 0.021 m.
    Cross; two quadrants with a single drilling each.

95. (Fig. 119) Nicosia E. 46; grey; L. 0.012 m. H. 0.017 m.
    Irregular lines and zigzags.

96. (Fig. 120) Nicosia E. 47; mottled dark grey; L. 0.010 m. H. 0.015 m.
    Bird incised in outline.

97. (Fig. 121) Nicosia E. 70; grey; L. 0.012 m. H. 0.024 m.
    Two stick-like figures on either side of a schematic tree.

98. (Fig. 122) Nicosia E. 71; pale grey; L. 0.017 m. W. 0.007 m. H. 0.029 m.
    Two drillings on one side of an incised line; six drillings on the other.

99. (Fig. 123) Larnaka (Pierides 1971); grey; L. 0.010 m. H. 0.021 m.
    Central dot; above, below, and on either side of this is a dot within a half circle (A. T. Reyes, 'Stamp-Seals in the Pierides Collection, Larnaca' *RDAC* (1991), 126, no. 21).[239]

100.(Fig. 124) Larnaka (Pierides 1976); mottled green; groove above base; no stringhole; L. 0.012 m. W. 0.011 m. H. 0.031 m.
    Quadruped (A. T. Reyes, 'Stamp-Seals in the Pierides Collection, Larnaca' *RDAC* (1991), 125, no. 15).

Fig. 117. Cat. 93. (2:1) Seal, impression.

Fig. 118. Cat. 94. (2:1).

Fig. 119. Cat. 95 (2:1).

Fig. 120. Cat. 96. (2:1).

Fig. 121. Cat. 97. (2:1).

Fig. 122. Cat. 98. (2:1).

Fig. 123. Cat. 99. (2:1) Seal, impression, drawing.

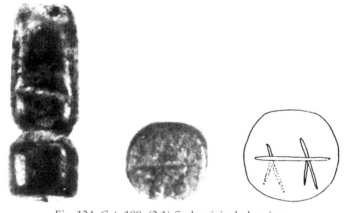

Fig. 124. Cat. 100. (2:1) Seal, original, drawing.

A North Syrian or Anatolian element may thus be isolated in early seals of the Cypro-Archaic period. This is particularly evident in the north, at Ayia Irini, where Lyre-Player seals of the eighth-century are well-attested. But the cubical seals of the south, already attested in the seventh century, show that foreign influence had spread well inland by the end of the CAI period. Cypriot involvement on the North Syrian coast and along Cilicia is not surprising. Cyprus no doubt participated in the trade emerging from Al Mina along the Orontes in North Syria during the eighth century, and the island's geographical proximity to the Cilician coast ensured close contact with that area as well.[240]

GREEN-JASPER SEALS

The green-jasper seals introduce a second strand of Levantine influence.[241] The ultimate origins of the material remain a well-known, still vexatious problem of Classical and Near Eastern archaeology, nor are all of these seals necessarily even made of what is properly called, from a geological standpoint, green jasper. Furthermore, to isolate Cypriot seals made of green jasper at this point may seem something of an anachronism and an anomaly to archaeologists. It may seem anomalous, since no other group of seals is distinguished here by material, and anachronistic, because when seals of green jasper are discussed as an entity in archaeological literature, the reference is generally to gems with devices cut in the distinctive Classicising style of the late sixth century B. C. and later. It is useful, however, to distinguish the seals of green jasper largely to signal them as a correlate to the green-jasper cylinders of the early first millennium B. C. on the Near Eastern mainland, also cut in a certain number of styles. Given the large number of green-jasper gems from the island, spanning different chronological periods, it is also possible to see the changes over the centuries in devices that appear within seals made of a particular type of material.

The beetles, set on high bases, are unusually large, with pronounced spines and tails that have been slightly pinched in. Many of the seals are likely to have Phoenician antecedents, and it is fair to describe the style of many of the devices on the Cypriot examples as Phoenician. Some examples, all with contexts dating to the sixth century, may even be called Graeco-Phoenician or Classical Phoenician; that is: the later gems have devices that show Phoenician or, at the very least, Near Eastern subjects that have been artistically treated in a Hellenic manner (104, 105, 106, 109 (?), 110, 113–118, 122, 126). Devices cut in local styles include 101, 102, 103, 119, 120, 123, and 125. There are also four scarabs of green jasper with devices showing Sub-Geometric figures: 20, 31, 36, 40. A possible sub-division of these seals may be the following whose devices may have been influenced by locally produced glazed seals of faience with hiero-glyphic devices: 107, 108, 112. These local green-jasper seals first appear early in the Cypro-Archaic period. Equally early is 111 from Paphos with a device cut in a Syrian style. Since few of the numerous examples of green-jasper scarabs and scaraboids from the mainland may be dated on the basis of archaeological contexts to periods earlier than Achaemenid times,[242] particular importance attaches to 111 which can assigned to the CAI period on the basis of associated finds.[243] Seal 121, an inscription-seal, also represents an early, purely Phoenician, tradition. The period of transition between the use of devices cut in an essentially non-Classical style and those cut in the more Classical style corresponds with period 5 at Ayia Irini, the first half of the sixth century. But 101 demonstrates the persistence of a local style into the CCI period.

Amathus

101. (Fig. 125) Limassol (?); Amathus T. 487 (tomb; CCI) scarab; L. 0.029 m.

Geometric motif; Cypro-syllabic inscription: *e-ke-pa-re* (V. Karageorghis, 'Chronique des fouilles et découvertes archéologiques à Chypre' *BCH* 111 (1987), 713, fig. 127 with comments by O. Masson in 709, n. 76).

Arsos

102. (Fig. 126) Larnaka 552 (once Nicosia 1939. x-6. 1); scarab; carinated spine; L. 0.017 m. W. 0.013 m. H. 0.009 m.

Griffin and lion, one on either side, attacking a fallen deer (?); linear border (V. Karageorghis,

Fig. 125. Cat. 101. (1:1) Original, impression.

Fig. 126. Cat. 102. (2:1) Seal, original, impression.

Fig. 127. Cat. 103. (2:1) Impression, drawing.   Fig. 128. Cat. 104. (2:1).

'A Cypro-Archaic I Tomb at Palaepaphos-Skales' *RDAC* (1987), 90; pl. 32).
The motif of two animals attacking from either side of a victim is Near Eastern, rather than Greek.[244] The lion's head, seen from above, is also a Near Eastern iconographic tradition.

Ayia Irini
See also 20.
103. (Fig. 127) Nicosia A. I. 1117 (period 4); scarab; no markings on back other than small notches to indicate division between prothorax and elytra; L. 0.013 m. W. 0.011 m. H. 0.008 m.
   Striding deer, body gouged out; linear border (*SCE* 2, 710, no. 1117; pl. 244, no. 5).

104. (Fig. 128) Nicosia A. I. 2657 (period 5); scaraboid; low-back; L. 0.014 m. W. 0.012 m. H. 0.007 m.
   Winged sea-horse (?); hatched border; plain exergue (*SCE* 2, 770, no. 2657; pl. 249, no. 13).

The motif is seen on another green-jasper gem, probably Phoenician in inspiration, in Paris,[245] but the execution of 104 is close to the Fine Style of Archaic Greek gems.[246] The hatched border, while characteristic of Late Archaic Greek gems, also tends to appear on the devices of Phoenician and Punic green-jasper seals.[247] The winged sea-horse had entered the Island Gem repertoire by the mid-sixth century, but its origins are obscure.[248]

105. (Fig. 129) Nicosia A. I. 2707 (period 5); scarab; gable-shaped back; large, lumpy beetle; forked line dividing elytra; L. 0.018 m. W. 0.013 m. H. 00.014 m.
      Two rampant lions facing each other; disc and crescent above; cross-hatched exergue; linear border (*SCE* 2, 772 no. 2707; pl. 250, no. 2).

The style of the lion recalls the way in which East Greek lions of the Late Archaic period are depicted. Note, especially, the sweep of the tails and the bristling manes.[249] The use of the disc and crescent-symbols as filling motifs is a Cypriot and Near Eastern practice.

106. (Fig. 130) Nicosia A. I. 2722 (period 5); scarab; black jasper (?); large, lumpy beetle; Y-shaped marking at back; L. 0.016 m. W. 0.012 m. H. 0.010 m.
      Seated (? stretching) lion; linear border (*SCE* 2, 772, no. 2722; pl. 250, no. 7).
      The style is Graeco-Phoenician.

107. (Fig. 131) Nicosia A. I. 2424 (period 4); scarab; L. 0.013 m. W. 0.010 m. H. 0.007 m.
      Two uraei; ankh in between; linear border (*SCE* 2, 764, no. 2424; pl. 247, no. 3).

108. (Fig. 132) Nicosia A. I. 2595 (period 4); scarab; double curving line to separate prothorax from elytra; L. 0.016 m. W. 0.012 m. H. 0.010 m.
      Bird standing between two objects (? uraeus or feather in front, crook behind); object above; ladder exergue, with three vertical lines; linear border (*SCE* 2, 769, no. 2595; pl. 248, no. 15).
      The device is possibly imitative of Egyptian or Egyptianising designs in which the god Horus, represented as a bird, appears alongside divine symbols; cf. 249. Ladder exergues tend to appear on seals early in the Archaic period.[250]

Kourion
109. (Fig. 133) London WA 132515 (1959. 2–14. 13); scarab; gold setting; dimensions unreported.
      Bull attacked by a panther; bird (? vulture) above bull (O. Masson, 'Nouvelles Variétés chypriotes' *Cahiers: Centre d'études chypriotes* 24, no. 2 (1995), 14–5; pl. 2, no. 1 and 3).

Marion
110. (Fig. 134) Nicosia D. 11; scarab; hatched double curving line to separate prothorax from elytra; L. 0.015 m. W. 0.012 m. H. 0.010 m.
      Seated bearded figure holding spear; throne with sides in the shape of sphinxes; hand of figure raised in front of incense burner; winged disc above; cross-hatched exergue; hatched border (Culican, 'Iconography', 57, fig. 2; 60 n. 54).
      This typically Phoenician motif cannot be closely dated. For a very similar device, see 122.[251]

Fig. 129. Cat. 105. (2:1) Impression, drawing.

Fig. 130. Cat. 106. (2:1) Impression.

Fig. 131. Cat. 107. (2:1) Impression, drawing.

Fig. 132. Cat. 108. (2:1) Impression, drawing.

Fig. 133. Cat. 109. (not to scale) Original.

Fig. 134. Cat. 110. (2:1) Impression, drawing.

Fig. 135. Cat. 111. (2:1) Seal, original, impression.

Paphos

111. (Fig. 135) Paphos Museum; Tomb 94, no. 42 (tomb, CAI); scarab; carefully carved beetle; L. 0.016 m. W. 0.012 m. H. 0.008 m.

Two heraldic griffins, one on either side of a stylised palmette; ladder exergue; linear border (V. Karageorghis, 'A Cypro-Archaic I Tomb at Palaepaphos-Skales' *RDAC* (1987), 89–90; 95).

The type shown on the seal owes more to Syrian depictions of the griffin, rather than specifically Phoenician ones.[252]

Salamis

112. (Fig. 136) Nicosia 1934. i-15. 4; scarab; base damaged; deep underscoring to legs; L. 0.017 m. W. 0.012 m. H. 0.007 m.
    Mummiform deity holding object in front of incense burner (?); plain exergue; linear border. For the device, cf. 297 and 298.

Tamassos

113. (Fig. 137) Berlin FG 103 (German excavations, 1889, Grave 13; found with CA jewellery); scarab; lightly flecked; ridged back; L. 0.017 m. W. 0.012 m. H. 0.009 m.
    Seated winged griffin; disc above head; cartouche with scarab in front of *neb*-sign as exergue (Zwierlein-Diehl, *AGDS* 2, 66, no. 136).

114. (Fig. 138) Berlin FG 102 (German excavations, 1889, Grave 11; found with sixth-century pots and black figure sherds of the late fifth century); scarab; L. 0.016 m. W. 0.012 m. H. 0.009 m.
    Bes-like creature battles rampant lion; star, disc, and crescent in field; cross-hatched exergue; linear border (Zwierlein-Diehl, *AGDS* 2, 65, no. 135).
    The iconography and filling motifs are Phoenician, although the treatment of the Bes-creature, particularly of its legs, owes something to Greek influence.[253]

Provenances unknown

See also 31, 36, and 40.

115. (Fig. 139) Oxford 1889. 414; scarab; L. 0.017 m. W. 0.013 m. H. 0.010 m.
    Isis and Horus; linear border; cross-hatched exergue (Buchanan and Moorey, *Ashmolean 3*, 82, no. 558; pl. 18).

116. (Fig. 140) Oxford 1891. 640; scarab; L. 0.016 m. W. 0.012 m. H. 0.010 m.
    Winged scarab; disc on either side; linear border (Buchanan and Moorey, *Ashmolean 3*, 82, no. 560; pl. 18).

117. Nicosia 1946. viii–13. 4; scarab; ridge back; double curving line separating prothorax from elytra; striated front legs; L. 0.016 m. W. 0.014 m. H. 0.013 m.
    Standing two-winged deity in front of attendant (?); winged disc above; linear border; cross-hatched exergue.

118. (Fig. 141) Nicosia D. 192; scarab; striated front legs; winglets shown by single notches; L. 0.019 m.
    Device worn: god with disc on head and staff in front of two-winged goddess with disc on head, perhaps Isis (cf. 115); disc and crescent above; linear border; cross-hatched exergue.

119. (Fig. 142) Nicosia D. 5; scarab; double line separating prothorax from elytra; double line separating elytra; ridge back; striated front legs; L. 0.021 m.
    Man battling rampant lion; winged disc above; linear border; cross-hatched exergue.

120. (Fig. 143) Nicosia D. 12; scarab; simple back; L. 0.014 m. W. 0.011 m. H. 0.007 m.
    Recumbent winged griffin, approaching object with circle above (? intended as ankh); disc above head; cross-hatched exergue; no linear border.

Fig. 136. Cat. 112.
(2:1) Impression.

Fig. 137. Cat. 113.
(2:1) Original.

Fig. 138. Cat. 114.
(2:1) Original.

Fig. 139. Cat. 115.
(2:1) Impression.

Fig. 140. Cat. 116.
(2:1) Impression.

Fig. 141. Cat.
118. (2:1).

Fig. 142. Cat. 119. (2:1).

Fig. 143. Cat. 120. (2:1).

The device of the following is unrecorded, but it has a Phoenician inscription:
121. Present location unknown; scarab (?); ring setting.
    Phoenician inscription: lmlk/rm ('appartenant à Milkiram' (A. Lemaire, 'Milkiram, nouveau
    roi phénicien de Tyr?' *Syria* 53 (1976), 89–90, no. 6).
    If Lemaire is right to identify this particular name as that of an eighth-century Phoenician
    ruler, the seal belongs to the early Cypro-Archaic period, but the loss of the seal and the
    conjectural reading detract from its historical value.

As a version of 110, the following may also belong; shape and material are unreported:

122. (Fig. 144) Beirut (?) (once Pérétié, found in Cyprus); scarab (?); L. 0.021 m. W. 0.016 m.
Seated male figure in conical headdress holding spear; throne with sides in shape of sphinx; ground line; Aramaic or Phoenician inscription; (?) *lgdsr* (F. Vattioni, ' I Sigilli Fenici' *AION* 41 (1981), 183, no. 26; Galling, 'Beschriftete Bildsiegel', 174, no. 13; Taf. 5).

123. (Fig. 145) Naples, National Museum 27001/1156; scarab; 'prasio'; L. 0.013 m. W. 0.011 m. H. 0.008 m.
Seated griffin; cross-hatched exergue; Cypro-syllabic inscription: (?) *mi-wa-te* (P. G. Guzzo, 'La Gemme a Scarabeo nel Museo Nazionale di Napoli' *MEFRA* 3 (1971), 352–3, no. 77; U. Pannuti, *La Collezione Glittica* 2 (Rome, 1994), 21).

124. (Fig. 146) Oxford 1891. 638; scarab; L. 0.017 m. W. 0.012 m. H. 0.007 m.
Bearded hero (? a Herakles figure) in smiting position and holding bow and club; object in field (Buchanan and Moorey, *Ashmolean 3*, 82, no. 559; pl. 18).

125. (Fig. 147) Nicosia D. 65; disc; grooves along the side; devices on both ends; L. 0.020 m. W. 0.013 m. H. 0.008 m.
(a) Standing human figure holding object; scorpion; tree in between; (b) sitting stick-like figure; object in field.
The shape is unusual in Iron-Age Cyprus, but may derive from the glyptic tradition of Anatolia and North Syria; note 43 and 188.

Fig. 144. Cat. 122. (2:1).

Fig. 145. Cat. 123. (2:1) Original, impression.

Fig. 146. Cat. 124. (2:1) Impression.

Fig. 147. Cat. 125. (2:1).

The resurgence in Cypriot glyptic in the Archaic period is underway by period 3 of Ayia Irini, that is, by the early seventh century B. C. Why there should have been a resurgence in the manufacture of seals at this time, after an apparent decline, is a matter of some speculation. In part, the accident of excavation within Cyprus may be to blame. As votive objects, stamp-seals are more likely to be found in sanctuaries than tombs. It is significant that over 300 seals were found in the sanctuary at Ayia Irini, whereas only one is reported from the cemetery at the same site. Since the majority of excavated sites in Cyprus are necropoleis, rather than settlements, there is some likelihood that this gap in current knowledge is to a certain extent illusory, rather than real. But even granting the possibility of continuity in glyptic practices through the early Iron Age, the sheer number of stamp-seals recorded from Cypro-Archaic contexts must suggest the development of a particular, need for such objects at that particular time.

The increase seems to signal a change in both the glyptic craft of Cyprus and the island's dedicatory practices. Since Cypriot seals of the time are allied largely with the Phoenician and the Syrian or Anatolian glyptic traditions, it may also be that advantages afforded by Cypriot participation within the economy fostered by Syria and Phoenicia promoted the further development of the island's vestigial glyptic tradition. From textual sources, it is clear that Cyprus was actively involved in the economic network of the Neo-Assyrian empire under Sargon II and his successors, and it may be thought that the use of stamp-seals was spurred by involvement in the politics of the Assyrian kings.[254] But a specifically Assyrian impetus is unlikely, since the sharp increase in glyptic material at Ayia Irini occurs well after this period, roughly a generation before the fall of Nineveh in 612 B. C.[255]

Where this resurgence began remains uncertain, and it need not have started in only one place. In the north, Ayia Irini provides the earliest stratified examples. In the south, Amathus and Kourion appear as the earliest sites, and an argument for Kition is possible.[256] These are all sites that could build on glyptic foundations laid, however weakly, in the Cypro-Geometric period (on the assumption that, perhaps, Ayia Irini fell within the kingdom of Lapethos). They were also important Phoenician staging-posts on the way to the western Mediterranean and, as commercial sites, with a certain value.[257] The resurgence of a glyptic tradition in the Cypro-Archaic period, therefore, may parallel to some extent the emergence of that tradition in the Late Bronze Age, when the cylinder and conoid were adopted to allow for participation within the economic systems of the time.

7

THE PHOENICIAN CONNECTION

By the eighth century, it is likely that a Phoenician glyptic tradition was well advanced, and the proximity of the Phoenician mainland to Cyprus and the colonial presence of Tyre and Sidon within the island strongly suggest that the beginnings of glyptic in Cyprus should be associated, at least in part, with a Phoenician presence.[258] The Phoenician glyptic style is traditionally defined by its use of Egyptianising, rather than Egyptian, motifs, but it is not always a straightforward matter to separate the one from the other. The devices on Phoenician hardstone seals usually appear with linear borders or borders with a rope-like pattern and plain or cross-hatched exergues. The zigzag exergue is less common than the cross-hatched one in Phoenician glyptic, but occasionally appears.[259] It seems more typical of Cyprus than the mainland.[260] Occasionally, an Egyptian *neb*-sign substitutes for the exergue, and a papyrus brake appears as a background filling motif.

A large number of such hardstone scarabs and scaraboids are known from Cyprus, and there is no doubt that Cypriots would have been familiar with this aspect of Phoenician art, given the widespread appearance of Phoenician seals in the Near East and the intense traffic between the island and the Levantine coast.[261] But it cannot, in most instances, be decided categorically that one or the other seal is an import from Phoenicia, rather than locally produced within the island. Nor can one readily decide whether a hardstone seal with an Egyptianising motif was carved by a Phoenician established in Cyprus or a Cypriot trained in the Phoenician styles. (Fig. 148) Cypro-syllabic inscriptions on certain seals are no guarantors of local production, since these may well have been added secondarily to the main device.

Fig. 148. (2:1) Onyx scarab of uncertain origin with a sphinx on either side of a tree (Boston 01. 7551). The motif is traditionally Phoenician, but the cutting of the device is in a Greek style. L. 0.018 m.

It can, however, be readily demonstrated that hardstone seals in the Phoenician manner were copied within the local serpentine tradition. A number of motifs traditionally asssociated with Phoenician iconography appears on serpentine scarabs, and these seem to be local copies, a less expensive alternative to the more expensive seals made of the harder stones that they imitated. Devices have exergues and linear borders, occasionally using the papyrus brake as a filling motif.

The lumpy beetle shapes, although of serpentine, are recognisably derived from the Phoenician type, often with ridge or gable spines and striations at the front where the legs should appear.

VERSIONS OF PHOENICIAN SEALS

To demonstrate the closeness of the Phoenician-style hardstone seals and the local serpentine sequences, the following lists identify a few Phoenician motifs that appear on both types of glyptic. Within each listed provenance, the hardstone examples, if any, are listed first. These are followed by the serpentines.

Animal Attacks

The representation of animal attacks has a long tradition in the Levant. For the iconography in the Phoenician tradition, see Markoe, *Bowls*, 39–40. The scheme in which one animal or monster is shown placing a paw on the back of another creature is particularly Near Eastern; cf. B. Teissier, 'Glyptic Evidence for a Connection between Iran, Syro-Palestine, and Egypt in the Fourth and Third Millennium' *Iran* 25 (1987), 36, fig. 69.

Amathus
126. (Fig. 149) Limassol; Amathus T. 237/94 (tomb; mid-CAI-early CAII); scarab; black; high
     plinth; L. 0.017 m. W. 0.012 m. H. 0.008 m.
     Lion lifting paw onto the back of a deer, its head turned back; linear border (Boardman,
     'Seals and Amulets', 162, pl. 4).

Arsos
127. (Fig. 150) Nicosia D. 165 (Cypriot excavations, 1917; sanctuary; CA); scarab; green quartz;
     double curving line separating prothorax from elytra; lightly carinated spine; L. 0.017 m.
     W. 0.012 m. H. 0.007 m.
     Griffin with paw raised on back of deer; linear border (*SCE* 3, 599; pl. 204, no. 23).

Kition (?)
128. (Fig. 151) Vienna, Kunsthistorisches Museum, ix. 1978 (once Ohnefalsch-Richter, purchased
     in Larnaka); scarab; light green; back is very worn; modern gold setting; L. 0.018 m. W.
     0.014 m. H. 0.010 m.
     Bull attacked by a lion from the front and a second lion from the back; plain exergue;
     hatched border (E. Zwierlein-Diehl, *Die antiken Gemmen des Kunsthistorisches Museums in
     Wien* 1 (Munich, 1973), 36, no. 16; Taf. 4; classified as 'Graeco-Phönikisch'[262]).
     The motif of an animal being attacked from both sides is Near Eastern. The hatched border,
     as on Archaic Greek gems, suggests a date within the sixth century.

Kourion
129. (Fig. 152) Nicosia 1963. x–7. 1; scaraboid; mottled green; L. 0.012 m. W. 0.01 m. H. 0.008 m.
     Lion biting the back of a running stag; three lines to show muscles in the body of the lion;
     similar lines showing muscles in the neck and body of the deer; drillings to show eyes and

Fig. 149. Cat. 126. (2:1) Seal, original, impression.

Fig. 150. Cat. 127. (2:1) Impression, drawing.   *Fig. 151. Cat. 128. (2:1) Original.*

Fig. 152. Cat. 129. (2:1) Seal, impression, drawing.   *Fig. 153. Cat. 131. (2:1) Original.*

feet; linear border (V. Karageorghis, 'Chronique des fouilles et découvertes archéologiques à Chypre' *BCH* 88 (1964), 292–3, fig. 5).

The device of 449 is similar and may have been cut by the same hand. Also related is Vollenweider, *Geneva* 3, no. 164.

130. Now lost; reportedly of sard; dimensions unknown.

Bovine animal attacked by lion (?); Cypro-syllabic inscription (reading uncertain): *ti-pi-si* (O. Masson, 'Nouvelles Variétés chypriotes' *Cahiers: Centre d'études chypriotes* 24, no. 2 (1995), 15–6; pl. 2, no. 2).

Lysi (Famagusta area)

131. (Fig. 153) Nicosia 1962. xi-3. 1; scarab; black; notched head; L. 0.021 m. W. 0.017 m. H. 0.010 m.

Upright lion places paw on back of running goat; linear border (V. Karageorghis, 'Chronique des fouilles et découvertes archéologiques à Chypre' *BCH* 87 (1963), 327–8; fig. 3a–c).

Mari (between Larnaka and Limassol)
132. (Fig. 154) London 333 (1899. 10–15. 2); scarab; banded agate; gold swivel setting; spine
    lightly carinated; L. 0.020 m. W. 0.012 m. H. 0.008 m.
    Roaring lion with one paw on back of fallen deer, the other paw raised to strike; head of
    deer turned back to face lion; papyrus brake in background; plain exergue; linear border
    (G. M. A. Richter, *Engraved Gems of the Greeks and the Etruscans* (New York, 1968), 33, no. 14).

Provenances unknown
For a glass scaraboid showing an animal attack, note A. T. Reyes, 'Stamp-Seals in the
Pierides Collection, Larnaca' *RDAC* (1991), 125, no. 17. (Fig. 155)
133. (Fig. 156) London 331 (1898. 2–23. 3); scarab; banded agate; tall beetle; ridge spine; striations
    in front; double curving line to mark prothorax; triple parallel lines dividing elytra; oblique
    cuttings for winglets; L. 0.019 m. W. 0.017 m. H. 0.010 m.
    Rampant lion and rampant griffin fighting each other; plain exergue; linear border; objects
    getween griffin and lion, uncertainly interpreted as Cypro-syllabic *ja-si* (G. M. A. Richter,
    Engraved Gems of the Greeks and the Etruscans (New York, 1968), 33, no. 13).

134. (Fig. 157) Nicosia D. 185; scarab; grey; short notches at back to indicate prothorax and
    elytra; legs not cut; L. 0.012 m.
    Device worn: quadruped leaping onto the back of another; drillwork for heads and
    haunches of animals.

Bes

On the common use of the Egyptian god Bes in Near Eastern art, see V. Wilson, 'The
Iconography of Bes in Cyprus and the Levant' *Levant* (1975), 77–103; V. Karageorghis,
*The Coroplastic Art of Ancient Cyprus VI. The Cypro-Archaic Period: Monsters, Animals,
and Miscellanea* (Nicosia, 1996), 12–3. The image of Bes seems particularly well-attested
in Amathus, although none of the seals below is known to be from that area.[263]

Ayia Irini
135. (Fig. 158) Nicosia A. I. 2243 (period 5); scarab; green; double line separating prothorax
    from elytra; double line to separate elytra; L. 0.012 m.
    Bes as Master-of-Animals, grasping two rampant lions (*SCE* 2, 757, no. 2243).

Cyrenaica
The following is reported as having been found in Cyrenaica, but its authenticity has
been doubted. The style is too summary to judge but not inappropriate to an Archaic
serpentine seal, and the zigzag exergue is at home in Cyprus. The inscription is
illegible. The seal is probably genuine and Cypriot.[264]
136. (Fig. 159) Paris, Bibl. Nat. (de Luynes 250); scarab; grey-green; notched head; slightly
    pinched tail; damaged head; double curving line separating prothorax from elytra; silver
    crescent-shaped hoop with gold swivel mount; L. 0.025 m. W. 0.019 m. H. 0.013 m.
    Bes as master of animals; linear border; zigzag exergue; inscription illegible (Masson, *ICS*,
    389, no. 456).

Fig. 154. Cat. 132.
(2:1) Impression.

Fig. 155. (2:1) Blue glass scaraboid
with a device showing a lion with its
paws raised onto the back of a running
deer (?) (Larnaka, Pierides Collection
1959). L. 0.015 m. W. 0.010 m. H.
0.006 m.

Fig. 156. Cat. 133.
(2:1) Impresssion.

Fig. 157. Cat. 134. (2:1).

Fig. 158. Cat. 135. (2:1) Impression, drawing.

Fig. 159. Cat. 136. (2:1) Original, impression.

Fig. 160. Cat. 137. (2:1) Impression.

Provenances unknown

137. (Fig. 160) London 277 (1898. 2–22. 2); scarab; milky chalcedony; carinated spine; no
stringhole; striated front legs; L. 0.017 m. W. 0.011 m. H. 0.008 m.
Winged Bes wrestling with griffin; cross-hatched exergue; hatched border (G. M. A. Richter,
Engraved Gems of the Greeks and the Etruscans (New York, 1968), 35, no. 30).
The device seems to be a variation on the more common motif of Bes wrestling with a
lion.[265]

138. (Fig. 161) London 348 (WA); frog-shaped; mottled agate; L. 0.020 m.
    Bes as master of animals; arms to his chest, holding forepaws of two rampant lions, both
    with heads averted and with curving, knobbed tails (Walters, *BMGems*, 42, no. 348; pl. 6).
    The frog amulet is attested in Mesopotamia and Egypt in much earlier contexts, but seems
    otherwise rare.[266]

139. (Fig. 162) Private collection; scarab; banded agate; silver bezel; L. 0.023 m. W. 0.015 m.
    Running Bes; two lions held by tail; ground line; Cypro-syllabic inscription in exergue: *zo-
    wa-po-o* (Ζωϝαφόω) (O. Masson, 'Nouvelles Variétés chypriotes' *Cahiers: centre d'études
    chypriotes* 24, no. 2 (1995), 7–8; pl. 1, no. 1–2).

Birds

For birds on Phoenician seals, cf. Buchanan and Moorey, *Ashmolean* 3, pl. 9, no. 275
(upper register); Bordreuil, *Sceaux ouest-sémitiques*, 37, no. 27; 29, no. 16. Birds are
more often found as filling motifs.

Amathus
140. (Fig. 163) London 343 (1894. 11–1. 398, British excavation, 1894; tomb 286; CA); scarab;
    black; deep incisions to indicate parts of the back; grooves above base; legs not cut; L. 0.016
    m. W. 0.013 m. H. 0.007 m.
    Two opposing birds; line in between (Forgeau, *Amathonte* 3, 156, no. 41).
    The seal was found with 438.

Salamis area
141. (Fig. 164) Nicosia D. 34; scarab; grey; back damaged; L. 0.017 m.
    Device worn: bird (?).

Provenances unknown
142. (Fig. 165) Once Southesk; scarab; reported as haematite; L. 0.011 m. W. 0.010 m.
    Bird in heraldic pose; wings hatched and pointed downwards; slanting feather (?) on
    either side; linear border (*Southesk*, 207, no. O. 21; pl. 17; A. P. di Cesnola, *Salaminia* (London,
    1884), 137, no. 7).

143. (Fig. 166) Oxford 1891. 626; scarab; black; L. 0.012 m. W. 0.009 m. H. 0.009 m.
    Bird; linear border.

144. (Fig. 167) Oxford 1891. 650; scarab; black; worn back; L. 0.012 m. W. 0.009 m. H. 0.004 m.
    Two birds; circular object (? ankh) in between; cross-hatched exergue; linear border
    (Buchanan and Moorey, *Ashmolean* 3, 81, no. 549; pl. 17).
    For Phoenician versions of two facing birds, see Bordreuil, *Sceaux ouest-sémitiques*, 26, no.
    12; 29, no. 16.

145. (Fig. 168) Nicosia D. 23; scarab; grey; legs not cut; notched head; double line dividing
    prothorax from elytra; L. 0.014 m.
    Schematic bird in heraldic pose.
    This seal may possibly date to the Late Bronze Age.

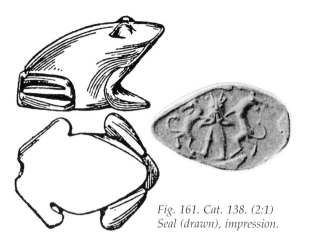

Fig. 161. Cat. 138. (2:1)
Seal (drawn), impression.

Fig. 162. Cat. 139. (2:1) Impression.

Fig. 163. Cat. 140. (2:1) Original.

Fig. 164. Cat. 141. (2:1).

Fig. 165. Cat. 142. (2:1) Impression.

Fig. 166. Cat. 143.
(2:1) Impression.

Fig. 167. Cat. 144.
(2:1) Impression.

Fig. 168. Cat.
145. (2:1).

Fig. 169. Cat.
146. (2:1).

146. (Fig. 169) Nicosia D. 73; scaraboid; black; L. 0.010 m.
Bird; lines in field (? Horus hawk).

147. (Fig. 170) Nicosia D. 26; scarab; black; L. 0.015 m.
Bird; one wing raised.

Fig. 170. Cat. 147. (2:1).

Fig. 171. Cat. 148. (2:1).

*Fig. 172. Cat. 149. (2:1)
Original.*

*Fig. 173. Cat. 150. (2:1)
Original.*

*Fig. 174. Cat. 151. (2:1)
Impression.*

*Fig. 175. Cat. 152. (2:1)
Impression.*

*Fig. 176. Cat. 153. (2:1)
Impression.*

Bulls

For the motif on Cypro-Phoenician bowls, see Markoe, *Bowls*, 28–9.

Ayia Irini

148. (Fig. 171) Nicosia A. I. 2562 (period 4). scarab; black; lumpy profile; L. 0.015 m. W. 0.015 m. H. 0.009 m.
Sriding bull; sideways crescent above; object in front; linear border (*SCE* 2, 768, no. 2562; pl. 248, no. 3).

149. (Fig. 172) Stockholm A. I. 2193 (period 4); scarab; black; high back; short notches to indicate parts of back; L. 0.017 m. W. 0.018 m. H. 0.009 m.
Striding bull; branch above; linear border (*SCE* 2, 756, no. 2193; pl. 245, no. 11, incorrectly drawn).

150. (Fig. 173) Stockholm A. I. (no accession number); scaraboid; black; L. 0.012 m. W. 0.010 m. H. 0.007 m.
Recumbent bull (?); linear border; scratch above back.

Kourion

151. (Fig. 174) New York N. E. 74. 51. 4405 (Kourion Treasure); scarab; black; notched head; L. 0.014 m. W. 0.011 m. H. 0.008 m.
Striding bull; summarily cut plant in front; star and curving line above; linear border (Myres, *HCC*, 448, no. 4405).

152. (Fig. 175) New York N. E. 74. 51. 4398 (Kourion Treasure); scaraboid; black; cross-hatching on back; L. 0.010 m. W. 0.008 m. H. 0.004 m.
Striding bull; tree above back; linear border (Myres, *HCC*, 447, no. 4398).

Lefkoniko

153. (Fig. 176) Nicosia 1960. v-24. 1; scarab; pale cornelian; L. 0.012 m.
Striding bull; linear border.

Pyrga

154. (Fig. 177) Larnaka (once Nicosia 1960. xi-21. 12); scarab; pale blue; L. 0.017 m. W. 0.012 m. H. 0.008 m.
Bull, head lowered, charging a tree; bird flying overhead; linear border (Charles, 'Pyrga', 29–30, no. 12, material reported as 'lapis lazuli'; device described as a lion walking toward a tree). The bull is closely related to bulls with lowered heads appearing on Phoenician bowls.[267] Seal 154 is in the Pyrga style.

Salamis

155. (Fig. 178) Nicosia D. 33; scarab; black; legs not cut; three short incisions to mark prothorax and elytra; large beetle; carefully

Fig. 177. Cat. 154. (2:1) Impression, drawing.

Fig. 178. Cat. 155. (2:1) Impression, drawing.

Fig. 179. Cat. 156.
(2:1) Impression.

Fig. 180. Cat. 157.
(2:1) Impression.

Fig. 181. Cat. 158.
(2:1) Impression.

Fig. 182. Cat. 159. (2:1) Impression, drawing.

cut head; L. 0.017 m. W. 0.014 m. H. 0.010 m.
Striding bull; branch above back; floral object in front; linear border.

Provenances unknown

156. (Fig. 179) Oxford 1891. 631; scarab; dark grey; deep groove at the side; summary back; legs not cut; L. 0.017 m. W. 0.014 m. H. 0.008 m.
Striding bull; flower (?) in front; crescent above (Buchanan and Moorey, *Ashmolean* 3, 81, no. 544; pl. 17).

157. (Fig. 180) Oxford 1891. 641; scarab; black; simple back; L. 0.020 m. W. 0.015 m. H. 0.011 m.
Charging bull, head lowered; large disc above; crude linear border (Buchanan and Moorey, *Ashmolean* 3, 81, no. 545; pl. 17).

158. (Fig. 181) Oxford 1891. 658; scarab; black; back very worn; L. 0.016 m. W. 0.012 m. H. 0.007 m.
Striding bull; disc and crescent above; objects (? scratches) in field; linear border (Buchanan and Moorey, *Ashmolean* 3, 81, no. 546; pl. 17).

159. (Fig. 182) Larnaka (Pierides 1960); diamond-shaped plaque; haematite; stringhole at one end; L. 0.022 m. W. 0.010 m.
Striding bull (A. T. Reyes, 'Stamp-Seals in the Pierides Collection, Larnaca' *RDAC* (1991), 125, no. 16).

Fig. 183. (2:1) Cow suckling calf on a green serpentine scarab of uncertain provenance (Nicosia D. 8). L. 0.016 m.

Cow Suckling Calf

On this well-known Near Eastern motif, see O. Keel, *Das Böcklein in der Milch Seiner Mutter und Verwandtes im Lichte eines altorientalischen Bildmotive* (Freiburg, 1980) and Markoe, *Bowls*, 43–4, pointing out its prevalence in Phoenicia. Note also Galling, 'Beschriftete Bildsiegel', Taf. 5, no. 33 and 35 and Nicosia D. 8, a serpentine scarab of unknown provenance (L. 0.016 m.). (Fig. 183).

Ayia Irini

160. (Fig. 184) Nicosia A. I. 2310 (period 4); scarab; black; carinated spine; L. 0.015 m. W. 0.011 m. H. 0.009 m.
  Cow suckling calf; hooves represented by drillings; linear border (*SCE* 2, 759, no. 2310; pl. 246, no. 30).

Marion

161. (Fig. 185) Nicosia D. 10 (German excavations, 1886; tomb; Ptolemaic); scarab; cornelian; lightly carinated spine; L. 0.013 m. W. 0.011 m. H. 0.008 m.
  Cow suckling calf; papyrus brake in back (Ohnefalsch-Richter, *KBH*, 366, no. 29; pl. 32. 29; Myres and Ohnefalsch-Richter, *CCM*, 136, no. 4582, classified as 'Egyptian style').
  Although the context is late, the scarab may belong to the Cypro-Archaic period, given its similarity to other seals of this time.

Provenances unknown

162. (Fig. 186) Present location unknown (once Berlin 6682; attributed by Cesnola to Kourion, by Pierides to Golgoi)[268]; scarab; described as 'de calcédoine et jaspe rouge'; heavy gold setting with pendant attachment; L. 0.015 m.
  Cow suckling calf; linear border; Cypro-syllabic inscription: *ku-pa-ra-ko-ra-o* (Κυπραγόραο) (Masson, *ICS*, 346–7, no. 357).

163. (Fig. 187) New York 74. 51. 4193 (attributed to Kourion by Cesnola, but Myres reports it as having been acquired in Smyrna);[269] scarab; agate; L. 0.018 m.
  Cow suckling calf; cow with drillings to show feet; branch in front; linear border; Cypro-syllabic inscription: *zo-wo-te-mi-se* (Ζωϝόθεμις) (Masson, *ICS*, 345, no. 354).

The following is included here as a variant on this common theme:

164. (Fig. 188) Paris, Bibl. Nat. (*Pauvert* 51); scarab; cornelian; V-shaped winglets; damaged head; low back; L. 0.012 m. W. 0.009 m. H. 0.005 m.

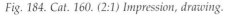

Fig. 184. Cat. 160. (2:1) Impression, drawing.   *Fig. 185. Cat. 161. (2:1).*

Lioness suckling cub; date-palm in the background; plain exergue; linear border (E. Babelon, *Collection Pauvert de la Chapelle* (Paris, 1899), 22–3, no. 51; pl. 5).

Deer

The motif is common on Near Eastern stamp-seals: see Galling 'Beschriftete Bildsiegel', 138–40.

Alakati-Galini Road (inland from Chrysochou, heading toward Kyrenia)
165. (Fig. 189) Nicosia 1937. ix-30. 1; scaraboid; black; L. 0.010 m.
   Stridiing deer with long, straight antlers; floral ornament in front; linear border (P. Dikaios, 'Prinicipal Acquisitions of the Cyprus Museum, 1937–1939' *RDAC* 1937–9 (1951), 202.

Amathus
166. (Fig. 190) Amathus T. 237/95 (tomb; mid CAI-early CAII); scarab; black; L. 0.013 m. W. 0.011 m. H. 0.007 m.
   Striding deer (?); linear border (Boardman, 'Seals and Amulets', 162, pl. 4).

Fig. 187. Cat. 163. (2:1) Impression.   Fig. 188. Cat. 164. (2:1) Original.

Fig. 186. Cat. 162. (2:1).

Fig. 189. Cat. 165. (2:1) Impression, drawing.

Fig. 190. Cat. 166. (2:1) Seal, original, impression.

167. (Fig. 191) London 338 (1894. 11–1. 373, British excavations, 1894; tomb 211; CA context)[270];
scarab; green; carinated spine; double line separating prothorax from elytra; notches to
indicate winglets; striations on front legs; L. 0.020 m. W. 0.009 m. H. 0.008 m.
Cow suckling calf; papyrus brake in background; double zigzag exergue; linear border
(Walters, *BM Gems*, 41, no. 338)

Ayia Irini
168. (Fig. 192) Nicosia A. I. 2533 (period 4); scarab; grey; lumpy profile; notched head; striations
on front legs; L. 0.015 m. W. 0.012 m. H. 0.008 m.
Striding deer, head turned back; muscles in body and neck carefully shown; two drillings
beside neck, one below body (*SCE* 2, 767; pl. 247, no. 18).
Cf. the cutting of 169.

Salamis
169. (Fig. 193) Nicosia (tomb 23. 52; CA); scarab; black; two notches for winglets; L. 0.015 m. H.
0.007 m.
Standing deer, grazing, head lowered; comb-like object above; linear border (Karageorghis,
Salamis 2, 51, no. 53; pl. 105, no. 53).

Tamassos
170. (Fig. 194) Berlin FG 129 (German excavations, 1889, tomb 15, section 4; found with black-
figure sherds of the second half of the sixth century); seal in the shape of a bull's head;
lapis lazuli; horns missing; extant dimensions: L. 0.019 m. W. 0.016 m. H. 0.011 m.
Stag; branch in front; linear border (Zwierlein-Diehl, *AGDS* 2, 62, no. 122).

Fig. 191. Cat. 167. (2:1) Impression.   *Fig. 192. Cat. 168. (2:1) Impression, drawing.*

Fig. 193. Cat. 169. (2:1) Seal, original, impression.

Fig. 194. Cat. 170. (2:1) Seal, original.

Figures With Branches, Staffs, Spears, Or Sceptres

The following devices are probably variants on the common Levantine motif showing a standing or seated male figure with a branch or sceptre in his hand (e.g., M. Dunand, *Fouilles de Byblos* 2 (Paris, 1954), 97–8, fig. 94, pl. 197; Bordreuil, *Sceaux ouest-sémitiques*, 27–8, no. 14). The device may derive from the Egyptian motif of a male figure carrying a lotus bloom or a sceptre.[271] The seated figure holding a branch-like object is possibly based on the common Phoenician seal-device showing a man with a spear, seated on a throne, in front of an incense burner: see Culican, 'Iconography', 57–73 = id., *Opera*, 218–34.

Amathus

171. (Fig. 195) Limassol; Amathus T. 285/79 (tomb; CA); scaraboid; grey-green; L. 0.015 m. W. 0.010 m. H. 0.005 m.
    Striding male figure, arm extended holding a branch; drillwork on branch and head of figure (Boardman, 'Seals and Amulets', 162, pl. 4).

172. (Fig. 196) London 295 (1894. 11–1. 633, British excavations, 1894; tomb 297; CA); scarab; black; notches to indicate winglets; base and head damaged; L. 0.014 m. W. 0.010 m. H. 0.008 m.
    Figure in tall, conical headdress, carrying sceptre with two short horizontal lines across the top; linear border; ground line (Walters, *BM Gems*, 35, no. 285; Forgeau, *Amathonte* 3, 158, no. 48).

Fig. 195. Cat. 171. (2:1) Seal, original, impression.

Fig. 196. Cat. 172. (2:1) Original.

Ayia Irini

173. (Fig. 197) Stockholm A. I. 2247 (period 5); scarab; black; crude markings on back; tail slightly pinched-in; L. 0.015 m. W. 0.011 m. H. 0.008 m.
Standing male figure holding branch; plain exergue; linear border (*SCE* 2, 757–8, no. 2247).

174. (Fig. 198) Nicosia A. I. 2296 (period 5); scaraboid; grey; L. 0.012 m. W. 0.009 m. H. 0.006 m.
Device worn: striding man wearing tall conical helmet; arm extended, carrying flower or mace; object in other hand (?); linear border; exergue (*SCE* 2, 759, no. 2296; pl. 246, no. 22).

175. (Fig. 199) Ayia Irini, Italian excavations 1972, tomb 10 (CG-CA); scarab; mottled blue; L. 0.015 m. W. 0.011 m. H. 0.009 m.
Standing male figure in long dress cut away at the hem, holding branch; linear border (G.S. Matthiae, 'Osservazioni Sulla Scarabeo della Tomba 10' in L. Rocchetti, *Le Tombe dei Periodi Geometrico ed Arcaico Della Necropoli A Mare di Ayia Irini "Paleokastro"* (Rome, 1978), 117–20).

176. (Fig. 200) Nicosia A. I. 2751 (period 4); scaraboid; black; deep groove above base; scoring on top; back partly damaged; L. 0.010 m. W. 0.010 m. H. 0.006 m. (*SCE* 2, 773, no. 2751; pl. 250, no. 13).
Standing figure, branch on either side.

177. (Fig. 201) Nicosia A. I. 2698 (period 4); scaraboid; grey-brown; L. 0.011 m. W. 0.009 m. H. 0.007 m.
Device worn: figure wearing a long robe, seated on chair; branch in front; branch (?) behind (*SCE* 2, 771, no. 2698; pl. 249, no. 27, shown on its side).

178. (Fig. 202) Nicosia A. I. 2728 (period 6); scaraboid; grey; L. 0.014 m.
Seated figure in long robe; branch on either side (*SCE* 2, 769, no. 2728).

Fig. 197. Cat. 173. (2:1) Original.

Fig. 198. Cat. 174. (2:1) Impression.

Fig. 199. Cat. 175. (2:1) Original, impression.

Fig. 200. Cat. 176. (2:1).

Fig. 201. Cat. 177. (2:1) Impression, drawing.

Fig. 202. Cat. 178. (2:1).

Idalion

179. (Fig. 203) Stockholm Idalion 1511 (sanctuary; context uncertain);
   scarab; black; ridge spine; double curving line to separate prothorax
   from elytra; L. 0.015 m. W. 0.012 m. H. 0.007 m.
   Device worn: figure with Egyptian hairstyle, holding staff with floral
   ornament; papyrus brake in background; exergue (?); linear border
   (*SCE* 2, 569, no. 1511; pl. 186, no. 11).
   For Phoenician examples, cf. Galling, 'Beschriftete Bildsiegel', Taf. 9, no.
   134–9. Because the device is simply outlined, rather than cut in intaglio,
   179 may directly imitate a faience model; cf. R. Giveon, *Egyptian Scarabs
   from Western Asia from the Collections of the British Museum* (Göttingen,
   1985), 76, no. 51; 114, no. 16.

*Fig. 203. Cat. 179.
(2:1) Original.*

Kition

180. (Fig. 204) Kition 505 (site 2, bothros 1; CAII); scarab; lapis lazuli; low beetle; L. 0.012 m. W.
   0.008 m. H. 0.005 m.
   Standing male figure in Egyptian wig and long skirt cut away at the hem, holding a sceptre
   (?) with a leaf-like top and resting a mace (?) on his shoulder; disc and crescent above; plain
   exergue; linear border (Clerc, *Kition* 2, 53–4, no. 505).

181. (Fig. 205) Kition 801 (site 2; bothros 1; CAII); scaraboid; lapis lazuli; very low; almost flat
   top; stringhole begun on either end, but does not traverse the length of the beetle; L. 0.012
   m. W. 0.008 m. H. 0.004 m.
   Standing male figure with tall helmet, carrying sceptre in front; ground line; linear border
   (Clerc, *Kition* 2, 70, no. 801).

Fig. 204. Cat. 180. (2:1) Seal, original, impression.

Fig. 205. Cat. 181. (2:1) Seal, original, impression.

Paphos

182. Nicosia 1937. viii-22. 2 (from Gila tou Tshiflikiou); scarab; grey; bottom damaged; extant L. 0.013 m.
Stick-like figure standing, wearing crested helmet and holding sceptre (? branch); hatching around edges.

Salamis

183. London 304 (1892. 5–19. 3, reported by Cesnola as having been found in a tomb);[272] scaraboid with sharply cut sides; black; summary scratches on top; L. 0.016 m. W. 0.012 m. H. 0.009 m.
Crudely-cut figure holding branch (? staff) in each hand; figure of man is striated; linear border (Walters, *BM Gems*, 36, no. 304).

Provenances unknown[273]

184. (Fig. 206) Nicosia D. 32; scarab; black; single straight line separating thorax from prothorax; short notches to separate elytra and to indicate head and winglets; L. 0.013 m.
Figure with branch; drillings used to show head, feet, hand, and base of branch.

185. (Fig. 207) Oxford 1891. 656; scaraboid; brown; L. 0.012 m. W. 0.010 m. H. 0.008 m.
Device very worn; figure wearing long robe, holding a branch in each arm (Buchanan and Moorey, *Ashmolean* 3, 81 no. 542; pl. 17).

186. (Fig. 208) Nicosia D. 67; scaraboid; black; L. 0.015 m. W. 0.011 m. H. 0.009 m.
Figure in long dress, with hatched skirt.

187. (Fig. 209) Nicosia D. 72; scarab; black; back damaged; deep notches to indicate prothorax and elytra; L. 0.015 m. W. 0.010 m. H. 0.006 m.
Figure wearing long, striated robe; hatched areas (? animals) on either side.

188. (Fig. 210) Nicosia D. 68; disc; grooves around circumference; black; devices cut on both ends; L. 0.014 m. H. 0.005 m.
(a) Figure between two branches; (b) four-winged scarab.
For the shape, cf. 43 and 125.

189. Paris, Bibl. Nat. (once Perdrizet); scarab; brown; L. 0.011 m.
Seated figure with branch (J. de Foville, 'Études de numismatique et de glyptique: Pierres gravées inédites du Cabinet de France' *Rev. Num.* 9 (1905), 293, no. 12; pl. 8).

190. (Fig. 211) Whereabouts unknown (once Péretié); scarab (?); dimension and material unreported.

Fig. 206. Cat. 184. (2:1).

Fig. 207. Cat. 185. (2:1) Impression.

Fig. 208. Cat. 186. (2:1).

Fig. 209. Cat. 187. (2:1).

Fig. 210. Cat. 188. (2:1).

Fig. 211. Cat. 190. (not to scale).

Fig. 212a. Cat. 191. (2:1).

Fig. 212b. Cat. 192. (1:1). Original.

Fig. 213. Cat. 193. (2:1).

Seated figure, arm holding branch; other arm raised; ladder exergue; branch behind chair; linear border (G. Colonna-Ceccaldi, 'Intaille phénicienne — Collection Péretié' *RA* 25 (1873), 30).

191. (Fig. 212a) Nicosia D. 63; scaraboid; green; L. 0.017 m.
Seated figure holding branch.

192. (Fig. 212b) New York 74. 51. 4147 (once Cesnola); lion-shaped; lapis lazuli; gold swivel setting; L. 0.011 m. H. 0.007 m.
Device very worn: single standing figure in long dress, holding spear; double ground line (Myres, *HCC*, 412, no. 4147, described as a 'sphinx shaped scarab').

193. (Fig. 213) Nicosia 1954. ix-17. 3; half-cylinder with devices at top and bottom; pale green; stringhole through centre; two grooves above stringhole L. 0.013 m. W. 0.009 m. H. 0.019 m.
(a) Standing man with crested helmet and wearing a striated long dress, holding staff; linear border (?); (b) winged insect (?); hatching on body.

Goats

Goats are well-attested as devices on Levantine seals.[274] Occasionally, in Phoenician iconography, they appear within a file of animals.[275]

Fig. 214. Cat. 194. (2:1) Original, drawing.

Amargeti (Paphos area)
194. (Fig. 214) Nicosia 1962. x-23. 2; scaraboid; black; L. 0.018 m. W. 0.013 m. H. 0.011 m.
Standing goat; hooves shown by drillings; linear border (V. Karageorghis, 'Chronique des fouilles et découvertes archéologiques à Chypre' *BCH* 87 (1963), 325–8, fig. 2).
For a very similar representation, cf. 206.

Amathus
See also Clerc, 'Aegyptiaca' 30–1 (T. 288/11, CAII context), for a scarab, 'probablement du lapis lazuli', with a reclining quadruped as a device, very likely a goat.
195. (Fig. 215) Limassol; Amathus T. 237/41 (tomb; mid-CAI-early CAII); scarab; black; deeply incised back; tall beetle with high plinth; L. 0.015 m. W. 0.011 m. H. 0.009 m.
Striding goat; slightly curved branch toward the back; linear border (Boardman, 'Seals and Amulets', 161, pl. 3).

196. (Fig. 216) Limassol; Amathus T. 242/82 (tomb; late CAI-early CAII); scarab; black; low back; very worn; L. 0.013 m. W. 0.010 m. H. 0.005 m.
Striding goat; linear border (Boardman, 'Seals and Amulets', 162, pl. 4).

197. (Fig. 217) Geneva 1897/ P. 836; scaraboid; black; L. 0.016 m. W. 0.012 m. H. 0.008 m.
Leaping goat (?); striations behind (? a branch) (Vollenweider, *Geneva* 1, 136, no. 182).

198. (Fig. 218) Nicosia D. 18; scarab; black; ridge back; legs not cut; L. 0.010 m.
Striding goat; body shown by three connected drilings.

Fig. 215. Cat. 195. (2:1) Seal, original, impression.

Fig. 216. Cat. 196. (2:1) Seal, original.

Fig. 217. Cat. 197. (2:1) Original.

Fig. 218. Cat. 198. (2:1) Impression, drawing.

199. (Fig. 219) London 1894. 11–1. 403 (British excavations, 1894; tomb 286; CA); low scaraboid; red; groove above base; L. 0.012 m. W. 0.009 m. H. 0.008 m.
Two goats *tête-bêche* (Forgeau, *Amathonte* 3, 147, no. 46).

The device of the following is much finer than the others:

200. (Fig. 220) Limassol; Amathus T. 288/12 (tomb; CAII); scarab; mottled black; L. 0.017 m. W. 0.013 m. H. 0.010 m.
Two rearing goats; heads turned back; branch in between; linear border (Boardman, 'Seals and Amulets', 162, pl. 4).

Ayia Irini

201. (Fig. 221) Stockholm A. I. 2257 (period 4); scaraboid; mottled grey-green; low back; L. 0.015 m. W. 0.012 m. H. 0.007 m.
Animal file: two striding goats; bird perched on back of second goat; linear border; bodies made up of drillwork (*SCE* 2, 758, no. 2257).
For another animal file, see 205.[276]

202. (Fig. 222) Nicosia A. I. 1120 (period 5); scaraboid; very pale green; L. 0.012 m. W. 0.010 m. H. 0.006 m.
Goat with bird perched on back; floral motif in front of goat; linear border (*SCE* 2, 710, no. 1120; pl. 244, no. 6).

203. (Fig. 223) Stockholm A. I. 2418; scarab; brownish-white serpentine (?); double curving line to divide prothorax from elytra; double line to separate elytra; L. 0.016 m. W. 0.011 m. H. 0.008 m.
Standing goat; hatched triangular area below (*SCE* 2, 763, no. 2418).

204. (Fig. 224) Nicosia A. I. 2263 (period 5); scaraboid; pale green; squarish; low back; base damaged; L. 0.013 m. W. 0.010 m. H. 0.007 m.
Stick-like standing goat (?) (*SCE* 2, 758, no. 2263; pl. 246, no. 11).

Fig. 219 Cat. 199. (2.1).

Fig. 220. Cat. 200. (2:1) Original, impression.

Fig. 221. Cat. 201. (2:1) Original.

Fig. 222. Cat. 202. (2:1) Impression, drawing.

Fig. 223. Cat. 203. (2:1) Original.

Fig. 224. Cat. 204. (2:1).

Possibly belonging as well is the following:

Kition
205. (Fig. 225) Kition 766 (site 2; bothros 1; CAII); scaraboid; grey; L. 0.017 m. W. 0.014 m. H. 0.008 m.
    Animal file: two quadrupeds striding to the left, the smaller one (? a goat) in front of the larger; tail of larger quadruped is knobbed; crescent (?) between animals (Clerc, *Kition* 2, no. 766).
    For another animal file, see 201.

Kourion
206. (Fig. 226) London 342 (1896. 2–1. 194, British excavations, 1896; site B; tomb 26; late CAII context); scarab; black; legs not cut; L. 0.014 m. W. 0.010 m. H. 0.007 m.
    Standing goat; drillings for hooves and eyes; body gouged deeper in the middle (Walters, *BM Gems*, 42, no. 342).
    Cf. the style of 194.

Paphos
207. (Fig. 227) Nicosia 1937. vi-8. 1; broken scarab or scaraboid; grey; L. 0.012 m. W. 0.010 m.
    Striding goat; branch in front; branch above back.

Provenances unknown
208. (Fig. 228) New York 27 (C. E. 1, once Cesnola); scarab; banded brown and white agate; gold box setting ornamented with granules and rope pattern in filigree; rope pattern incised along the upper edge; L. 0.020 m. W. 0.015 m. H. 0.005 m.

Fig. 225. Cat. 205. (2:1) Seal, original, impression.

Fig. 226. Cat. 206. (2:1) Original.

Fig. 227. Cat. 207. (2:1) Impression, drawing.

Fig. 228. Cat. 208. (2:1) Impression.

Two rampant ibexes back-to-back with heads turned to face each other; papyri in field; ladder exergue; linear border (G. M. A. Richter, *Catalogue of Engraved Gems* (New York, 1956), 8, no. 27; pl. 5).

For back-to-back rampant ibexes on a seal with a Hebrew inscription, see Bordreuil, *Sceaux ouest-sémitiques*, 50, no. 49.

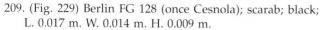

Fig. 229. Cat. 209.
(2:1) Original.

209. (Fig. 229) Berlin FG 128 (once Cesnola); scarab; black; L. 0.017 m. W. 0.014 m. H. 0.009 m.
Striding goat; branch above back; branch in front and behind; linear border (Zwierlein-Diehl, *AGDS* 2, 62, no. 123; Taf. 29).

210. (Fig. 230) Larnaka (Pierides 1958); scaraboid; black; low back; L. 0.019 m. W. 0.017 m. H. 0.008 m.
Goat (?); stick-like feet; tree with two branches above back; linear border (A. T. Reyes, 'Stamp-Seals in the Pierides Collection, Larnaca' *RDAC* (1991), 124, no. 14).

211. (Fig. 231) Nicosia D. 46; scaraboid; black; L. 0.013 m.
Two goats facing each other.

The following is of schist, but clearly related to the main serpentine series:

212. (Fig. 232) Oxford 1891. 652; scaraboid; dark grey schist; L. 0.013 m. W. 0.010 m. H. 0.006 m.
Striding goat; tree in front; fox (?) above; tortoise (?) behind (Buchanan and Moorey, *Ashmolean* 3, 81, no. 547; pl. 17).
Suitable sources of schist are known west of Marion.

213. (Fig. 233) Nicosia D. 210; scarab; black; L. 0.013 m.
Recumbent goat; tail curving up; linear border.

Fig. 230. Cat. 210. (2:1) Seal, impression, drawing.

Fig. 231. Cat. 211. (2:1).   *Fig. 232. Cat. 212. (2:1) Impression.*   *Fig. 233. Cat. 213. (2:1).*

Griffins

On the extensive literature concerning the Near Eastern griffin, see especially Buchanan and Moorey, *Ashmolean* 3, 41; I.J. Winter, 'Phoenician and North Syrian Ivory Carving in Historical Context: Questions of Style and Distribution' *Iraq* 38 (1976), 6–11; and E. Gubel, 'Notes on a Phoenician Seal in the Royal Museum for Art and History, Brussels (CGPH.1)' *OLP* 16 (1985), 91–110.

Amathus

214. London 289 (1894. 11–1. 413, British excavations, 1894; tomb 242; CA); scarab; black; short notch at each side to indicate position of prothorax; no line to mark elytra; stringhole; L. 0.015 m. W. 0.011 m. H. 0.007 m.
Griffin; head and wing only visible; linear border (?) (Walters, *BM Gems*, 36, no. 289).
The seal was found with 46. Walters pointed out that the device of 214 seems to have been left unfinished; it provides evidence for local production at Amathus.

Fig. 234. Cat. 215. (2:1) Impression.

Fig. 235. Cat. 216. (not to scale) Impression.

Fig. 236. Cat. 218. (2:1) Original.

215. (Fig. 234) New York N. E. 74. 51. 4401; scarab; black; oblique line to indicate winglets; L. 0.020 m. W. 0.014 m. H. 0.010 m.
Two griffins facing each other; discs above heads; date-palm in between; zigzag exergue; linear border (?) (Myres, *HCC*, 448, no. 4401).

216. (Fig. 235) Limassol; Amathus 82. 30. 1 (French excavations Chantier B Nord; isolated find); 'intaille de lapis lazuli'; dimensions unreported.
Striding winged griffin; disc above head; tail curving forward onto back; floral ornament (? ankh) in front; linear border (P. Aupert *et al.*, 'Rapport sur les travaux de la mission de l'école française et du ministère des relations extérieures à Amathonte en 1982' *BCH* 107 (1983), 967).
The material, rare in Cyprus, allies it to 180, 181, and 303 from Kition, all with Egyptianising motifs; note also 170 from Tamassos.

Ayia Irini

217. Nicosia A. I. 2111 (period 5); scarab; blue; L. 0.010 m.
Device very worn; recumbent griffin (?); cross-hatched exergue; linear border (*SCE* 2, 574, no. 2111).

218. (Fig. 236) Stockholm A. I. 2686 (period 5); scarab; mottled green; plain back; short oblique stroke on each side to mark division between prothorax and elytra; sumarily-cut head; L. 0.020 m. W. 0.015 m. H. 0.011 m.
Seated griffin; line above head (? representing disc); ladder exergue; linear border (*SCE* 2, 771, no. 2686). On the ladder exergue, see on 108.

219. (Fig. 237) Stockholm A. I. 2723 (listed as no. 2721 in *SCE* 2; context therefore uncertain); scarab; green chalcedony; double curving line separating prothorax from elytra; double line separating elytra; large beetle; slightly pinched tail; L. 0.019 m. W. 0.014 m. H. 0.010 m. Two griffins flanking a tree; bodies represented by drill-work; tree schematically cut; plain exergue (*SCE* 2, 772, no. 2721).

The following griffin-type seems local to Cyprus:

220. (Fig. 238) Nicosia A. I. 2755 (listed as no. 2687 in *SCE*; context therefore uncertain) scaraboid; grey; L. 0.013 m. W. 0.010 m. H. 0.007 m.
Standing, winged griffin with horns (? perked ears); circle beneath; linear border (*SCE* 2, 771, no. 2687; pl. 249, no. 23).

Arsos

221. (Fig. 239) Nicosia D. 168 (Cypriot excavations, 1917; sanctuary; CA); scarab; black; L. 0.014 m.
Winged griffin; disc above head; ground line; linear border (*SCE* 3, 598d; pl. 204. 23d).

Idalion

222. (Fig. 240) Stockholm; Idalion 1 (sanctuary on acropolis; period 6; CAII); scarab; chalcedony; large beetle; lightly gabled spine; notching in front; double curving line dividing prothorax from elytra; L. 0.022 m. W. 0.018 m. H. 0.012 m.
Winged griffin with apron; winged disc above head; exergue with parallel zigzag lines (*SCE* 2, 532, no. 1; pl. 186, no. 5).

Fig. 237. Cat. 219.
(2:1) Original.

Fig. 238. Cat. 220. (2:1)
Impression, drawing.

Fig. 239. Cat. 221. (2:1).

Fig. 240. Cat. 222. (2:1)
Original, impression.

223. Nicosia 1934. iv-4. 1 (acropolis); scarab; white agate; sharply carinated spine; L. 0.020 m.
W. 0.015 m. H. 0.010 m.
Seated winged griffin wearing double crown; ankh in front; zigzag exergue; linear border.

Kition

224. (Fig. 241) Nicosia D. 20; scarab; black; carinated spine; short, oblique lines to indicate
winglets; L. 0.020 m. W. 0.013 m. H. 0.010 m.
Winged griffin wearing double crown; comb-like object above; ladder exergue; linear border.

Kourion

225. (Fig. 242) New York 74. 51. 4168 (Kourion Treasure); scaraboid; black and white banded
agate; heavy bronze swivel setting with pendant attachment; L. 0.017 m. W. 0.013 m. H.
0.008 m.
Device worn: striding griffin (?); ankh in front (Myres, *HCC*, 415, no. 4168).

226. (Fig. 243) New York 74. 51. 4188 (Kourion Treasure); scarab; cornelian; heavy bronze
swivel setting; L. 0.015 m. W. 0.011 m. H. 0.007 m.
Seated griffin with head turned back; ankh in front; double ground line; linear border
(Myres, *HCC*, 418, no. 4188).

227. (Fig. 244) New York 74. 51. 4189 (Kourion Treasure); scarab; cornelian; striated front legs;
carinated spine; heavy bronze swivel setting; L. 0.015 m. W. 0.010 m. H. 0.007 m.
Seated winged griffin wearing double crown; incense burner in front; *neb*-sign as exergue;
linear border (Myres, *HCC*, 418, no. 4189; Clerc, *Kition* 2, 169, no. 7F).

228. (Fig. 245) New York 74. 51. 4191 (Kourion Treasure); scarab; green plasma; heavy bronze
setting with gold mount; carinated spine; double curving line to distinguish prothorax
from elytra; notches on front legs; L. 0.012 m. W. 0.008 m. H. 0.007 m.
Device worn: recumbent winged griffin with double crown; object (? ankh) in front; ground
line; linear border (Myres, *HCC*, 419, no. 4191; L. P. di Cesnola, *Cyprus* (London, 1877), pl.
37, no. 18).

229. (Fig. 246a) New York 74. 51. 4187 (Kourion Treasure); scarab; cornelian; carinated spine;
bronze swivel setting; striated front legs; L. 0.014 m. W. 0.010 m. H. 0.007 m.
Seated griffin; ankh in front; zigzag exergue; linear border (Myres, *HCC*, 418, no. 4187).

The following is made of metal, its motif cut in outline:

230. (Fig. 246b) New York 74. 51. 4143 (Kourion Treasure); scarab; gold; gold swivel setting;
low back; V-winglets; L. 0.010 m. W. 0.008 m. H. 0.006 m.
Striding griffin; disc above head; ankh in front; zigzag exergue with some horizontal
scratches; linear border (Myres, *HCC*, 413, no. 4143).

Marion

231. Stockholm M 62. 40 (tomb; first burial period; early/mid CAII); scarab; cornelian; carinated
spine; heavy gold setting with pendant attachment; L. 0.014 m. W. 0.009 m.
Seated griffin, disc above head; cross-hatched exergue; linear border (*SCE* 2, 370, no. 40; pl.
70, no. 1–2; Clerc, *Kition* 2, 169, fig. 7A).

Pyrga

232. (Fig. 247) Larnaka (once Nicosia 1960. xi-21. 7); scarab; black; details indicated by short

incisions; legs not cut; L. 0.019 m. W. 0.015 m. H. 0.010 m.

Seated griffin, wings extended on either side of the body; crescent above; cross-hatched exergue; linear border (V. Karageorghis, 'Chronique des fouilles et découvertes archéoloques à Chypre' *BCH* 85 (1961), 263, fig. 8; Charles, 'Pyrga', 25–7, no. 7).

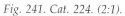

Fig. 241. Cat. 224. (2:1).

Fig. 242. Cat. 225. (1:1) Original.

Fig. 243. Cat. 226. (1:1) Original.

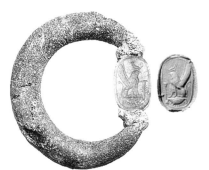

Fig. 244. Cat. 227. (1:1) Original.

Fig. 245. Cat. 228. (1:1) Original.

Fig. 246a. Cat. 229.
(1:1) Original.

Fig. 246b. Cat. 230.
(1:1) Impression.

Fig. 247. Cat. 232.
(2:1) Impression.

Salamis

233. (Fig. 248) Famagusta 866 (tomb; CA); scarab; 'pierre'; L. 0.017 m.
   Striding griffin with hatched wing; ankh (?) in front; linear border (V. Karageorghis, 'Chronique des fouilles et découvertes archéologiques à Chypre' *BCH* 95 (1971), 361–2; fig. 56).

Provenances unknown

234. Nicosia D. 102; scarab; mottled grey jasper; ridge back; L. 0.017 m.
   Seated griffin; ankh in front; cross-hatched exergue; linear border.

235. (Fig. 249) Oxford 1889. 407; scarab; brownish chalcedony; L. 0.017 m. H. 0.012 m. W. 0.008 m.
   Two seated griffins facing each other; discs above heads; date-palm in between; linear border (Buchanan and Moorey, *Ashmolean* 3, 81, no. 553).

236. (Fig. 250) Oxford 1891. 627; scarab; brownish-red; deep groove around side; legs not cut; L. 0.015 m. W. 0.012 m. H. 0.008 m.
   Two standing griffins facing each other, discs above heads; tails in S-shape; heads represented by drillings (Buchanan and Moorey, *Ashmolean* 3, 81, no. 543; pl. 17).

237. (Fig. 251) Oxford 1891. 636; scarab; dark green; L. 0.014 m. W. 0.011 m. H. 0.007 m.
   Seated griffin; disc above head; cross-hatched (?) exergue; linear border (?) (Buchanan and Moorey, *Ashmolean* 3, 81, no. 554; pl. 17).

238. (Fig. 252) New York N. E. 74. 51. 4400; scarab; black; back worn smooth; L. 0.015 m. W. 0.010 m. H. 0.008 m.
   Device worn: winged griffin, disc above head (Myres, *HCC*, 448, no. 4400).

Fig. 248. Cat. 233.   *Fig. 249. Cat. 235.*   *Fig. 250. Cat. 236.*
(2:1) Impression.   *(2:1) Impression.*   *(2:1) Impression.*

Fig. 251. Cat. 237. (2:1) Impression.   *Fig. 252. Cat. 238. (2:1) Impression.*

Hawk-Headed Figure

The hawk-headed figure, presumably a deity, appears frequently on Cypriot and Phoenician media; note, e.g., Markoe, *Bowls*, 88; Galling, 'Beschriftete Bildsiegel', Taf. 8, no. 100–2.

Amathus

See also Clerc, 'Aegyptiaca', 18–9 (T. 236/59. 1, CAII context), a scarab of orange cornelian, showing two hawk-headed (?) figures on either side of a thymiaterion. (Fig. 253)

The following is unusual in having a double-head.[277]

239. (Fig. 254) London 267 (1894. 11–1. 381, British excavations, 1894; tomb 287; second sarcophagus; CAII); scaraboid; burnt agate; gold mount; L. 0.013 m. W. 0.010 m. H. 0.006 m.

Four-winged diety (?) with two hawk-heads (?) in running-kneeling position; *neb*-sign used as exergue; linear border ; uraei above heads (?) (Walters, *BM Gems*, 42–3, no. 267; Murray *et al.*, *Excavations*, 98, 126; fig. 3).

The seal was found with 269 and 425.

240. (Fig. 255) London 284 (1894. 11–1. 294, British excavations, 1894; tomb 95); scarab; black; double curving line dividing prothorax from elytra; double line separating elytra; notched head; legs not cut; ridge spine; L. 0.016 m. W. 0.012 m. H. 0.009 m.

Clumsy engraving: hawk-headed figure in running-kneeling position; crudely-cut hatched border (Walters, *BM Gems*, 55, no. 284).

Fig. 253. (2:1) Cornelian scarab from Amathus with two hawk-headed (?) figures on either side of a thymiaterion (T. 236/59. 1). L. 0.016 m. W. 0.012 m. H. 0.009 m.

Fig. 254. Cat. 239. (2:1) Impression.   *Fig. 255. Cat. 240. (2:1) Original.*

Kourion

241. (Fig. 256) New York N. E. 74. 51. 4407; scarab; sard; L. 0.016 m. W. 0.010 m.
    Hawk-headed figure kneeling holding disc above head; linear border; no exergue (Myres, *HCC*, 448, no. 4407; Markoe, *Bowls*, 371, no. 18).
    The figure is very close in appearance to the hawk-headed figure on the inner register of a silver bowl from Amathus.[278]

242. (Fig. 257) New York 74. 51. 4149 (Kourion Treasure); scarab; blue chalcedony; heavy gold swivel setting; high beetle; elaborate markings on back; slightly pinched-in lines at the tail; V-shaped winglets; slight hatching on line dividing prothorax from elytra; notched front legs; L. 0.019 m. W. 0.009 m. H. 0.009 m.
    Hawk-headed figure kneeling opposite male (?) figure in Egyptian wig; blank cartouche with two papyri (?) at the top, between the figures; ankh behind each figure; winged disc above; linear border; ladder exergue (Myres, *HCC*, 41304, no. 4149).

243. (Fig. 258) New York 74. 51. 4150 (Kourion Treasure); scarab; milky white chalcedony; heavy gold setting; double curving line dividing prothorax from elytra; double line separating elytra; V-winglets; gable spine; L. 0.020 m. W. 0.014 m. H. 0.008 m.
    Two hawk-headed figures, discs above heads, facing each other; baetyle in between; disc and two rearing uraei above baetyl; *atef* crown above disc; winged disc at the top; *neb*-sign as exergue; linear border (Myres, *HCC*, 414, no. 4150).
    For a close copy, see Galling, 'Beschriftete Bildsiegel', 187, no. 102; Taf. 8 (with a Phoenician inscription).

Salamis

244. (Fig. 259) London 274 (1881. 8–24. 38, British excavations, 1881; reported by Walters as

Fig. 256. Cat. 241. (2:1) Impression.   *Fig. 257. Cat. 242. (1:1) Original.*

Fig. 258. Cat. 243. (2:1) Impression.   *Fig. 259. Cat. 244. (2:1) Impression.*

having been found in a Graeco-Roman tomb); scarab; milky chalcedony; spine and back damaged; tall beetle; double curving line to separate prothorax from elytra; L. 0.017 m. W. 0.013 m. H. 0.010 m.

Seated hawk-headed figure holding sceptre; disc above head; arm raised in front of incense burner (?); winged disc above; ground line; linear border (Walters, *BM Gems*, 33, no. 274; pl. 5).

For a similar seated figure, cf. E. Gubel, *Les Phéniciens et le monde méditerranean* (Brussels, 1986), 223, no. 254 (green jasper from Tortosa).

Horus Bird

The bird, traditionally a hawk, is usually shown standing on an outcrop, with a crook and flail, and wearing the Egyptian double crown. The hawk is associated with the Egyptian god Horus. For the Phoenician type, *cf.* J. Boardman, *Escarabeos de Ibiza, Procedentes de Ibiza* (Madrid, 1984), Lam. 5. 25a. In the west, the motif is known primarily from contexts that date to the fourth century B.C. (e.g., Boardman, above, 289; J. Vercoutter, *Les Objets égyptiens et égyptisants du mobilier carthaginois* (Paris, 1945), 214–5, no. 554–6), but the type probably appears earlier in the eastern Mediterranean. For other representations, see Markoe, *Bowls*, 42–3.

Amathus

245. (Fig. 260) London 286 (1900. 5–21. 4); scarab; banded brown and white agate; carinated spine; low back; double curving line dividing prothorax from elytra; striated front legs; L. 0.013 m. W. 0.009 m. H. 0.006 m.
    Horus hawk on omphalos; uraeus in front; linear border (Walters, *BM Gems*, 35, no. 286; pl. 6).

246. (Fig. 261) London 1969. 4–11. 261 (British excavations; tomb 311); scarab; black; curving double line separating prothorax from elytra; double line dividing elytra; ridge spine; L. 0.011 m. W. 0.008 m. H. 0.005 m.
    Crude Horus hawk; worn at base (Forgeau, *Amathonte 3*, 158, no. 50).

Ayia Irini

247. (Fig. 262) Stockholm A. I. 2632 (number does not correspond to no. 2632 in *SCE* 2, 770; context therefore uncertain) scarab; black; back worn; L. 0.016 m. W. 0.012 m. H. 0.008 m.
    Horus bird on cross-hatched outcrop; disc and crescent above; linear border.

Fig. 260. Cat. 245. (2:1) Impression.

Fig. 261. Cat. 246. (2:1).

Fig. 262. Cat. 247. (2:1) Original.

Fig. 263. Cat. 248. (1:1) Original.   Fig. 264. Cat. 249. (2:1).   Fig. 265. Cat. 250. (2:1).

Kourion

248. (Fig. 263) New York 74. 51. 4164 (Kourion Treasure); scarab; cornelian; carinated spine; heavy gold swivel setting with pendant attachment; L. 0.020 m. W. 0.015 m. H. 0.010 m. Horus hawk with crook and flail; rearing uraeus in front; circular and semicircular objects behind (Myres, *HCC*, 415, no. 4164; Clerc, *Kition* 2, 169, no. 7B).

Pera (near Tamassos)

249. (Fig. 264) Nicosia D. 131; scarab; onyx; base damaged; L. 0.013 m. Seated Horus hawk wearing double crown; ankh in front; object behind.

Provenance unknown

250. (Fig. 265) Nicosia D. 13; scarab; brown jasper with white patch; short notches at back to indicate prothorax and elytra; two grooves for legs; base of device damaged; L. 0.015 m. Horus bird (?).

Lions

On the Levantine basis for this motif, see Markoe, *Bowls*, 39–41; Buchanan and Moorey, *Ashmolean* 3, 40; A. Lemaire, 'Nouveau Sceau nord-ouest sémitique avec un lion rugissant' *Semitica* 29 (1979), 67–9; I. Cornelius, 'The Lion in the Art of the Ancient Near East: A Study of Selected Motifs' *Journal of Northwest Semitic Languages* 15 (1989), 53–85. On Phoenician seals, the lion is more often represented striding, rather than recumbent.

Amathus

251. (Fig. 266) Limassol; Amathus T. 159/50 (tomb; CC); scarab; black; carinated spine; L. 0.011 m.
Recumbent lion, head turned back with mouth open; papyrus brake in background (V. Karageorghis, 'Chronique des fouilles et découvertes archéologiques à Chypre' *BCH* 103 (1979), 678–81, fig. 32; Clerc, 'Aegyptiaca', 9–10).

Fig. 266. Cat. 251. (2:1) Seal, original, impression.   *Fig. 267. Cat. 252. (2:1) Original, impression.*

Fig. 268. Cat. 253.   *Fig. 269. Cat.*   *Fig. 270. Cat. 255. (2:1)*
(2:1) Original.   *254. (2:1).*   *Impression, drawing.*

252. (Fig. 267) Limassol; Amathus T. 288/10 (tomb; CAII); scarab; black; L. 0.013 m. W. 0.010 m. H. 0.007 m.
     Striding lion; flower in front; disc over back; linear border (Boardman, 'Seals and Amulets', 162, pl. 4).

253. (Fig. 268) London 336 (1894. 11–1. 617, British excavations, 1894; tomb 263; CA context)[279]; scarab; black; lumpy profile; carinated spine; L. 0.015 m. W. 0.011 m. H. 0.007 m.
     Striding lion; branch in front and at the back; branch above back; cross-hatched exergue; linear border (Walters, *BM Gems*, 41, no. 336; Forgeau, *Amathonte* 3, 153, no. 314; exergue should be cross-hatched).

Ayia Irini
254. (Fig. 269) Nicosia A. I. 2284 (period 4); scarab; grey; notched head; L. 0.014 m. W. 0.010 m. H. 0.009 m.
     Striding lion; linear border (*SCE* 2, 758–9, no. 2284; pl. 246, no. 8).

255. (Fig. 270) Nicosia A. I. 2528 (period 4); scarab; grey; back worn smooth ; L. 0.017 m. W. 0.013 m. H. 0.009 m.
     Device worn: striding lion (*SCE* 2, 767, no. 2528; pl. 247, no. 15).

Kourion
256. Kourion K81 (sanctuary of Apollo); scaraboid; pale green; L. 0.019 m. W. 0.012 m. H. 0.009 m.
     Striding lion; cross-hatched mane; a single curving line for tail; stylised date-palm incised above; linear border.

257. Kourion K79 (sanctuary of Apollo); scaraboid; light green; L. 0.012 m. W. 0.009 m. H. 0.006 m.
     Striding lion, head turned back; open mouth; very slim body; mane shown by horizontal

Fig. 271. Cat. 258.
(2:1) Impression.

Fig. 272. Cat. 259.
(2:1) Original.

Fig. 273. Cat. 260.
(2:1) Impression.

Fig. 274. Cat. 261.
(2:1) Original.

lines; curled feet ending in drilling; ribs depicted; muscles on the back leg shown with a V-shaped incision; S-shaped knobbed tail; object in front (?); linear border.

Provenances unknown

258. (Fig. 271) Boston 98. 738; scarab; cornelian; L. 0.012 m. W. 0.008 m.
Recumbent lion, mouth open, tongue lolling; papyrus brake in background; cross-hatched exergue; linear border (G. M. A. Richter, *Engraved Gems of the Greeks and the Etruscans* (New York, 1968), 33, no. 12).

259. (Fig. 272) Geneva 1897/ P. 836; scarab; cornelian; carinated spine; L. 0.014 m. W. 0.010 m. H. 0.008 m.
Striding lion; floral (?) object in front; V-shaped cutting above; oblique line behind; linear border (Vollenweider, *Geneva* 1, 117, no. 148).

260. (Fig. 273) London WA 134361; scarab; cornelian; elongated beetle; L. 0.021 m.
Two rampant lions; date-palm in between; winged disc above; zigzag exergue; linear border (Boardman, *AGGems*, 22, no. 22; pl. 1).

261. (Fig. 274) Munich A. 1282 (once Rhusopoulos); scarab; black; L. 0.019 m. W. 0.014 m. H. 0.008 m.
Seated lion; plant in front; ground line; hatched area above; linear border (Brandt, *AGDS* 1, 33, no. 109; Taf. 13).

262. (Fig. 275a) Berlin FG 77; scarab; black; L. 0.020 m. W. 0.016 m. H. 0.010 m.
Device worn: two rampant lions (?); linear border; cross-hatched exergue (Zwierlein-Diehl, *AGDS* 2, 62, no. 124; Taf. 30).

263. (Fig. 275b) New York N. E. 74. 51. 4377; oval stamp-seal with handle; low back; black; two diamond-shaped cuttings along the sides to provide a handle; stringhole; L. 0.030 m. W. 0.020 m. H. 0.006 m. Crudely-cut striding lion (?) (Myres, *HCC*, 444, no. 4377).
For the shape, cf. Buchanan and Moorey, *Ashmolean* 3, pl. 7, no. 211 (early Iron Age). Roughly comparable also is J. Boardman, 'Near Eastern and Archaic Greek Gems in Budapest' *Bull. du Musée Hongrois des Beaux-Arts* 32–3 (1969), 7–8, no. 1; fig. 4a–b with comments ad loc.

Fig. 275a. Cat. 262.
(2:1) Original.

Fig. 275b. Cat. 263
(1:1) Impression.

Man Confronting Rampant Animal

On the Phoenician basis for the iconography, see G. E. Markoe, 'A Terracotta Warrior from Kazaphani, Cyprus, with Stamped Decoration in the Cypro-Phoenician Tradition' *RSF* 16 (1988), 15–9; Clerc, *Kition* 2, 45, no. 468. Note also an Egyptianising glazed scarab from Kition in Clerc, *Kition* 2, 45, no. 468.

Fig. 276. Cat. 264. (not to scale).

Ayios Dhimitrios (Limassol area)

264. (Fig. 276) Nicosia 1955. i-11. 4; scaraboid; pale green; base damaged.

Lion with one paw raised confronts man (? with Egyptian hairstyle) carrying a sword; moon and crescent above; exergue with slanting lines.

Kourion

265. (Fig. 277) New York N. E. 74. 51. 4403; scarab; black; ridge spine; legs not cut; double curving line separating prothorax from elytra; double line dividing elytra; L. 0.012 m. W. 0.009 m. H. 0.007 m.

Fig. 277. Cat. 265. (2:1) Impression.

Warrior wearing long, hatched skirt slays griffin atop cross-hatched outcrop; plain exergue; linear border (Myres, *HCC*, 448, no. 44034; Markoe, *Bowls*, 371, no. 19).

For the cross-hatched outcrop, cf. 266 and 267.

Lapethos

266. (Fig. 278) Berlin FG 101; scarab; red quartz; L. 0.017 m. W. 0.013 m. H. 0.009 m.

Man in Egyptian wig and skirt grasps a rampant lion by the paw and prepares to slay it with his sword; the figures stand on a cross-hatched mound; winged disc above (Ohnefalsch-Richter, *KBH*, pl. 104, no. 3 for the provenance; Zwierlein-Diehl, *AGDS* 2, 65, no. 133, classified as 'Graeco-Phönikisch').

Fig. 278. Cat. 266. (2:1) Original.

Provenances unknown

The following is close to 266 in style:

267. Whereabouts unknown; scarab; cornelian; dimensions not reported.

Man seizes griffin by the neck; one arm raised; figure stands on a cross-hatched outcrop; branch on either side; linear border (*Hotel Drouot Sales Catalogue for 8 May 1905* (Paris, 1905), 8, no. 44; pl. 3).

The cross-hatched outcrops of 266 and 267 may be attempts to enliven the composition by treating the standard cross-hatched exergue imaginatively.

268. Nicosia D. 4; scarab; mottled brown jasper; ridge back; large beetle; L. 0.018 m. W. 0.015 m. H. 0.012 m.

Striding human figure grasps rampant lion by paw and prepares to stab it; disc and crescent above; hatched exergue; linear border.

Scarabs

Fig. 279. Cat. 269. (2:1)
Impression.

On the iconography of the Phoenician four-winged scarab, see Buchanan and Moorey, *Ashmolean* 3, 40. For the motif with a human head, cf. Boardman, *AGGems*, 73, no. 173 = G. M. A. Richter, *Catalogue of the Engraved Gems* (New York, 1956), 19, no. 23; pl. 4 (possibly Cypriot cornelian scarab with device showing a scarab with human head and forearms; inscription: either as two sigmas or Cypro-syllabic *zo*).

Fig. 280. Cat. 270. (2:1).

Amathus
The following was found with 239 and 425:
269. (Fig. 279) London (British excavations, 1894; tomb 287; second sarcophagus; CAII); scarab; sard; gold mount; L. 0.013 m. W. 0.009 m.
Four-winged scarab; disc above and below; linear border; zigzag exergue (Murray et al., *Excavations*, 126; pl. 4, Amathus no. 2; pl. 14, fig. 24).

Paphos
270. (Fig. 280) Nicosia D. 97; scarab; rock crystal; double line dividing prothorax from elytra; L. 0.012 m. W. 0.010 m. H. 0.010 m.
Four-winged scarab; disc above; incense burner (?) below; papyri on either side.

Provenance unknown
271. (Fig. 281) Geneva 1897/ P. 850; scarab; 'stéatite verte'; corroded silver setting; L. 0.015 m. W. 0.010 m. H. 0.011 m.
Four-winged scarab with human head and arms; head in profile with Egyptian hairstyle; arms raised to carry disc; linear border (Vollenweider, *Geneva* 1, 119, no. 151; pl. 61).
If the seal-setting is not modern, this gem is a rare example of a serpentine seal with a precious metal setting.

Fig. 281. Cat. 271. (2:1)
Original, impression.

Sphinx

On the iconography of the Phoenician sphinx, see Buchanan and Moorey, *Ashmolean* 3, 41; V. Karageorghis, *The Coroplastic Art of Ancient Cyprus VI. The Cypro-Archaic Period: Monsters, Animals, and Miscellanea* (Nicosia, 1996), 9–11; cf. also H. Pittman, *Ancient Art in Miniature* (New York, 1987), 75, no. 83.

Amathus
See also Clerc, 'Aegyptiaca', 3–4, no. T. 114/15 (early CAI context, 750/725–650 B. C.), with material described as 'pierre grise mouchetée de noir, présentant des trous et porosités sur la face non polie' and in a silver mount; the device shows a seated sphinx.

272. Limassol; AM 808 (French excavations, 1983; near city wall; late CAII);[280] scarab; black; triple line dividing elytra; L. 0.019 m. W. 0.013 m. H. 0.010 m.
    Two seated sphinxes facing each other; zigzag line above (Forgeau, *Amathonte* 3, 170, no. 85). The forepaws are not raised, as is usual. The hairstyles indicates Greek influence of the early fifth century.

Ayia Irini

273. (Fig. 282) Nicosia A. I. 2223 (period 4); scarab; black and white veined stone; L. 0.017 m. W. 0.013 n. H. 0.010 m.
    Recumbent sphinx; ankh in front; ladder exergue; linear border (*SCE* 2, 759, no. 2223, pl. 245, no. 24).

Erimi (Limassol area)

274. Nicosia 1935. v-22. 8; scaraboid; grey; L. 0.014 m.
    Device worn; seated sphinx with curved wing and one paw raised.

275. (Fig. 283) Nicosia 1933. viii-24. 1; scaraboid; grey; tall back; L. 0.017 m. H. 0.009 m. Similar to 274.
    Related sphinxes appear as emblems for the coinage of Idalion, the earliest of which come from a Larnaka coin hoard with a *terminus ante quem* of 480–70 B.C.[281]

Kition

276. (Fig. 284) Oxford 1889. 423; scarab; white agate; L. 0.014 m. W. 0.010 m. H. 0.006 m.
    Recumbent sphinx with double crown; papyrus plants; ladder exergue; linear border (Buchanan and Moorey, *Ashmolean* 3, 82, no. 555; pl. 17).

Kourion

277. (Fig. 285) New York 74. 51. 4139 (Kourion Treasure); scarab; green plasma; damaged head; V-winglets; L. 0.015 m. W. 0.011 m. H. 0.008 m.

Fig. 282. Cat. 273. (2:1).

Fig. 283. Cat. 275. (2:1) Impression, drawing.

Fig. 284. Cat. 276. (2:1) Seal, impression.

Fig. 285. Cat. 277. (1:1) Original.

Two facing sphinxes seated, each with forepaw raised; stylised tree in between; hatched exergue; linear border (Myres, *HCC*, 412, no. 4139).

278. Kourion Misc. 3 (sanctuary of Apollo; context uncertain); scarab; grey; large beetle; back damaged slightly; winglets shown with single, short, oblique line; single groove above base; L. 0.031 m. W. 0.022 m. H. 0.015 m.
Striding sphinx; branches in front and behind; ladder exergue; linear border.

279. (Fig. 286) Geneva 1897/P. 854 (from Episkopi); scarab; green; L. 0.013 m. W. 0.010 m. H. 0.007 m.
Schematic sphinx (?) (Vollenweider, *Geneva* 1, 137–8, no. 184; pl. 72).

280. (Fig. 287) New York N. E. 74. 51. 4402; scarab; black; double curving line to divide prothorax from elytra; double line separating elytra; carinated spine; L. 0.015 m. W. 0.011 m. H. 0.008 m.
Device worn: seated sphinx with straight wings; ground line; linear border (Myres, *HCC*, 448, no. 4402).

Provenances unknown[282]
281. (Fig. 288) Nicosia D. 59; scarab; cornelian; carinated spine; L. 0.017 m.
Device worn: two seated sphinxes; date-palm in between (Boardman, *AGGems*, 23, no. 30; pl. 1).

282. (Fig. 289) Berlin FG 135 (once de Montigny); scaraboid; black; L. 0.014 m. W. 0.011 m. H. 0.006 m.
Sphinx with short Greek hair style, sharply curved wing, one paw raised; linear border (Zwierlein-Diehl, *AGDS* 2, 64, no. 131; Taf. 31).

Fig. 286. Cat. 279. (2:1) Seal, original, impression.   *Fig. 287. Cat. 280. (2:1) Impression.*

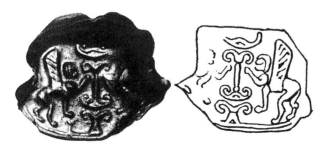 

Fig. 288. Cat. 281. (2:1) Original, drawing.   *Fig. 289. Cat. 282. (2:1) Original.*

283. (Fig. 290) London 448 (1894. 3–16. 1); low scaraboid; black; L. 0.016 m. W. 0.011 m. H. 0.006 m. Sphinx with short Greek hairstyle and one paw raised; tail curved forward, making a loop; linear border (G. M. A. Richter, *Engraved Gems of the Greeks and the Etruscans* (New York, 1968), 65, no. 168).

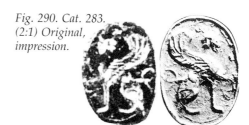

Fig. 290. Cat. 283. (2:1) Original, impression.

Worshippers

For the iconography, see Galling, 'Beschriftete Bildsiegel', 155–9; Taf. 8, no. 102 (Phoenician); Buchanan and Moorey, *Ashmolean* 3, 42, no. 272; Bordreuil, *Sceaux ouest-sémitiques*, 62, no. 67 (jasper, with a Moabite inscription); 82, no. 97; R. D. Barnett, *Catalogue of the Nimrud Ivories*, 2d ed. (London, 1975), 237 Suppl. 52; pl. 136 (Byblos). Cf. also J. Boardman, *Escarabeos de Piedra Procedentes de Ibiza* (Madrid, 1984), 45, no. 64 (green jasper, classified as 'Orientalising').

Amathus

284. (Fig. 291) Limassol; Amathus T. 276/342 (tomb; CA); scarab; red/white agate; well-cut beetle; L. 0.015 m. W. 0.010 m. H. 0.007 m.
Man in long, cut-away skirt holds mace (?); incense burner in front; crescent above; flower behind; crude cross-hatched exergue (? two stars and a stroke in exergue); linear border (Boardman, 'Seals and Amulets', 162, pl. 6).

285. (Fig. 292) Limassol; Amathus T. 172/14 (tomb; CCI); scarab; black; low beetle, very worn; L. 0.017 m. W. 0.012 m. H. 0.006 m.
Striding male figure wearing a high conical headdress; one arm raised; drilling in front of head; object in front; remains of exergue (?) (Boardman, 'Seals and Amulets', 161, pl. 3).

286. (Fig. 293) Limassol; Amathus T. 212/77 (tomb; CAII-early CCI); scarab; mottled grey; deep scoring at back; large head; high plinth; L. 0.020 m. W. 0.015 m. H. 0.009 m.
Two figures facing each other, both with one arm raised; incense burner between them; heads represented by drillings; winged disc (?) above (Boardman, 'Seals and Amulets', 161, pl. 3).

287. (Fig. 294) Limassol; Amathus 79. 10. 1 (Chantier B Nord; CC); scarab; black; dimensions not reported.

Fig. 291. Cat. 284. (2:1) Original, impression.

Fig. 292. Cat. 285. (2:1) Original, impression.

Fig. 293. Cat. 286. (2:1) Seal, original, impression.

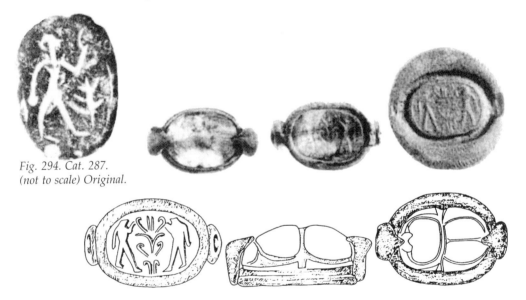

Fig. 294. Cat. 287.
(not to scale) Original.

295. Cat. 288. (2:1) Seal, original, impression, drawing.

Human figure with one arm raised and wearing a conical helmet approaches a small tree; linear border (P. Aupert *et al.*, 'Rapport sur les travaux de la mission de l'école française et du ministère des relations extérieures à Amathonte en 1979' *BCH* 104 (1980), 814, fig. 20; Forgeau, *Amathonte 3*, 169–70, no. 83).

Kourion

288. (Fig. 295) Nicosia (American excavations, 1981; near Archaic altar; late seventh-early sixth century); scarab; rock crystal; silver bezel; L. 0.013 m.
   Two standing figures, one on either side of a stylised palmette; each has one arm raised (D. Buitron, 'The Archaic Precinct at Kourion: 1981 Excavations' *RDAC* (1982), 144–7; V. Karageorghis, 'Chronique des fouilles et découvertes archéologiques à Chypre' *BCH* 106 (1982), 727–8, fig. 96; E. Gubel, 'The Seals' in D. Buitron-Oliver, *The Sanctuary of Apollo-Hylates at Kourion* (Jonsered, 1996), 163–4, no. 2).

Fig. 296. Cat. 289. (1:1) Original.   *Fig. 297a. Cat. 290. (1:1) Original.*

Local imitations of this Egyptianising motif are also well-attested in the glazed scarabs of Kourion. Particularly notable are two glazed scarabs of careful workmanship from the CAI levels of Kourion-Kaloriziki (K1166 and K1167); of these, the motif of K1167 closely resembles 288.[283]

289. (Fig. 296) New York 74. 51. 4166 (Kourion Treasure); scarab; cornelian; bronze swivel setting with pendant attachment; gold mount; carinated spine; double curving line to divide prothorax from elytra; double line separating elytra; V-winglets; L. 0.019 m. W. 0.013 m. H. 0.008 m.

Two bearded worshippers facing each other; both with one arm raised; date-palm in between; figures wearing tall headdresses and long dresses cut away to show one leg; winged disc above; papyrus plants (?) below figures; ladder exergue (Myres, *HCC*, 415, no. 4166).

Cf. 284.

290. (Fig. 297a) New York 74. 51. 4192 (Kourion Treasure); scarab; cornelian; heavy bronze swivel setting; carinated spine; L. 0.016 m. W. 0.013 m. H. 0.008 m.

Seated figure, arm raised, facing standing male worshipper, also with arm raised; figures with tall, flat-topped headdresses; incense burner (?) between them; winged disc with fan-tail above; linear border; zigzag exergue (Myres, *HCC*, 419, no. 4192).

The winged disc with a fan-tail is a North Syrian feature; cf. I. J. Winter, 'Phoenician and North Syrian Ivory Carving in Historical Context: Questions of Style and Attribution' *Iraq* 38 (1976), 4. The headdresses with wide brims find parallels in some Archaic sculpture and the Kourion terracottas.[284]

From the examples listed, it is clear that Phoenician influence is most prevalent in the area around Amathus and Kourion, where both hardstone and serpentine seals appear in a certain quantity. The seals of Ayia Irini, however, though comparable to the hardstone Phoenician examples, are largely made of serpentines. As an area, it specialised more in serpentine stamps.

To have emphasised, in the previous chapter, the rationality of the marketplace – increased trade and the need for seals as administrative tools – as a mechanism explaining the widespread use of seals in Archaic Cyprus may seem to undervalue the irrationality of the mind as an alternative. The fashion for Phoenician and Phoenician-style seals may have been no more than precisely that: a fashion. As a reading of Theophrastos and Pliny on stones readily shows, beliefs (not to say superstitions) attached themselves to ancient materials, and many hardstones, translucent and brilliant as they are, appealed as aesthetic objects and as possessions advertising some social standing. One thinks, perhaps, of an Early Iron Age equivalent to Crispinus in Juvenal's first satire:

> that Delta-bred house-slave, silt washed down by the Nile –
> now hitches his shoulders under Tyrian purple, airs
> a thin gold ring in summer on his sweaty finger
> ('My dear, I couldn't bear to wear my heavier jewels.').

Juvenal uses the word *gemmae* for the word translated above as 'jewels', from which it is clear that Crispinus was flaunting rings with hardstones, no doubt carved with a variety of wonderful and fantastic devices.[285]

There were clearly many reasons, rational and irrational, for which one acquired a Phoenician or Phoenician-like seal, and the adoption or purchase of a stamp could depend solely neither on one reason nor on another, but on several at once. For some, what would have mattered were the magical or religious qualities of the seals, valuable as dedications as well as possessions. It was not so much that a name was inscribed or that a device was lifelike, but that the script somehow encapsulated the qualities of the owner, and the device likewise captured the essence of its image.[286]

The repetition of devices may also imply that, for others, the choice of device was forced upon them. Similar devices may denote matching authority or equivalent responsibilities.[287] In the absence of sealings with closely matching devices, that is a possibility that cannot yet be shown. Possibly too, the consistency and repetition of the images mean that the seals are visual equivalents of ritual incantations, each device generally representing a hope for a particular deity's protection or a desire for the fulfillment of a certain wish. They are like a prayer, learnt long ago and repeated automatically thereafter, a token gesture and no more than a habit, but comforting and reassuring nonetheless.[288]

8

MISSING PAIRS

It is easy to see the influence of Phoenicia when serpentine versions of Phoenician seals are juxtaposed against their hardstone counterparts. There are, however, other seals found on Cyprus that are cut from the harder stones and seem Phoenician on the basis of their materials, shapes, and devices, but are without matching seals carved in the local serpentine idiom. Similarly, there are Cypriot serpentine seals with devices Phoenician in nature but lacking corresponding hardstone seals that one may point to as models. Those seals that seem Phoenician but have no counterparts in either serpentine or any of the harder stones have been isolated below as a sort of coda to the preceding chapter, with the expectation that, in time, the missing parts of the respective pairs will come to light.

SEALS CUT FROM HARDER STONES

The seals listed below are all carved from harder stones such as chalcedony or cornelian and are either found on Cyprus or else reported as having been recovered from the island. They may be either imports from Phoenicia or else locally cut, but the absence of serpentine versions means that one cannot assess to any significant extent their impact on the iconography of Cypriot glyptic. The prevalence of material from Kourion is again evident. As a Phoenician colony, the material from Kition may well have been imported.

Baboon

For the iconography, cf. R. Giveon, *Egyptian Scarabs from Western Asia Minor from the Collection of the British Museum* (Göttingen, 1985), 124–5, no. 47. It is unusual to find the baboon, usually associated with the Egyptian deity Thot, as the primary device on a Near Eastern seal. It is more common as a filling motif.[289]

Kourion
291 (Fig. 297b). New York 74. 51. 4151 (Kourion Treasure); scarab; cornelian; short lines to show winglets; striations on front legs and head; heavy gold setting; L. 0.015 m. W. 0.010 m. H. 0.008 m.

Fig. 297b. Cat. 291.
(1:1) Impression.

Baboon, disc and crescent above head; possible Cypro-syllabic inscription: (?) *e*; ground line (Myres, *HCC*, 414, no. 4151).
For a very close glazed scarab, cf. Clerc, *Kition* 2, 97, no. 1011. As a filling motif, the baboon will eventually become part of an East Greek Orientalising repertoire.[290]

Divine Boat

The divine boat is particularly associated with the Egyptian gods Horus and Isis. For the boat alone on a Phoenician seal, see Galling, 'Beschriftete Bildsiegel', Taf. 8, no. 104; cf. also J. Boardman, *Escarabeos de Piedra, Procedentes de Ibiza* (Madrid, 1984), 82; Lam. 4, no. 21–3.

298. Cat. 292.
(1:1) Original.

Kourion
292. (Fig. 298) New York 74. 51. 4190 (Kourion Treasure); scarab; banded agate; lumpy profile; heavy bronze swivel setting; L. 0.014 m. W. 0.012 m. H. 0.008 m.
Divine boat; disc and uraei above; disc and crescent and winged disc at the top; row of alternating large and small papyri plants below boat; ground line; linear border (Myres, *HCC*, 418, no. 4190).

Isis Suckling Horus

On this standard Egyptianising motif in Phoenician art, cf. R. D. Barnett and C. Mendleson, eds., *Tharros* (London, 1987), pl. 56. 6; Culican, 'Iconography', 57, fig. 1. For variants, see also Markoe, *Bowls*, 44–5.

Kition
293. (Fig. 299) Oxford 1896–1908 C. 338 (impression only; original missing; British excavations, 1894; tomb 56; Turabi Tekke; CA); scaraboid; haematite; ring setting; L. 0.012 m. W. 0.008 m. H. 0.004 m.
Isis suckling Horus; vegetation in front with bird (?) above; ankh behind; linear border; cross-hatched (?) exergue (Buchanan and Moorey, *Ashmolean* 3, 87, no. 581).

Fig. 299. Cat. 293.
(2:1) Impression.

Fig. 300. Cat. 294. (1:1) Original.

Kourion

294. (Fig. 300) New York 74. 51. 4140 (Kourion Treasure); scarab; blue chalcedony; carinated
spine; double curving lines to separate prothorax from elytra; two curving lines to divide
elytra; L. 0.015 m. W. 0.011 m. H. 0.008 m.
Isis suckling Horus in sacred boat; hawk-headed deity in front; male deity (?) behind; discs
above heads; bird on either extremity of the boat (Myres, *HCC*, 412–3, no. 4140).

Maat-Figures

Rare on hardstone seals, the Egyptian Maat-figure is usually seen as a filling motif.
These examples may be imitative of faience models; note, in particular, the excising of
the exergue of 295, and cf. Rowe, *Scarabs*, pl. 24, no. SE. 2. See also Clerc, 'Aegyptiaca',
35–6 (T. 297/21, CAII), a scarab of amethyst with two Maat-figures below two rearing
uraei. (Fig. 301) For a possible Maat-figure on a Cypriot scarab of serpentine, see
Clerc, 'Aegyptiaca', 42–3 (T. 321/114, CGIII-CA).

Fig. 301. (2:1) Amethyst scarab from Amathus with a Maat-figure on either side of a djed-pillar and rearing uraei above (T. 297/21). L. 0.015 m. W. 0.012 m. H. 0.008 m.

Kourion

295. (Fig. 302) London 151 (1896. 2–1. 1, British excavations, 1896; site D;
tomb 28);[291] scarab; sard; low beetle; L. 0.015 m. W. 0.011 m. H. 0.008
m.
Seated Maat-figure with disc and crescent above head; winged disc
above head; feather (?) on either side; cut-out exergue; linear border
(Walters, *BM Gems*, 20–1, no. 151; pl. 4).

*Fig. 302. Cat. 295.
(2:1) Impression.*

Very similar, but more lumpy in its shape, is the following:

296. (Fig. 303) London 154 (1902. 9–15. 3); scarab; sard; striated front legs;
gold swivel setting; L. 0.015 m. W. 0.012 m. H. 0.007 m.
Maat-figure; ankh above knees; *nefer*-sign (?) behind; feather in front;
inverted *neb*-sign (?) below; linear border (Walters, *BM Gems*, 21, no.
154; pl. 4).

Mummiform Deity

The deity probably represents Ptah. For a scarab showing the same
mummiform deity, cf. Galling, 'Beschriftete Bildsiegel', 187, no. 100,
with a Phoenician inscription, said to be from Aleppo. Cf. also
Bordreuil, *Sceaux ouest-sémitiques*, 35–6, no. 25.

*Fig. 303. Cat. 296.
(2:1) Impression.*

Fig. 304. Cat. 297.
(2:1) Impression.

Kition

297. (Fig. 304) Oxford 1899. 717; scarab; cornelian; deep groove for legs; simple beetle; L. 0.016 m. W. 0.012 m. H. 0.006 m. Mummiform deity holding sceptre; plant (?) in front; rod behind (Buchanan and Moorey, *Ashmolean* 3, 82, no. 561; pl. 18).

The following may be Cypro-Archaic, although found in a Late Cypriot context:

298. (Fig. 305) Kition 962 (site 2; 'entre les sols II et III de l'atelier 15 du Chypriote Récente III'); scarab; cornelian; bottom damaged; L. 0.015 m. W. 0.012 m. H. 0.008 m.

Mummiform deity holding sceptre; another deity (?) in front approaches also carrying a sceptre; traces of exergue; linear border (Clerc, *Kition* 2, 82, no. 962).

Fig. 305. Cat. 298. (2:1) Seal, original, impression.

Cf. also:

Fig. 306. Cat. 299. (2:1).

Provenance unknown

299. (Fig. 306) Nicosia D. 2; scarab; white jasper with brown patches; L. 0.018 m. Standing deity holding sceptre; figure in tall conical headdress; linear border; plain exergue.

Uraei

On the Phoenician iconography and the significance of the uraeus, see Buchanan and Moorey, *Ashmolean* 3, 40. For winged uraei on Phoenician gems, see Galling, 'Beschriftete Bildsiegel', Taf. 6, no. 64–6. See also Clerc, 'Aegyptiaca', 35–6 from Amathus (T. 297/21, CAII), a scarab of pale amethyst, showing two rearing uraei facing each other above two seated Maat-figures on either side of a pillar (Fig. 301).

Kourion

300. (Fig. 307) New York 74. 51. 4145 (Kourion Treasure); scarab; green plasma; gold swivel setting; low beetle; L. 0.013 m. W. 0.009 m. H. 0.006 m.

Fig. 307. Cat. 300.
(1:1) Original.

Fig. 308. Cat. 301.
(1:1) Original.

Fig. 309. Cat. 302. (1:1)
Original, impression.

Rearing winged uraeus; cross and dagger-shaped objects (? pseudo-hieroglyphs) in field; plain exergue; linear border (Myres, *HCC*, 412, no. 4145).

301. (Fig. 308) New York 74. 51. 4167 (Kourion Treasure); scarab; onyx; bronze swivel setting, now broken; oblique notches to indicate winglets; L. 0.018 m. W. 0.013 m. H. 0.008 m.
Cartouches with pseudo-hieroglyphs; uraeus on either side; linear border (Myres, *HCC*, 415, no. 4167; Clerc, *Kition* 2, 169, no. 7C).

302. (Fig. 309) New York 74. 51. 4217 (Kourion Treasure); scarab; brown and white banded agate; gold swivel setting; L. 0.012 m. W. 0.009 m. H. 0.006 m.
Rearing uraeus with cross-hatched body; plant in front with lower part of stem serving as shallow exergue; linear border (Myres, *HCC*, 420, no. 4217).

Uzat-eye

The *uzat*-eye seems infrequent as the principal device of a Phoenician seal, but for the eye as the primary motif on a faience scarab from Kition bothros 1 (CAII context), see Clerc, *Kition* 2, 66, no. 786; cf. also J. Vercoutter, *Les Objets égyptiens et égyptisants du mobilier carthaginois* (Paris, 1945), 250, no. 697. These seals may have been intended as imitations of faience models.

Kition
303. (Fig. 310) Kition 755 (site 2; surface find); scaraboid; lapis lazuli; L. 0.010 m.
Uzat-eye; linear border (Clerc, *Kition* 2, 62, no. 755).

Fig. 310. Cat. 303. (2:1) Seal, original, impression.

Winged Deities

On winged deities in the Near East and the distinctive Phoenician, North Syrian, and Assyrian types, see Culican, 'Iconography', 98–100; id., 'Seals in Bronze Mounts' *RSF* 5 (1977), 3; Buchanan and Moorey, *Ashmolean* 3, 40; G. Herrmann and J. E. Curtis, 'Reflections on the Four-Winged Genie: A Pottery Jar and an Ivory Panel from Nimrud' *Iranica Antiqua* 33 (1998), 107–34.

Kourion
304. (Fig. 311) New York 74. 51. 4197 (Kourion Treasure); scarab; grey and white onyx; heavy

Fig. 311. Cat. 304. (1:1) Original.

bronze swivel setting; carinated spine; L. 0.017 m. W. 0.013 m. H. 0.012 m.

Kneeling two-winged deity; one arm raised; very shallow cutting; ground line; linear border (Myres, *HCC*, 419, no. 4197).

305. Now lost; chalcedony; silver mounting; 'five-eighths of an inch long'.

Two winged figures facing each other; small figure of Horus-Harpocrates in between (O. Masson, 'Nouvelles Variétés chypriotes' *Cahiers: Centre d'études chypriotes* 24, no. 2 (1995), 15; pl. 2, no. 4).

Provenance unknown

306. (Fig. 312) London 281 (1902. 9–15. 1); scarab; mottled green plasma; ridge spine; double curving line to divide prothorax from elytra; oblique notches for winglets; L. 0.016 m. W. 0.013 m. H. 0.008 m.

Fig. 312. Cat. 306. (2:1) Impression.

Kneeling four-winged deity wearing *atef*-crown and carrying disc in front of the body; uraeus on either side of the head; *neb*-sign as exergue; papyrus blossom on either side of *neb*-exergue; linear border (Walters, *BM Gems*, 34–5, no. 281; pl. 5).

SERPENTINE SEALS

It is easy to imagine any of the motifs below as a device on a hardstone seal. They are all carved of serpentines with devices that show characteristics typical of the mainland Phoenician glyptic series: the cross-hatched exergues, Egyptianising filling motifs, linear borders. The range of sites demonstrates that, aside from Kourion and Amathus, where the Phoenician style is peculiarly at home, there are also traces of its infiltration in Ayia Irini, Salamis, and, not surprisingly, the area around the Phoenician colony of Kition.

Baetyl

On the baetylic image in Phoenician art, see Culican, 'Iconography', 73–80.

Fig. 313. Cat. 307. (2:1) Original.

Salamis

307. (Fig. 313) London 271 (1892. 5–19. 5, reported by Cesnola as having been found in a tomb); scaraboid; dark green; L. 0.017 m. W. 0.012 m. H. 0.007 m.

Baetyl with uraeus on either side; winged disc above; cross-hatched exergue (Walters, *BM Gems*, 33, no. 271, described as a 'sun-boat').

Fish-Man

For the motif, cf. Galling, 'Beschriftete Bildsiegel', 155; 188, no. 110; Taf. 8 = Bordreuil, *Sceaux ouest-sémitiques*, 37–8, no. 28. See also E. Gubel, 'La Glyptique et la genèse de l'iconographie monétaire phénicienne I' *Studia Phoenicia* 9 (1992) = T. Hackens and G. Moncharte, eds., *Numismatique et histoire économique phénicienne et puniques* (Louvain, 1992), 8; pl. 4, no. 12.

Provenance unknown

308. (Fig. 314) Cambridge; Fitzwilliam Museum E. 97. 1955; scarab; dark green; L. 0.021 m. W. 0.012 m. H. 0.017 m.

Fish-man, holding necklace (? dolphin); double ground line; cross-hatched exergue; Cypro-syllabic inscription: *pi-lo-i* (Φιλώι) (O. Masson, 'Un Scarabée de Cambridge à inscription chypriote syllabique' *Kadmos* 25 (1986), 162–3; P. Bordreuil and E. Gubel, 'Bulletin d'antiquités archéologiques du Levant inédites ou méconnues IV' *Syria* 64 (1987), 311; M. Henig, *Classical Gems* (Cambridge, 1994), 4, no. 8)).

For a comparable device on a Cypriot bronze ring, see R. Laffineur, 'Bijoux et Orfèvrerie' in V. Karageorghis, O. Picard, and C. Tytgat, *La Nécropole d'Amathonte: Tombes 113–367 VI: Bijoux, Armes, Verre, Astragales, et Coquillages, Squelettes* (Nicosia, 1992), 12, with a female version, from a Cypro-Classical tomb.

Fig. 314. Cat. 308. (2:1) Impression.

Floral Patterns

On floral ornamentation in Phoenician seals, see Galling, 'Beschriftete Bildsiegel', 149–50. The use of branches (?) as a device may derive from the papyrus-brake motif common in Phoenician iconography.[292] For an unprovenanced scarab of black serpentine, note also A. T. Reyes, 'Stamp-Seals in the Pierides Collection, Larnaca' *RDAC* (1991), 125–6, no. 19. (Fig. 315)

Fig. 315. (2:1) Black serpentine scarab with two crude palmettes (Larnaka, Pierides Collection). L. 0.017 m. W. 0.013 m. extant H. 0.008 m.

Amathus

309. (Fig. 316) Limassol; Amathus T. 182/40 (tomb; Roman ?);[293] scarab; black; low beetle: L. 0.009 m. W. 0.007 m. H. 0.004 m.

Tree(?); branches on one side bent back (Boardman, 'Seals and Amulets', 161, no. 182/40; pl. 3, no. 6).

Fig. 316. Cat. 309. (2:1) Seal, original.

Fig. 317. Cat. 310. (2:1) Original.

Ayia Irini
310. (Fig. 317) Stockholm A. I. 2425 (period 4); scaraboid; mottled blue-grey; low back; very polished; L. 0.012 m. W. 0.008 m. H. 0.005 m.
Three branches; vertical line between branches; linear border (*SCE* 2, 764, no. 2425).

Frontal Faces

Scarab motifs using the heads of deities such as Hathor or Bes are well-attested for Phoenician glyptic.[294] Serpentine seals with crude schematic faces as their devices may be imitative of these and were perhaps used as apotropaic charms. Cf. also 446, side (a) and 447, side (d).

Fig. 318. Cat. 311. (2:1) Impression, drawing.

Amathus
311. (Fig. 318) Nicosia 1950. xi-10. 2 (reported as from Aoratos, Limassol); scarab; black; legs not cut; L. 0.013 m.
Schematic bearded face.
The head may represent either a Gorgon or Bes figure (if the device has been presented the right way up); cf. 314.

Ayia Irini
312. (Fig. 319) Nicosia A. I. 2280 (period 4); cylinder pinched-in at the middle; pale green; stringhole across pinched section; devices at either end; D. 0.012 m. H. 0.014 m.
(a) Seated lion; tail in S-shaped curve; head turned back; circular border; (b) frontal demon's head with horns (? upright ears); disc above; uraeus on either side; circular border (*SCE* 2, 758, no. 2280; pl. 243, no. 16).
The shape may derive from an Anatolian tradition, but the distinctive pale green colour allies it with local production.[295] For the seated lion, *cf.* Vollenweider, *Geneva* 3, 89, no. 127 (unprovenanced, but perhaps Cypriot).

Kition
313. (Fig. 320) Kition 2021 (site 2; outside the norther wall of the Phoenician temple, between floors 3 and 1; CGIII-Hellenistic); scaraboid; grey; L. 0.014 m. W. 0.011 m. H. 0.008 m.
Schematic face (?), consisting of two dots for eyes; a triangular nose; a small curve for the mouth (Clerc, *Kition* 2, 107, no. 2021).

Provenance unknown
314. (Fig. 321) Oxford 1891. 629; scarab; dark-grey; legs not cut; deep grooves above the base; L. 0.017 m. W. 0.014 m. H. 0.009 m.
Schematic face; hair shown with hatching (Buchanan and Moorey, *Ashmolean* 3, 81, no. 551; pl. 17).

Fig. 319. Cat. 312. (2:1)
Impression, drawing.

Fig. 320. Cat. 313. (2:1) Seal, original, impression.

Fig. 321. Cat. 314.
(2:1) Impression.

Horses

On the horse in Cypro-Phoenician iconography, see Markoe, *Bowls*, 41–2.

Amathus

315. (Fig. 322) Limassol; Amathus T. 142/39 (tomb; late CAI-early CAII); scarab; dark grey; deeply incised back; L. 0.016 m. W. 0.011 m. H. 0.008 m.
Striding horse; branch over back; linear border (Boardman, 'Seals and Amulets', 161, pl. 3).

316. (Fig. 323) Limassol; Amathus T. 237/16 (tomb; mid-CAI-early CAII); scarab; black; deeply incised back; L. 0.013 m. W. 0.010 m. H. 0.006 m.
Striding horse; branch over back; line in front (Boardman, 'Seals and Amulets', 161, pl. 3).

317. (Fig. 324) Limassol; Amathus T. 237/92 (tomb; mid-CAI-early CAII); scarab; black; L. 0.009 m. W. 0.007 m. H. 0.008 m.
Striding horse; branch over back (Boardman, 'Seals and Amulets', 162, pl. 4).

Arsos

318. (Fig. 325) Nicosia D. 166 (Cypriot excavations, 1917; sanctuary; CA); scarab; black; notched head; L. 0.014 m.
Striding horse; tail with sharp, downward turn; linear border (*SCE* 3, 598; pl. 204. 23b).

319. (Fig. 326) Nicosia D. 171 (Cypriot excavations 1917; sanctuary; CA); scarab; black; L. 0.015 m.
Striding horse; V-shaped object (? bird) above; linear border (*SCE* 3, 599. l; pl. 204. 23l).

Ayia Irini

320. (Fig. 327) Nicosia A. I. 2557 (period 4); scarab; grey; L. 0.017 m. W. 0.014 m. H. 0.007 m.

Fig. 322. Cat. 315. (2:1) Seal, original, impression.

Fig. 323. Cat. 316. (2:1) Seal, original, impression.

Fig. 324. Cat. 317. (2:1) Seal, original, impression.

Fig. 325. Cat. 318. (2:1) Seal, original, drawing.

Fig. 326. Cat. 319. (2:1) Seal, original, drawing.

Fig. 327. Cat. 320. (2:1) Impression, drawing.

Device worn: running horse; vertical scratch (? wing) above back; linear border (?) (*SCE* 2, 768, no. 2557; pl. 247, no. 29; S. M. Lubsen-Admiraal and J. Crouwel, *Cyprus and Aphrodite* ('s-Gravenhage, 1989), 170–1, no. 169.

321. (Fig. 328) Nicosia A. I. 2275 (period 5); scarab; grey; L. 0.013 m.
Striding horse; tail with sharp downward turn; drilling above; crude linear border (*SCE* 2, 758, no. 2275).

Salamis

322. (Fig. 329) Nicosia (Salamis T. 89. 32; CCI); scarab; grey-green; L. 0.017 m.
Device worn: two opposed, standing horses (?), heads averted (Karageorghis, *Salamis* 2, 139; pl. 170, no. 32).

Provenances unknown

323. (Fig. 330) Nicosia D. 22; scarab; grey; legs not cut; straight line to divide prothorax from elytra; double line separating elytra; L. 0.018 m.
Horse approaching vegetation (?); long-necked bird above.
It is not impossible that 323 should date to the Late Bronze Age.

324. (Fig. 331) Nicosia D. 209; scarab; black; striations head; hatching on elytra; elytra divided from prothorax by a single straight line; legs indicated by grooves above base; L. 0.011 m.
Striding horse approaching flower (?); curving branch (? scorpion) above.
The device may derive from the Horse-Group motif.

Fig. 328. Cat. 321. (2:1) Impression, drawing.

Fig. 329. Cat. 322. (2:1) Seal, original.

Fig. 330. Cat. 210. (2:1) Seal, impression, drawing.

Fig. 331. Cat. 324. (2:1).

Smiting Figure

On the iconography, see above on 23.

Idalion

325. Whereabouts uncertain; Idalion 1524 (sanctuary; period 6a; late CAII); scarab; grey; chipped
    back; L. 0.014 m.
    Figure in smiting pose, wearing tall, conical headdress (*SCE* 2, 569, no. 1524; 833; pl. 186,
    no. 9).

9
EGYPT AND MESOPOTAMIA

Even accepting the predominance of Phoenician, as well as Anatolian or North Syrian, influence on Cypriot glyptic, one still needs to consider the possibility that other glyptic traditions active in the Mediterranean affected the island's stamp-seal production, however minimally. This chapter considers two such areas left largely unconsidered thus far: Egypt and Mesopotamia. Since Cyprus is positioned amidst trading routes emerging from both these areas, it is worth looking at the extent to which they may have exerted any influence on the Cypriot stamp-seals.

EGYPTIAN INFLUENCE

To define a style as Phoenician is, in essence, to define by a negative. What does not correspond precisely to the iconography of Egypt is therefore Egyptianising and thus Phoenician. But is it possible that the Egyptianising qualities of particular devices result from contact with Egypt itself, rather than Phoenicia? Typically with low, uncarinated, crudely-marked backs, and summary legs, the Egyptian glazed scarabs could easily be copied in serpentine. This is certainly true of a Middle Bronze Age scarab from Cyprus, now in London, but whose precise provenance is unknown. Its device shows a goat incised in outline, with a branch in front and a cobra above its back, the whole enclosed in a linear border (Fig. 332). But the use of incision to outline the animal could have derived from a similar technique used in the Levant, rather than in Egypt itself, and the profile of the seal and markings on its back, unusual for serpentine scarabs, are equally explicable as imitations of faience originals from the Levant.[296] The same practice of imitating Egyptian products is very likely true for periods later than the Middle Bronze Age. The problem is made more difficult by the long history of cultural borrowing between the Levant and Egypt, from the Bronze Age onwards, in glyptic as well as other arts.[297]

Fig. 332. (2:1) Scarab of dark green serpentine of unknown provenance, with device showing a striding goat (London 245). L. 0.020 m. W. 0.014 m. H. 0.008 m.

Thus, the identification of serpentine seals that copy or imitate faience or glazed scarabs that are definitely Egyptian, rather than Levantine, is especially difficult. Because in Cyprus, as in the western Mediterranean, scarabs and scaraboids of steatite, faience, and frit that actually originate in Egypt are found side-by-side with the serpentine seals, there is every likelihood that a thread of direct Egyptian influence on local Cypriot glyptic runs parallel with the more overt Phoenician or North Syrian and Anatolian strands.[298] Cypriot factories, for example, could reproduce particular Egyptian glazed scarabs closely; the island's glazed scarabs, for example, show affinities with glazed scarabs from Naukratis and other Egyptian types.[299] It is therefore not impossible that some of the serpentine and hardstone seals of Cyprus are meant as approximations of Egyptian, rather than Egyptianising, models.

It is generally true to say that the devices on the serpentine seals do not at all resemble Egyptian hieroglyphs. But a small number may nonetheless be described as 'hieroglyphic', recalling certain images on Egyptian glazed seals. Note, for example, 295. Some of the striding animals on the Cypriot serpentine stamps may also be imitative of the striding animals on the glazed scarabs, particularly when a disc appears above the animal (e. g., 157, 466). Other points of similarity between the serpentine series from Cyprus and glazed scarabs and scaraboids that are found throughout the Levant and Egypt include the use of geometric patterns as the sole device (e. g., 498–510); the use of motifs that appear in two or three registers with each register denoted by two or three lines (e. g., 47, 61, 88); the use of certain Egyptian deities or composite creatures as the principal device of the scarab or scaraboid (e. g., Maat or Ptah figures: 295–9); and the use of seals cut in the shape of heads (e. g., 4–12).[300] Since Cypriot seals of glazed materials already appear by the early seventh century in Italy, some of the later serpentine devices from Cyprus itself may well have been influenced by these earlier glazed seals. In certain instances, however, both the Cypriot glazed scarabs and the serpentine examples may have been influenced by common Egyptian or Egyptianising sources.[301]

Direct Egyptian influence on the serpentine seals cannot be ruled out, therefore. The regular traffic between Cyprus and Egypt throughout the Archaic period ensures that possibility. But a more refined understanding of the differences between actual Egyptian products and their imitations is necessary before the matter can be settled. Ultimately, the Cypriot serpentine seals exerted some influence on the local glazed scarabs, and later faience seals acquire devices that are less hieroglyphic and more orientalising or even Classical in appearance, with *neb*-exergues disappearing, for example, and hatched borders becoming more in vogue.[302]

It has also been suggested that, in the sixth century especially, the Egyptian element in Cypriot glyptic became stronger, and this has been explained in terms of Amasis' rule over the island; at this time too, 'an Egyptian Cyprus may have been more readily open to the Greeks of East Greece and Aegina who had cornered the trade with Egypt at Naukratis.'[303] Perhaps then, at least some of the Egyptianising devices reflect this period of Cypriot history. To prove this, however, one needs to define more closely the character of Phoenician seals belonging to the sixth century. Little is known of mainland Phoenician art at that time, and Phoenician seals are no exception to this general rule. But nothing suggests that the Egyptianising element within Phoenicia itself would have been any less prominent than that found in Cyprus for the sixth century. Furthermore, it may be correct to prefer a minimalist interpretation to the Herodotean passage alluding to a 'domination' over the island by the Egyptian Pharaoh Amasis. If that reference is, in fact, less malevolent than is normally understood, then it is difficult to see the Egyptian or Egyptianising elements within Cyprus during the sixth century as any heavier or lighter than they had been in previous centuries.

MESOPOTAMIAN SEALS

The evidence for significant direct influence from the Neo-Assyrian empire has already been discussed and set aside.[304] But unequivocally attested from excavations on the island are a number of seals cut in what is generally known as a Neo-Babylonian style. To what extent do these seals reflect contact and influence with the Neo-Babylonian empire?

Neo-Babylonian Seals

The term 'Neo-Babylonian' is a loose one, since chronologically, the seals cut in this distinctive style range from the second half of the seventh century until the Achaemenid period. The seals are usually conoid, of chalcedony or quartz, often with eight facets forming an octagonal base, and with devices cut in a very modelled style. Typically, devices show a worshipper with one hand raised in front of religious symbols. The cutting emphasises the different parts of the motif by the use of rounded, drilled forms.[305]

Amathus

326. Amathus (Cypriot excavations, 1983; tomb 11, no. 19; context
     unreported); conoid; dimensions, material, and device unreported (V.
     Karageorghis, 'Chronique des fouilles et découvertes archéologiques a
     Chypre' *BCH* 112 (1988), 804, n. 17).
     The device of the following seal from Amathus seems derivative of the
     lunar standard that appears on Neo-Babylonian seals and may be noted
     here:[306]

Fig. 333. Cat. 327. (2:1) Impression.

327. (Fig. 333) New York N. E. 74. 51. 4404; scarab;
     pale green; legs not cut; L. 0.008 m. W. 0.010
     m. H. 0.008 m.
     Horned table (?); papyrus plant (?) on either
     side below horns (Myres, *HCC*, 448, no. 4404).

The device may be imitative of those Neo-Babylonian seals; see, however, also Appendix 5.

Ayia Irini
328. (Fig. 334) Nicosia A. I. 2684 (period 5); conoid;

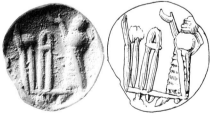

*Fig. 334. Cat. 328. (2:1)
Impression, drawing.*

faience; slightly convex base; H. 0.020 m. D. 0.014 m.

Male worshipper; arms raised in front of divine symbols (*SCE* 2, 771, no. 2684; pl. 243, no. 13).

Since 328 is of faience, it may well be a local Cypriot product, imitative of Neo-Babylonian conoids, rather than an import.

Kition

329. (Fig. 335) Oxford 1896–1908 C. 337 (tomb 4, Turabi Tekke; 'late Hellenistic or Graeco-Roman'); octagonal conoid; bluish chalcedony; L. 0.024 m. H. 0.020 m.

Worshipper with one arm raised; in front, deity standing on a crescent; star above; 'cactus'-plant below (Buchanan and Moorey, *Ashmolean* 3, 82, no. 564).

Paphos

330. (Fig. 336) Paphos Museum; PM 2593/3 (tomb; Hellenistic ?); octagonal conoid; chalcedony; H. 0.021 m.

Divine symbols, crescent standard in between; perhaps unfinished (V. Karageorghis, 'Chronique des fouilles et découvertes archéologiques à Chypre' *BCH* 112 (1988), 804, n. 17).

Voroklini (north of Larnaka)

331. (Fig. 337) Larnaka E. 3 (tomb); octagonal conoid; chalcedony; L. 0.020 m. W. 0.015 m. H. 0.029 m.

Two worshippers, one on either side of a spade (symbol of the god Marduk); crescent above (V. Karageorghis, 'Chronique des fouilles et découvertes archéologiques à Chypre' *BCH* 112 (1988), 804, n. 17).

Provenances unknown[307]

332. (Fig. 338) Oxford 1891. 647; octagonal conoid; onyx; L. 0.020 m. W. 0.010 m. H. 0.026 m.

Worshipper, symbols and lamp on altar; star above (Buchanan and Moorey, *Ashmolean* 3, 82, no. 565).

Fig. 335. Cat. 329. (2:1) Impression.

Fig. 336. Cat. 330. (2:1) Impression.

*Fig. 337. Cat. 331.
(2:1) Impression.*

*Fig. 338. Cat. 332.
(2:1) Impression.*

*Fig. 339. Cat. 333.
(2:1) Impression.*

Fig. 340. Cat. 334. Original, impression.

333. (Fig. 339) Oxford 1891. 655; conoid; brown-blue chalcedony; L. 0.014 m. W. 0.012 m. H. 0.017 m.
Star pattern (? described as a 'highly stylised four-winged figure'); ground line (Buchanan and Moorey, *Ashmolean* 3, 82, no. 566).

334. (Fig. 340) Aberdeen (Marischal College, Anthropological Museum); octagonal conoid; chalcedony; H. 0.025 m.
Worshipper with one arm raised in front of divine symbols on altar; two crescents above; object behind figure; Cypro-syllabic inscription: *zo-si-ke-re-wo-to-se* (Ζωσικρέϝο(ν)) (Masson, *ICS*, 344 and 421, no. 353).
The inscription may have been added later and need not argue for local manufacture.

Fig. 341. Cat. 335. (2:1) Impression.

335. (Fig. 341) Geneva 1881/P. 400; conoid; 'chalcedoine brulée et veinée'; slightly convex base; D. 0.018 m. H. 0.024 m.
Bearded worshipper with one arm raised in front of altar and divine symbols; *mushhushshu*-dragon of god Marduk above altar and supporting the spade of Marduk and symbol of Nabu (stylised wedge or stylus); crescent above; diamond behind (Vollenweider, *Geneva* 1, 74, no. 81).

The excavations at Ayia Irini provide the only reliable context for Neo-Babylonian seals from within Cyprus. Seal 328, probably a local imitation, belongs to period 5, corresponding to the first half of the sixth century, and is therefore precisely contemporary with the Neo-Babylonian empire. Since, however, Neo-Babylonian seals are widely known in the Levant and Iran, they cannot be taken as primary evidence for close interaction between Mesopotamia and Cyprus, although there are other indications of contact between these two areas. They are, above all, not indicators of control, administrative or otherwise, although, historically, it is clear that Cyprus was a crucial staging post in the trading network that extended from Mesopotamia into the Greek world, not only in the Late Bronze Age, but also in the Iron Age.[308]

There is therefore no firm evidence to suppose direct Mesopotamian or Egyptian influence on Cypriot glyptic traditions of the Archaic period, but neither possibility can be excluded. Certainly any Assyrian or Babylonian elements that appear on local Cypriot stamp-seals result largely from the mediation of Syria and Palestine.[309] The same may be true for the influence of Egypt. Furthermore, precisely because of the importance of Cyprus as such a staging-post for traffic moving between the Aegean, Egypt, and the Near East, it is necessary to investigate, as well, Cypriot stamp-seals in relation to the Greek tradition. What connections were there between the two, and how, if at all, did one affect or influence the other?

10
THE GREEK IMPACT

The histories of Cyprus and Greece had been closely intertwined since the Bronze Age. Even in Classical times, Cypriots still used a syllabic script to write Greek, a relic from when the alphabet, as an innovation, had not yet superseded other types of writing. When Cypriots spoke Greek, mainland Greeks deemed their use of the language unusual and idiosyncratic, and the word 'solecism' in English may still reflect this prejudice, if its etymology is from Soloi in Cyprus, not Soloi in Cilicia.[310] Contrary to what one might have expected, the historical closeness of the Cypriots and Greeks is not reflected to any great extent in the serpentine scarabs and scaraboids from the island. The number of such seals with devices that reflect Greek conventions is surprisingly small and contrasts with the large number of serpentine stamps with devices that closely copy Phoenician seals and the equally significant number of hardstone seals with devices in Greek styles. In contrast also to the Phoenician-style seals which are already attested by the early CAI period, the archaeological dates available for the serpentine seals influenced by Greece suggest that they are confined chronologically to the CAII period.

SERPENTINE SEALS WITH DEVICES
WITH GREEK SUBJECTS AND STYLES

Examples of serpentine scarabs and scaraboids with devices with Greek subjects and styles include the following:

Amathus
336. (Fig. 342) Limassol; Amathus T. 223/86 (tomb; CAII); scaraboid; black; L. 0.012 m. W. 0.010 m. H. 0.006 m.
    Centaur (?) holding a small animal (?) in front of him; crescent behind; linear border (Boardman, 'Seals and Amulets', 161, pl. 3).

Fig. 342. Cat. 336. (2:1)
Seal, original, impression.

Fig. 343. Cat.
337. (2:1)
Impression,
drawing.

Fig. 344. (2:1) Seal of 'glass paste',
provenance uncertain, with a figure
carrying a bow and arrow and hunting a
winged deer (Berlin FG 126). L. 0.026 m.
W. 0.013 m. H. 0.010 m.

Fig. 345. Cat. 338.   Fig. 346. Cat. 339.
(2:1) Original.   (2:1) Impression.

Ayia Irini

337. (Fig. 343) Nicosia A. I. 2639 (period 6);
     scaraboid; black; L. 0.011 m. W. 0.009 m.
     H.0.008 m.
     Centaur; branch in hand (*SCE* 2, 770, no. 2639;
     pl. 249, no. 7).

Seals 338 and 339, although not of stone,
demonstrate that devices cut in a purely
Greek style could be used on other materials.
A seal in the shape of a long bead, now in
Berlin and described as being made of 'glass
paste' has also been thought to represent
Herakles hunting the deer as one of his
labours. (Fig. 344)

338. (Fig. 345) Stockholm A. I. 2607 (period 5);
     grey glazed scarab; striated legs; slightly
     raised spine; L. 0.015 m. W. 0.010 m. H. 0.007
     m.
     Striding youth approaching dog (*SCE* 2, 769,
     no. 2607).

339. (Fig. 346) Stockholm A. I. 2678 (period 5);
     scaraboid; clear glass; nearly flat top; L. 0.014
     m. W. 0.012 m. H. 0.007 m.
     Striding bearded figure carrying dead animal
     (?); head of man is turned back; dot and
     chevron behind arm; hatched border (*SCE* 2,
     771, no. 2678).

The animals on the next two seals are listed here, since they seem related to the
lions often found as devices on Archaic Greek gems.[311]

Paphos

340. London market, 1910; scarab; 'dark steatite'; L. 0.014 m.
     Lion leaping onto the back of a goat; linear border (Boardman, *AGGems*, 127, no. 397).

Pyrga

341. Larnaka (once Nicosia 1960. xi-21. 10); scarab; black; L. 0.015 m. W. 0.010 m. H. 0.008 m.
     Striding, roaring lion, tail curved forward (Charles, 'Pyrga', 28–9, no. 10).

Provenances unknown

342. (Fig. 347) Nicosia D. 39; scarab; black; L. 0.016 m. Striding centaur; branch behind.

343. (Fig. 348) Larnaka (? once Pierides Collection); prob. dark serpentine; shape and dimensions
     unreported.
     Very linear style: centaur; man in front (V. Karageorghis, 'Notes on Some Centaurs from
     Cyprus' in *Charisterion eis A. K. Orlandon* 2 (Athens, 1966), 168, fig. 1).

The range of motifs on these few scarabs and scaraboids is limited. Four of the eight show a centaur carrying a raised branch, typically Greek in its iconography.[312] The subject was a popular one in other Cypriot media of the time.[313] Other devices show lions. The two human figures are not on serpentine at all, but on other materials.

Fig. 347. Cat. 342. (2:1).

The small number of devices with Greek subjects in serpentine seals, taken together with the large number of Greek-style seals cut from harder stones, suggests that in the middle of the CAII period, Greek devices were preferred on hardstones, not serpentine ones. These hardstone seals have devices cut in styles particularly characteristic of the East Greek islands and largely span the latter half of the sixth century B. C. But they cannot simply be treated *en masse* as Cypriot. Given the extensive contact attested textually and archaeologically between Cyprus and the Greek world, there is every likelihood that some of these were imported into the island, while others were cut within Cyprus in imitation of Greek gems. As with Phoenician hardstone seals, it is not easy to decide whether the latter

Fig. 348. Cat. 343. (not to scale) Impression.

were cut by Cypriots influenced by Greek styles, Greeks living on the island, Phoenicians influenced by Greece, or any such combination of circumstances. Devices that deviate from standard Greek iconography and appear to reflect confusions between eastern traditions and Hellenic norms may represent local Cypriot products, but even in these instances an element of doubt necessarily remains. Those seals with Cypro-syllabic characters were very likely owned by Cypriots but they could well have had these inscriptions carved after purchasing the seals.

There is, however, some correspondence between devices on these hardstone seals and the devices on Cypriot coinage of the time. Similar animal studies and divinities appear on both coins and seals. This congruence between numismatic and glyptic arts on the island suggests that, with hardstone seals in Greek styles, we are dealing with actual Cypriot products in these particular cases.[314]

THE SEMON MASTER

These problems of interpretation are neatly exemplified by the career of the Archaic gem-cutter known as the Semon Master. There are no examples of the Semon Master's work with archaeological contexts, but because a number of gems found in Cyprus have been attributed to him, it has been conjectured that he worked on the island.[315] This is possible, but it is important to remember that the one gem signed by Semon is from the area around Troy in Asia Minor, and its inscription uses Greek lettering, not the Cypriot syllabary (Fig. 349). He may not be Cypriot at all, therefore, and his work may simply have been popular in Cyprus. Listed here are those seals attributed or related to the work of the Semon Master and found in the island.[316]

Fig. 349. (2:1) Agate scarab carved with the name of Semon, from the Troy area. The device shows a naked woman gathering water from a lion-headed spout. L. 0.014 m. W. 0.011 m. H. 0.008 m.

Fig. 350. Cat. 344. (2:1) Impression.

Fig. 351. Cat. 345. (2:1) Original.

Fig. 352. Cat. 346. (2:1) Original.

Fig. 353. Cat. 347. (2:1) Impression.

Fig. 354. Cat. 348. (2:1) Impression.

Amathus

344. (Fig. 350) Nicosia J. 777; scaraboid; cornelian; L. 0.011 m.
 Naked girl kneeling and adjusting her hair as she looks into a mirror; hatched border (Boardman, *GGFR*, 184; pl. 363).[317]

345. (Fig. 351) London 527; scaraboid; plasma; L. 0.018 m. W. 0.014 m.
 Youth wearing a pointed cap draws a bow; dog beside him; linear border (Boardman, *GGFR*, 184; pl. 363).

Marion

346. (Fig. 352) Nicosia 1964. i-24. 14; scaraboid; green chalcedony; L. 0.015 m. W. 0.012 m. H. 0.007 m.
 Crouching Hermes, wearing petasos and chlamys and holding a caduceus; hatched border (Boardman, *GGFR*, 184; pl. 365; V. Karageorghis, *Greek Gods and Heroes in Ancient Cyprus* (Athens, 1998), 94, no. 52).

Provenances unknown

347. (Fig. 353) Boston 27. 674; ringstone with convex face; cornelian; L. 0.016 m.
 Herakles throwing the Nemean lion over his shoulder; hatched border (Boardman, *AGGems*, 94, no. 254; pl. 17; V. Karageorghis, *Greek Gods and Heroes in Ancient Cyprus* (Athens, 1998), 86, no. 41).

348. (Fig. 354) Boston 27. 682; scaraboid; cornelian; L. 0.014 m. W. 0.015 m.
 Achilles slaying Penthesilea, or possibly generic scene of Greek spearing an Amazon; star

Fig. 355. Cat. 349.
(2:1) Impression.

Fig. 356. Cat. 350.
(2:1) Impression.

Fig. 357. Cat. 351.
(2:1) Impression.

in field; pellets between two parallel lines acting as a ground line (Boardman, *AGGems*, 94, no. 255; pl. 17; V. Karageorghis, *Greek Gods and Heroes in Ancient Cyprus* (Athens, 1998), 92–3, no. 51).

349. (Fig. 355) New York 74. 51. 4223 (= New York 41 = C. E. 16); scaraboid; cornelian; gold swivel setting; no stringhole; L. 0.019 m.
Winged Eros carrying away a naked girl holding a lyre; her hair is bound in a *sakkos*; linear border (Boardman, *GGFR*, 184; pl. 359; V. Karageorghis, *Greek Gods and Heroes in Ancient Cyprus* (Athens, 1998), 91, no. 49)

The following seals are related to the work of the Semon Master; 351 is listed for its possible Cypro-syllabic inscription.
350. (Fig. 356) London 500; scaraboid; plasma; no stringhole; L. 0.017 m. W. 0.012 m.
Collapsing warrior wearing Attic helmet and carrying Boiotian shield and machaira; linear border (Boardman, *GGFR*, 184; pl. 369).

351. (Fig. 357) Once Tyszkiewicz, Warren, Evans (impression in Oxford); scaraboid; chalcedony; L. 0.017 m.
Collapsing warrior, wearing Attic helmet and carrying Boiotian shield and machaira; linear border; worn Cypro-syllabic inscription: (?) *no-to-sa-to-i* (Boardman, *AGGems*, 97, no. 265; pl. 18).
The device is similar to 350, but finer.

Other hardstone seals with devices in Greek styles from the island show similar motifs: Greek mythological figures, youthful figures, and animals. Each of these types of scenes is considered in detail below.

MYTHOLOGY

Certain patterns are evident from the examples listed below. Such archaeological contexts as there are fall consistently towards the latter half of the Cypro-Archaic period or later. Arguments from the stylistic representation of the figures agree with this dating. A number of these seals use Egyptianising motifs such as the uraeus, the winged disc, the *uzat*-eye or the ankh as filling ornaments within the oval space of the

Fig. 358. Cat. 352. (2:1) Original, impression.   *Fig. 359. Cat. 353. (2:1) Impression.*

scarab or scaraboid. These seals especially have some claim to actual Cypriot manufacture.

The depiction of mythological stories with a strong narrative content was also particularly Cypriot speciality. Usually, scenes have three characters, often above a cross-hatched exergue, within a linear border. Egyptianising motifs are used to fill in the field behind the figures.

Amathus

352. (Fig. 358) Limassol (Amathus 283/151. 1; tomb; late CAII-CCI); scarab; pale agate; silver wire through stringhole; raised spine; L. 0.018 m. W. 0.014 m. H. 0.009 m.
Athena, Perseus, and the Gorgon; Athena with tall headdress and long robe, holding one hand up; linear border; no exergue (Boardman, 'Seals and Amulets', 163, pl. 6; V. Karageorghis, *Greek Gods and Heroes in Ancient Cyprus* (Athens, 1998), 97–8, no. 56).
In Cyprus, a cult of Perseus is attested only in much later inscriptions from nearby Kourion.[318] For the subject, popular in the island during the Cypro-Archaic period, cf. 364 and one side of a sarcophagus from Golgoi.[319]

353. (Fig. 359) London 447 (British excavations, 1894; tomb 256; CAII); diamond-shaped plaque; banded agate; L. 0.017 m.
Running four-winged goddess wearing winged cap (?); arms bent at waist; two more wings projecting horizontally at the waist; ground line; linear border (Boardman, *AGGems*, 31, no. 41; pl. 3).
Seal 353 was found with 355 and 406. It is the earliest of the seals cut in a Greek style and may on stylistic grounds may be dated to the second quarter of the sixth century.[320]

354. (Fig. 360) London 437; scarab; onyx; swivel setting with gold mount and bronze hoop; side of mount in filigree ornamented in two registers: (a) tendrils; (b) cable pattern; L. 0.017 m. W. 0.012 m. H. 0.008 m.
Two-winged Athena; gorgoneion (?) behind high-crested helmet; snakes on aegis (?) behind figure; spear in right hand; skirt held out with left hand; bare feet; hatched border; Ionic (?) inscription: *xi* (Boardman, *GGFR*, 183; pl. 334; V. Karageorghis, *Greek Gods and Heroes in Ancient Cyprus* (Athens, 1998), 113, no. 70).

355. (Fig. 361) London 299 (British excavations, 1894; tomb 256; sarcophagus 3; CAII); scaraboid; cornelian; low back; gold mount; L. 0.015 m. W. 0.012 m. H. 0.004 m.

Fig. 360. Cat. 354. (1:1) Original; (2:1) Impression.

Fig. 361. Cat. 355. (2:1) Impression.

Fig. 362. Cat. 356. (2:1). Original, Impression.

Fig. 363. Cat. 357. (2:1) Impression.

Herakles grips lion behind back and stabs the animal with his sword; two *uzat*-eyes behind the herop linear border (Boardman, *AGGems*, 104, no. 299).
This seal was found with 353 and 406.

Kourion
356. (Fig. 362) New York 74. 51. 4152; scarab; plasma; gold setting; L. 0.015 m. W. 0.012 m. H. 0.007 m.
Atalante, long-haired and wearing a short dress, grapples with a bearded man (? Peleus); boar's head in between; rearing winged uraeus on either side (*LIMC* 2, 946, no. 75, s. v., 'Atalante').
The boar's head may allude anachronistically to the hunt for the Calydonian boar. The addition of winged uraei to an otherwise wholly Greek scene is a Cypriot practice. There seems no evidence to associate Atalante specifically with Kourion or with Cyprus in general. On stylistic grounds, the figures date to the early Classical period.
357. (Fig. 363) London 375 (British excavations, 1895; tomb 83; CAII); scarab; agate; carinated spine; L. 0.012 m. W. 0.009 m.
Running Herakles wearing lion-skin and carrying club and bow (Boardman, *AGGems*, 104, no. 301; pl. 20; V. Karageorghis, *Greek Gods and Heroes in Ancient Cyprus* (Athens, 1998), 86–7, no. 42).

Fig. 364. Cat. 358. (2:1) Impression.

Fig. 365. Cat. 359. (2:1) Original.

Fig. 366. Cat. 360. (2:1) Impression.

Fig. 367. Cat. 361. (2:1) Impression.

Fig. 368. (2:1) Scarab of black serpentine, of uncertain provenance, showing Eros holding a lyre (Geneva 20463). L. 0.015 m. W. 0.012 m. H. 0.007 m.

Marion

358. (Fig. 364) Once Pierides; scarab; material unreported; carinated spine; L. 0.020 m.

Theseus, with quiver and sword, battles the Minotaur, Ariadne looking on; linear border; cross-hatched exergue; Cypro-syllabic inscription: *ti-we-i-te-mi-wo-se* (Διϝειθέμιϝος) (T. L. Shear, 'A Terra-Cotta Relief from Sardes' *AJA* 27 (1923), 142–3; Boardman, *AGGems*, 45, no. 71; pl. 5; V. Karageorghis, *Greek Gods and Heroes in Ancient Cyprus* (Athens, 1998), 86–7, no. 43).

The name is the same as that of a king from Kourion, but there is no reason to believe that this seal is necessarily a royal one and names the same king.[321]

359. (Fig. 365) Once Kammitsis, Nicosia; scarab; cornelian; L. 0.016 m.

Herakles, wearing lion-skin, aims an arrow against the centaur Nessos; Deianeira runs toward Herakles, but looks back at Nessos; bird and ankh in field; linear border; cross-hatched exergue (Boardman, *GGFR*, 182; pl. 329; V. Karageorghis, *Greek Gods and Heroes in Ancient Cyprus* (Athens, 1998), 85, no. 40).

On the popularity of Herakles throughout Cyprus in the Archaic period, see, in general, *LIMC* 4–5, s. v., 'Herakles', S. Dalley, 'Near Eastern Patron Deities of Mining and Smelting in the Late Bronze and Early Iron Ages' *RDAC* (1987), 64–6; S. Sophocleous, *Atlas des représentations chypro-archaïques des divinités* (Göteborg, 1985), 28–56.

360. (Fig. 366) London 467; scarab; cornelian; carinated spine; L. 0.014 m. W. 0.010 m.

Winged goddess running; object in hand (? bowl or diadem); linear border (Boardman, *GGFR*, 183; pl. 334).

Paphos (?)
361. (Fig. 367) Boston 27. 680; scarab; cornelian; carinated spine; L. 0.012 m.

Flying Eros, with branch and pedum (?); cloak over shoulder (Boardman, *AGGems*, 98, no. 274; pl. 19).

The motif of the winged Eros was popular in Greek glyptic;[322] cf. 349 and 362. A number of cruder examples are known on Cypriot finger-rings, particularly from Marion.[323] Possibly Cypriot as well is the Eros shown on a black serpentine scarab in Geneva (Fig. 368).[324]

Salamis

362. (Fig. 369) Salamis Tomb 73. 10 (early CCI); oval ringstone; cornelian; silver setting; L. 0.009 m.

Flying Eros holding lyre and diadem; linear border (Karageorghis, *Salamis* 2, 114, 116).

Tortosa (Phoenician coast)

363. (Fig. 370) Paris, Bibl. Nat. (De Luynes 114); flat ringstone; rock crystal; gold mount with heavy, crescent-shaped silver hoop; L. 0.015 m. W. 0.011 m. H. 0.003 m.

Herakles throwing the lion over his shoulder; club behind him; Cypro-syllabic inscription; *to-pe* (?); hatched border; ground line (Boardman, *AGGems*, 104, no. 295; pl. 20).

Provenances unknown[325]

364. (Fig. 371) Nicosia D. 15; scarab; amethyst; carinated spine; L. 0.014 m.

A hero (? Perseus), wearing a lion-skin and with winged heels, averts his head and decapitates the Gorgon; a draped female figure looks on; linear border; cross-hatched exergue (Boardman, *GGFR*, 179; fig. 187; V. Karageorghis, *Greek Gods and Heroes in Ancient Cyprus* (Athens, 1998), 97, no. 55).

The seal-cutter has confused Perseus and Herakles (who is, however, the great-grandson of Perseus through Alkmene and Elektryon: Apoll. 2. 4. 5). For an encounter between Herakles and the Gorgon, see Apoll. 2. 5. 12. There may also be a confusion with the iconography of Gilgamesh here. The figure rests his foot on Medusa's leg, just as Gilgamesh does on Humbaba's leg, and the figure on the left could be derived from Ishtar, who tries to stop Gilgamesh killing the Bull of Heaven. See D. Collon, *First Impressions* (London, 1987), no. 855, 856, and 857. For a similar concatenation on a seal of attributes relating to Gilgamesh and Herakles, the Near East and Greece, note a chalcedony scarab now in the Bibliothèque Nationale, Paris , showing a four-winged Bes-like creature, naked holding a lion in either hand by the tail. (Fig. 372)

Fig. 369. Cat. 362. (2:1) Original, impression.

Fig. 370. Cat. 363. (2:1) Impression.

Fig. 371. Cat. 364. (2:1) Impression.

Fig. 372. (2:1) Chalcedony scarab with device showing a four-winged creature with a Bes-head, in the Master-of-the-Animals pose (Paris, Bibliothèque Nationale). L. 0.018 m.

365. de Clercq 2797; scarab; rock crystal; L. 0.016 m.
    Herakles advances on Nessos; object in field; linear border; cross-hatched exergue
    (Boardman, *AGGems*, 46, no. 73).

366. (Fig. 373) Boston 95. 80; octagonal conoid; chalcedony; L. 0.019 m.
    Herakles holding a small lion by its mane and with a club in his other hand; he faces a
    Gorgon carrying a small lion by the tail in each hand (J. Boardman, 'Pyramidal Stamp-
    Seals in the Persian Empire' *Iran* 8 (1970), 26; 40, no. 12; V. Karageorghis, *Greek Gods and
    Heroes in Ancient Cyprus* (Athens, 1998), 84, no. 39).
    For the subject , cf. 364 above. The figures are early Classical in style. The shape of the seal
    is standard within the Achaemenid Empire.

367. (Fig. 374) Karlsruhe 63/57; scarab; chalcedony; L. 0.015 m.
    Centaur brandishing club; uncertain Cypro-syllabic inscription: *ta-u-ma-o-se* (? Θαυμάος)
    (H. W. Catling, 'The Seal of Pasitimos' *Kadmos* 11 (1972), 62, no. 5; fig. 2).

368. (Fig. 375) London 519; scaraboid; agate; damaged; L. 0.018 m. W. 0.014 m. H. 0.007 m.
    Centaur carrying off a woman; hatched border (Boardman, *AGGems*, 106, no. 307; pl. 21).

369. (Fig. 376) Oxford 1966. 595; scaraboid; chalcedony; L. 0.015 m. W. 0.011 m. H. 0.006 m.
    Six-winged deity with winged cap (? part of head); winged feet; disc held in arms; object in
    front (caduceus, perhaps added later?); linear border (Boardman and Vollenweider,
    Ashmolean Gems, 12, no. 60).

For the iconography, cf. 304 and 306. Possibly Cypriot as well is Boardman, *AGGems*,
36, no. 63; pl. 4: two-winged deity, perhaps with Cypro-syllabic *si* in field (Fig. 377).[326]

Fig. 373. Cat. 366.
(2:1) Impression.

Fig. 374. Cat. 367. (2:1).

Fig. 375. Cat. 368.
(2:1) Impression.

Fig. 376. Cat. 369.
(2:1) Impression.

Fig. 377. (2:1) A two-winged deity on a chalcedony
scarab (Paris, Bibliothèque Nationale). L. 0.015 m.

370. (Fig. 378) Berlin FG 140; scaraboid; rock crystal; L. 0.018 m. W. 0.012 m. H. 0.010 m.
Satyr reclining on one arm and lifting up a kantharos; krater above legs; hatched border (Zwierlein-Diehl, *AGDS* 2, 47, no. 77).

371. (Fig. 379) Athens, Num. Mus. (Tzivanopoulos 6); scaraboid; mottled red-brown limestone; L. 0.015 m.
Satyr raises an amphora onto his shoulders; Cypro-syllabic inscription: *o-na-sa-to-se* (Ὀνάσα(ν)τος) (Boardman, *GGFR*, 183; pl. 340; Masson, *ICS*, 349 and 421, no. 362).
The inscription seems to have been added later.

372. (Fig. 380) New York 58 (74. 51. 4194); scarab; agate; heavy gold hoop with silver swivel mount; gable spine; double line dividing elytra; single curving line to separate prothorax from elytra; L. 0.013 m. W. 0.010 m. H. 0.007 m.
Composite creature: forepart shows a winged horse; body ends in three snakes (? a fish-tail); linear border (Boardman, *AGGems*, 67, no. 154).

373. (Fig. 381) New York 74. 51. 4220; scaraboid; cornelian; gold box setting with spirals in filigree; L. 0.017 m. W. 0.010 m. H. 0.003 m.
Winged goddess wearing chiton and himation; left arm holds a flower; rearing snake behind (Boardman, *AGGems*, 91, no. 241; pl. 15; Richter, *Engraved Gems*, 64, no. 162).

374. (Fig. 382) Berlin 145 (FG 143); scarab; chalcedony; back of beetle damaged; L. 0.017 m. W. 0.012 m. H. 0.008 m.
Herakles swings a lion by its tail in one hand; club raised with the other; linear border (Zwierlein-Diehl, *AGDS* 2, 68, no. 145).

Fig. 378. Cat. 370. (2:1) Original, impression. *Fig. 379. Cat. 371. (2:1) Impression.*

Fig. 380. Cat. 372.
(2:1) Impression.

Fig. 381. Cat. 373.
(2:1) Impression.

Fig. 382. Cat. 374.
(2:1) Original.

Fig. 383. Cat. 375.   Fig. 384. Cat. 376.   Fig. 385. Cat. 377. (not
(2:1) Impresssion.   (2:1) Impression.   to scale) Impression.

375. (Fig. 383) New York 71 (C. E. 18); scaraboid; cornelian; gold setting; mount ornamented along the side with granules and tongues in filigree; L. 0.019 m. W. 0.011 m. H. 0.007 m. Herakles with raised club; bow and lion-skin hanging from arm; face and left leg in profile; hatched border (Boardman, *AGGems*, 107, no. 318; V. Karageorghis, *Greek Gods and Heroes in Ancient Cyprus* (Athens, 1998), 87–8, no. 44).

376. (Fig. 384) Oxford 1966. 596; scaraboid; moss agate; L. 0.025 m. W. 0.019 m. H. 0.014 m. Europa on the bull; fish in front; linear border (Boardman and Vollenweider, *Ashmolean Gems*, 16, no. 75).

377. (Fig. 385) Once Pierides; shape and material unknown.
Kneeling four-winged female (?) deity holding sun disc; two winged horses beneath, basket in between; star below basket (Culican, 'Iconography', 97–100).
As Culican noted, the deity is certainly Near Eastern, and the winged horse is known in Near Eastern iconography, but the stylistic treatment is Greek.[327]

The gods and heroes depicted include Eros, Athena, Hermes, Herakles, Perseus, and Atalante. Herakles is a particular favourite. The presence of these particular mythological figures is largely explicable within a Cypriot milieu. As the offspring of Aphrodite, Eros is appropriate on a gem from Cyprus, Aphrodite's island. Athena seems to have been conflated within the island with the Phoenician goddess Anat.[328] Hermes was used as a device for local coinage, examples of which were discovered by Lang at Idalion.[329] The worship of Herakles, in various forms, was also popular in the Cypro-Archaic period.[330] Perseus is rarely mentioned, but known at Kourion.[331] Atalante seems otherwise unattested, but as an Arcadian myth, her story may have found favour in Cyprus.[332]

Centaurs and sphinxes are the only monsters to appear extensively on Cypriot gems in particularly Greek guise. The use of the Greek sphinx with its pronounced curving wings and short hairstyle probably emerged from influence exercised by contact with the East Greek islands in the second half of the sixth century. The centaur seems always to have been peculiarly associated with the mythology of Cyprus.[333] There are terracottas from Ayia Irini in the shape of a horned human with the body of a horse, dating to the Cypro-Geometric II and Cypro-Geometric III periods.[334] These are ultimately related to the Greeek centaur, but at this time, they seem to represent a purely local creature.[335] Cyprus may have played an important role in the development of what came to be the iconography of the Greek centaur.[336] It need not be coincidental then that gems showing Herakles and Perseus involve a centaur and a Gorgon, who is depicted with a horse-body, rather than a regular human frame.[337]

ANIMALS

Some of the animals depicted here may be described as Graeco-Phoenician, descendants of the Phoenician seals showing animals and animal-attacks that had appeared earlier in the Cypro-Archaic period. Other devices, notable 379 and 380 are more Syrian in character, but still with a Greek flavour.

Fig. 386. Cat. 378. (2:1) Impression.

Amathus

378. (Fig. 386) London 305 (1894. 11–1. 79, British excavations, 1894; tomb 31; CA); scaraboid; black jasper; L. 0.012 m. W. 0.008 m. H. 0.006 m.
   Lion leaping onto the back of a deer; linear border (Walters, *BM Gems*, 38, no. 305; Murray *et al.*, *Excavations*, 98; pl. 4; fig. 6).

379. (Fig. 387) London 339 (1894. 11–1. 490, British excavations, 1894; tomb 225; CA); scarab; haematite; legs not cut; parallel inverted Y-shaped lines to separate prothorax from elytra; notching along plinth; L. 0.015 m. W. 0.013 m. H. 0.007 m.
   Device very worn: two oxen, heads averted (Walters, *BM Gems*, 42, no. 339).

Fig. 387. Cat. 379. (2:1) Original.

380. (Fig. 388) Nicosia (Amathus T. 11. 77; third burial; mid-CAII); scarab; haematite; L. 0.015 m.
   Two oxen *tête-bêche*; linear border (*SCE* 2, 75, no. 77; Forgeau, *Amathonte* 3, 167, no. 75).

Beirut

381. (Fig. 389) de Clercq 2794; scaraboid; chalcedony; L. 0.014 m.
   Panther scratches nose with its hind leg; cock on back; monkey in front; Cypro-syllabic inscription: *ka-pa-sa* (?) (Boardman, *GGFR*, 185; pl. 385; Masson, *ICS*, 350, no. 365).
   Boardman suggests that 391 and 393 may be by the same hand. On the occasional appearance of monkeys in Cypriot art, see V. Karageorghis, 'Monkeys and Bears in Cypriote Art' *OpAth* 20 (1994), 63–9.

Fig. 388. Cat. 380. (2:1).

Fig. 389. Cat. 381. (2:1) Original.

Golgoi

382. (Fig. 390) Boston 21. 1196; scaraboid; chalcedony; L. 0.016 m.

Running lion; eagle carrying snake overhead; ground line (Boardman, *AGGems*, 132, no. 428; pl. 31).

Beazley noted the similarity of the lion to 347 by the Semon Master and drew the relevant comparisons to coinage of Amathus which depicts an eagle above a lion.[338] The Amathus lion is shown recumbent, rather than striding as in 382, but the general relationship is clear. Current evidence suggests that the coinage of Amathus began around 460 B.C.;[339] the Boston lion may be somewhat earlier. Beazley also compared the animal to a similar striding lion on a coin issue then thought to be from Golgoi on the basis of the Γ-sign on the obverse and reverse.[340] But this attribution is by no means certain, since the Γ-sign may simply denote a particular numismatic series, rather than a mark of the original mint.[341]

Kourion

The following may be compared with 382, to which it is particularly close:

383. (Fig. 391) London 539; scaraboid; chalcedony; gold swivel setting; L. 0.019 m. W. 0.013 m. H. 0.010 m.

Lion dragging a dead stag by the throat; linear border (Boardman, *GGFR*, 185; pl. 389).

The following seal is probably from the Kourion area:

384. (Fig. 392a) London 523; scaraboid; cornelian; L. 0.012 m. W. 0.008 m.

Composite animal: bull with body of a cock (Boardman, *AGGems*, 154, no. 585; pl. 37).

385. (Fig. 392b) New York 74. 51. 4209 (Kourion Treasure); half-barrel; heavy gold swivel setting; banded agate; L. 0.016 m. W. 0.008 m. H. 0.007 m.

Two recumbent lions facing each other; plant (?) in between; linear border (Myres, *HCC*, 420, no. 4209).

For the half-barrel shape and the style of 385, cf. Boardman, *GGFR*, 199 on sliced barrels. See also 430.

Marion

386. (Fig. 393) de Clercq 2793; scaraboid; onyx; L. 0.014 m.

Panther leaps onto a mule, shown lying on its back; Cypro-syllabic inscription: *a-ri-si-to-wa-na-to* (Ἀροστοϝάνα(κ)το(ς)) (Masson, *ICS*, 161, no. 121; Boardman, *AGGems*, 131, no. 422).

The same hand may have also cut 394; cf. also 381, 391, and 393.

387. (Fig. 394) Nicosia 1964. xii–4. 10; scarab; cornelian; high back; carinated spine; L. 0.015 m. W. 0.012 m. H. 0.010 m.

Fig. 390. Cat. 382. (2:1) Impression.

Fig. 391. Cat. 383. (2:1) Impression.

Fig. 392a. Cat. 384. (2:1) Impression.

Fig. 392b. Cat. 385. (1:1) Impression.

Bull scratching muzzle with hind leg; star in field; hatched border (Boardman, *GGFR*, 186; pl. 400).

388. (Fig. 395) Nicosia J. 816 (Tomb 86, Necropolis 2; CA); scarab; cornelian; L. 0.013 m.
Goat with head turned back; hatched border (Boardman, *AGGems*, 150, no. 568; Ohnefalsch-Richter, *KBH*, 366–7, pl. 32. 30).

389. (Fig. 396) Once Konstantinides; scarab; cornelian; gold setting; dimensions unreported.
Animal protomes: joined heads of a lion and boar; linear border (Ohnefalsch-Richter, *KBH*, 367; pl. 32. 32).

390. (Fig. 397) Paris, Bibl. Nat. (Chandon de Briaille 222; once Cesnola, *Southesk* A. 35); scarab; cornelian; modern gold setting; carinated spine; double line separating prothorax from elytra; striated head; notched front legs; L. 0.016 m. W. 0.011 m. H. 0.007 m.
Panther leaps onto the back of a stumbling boar; cross-hatched exergue; linear border; Cypro-syllabic inscription: *pu-nu-to-ni-ko-e-mi* (Πνυτονίκω ἠμί) (Boardman, *AGGems*, 130, no. 421; pl. 30; Masson, *ICS*, 346 and 421, no. 356; Bibliothèque Nationale de France, *Art antique de Chypre* (Paris, 1994, 66, no. 49).

391. (Fig. 398) London 450; scaraboid; black jasper; L. 0.015 m. W. 0.013 m.
Panther leaping onto the belly of another panther, shown on its back; hatched border; Cypro-syllabic inscription: *a-ri-si-to-ke-le-o* (Ἀριστοκλῆος) (Boardman, *GGFR*, 185; pl. 384; Masson, *ICS*, 347–8, no. 359).
Possibly by the same hand are 381 and 393.

Note also the following two ringstones:

392. Nicosia 1955. xii–28. 9; ringstone of black glass; oval; convex face; flat back; bevelled edges; L. 0.014 m.
Panther; ground line (Boardman, *AGGems*, 131, no. 426).

Fig. 393. Cat. 386. (2:1) Impression, drawing.

Fig. 394. Cat. 387. (2:1) Impression.

Fig. 395. Cat. 388. (2:1).

Fig. 396. Cat. 389. (not to scale).

Fig. 397. Cat. 390. (2:1) Original.

Fig. 398. Cat. 391. (2:1) Impression.

Fig. 399. Cat. 393. (1:1)
Original; (2:1) Impression.

Fig. 400. Cat. 394.
(2:1) Impression.

Fig. 401. Cat. 395.
(2:1) Impression.

Fig. 402. Cat. 396.
(2:1) Impression.

Fig. 403. Cat. 397.
(2:1) Impression.

Fig. 404. Cat. 398.
(2:1) Impression.

Fig. 405. Cat. 399.
(2:1) Impression.

393. (Fig. 399) Nicosia 1960. vi-21. 1; ringstone of cornelian; oval; convex face; gold setting; L. 0.013 m.
Panther scratching nose; murex shell below (Boardman, *GGFR*, 185; pl. 386).
The same hand may have cut 381 and 391.

394. (Fig. 400) Boston; scarab; chalcedony; L. 0.014 m.
Lion leaping onto the back of a horse; the horse's head is turned back; hatched border (Boardman, *GGFR*, 186; pl. 391).
Cf. the style of 386 from Marion.

395. (Fig. 401) Nicosia R. 86; scaraboid; cornelian; beetle damaged; L. 0.010 m.
Crouching lion; hatched border (Boardman, *AGGems*, 133, no. 443; pl. 31).

396. (Fig. 402) London 484; scarab; cornelian; carinated spine; L. 0.012 m. W. 0.009 m.
Bull with head thrown back; hatched border (Boardman, *AGGems*, 144, no. 476; pl. 33).

397. (Fig. 403) Oxford 1891. 659; scarab; cornelian; damaged; extant dimensions: L. 0.014 m. W. 0.009 m. H. 0.008 m.
Standing bull with head turned back; objects in field (? an inscription); hatched border (Boardman and Vollenweider, *Ashmolean Gems*, 17, no. 80).

398. (Fig. 404) Nicosia D. 58; scarab; milky chalcedony; simple beetle; L. 0.011 m. W. 0.009 m. H. 0.006 m.
Composite animal: winged cock-horse; one wing raised, the other lowered; linear border (Boardman, *AGGems*, 154, no. 583; pl. 37).
The cock-horse is also known on a similar scarab from Etruria: Boardman, *AGGems*, 154, no. 584.

399. (Fig. 405) London 446; scarab; cornelian; carinated spine; L. 0.013 m.
Horse rolling (Boardman, *AGGems*, 145, no. 503; pl.33).

400. (Fig. 406) New York 25 (74. 51. 4195); scarab; cornelian; carinated spine; legs shallowly cut; bronze swivel setting; L. 0.018 m. W. 0.012 m. H. 0.007 m.

Lion leaping onto another lion shown on its back (Boardman, *AGGems*, 127, no. 400; pl. 29).

401. (Fig. 407) Nicosia 1955. iii-8. 1; scaraboid; cornelian; L. 0.014 m.
Kneeling bull (Boardman, *AGGems*, 148, no. 523; pl. 35).

402. (Fig. 408) New York 105 (74. 51. 4198); scaraboid; chalcedony; L. 0.023 m. W. 0.015 m. H. 0.007 m.
Horse falling to its knees; ground line; linear border; Greek inscription in awkward lettering (ΣΤΗΣΙΚΡΑΤΗΣ): (Boardman, *AGGems*, 150, no. 561; pl. 36).

403. (Fig. 409) Harari Collection 3; scaraboid; cornelian; L. 0.011 m. W. 0.008 m. H. 0.007 m.
Horse rolling and twisting; hind legs together; hatched border (J. Boardman and D. Scarisbrick, *The Ralph Harari Collection of Finger Rings* (London, 1977), 13–4, no. 3).

404. (Fig. 410) London 341 (1900. 5–23. 2); scarab; cornelian; elongated beetle; hatched line separating prothorax from elytra; ridge spine; L. 0.015 m. W. 0.007 m. H. 0.006 m.
Ram's head; hatched border (Boardman, *AGGems*, 147, no. 520; pl. 34).
A similar ram's head appears on the reverse of coins from Salamis, on a type first known from the end of the CAII period.[342] The profile view of 405 from Marion is also comparable, although in the shape of a sheep's head.

405. (Fig. 411) London *BMCat Jewellery* 1599; pendant in the form of a sheep's head; gold; setting of twisted wire coiled at the sides and inserted into stringhole; W. 0.012 m.
Panther and dog-headed man in battle; double hatched border (Boardman, *GGFR*, 183; pl. 341).
Cf. the profile view with the ram's head shown in 404 and on the coinage of Salamis, which began around the third quarter of the sixth century.[343] The ram may have had peculiar significance to Marion, since its coinage alludes to the legend of Phrixos and the golden fleece.[344]

Among these animal motifs, there is marked East Greek influence. The bristling manes of lions, in particular, have been traced back to East Greece. The popularity of the panther figure recalls similar animals on Greek orientalising pottery.[345]

Fig. 406. Cat. 400. (2:1) Impression.

Fig. 407. Cat. 401. (2:1) Impression.

Fig. 408. Cat. 402. (2:1) Impression.

Fig. 409. Cat. 403. (2:1) Original.

Fig. 410. Cat. 404. (2:1) Impression.

Fig. 411. Cat. 405. (2:1)
Seal, original, impression.

YOUTHS

These hardstone seals favour as subjects youths at work or leisure cut in a Greek style. cf. 338 and 339. The series probably began around the middle of the sixth century and was still current in the early fifth century. Scarabs with related subjects are widely known from the Greek mainland, the western Mediterranean, and the Levantine coast.[346]

Amathus

406. (Fig. 412) London 481 (British excavations, 1894; tomb 256; CAII); scarab; cornelian; carinated spine; L. 0.017 m. W. 0.012 m.
   Youth stoops to pick up discus; strigil (?) behind him; hatched border (Boardman, *GGFR*, 183; pl. 336).
   Seal 406 was found with 353 and 355.

Kition

407. (Fig. 413) Oxford 1889. 713 (once Chester); scarab; cornelian; ridge spine; L. 0.012 m. W. 0.009 m. H. 0.008 m.
   Youth kneels and draws his bow; hatched border (Boardman and Vollenweider, *Ashmolean Gems*, 14, no. 68).

Kourion

408. (Fig. 414) London 502 (British excavations, 1895; tomb 73; CAII); scaraboid; rock crystal; unpierced; L. 0.022 m. W. 0.017 m.
   Youth wearing fillet and leaning on a stick, holds a hare in front of a leaping dog; Cypro-syllabic inscription: *la-wa-ti-ri-so* (Λαϝανδρίσο(ς)) (Boardman, *AGGems*, 99, no. 287).

Marion

409. London 325; scarab; cornelian; carinated spine; double line separating prothorax from elytra; double line separating elytra; heavily incised side notches to show wing cases; stringhole filled with corroded wire; L. 0.014 m. W. 0.009 m. H. 0.008 m.
   Youth stoops to fasten his sandal; double linear border (Boardman, *AGGems*, 82, no. 218).

410. (Fig. 415) Cambridge, Massachusetts (Fogg); scarab; cornelian; L. 0.015 m.
   Youth kneels and tests an arrow; a bow is slung over his wrist (Boardman, *AGGems*, 99, no. 281; pl. 19).

411. (Fig. 416) Nicosia J. 388; scaraboid; cornelian; L. 0.009 m.
   Bust of a youth; linear border (Boardman, *AGGems*, 105, no. 304; pl. 20).

The following may be noted for its Cypro-syllabic inscription:

Aleppo (Syria)
412. (Fig. 417) de Clercq 1795; scaraboid; cornelian; L. 0.014 m.
   Youth carrying a shield stoops to pick up a Corinthian helmet; ground line; Cypro-syllabic inscription: *a-ke-se-to* (Ἀκέστω) (Boardman, *GGFR*, 184; pl. 367; Masson, *ICS*, 350, no. 364). Seal 412 was probably cut by the same hand as Boardman and Vollenweider, *Ashmolean Gems*, 14, no. 70.

Provenances unknown[347]
413. (Fig. 418) New York 40 (74. 51. 4225); scaraboid; white stone; gold swivel setting; mount decorated on side with spirals in filigree; L. 0.011 m. W. 0.009 m. H. 0.004 m.
   Figure bending over lekane and washing hair; hatched border (Boardman, *AGGems*, 107, no. 319).

414. (Fig. 419) Nicosia D. 56; scarab; cornelian; carinated spine; L. 0.011 m. W. 0.007 m. H. 0.006 m.
   Youth kneeling; hatched border (Boardman, *GGFR* 182; pl. 327).

415. (Fig. 420) New York 35 (74. 51. 4221); scarab; cornelian; carinated spine; gold setting ornamented along the sides with spirals in filigree; L. 0.014 m. W. 0.010 m. H. 0.006 m.

Fig. 412. Cat. 406.   Fig. 413. Cat. 407.   Fig. 414. Cat. 408.   Fig. 415. Cat. 410.
(2:1) Original.   (2:1) Impression.   (2:1) Impression.   (2:1) Impression.

Fig. 416. Cat. 411.   Fig. 417. Cat. 412.   Fig. 418. Cat. 413.   Fig. 419. Cat. 414.   Fig. 420. Cat. 415.
(2:1) Impression.   (2:1) Impression.   (2:1) Impression.   (2:1) Impression.   (2:1) Impression.

Fig. 421. Cat. 416. (2:1) Impression.

Fig. 422. Cat. 418. (2:1) Impression.

Fig. 423. Cat. 419. (2:1) Impression.

Fig. 424. Cat. 420. (2:1) Impression.

Fig. 425. Cat. 421. (2:1) Impression.

Youth leaning on a stick stoops to fasten a sandal; hatched border (Boardman, *AGGems*, 82, no. 216).

416. (Fig. 421) New York 38 (74. 51. 4173); scaraboid; plasma; gold setting, now broken; L. 0.013 m. W. 0.010 m. H. 0.007 m.
Youth standing between two rearing horses, holding each by its bridle (Boardman, *AGGems*, 69, no. 135, pl. 10; Richter, *Engraved Gems*, 51, no. 98).

417. de Clercq 2815; scaraboid; sardonyx; convex face; L. 0.014 m.
Naked youth, carrying strigil and aryballos, offers food to a dog; ground line; linear border (Boardman, *AGGems*, 96, no. 262).

418. (Fig. 422) Nicosia D. 55; scarab; agate; carinated spine; L. 0.016 m. W. 0.012 m. H. 0.009 m.
Youth sitting on a stool and working on a helmet with a hammer (Boardman, *GGFR*, 184; pl. 370).

419. (Fig. 423) New York 45 (74. 51. 4201); scaraboid; moss agate; flat back; L. 0.015 m. W. 0.010 m. H. 0.004 m.
Youth crouching; unfinished, perhaps intended to be shown as in 418 (Boardman, *AGGems*, 99, no. 282; pl. 19).

420. (Fig. 424) New York 66 (74. 51. 4200); scaraboid; dark chalcedony; L. 0.016 m. W. 0.012 m. H. 0.007 m.
Youth leaning on a stick and offering food to a dog; linear border (Boardman, *AGGems*, 99, no, 286; pl. 19; Richter, *Engraved Gems*, 53, no. 107).
The subject is treated in a different style from that of 417.

421. (Fig. 425) London 692 (1906. 4–11. 3); scarab; cornelian; elaborate, careful cutting; hatching along line separating prothorax from elytra; high base; carinated spine; L. 0.014 m. W. 0.011 m. H. 0.008 m.
Man bending down to carve animal (?); Greek (?) letttering in field: IEV..(perhaps one or two letters missing) (Walters, *BM Gems*, 86, no. 692; pl. 12).
Walters suggested this may have been an Etruscan import into Cyprus; the beetle-carving is more elaborate than usual for Cypriot seals.

422. (Fig. 426) New York 74. 51. 4222 (= New York 29 = C. E. 7); scarab; cornelian; carinated spine; gold box setting ornamented with spirals and chevrons in filigree; gold hoop; L. 0.019 m. W. 0.012 m. H. 0.004 m.

Fig. 426. Cat. 422.
(2:1) Impression.

Fig. 427. Cat. 423. (2:1).

Fig. 428. Cat. 424.
(2:1) Impression.

Naked youth pulling the hair of a naked girl crouched in front of him; hatched border (Boardman, *GGFR*, 181; pl. 308).

423. (Fig. 427) Nicosia D. 71; scaraboid; blue glass; L. 0.017 m. W. 0.014 m. H. 0.008 m.
Very worn: standing youth (?), leaning on stick; right knee bent.

Possibly related is the following:

424. (Fig. 428) Paris, Bibl. Nat. (ex Louvre 1497); scarab; cornelian; carinated spine; L. 0.014 m.
Youth wearing Scythian cap kneels and draws a bow; bow case beside him; star in field; Cypro-syllabic (?) inscription: *lo-to* (Boardman, *AGGems*, 78, no. 184; pl. 12).

These youths presage the passage of Cypriot glyptic into the Classical Greek mainstream. The future development of the stamp-seals of the island is to be marked on the hardstones, not on the serpentine seals. The disparity between seals cut from these two types of materials becomes increasingly great, with the finer styles adopted for the hardstones, the more summary reserved for the serpentines.

FROM ARCHAIC TO CLASSICAL

By the early Classical period, motifs on the stamp-seals from Cyprus are largely Hellenic in style, despite having motifs that might have been originally Levantine in character.[348] The devices are not simply slavish imitations of Greek mainland fashions.[349] Two seals, one from Amathus, the other from Kourion, both depicting scenes of war, may be taken as exemplary.

Amathus

425. (Fig. 429) London 449 (British excavations; tomb 287; second sarcophagus; CAII); roughly diamond-shaped ringstone; sard; gold box setting; L. 0.019 m. W. 0.009 m. H. 0.006 m.
Warship; galley of oars emerging from portholes; three warriors at the top wearing crested Greek helmets and carrying spears and round shields

Fig. 429. Cat. 425. (2:1) Original.

(Boardman, *GGFR*, 287; pl. 457).

The style and shape indicate an early Classical date. For the motif, cf. side (a) of 437, also from Amathus. See also Walters, *BM Gems*, 59–60, no. 991 (? Asia Minor) and G. M. A. Richter, *Catalogue of Engraved Gems* (New York, 1956), 41, no. 43; pl. 7 and comments ad loc. Compare also the motif on a fourth-century Phoenician coin: J. Elayi and A. Lemaire, 'Graffiti monétaires ouest-sémitiques' in T. Hackens and G. Moncharte, eds., *Numismatique et histoire économique phéniciennes et puniques* (= *Studia Phoenicia* 9) (Louvain, 1992), 73–4, no. 50; pl. 18. The seal was found with 239 and 269.

Kourion

426. (Fig. 430) New York 74. 51. 4146 (Kourion Treasure); scarab; cornelian; lumpy profile; lightly carinated spine; some notching on head; gold swivel setting; L. 0.016 m. W. 0.010 m. H. 0.009 m.
    Device worn: two opposing warriors in smiting position, one wearing a crested helmet, the other a cloth (?) headdress; both hold round shields and carry two spears; ground line; linear border (?) (Myres, *HCC*, 412–3, no. 4146).

A series of heads in profile is equally striking, although none have precise provenances from within Cyprus. The example from Syria is noted for its Cyprosyllabic inscription.

Syria

427. (Fig. 431) Paris, Bibl. Nat. (Pauvert 89); scarab; cornelian; carinated spine; slightly pinched tail; lumpy profile; no markings on back; L. 0.009 m. W. 0.007 m. H. 0.006 m.
    Bearded head; hair and beard in shape of birds; Cypro-syllabic inscription: *ta-ma* (Boardman, *AGGems*, 83–4, no. 226; pl. 14; Bibliothèque Nationale de France, *Art antique de France* (Paris, 1994), 66, no. 50; Masson, *ICS*, 421, no. 367b).
    On the use of composite heads as a gem-motif in the Classical world, see D. Collon, 'A Hoard of Sealings from Ur' in M.-F. Boussac and A. Invernizzi, *Archives et sceaux du monde hellénistique* = *BCH Supplément* 29 (Paris, 1996), 75–6, fig. 12.

Provenances unknown

428. (Fig. 432) Cambridge, Massachusetts (Fogg); scaraboid; agate; L. 0.015 m.
    Conjoined heads of a bearded man and a woman; linear border (Boardman, *AGGems*, 67, no. 149).

429. (Fig. 433) Paris, Bibl. Nat. (Pauvert 74); scaraboid; white agate; L. 0.015 m. W. 0.011 m. H. 0.007 m.

Fig. 430. Cat. 426. (1:1)   *Fig. 431. Cat. 427.*   *Fig. 432. Cat. 428.*   *Fig. 433. Cat. 429.*
Original, Impression.   *(2:1) Impression.*   *(2:1) Impression.*   *(2:1) Impression.*

Male head, wearing Corinthian helmet; Greek inscription: ΠΥΘΟΝΑΞ (Boardman, *AGGems*, 83, no. 224; pl. 14).

Other seals continue the tradition of animal studies and mythological creatures:

Kourion

430. (Fig. 434) New York CE 24 (74. 51. 4210) (Kourion Treasure); half-barrel; orange chalcedony; heavy bronze swivel setting; L. 0.020 m. W. 0.009 m. H. 0.006 m.
Standing crane (Myres, *HCC*, 420, no. 4210).
See also 385 for the shape.

Provenances unknown

431. (Fig. 435) Péronne (once Danicourt); pyramidal; blue chalcedony; L. 0.019 m.
Griffin attacking stag from behind; sun disc in field; Cypro-syllabic inscription: *a-ke-se-to-ta-mo* (Ἀκεστοδάμω) (Boardman, *GGFR*, 351–2; pl. 847; Masson, *ICS*, 349–50, no. 363).[350]

432. (Fig. 436) Oxford 1891. 648; scaraboid; blue glass; L. 0.014 m. W. 0.012 m. H. 0.008 m.
Seated sphinx; paw raised; linear border (Buchanan and Moorey, *Ashmolean* 3, 82, no. 557; pl. 17).
The sphinx probably dates to late Classical times. On the increased use of glass for the manufacture of Levantine conoids and scaraboids in the fifth and fourth centuries, see Buchanan and Moorey, *Ashmolean* 3, 75. For another Classical sphinx on a seal from Cyprus, see Walters, *BM Gems*, 64, no. 521.

Fig. 434. Cat. 430.
(1:1) Original;
(2:1) Impression.

Fig. 435. Cat. 431.
(2:1) Impression.

Fig. 436. Cat. 432.
(2:1) Impression.

At the end of the sixth century, Cyprus had fallen within the orbit of the Persian Empire. As part of the empire, it was open to influences from Susa, as well as other Persian royal capitals, and a small number of seals from Cyprus are known with devices in the Court-style typical of the Achaemenid Empire in general.[351] Some of these seals, however, may simply have been imported.[352]

Seals manufactured from hardstones gradually increased in production, perhaps even superseding the serpentine scarabs and scaraboids in general popularity within the island. In this way, Cypriot glyptics conform to a pattern evident elsewhere in the Near East and the Aegean, in which seal-cutters progress from the cutting of softer to harder stones. It is very likely that Cyprus was instrumental in promoting this fashion for hardstone seals further west, since, in the Greek-speaking world, it is among the first places to have had extensive experience of hardstone seals. Given increasing demand for hardstone seals within the Mediterranean in general, production within Cyprus may have increased commensurately.

11
CUBICAL SEALS

Although hardstone seals with devices cut in a Greek style may have been favoured in the sixth century, serpentine production never ceases entirely. Phoenician motifs never completely disappear, but they may be treated in a more Hellenic manner. In the late sixth century, in fact, one particular type of Cypriot stamp-seal may use both Phoenician and Greek motifs. These are the cubical seals, all manufactured from serpentine. They usually have devices cut on two or more sides, but are clearly related to pyramidal and tabloid seals in conception.[353] The shapes differ simply in whether or not a handle is present or whether the sides taper. The majority fall within the CAII period. The type may be descended from the tabloid seals manufactured within the island during the Late Bronze Age and possibly later, if they are not ultimately to be derived from the Anatolian tradition of stamp-seals.[354] Cubical seals were also known in the Levant, but the number of Cypriot examples extant suggests that the type with devices carved on several faces was a glyptic speciality of the island. (Figs. 437–439) The cubical stamps belonging to the Sounion Group of Archaic Greek seals (mid-seventh to the sixth centuries) may owe inspiration to the Cypriot tradition.[355]

CUBICAL SEALS OF UNCERTAIN PROVENANCE, PROBABLY FROM THE LEVANTINE COAST.

Fig. 437. (object at approximately 1:1) Pyramidal seal of grey serpentine (London, Bürgin Collection). Devices show a four-winged genius; a lunar standard with branches, circles, a star and a baboon of Thot in the field; Bes holding flails; a striding griffin; a cock with a disc and crescent above. L. 0.012 m. W. 0.010 m. H. 0.020 m.

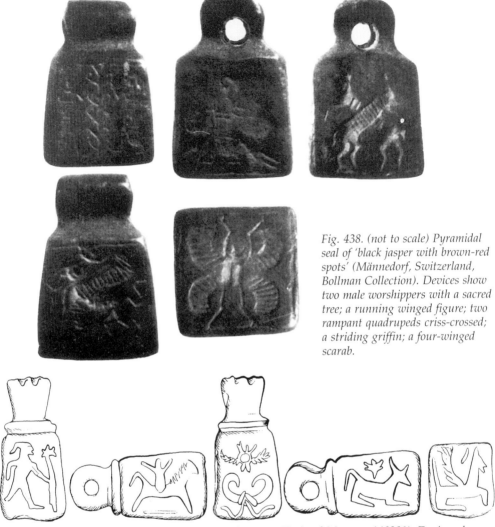

Fig. 438. (not to scale) Pyramidal seal of 'black jasper with brown-red spots' (Männedorf, Switzerland, Bollman Collection). Devices show two male worshippers with a sacred tree; a running winged figure; two rampant quadrupeds criss-crossed; a striding griffin; a four-winged scarab.

Fig. 439. (1:1) Pyramidal seal of black serpentine (Warsaw National Museum 148391). Devices show a striding human figure grasping a staff; a horse and rider; a pair of horns (?) with a winged disc above; a recumbent bull; a recumbent sphinx. L. 0. 019 m. H. 0.028 m.

Amathus[356]

433. (Fig. 440) Nicosia E. 61 (1933. v-6. 3); pyramidal; black; looping lug handle; L. 0.016 m. W. 0.022 m. H. 0.043 m.

(a) Recumbent sphinx; (b) lion with hatched mane; hatched area (? papyrus brake) above; (c) striding human figure in long dress; (d) cut in a different style: winged uraeus (?); (e) (base) four winged scarab.

Side (d) may have been recut, since it is in a different style. For the use of hatching and striated lines on the figures cf. 441 from nearby Erimi.

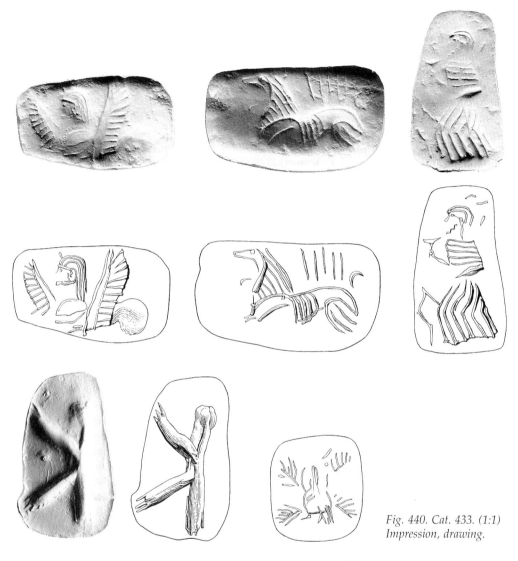

Fig. 440. Cat. 433. (1:1) Impression, drawing.

434. (Fig. 441) Limassol; Amathus Tomb 232/146 (tomb; late CAI-early CAII); pyramidal; green; L. 0.013 m. W. 0.013 m. H. 0.014 m.
Device on base only: two human stick-figures side by side (Boardman, 'Seals and Amulets', 159, pl. 1).

Fig. 441. Cat. 434. (1:1) Seal, original, impression.

435. (Fig. 442) Limassol; Amathus Tomb 232/54 (tomb; late CAI-early CAII); irregularly-shaped tabloid; grey; stringhole across short axis; L. 0.033 m. W. 0.027 m. H. 0.011 m.
(a) Two human, stick-like figures, arms raised and joined; figure on the left with a stick; groundline; beneath groundline, inverted tree, star on either side; linear border; (b) two human stick-like figures, arms joined; circle in between; sideways tree as groundline;

Fig. 442. Cat. 435. (1:1) Seal, impression.

scorpion (?) on left border beside tree; quadruped with long ears or horns and a hump (?); linear border (Boardman, 'Seals and Amulets', 160, pl. 2).

436. (Fig. 443) Limassol; Amathus T. 223/81 (tomb; CAII); pyramidal; black; L. 0.010 m. W. 0.008 m. H. 0.015 m.
(a) Stick-like human figure; one hand raised, the other lowered; line in front; head and arms shown as drillings; (b) multiple zigzags; (c) cross with chevron; (d) tree; linear border; (e) (base) striding goat (Boardman, 'Seals and Amulets', 159, pl. 1).
For a serpentine pyramidal stamp-seal similar in style and iconography, cf. Vollenweider, *Geneva* 3, 52–3, no. 84, attributed to North Syria.

437. (Fig. 444) Limassol (Tomb 297/9; CAII-CCI); pyramidal; loop handle; greyish black; L. 0.017 m.
(a) Striding lion; flower in front; linear border; (b) four rearing uraei (? vegetal pattern); (c) summary tree; linear border; (d) ship with sails (?); linear border; (e) warship (?); linear border; linear border (Boardman, 'Seals and Amulets', 160, pl. 2).

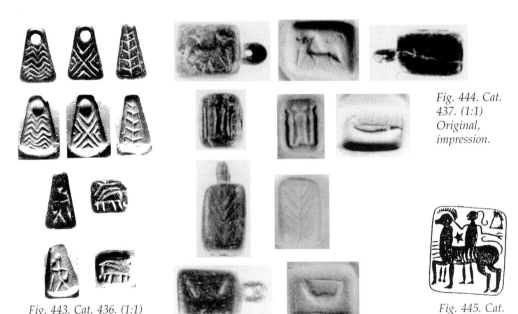

Fig. 444. Cat. 437. (1:1) Original, impression.

Fig. 443. Cat. 436. (1:1) Original, impression.

Fig. 445. Cat. 438. (1:1).

The motif of the lion approaching a flower and the rearing uraei on the base are certainly Phoenician-inspired. Other motifs are more summary, although the warship (?) may be compared to 425 also from Amathus.

438. (Fig. 445) London (British excavations; tomb 286; CA); pyramidal; grey; L. 0.023 m. W. 0.020 m.
(base) Horse with bristling mane carrying rider; triangle, star, other objects in field (Murray *et al.*, *Excavations*, 99, fig. 147, no. 40).
Seal 438 was found with 140.

Like 444 below, the following seal uses both Greek and Phoenician motifs as devices:
439. (Fig. 446) Limassol; Amathus T. 212/2 (tomb; CAII-early CCI?); black jasper; L. 0.015 m. W. 0.010 m. H. 0.007 m.
(a) Athena wearing crested helmet, long dress; mantle hanging from arm; spear in right hand; hoplite shield in left; linear border; (b) owl or falcon perched on outcrop; frontal face; linear border; (c) female winged deity with long hair holding flowers andwearing a long skirt; one wing raised, the other lowered; linear border; (d) four-winged female deity holding flowers and wearing a long skirt; linear border (Boardman, 'Seals and Amulets', 160, pl. 2; V. Karageorghis, *Greek Gods and Heroes in Ancient Cyprus* (Athens, 1998), 112, no. 69).
The style of the Athena-figure places the seal within the second half of the sixth century.

Ayia Irini (?)
The following is in the Medelhavsmuseet, among the Ayia Irini seals. It has no accession number, nor is there any indication of its precise provenance, but the style and shape are certainly Cypriot, and the seal may well have come from the sanctuary at Ayia Irini.
440. (Fig. 447) Stockholm; cubical stamp with knob handle; stringhole through handle; devices on all sides except the top; grey; (base) L. 0.016 m. W. 00.012 m. (top) L. 0.013 m. W. 0.010 m. H. 0.020 m., without handle; 0.028 m., with handle.

Fig. 446. Cat. 439. (1:1) Original, impression.

Fig. 447. Cat. 440. (1:1) Original.

(a) (side) Two rampant lions (?), heads facing each other; linear border; (b) (side) tree; linear border; (c) (side) striding quadruped; linear border; (d) (side) standing helmeted figure; no linear border; (e) (base) star pattern; linear border.

Erimi (Limassol area)

441. (Fig. 448) Nicosia 1933. iii-18. 1; black; ribbed lug handle; L. 0.027 m. W. 0.011 m. H. 0.040 m.

(a) Two male figures, both in skirts cut away at the hems, one on either side of a stylised date-palm; each figure with one raised arm; (b) male figure in short dress as master of animals taming two lions; head and legs of male figure in profile; body frontal; (c) animal-headed figure carrying sceptre (?) and wearing a dress reaching below the knees; (d) goat-headed figure in short dress; (e) (base) human figure in long, striated dress; hatched area above shoulder (? wing of raised arm).

Characteristic of the devices are the deeply cut striations that appear on the clothes of the human figures and on the manes of the animals. Stylistically related is 433 from nearby Amathus, which also uses hatching on the figures. The worshippers of side (a) and the master of animals on side (b) are long-standing Near Eastern motifs; the animal-headed figures of (c) and (d) are better known from Cypro-Archaic terracottas, although the goat's head is difficult to parallel.[357]

Fig. 448. Cat. 441. Impression, drawing.

Kalavassos (between Limassol and Larnaka)

442. (Fig. 449) Limassol; CS 1745 (tomb; CAII-CCI); no handle; greyish-black; L. 0.014 m. W. 0.010 m. H. 0.006 m.

(a) Female warrior riding horse; (b) striding bull; (c) striding boar with bristling mane; (d) woman wearing himation and chiton (V. Karageorghis, 'Chronique des fouilles et découvertes archéologiques à Chypre' *BCH* 94 (1970), 210, fig. 34; Gubel, 'Cubical Stamps', 196).

It is evident from 442 that the cubical seal tradition continued in Cyprus after the Cypro-Archaic period. The animal motifs are related to the Fine Style animal studies in Greek gems of the late sixth and early fifth centuries.[358]

Kourion

443. (Fig. 450) Kourion K83 (JKde Q30) (sanctuary of Apollo; 7th c.); pyramidal; grey; lug broken off; L. 0.021–0.023 m. W. 0.018–0.019 m. H. 0.028 m.

(a) Scroll pattern; linear border; (b) running horse; three drillings in field; linear border; (c) winged sphinx; cross-hatched ground; linear border; (d) sub-geometric warrior wearing a crested helmet, in running-kneeling position; spear (?) in hand; object behind (?); linear border; (e) (base) leaf pattern (Gubel, 'Cubical Stamps', 201; E. Gubel, 'The Seals' in D. Buitron-Oliver, *The Sanctuary of Apollo-Hylates at Kourion* (Jonsered, 1996), 165–7, no. 4).

Gubel has described this seal as cut in the Pyrga-style. But 443 contains little that is characteristic of that group, although drillings, a Pyrga characteristic, occasionally appear in the field. The cross-hatched ground, which allies the cubical seal to the tradition of Phoenician scarabs, is also rare on seals from Pyrga. The Sub-Geometric warrior is related to the series described above.

Fig. 449. Cat. 442. (1:1)
Original, impression.

Fig. 450. Cat. 443.
(1:1) Seal, original.

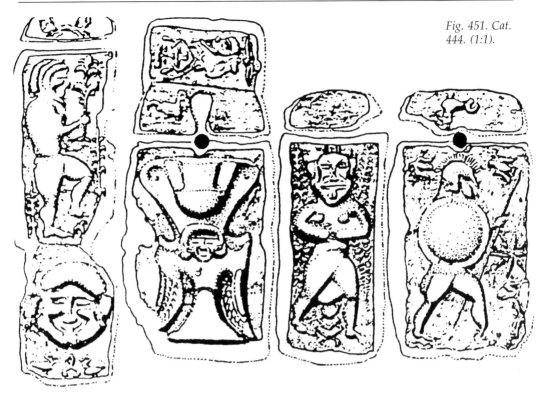

Fig. 451. Cat. 444. (1:1).

The following seal, like 439, combines Phoenician and Greek motifs.

444. (Fig. 451) Kourion St. 846 (sanctuary of Apollo); black; top section with undercut sides to provide a handle; approx. L. 0.040 m. W. 0.035 m. H. 0.060 m.

(a) (top) Frontal Gorgon figure; birds (?) on bevelled sides; (b) male figure shown in profile carrying blossom; branch in front; branch behind; (c) winged Horus (?) figure; (d) frontal Bes, carrying flails (?); branches in field; (e) Greek hoplite wearing a crested helmet, carrying spear and shield; two birds in field; star in front; (f) (base) Gorgon head; two small ducks (?) beneath, one on either side of a symbol (Gubel, 'Cubical Stamps', 197; M. Arwe, 'A Cypriote Cubical Stamp-Seal' in J. C. Biers and D. Soren, eds., *Studies in Cypriote Archaeology* (Los Angeles, 1981), 141–4).

The depiction of the Greek hoplite warrior dates the seal to the last half of the sixth century.

Pyrga
62, 63, 64.

Provenances unknown

Note 70 and 71. The following may be safely attributed to Cypriot manufacture on the basis of their styles and shapes:[359]

445. (Fig. 452) Oxford 1909. 372; dark green; perforated knob on top; linear striations on top surface, below knob; L. 0.033 m. W. 0.028 m. H. 0.051 m.

(a) Standing hawk-headed figure, with crown (?), holding sceptre with wing and disc at the top; linear border; (b) griffin wearing double crown; knobbed tail in an S-shaped curve; ankh in field; linear border; (c) hawk with crook and flail at the back, wearing crown (?),

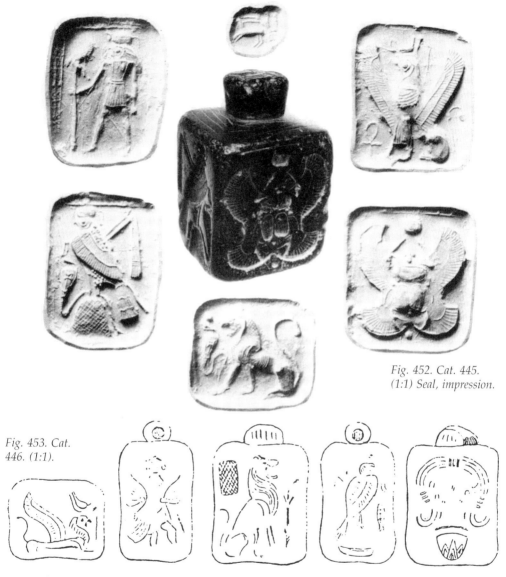

Fig. 452. Cat. 445.
(1:1) Seal, impression.

Fig. 453. Cat.
446. (1:1).

perched on a hatched outcrop; uraeus in field; linear border; (d) four-winged scarab; disc above; dot below; linear border; (e) (base) seated lion; uraeus in front; (f) (top of knob) chariot carrying two figures (Buchanan and Moorey, *Ashmolean* 3, 83, no. 569; pl. 18; Gubel, 'Cubical Stamps', 215, fig. 13).

The chariot motif allies the seal with the chariot series. Gubel argued for a date in the eighth century, but this seems too early.

446. (Fig. 453) London 1912. 2–28. 1 (WA) = British Museum 104461; black; ribbed suspension tube; L. 0.024 m. W. 0.020 m. H. 0.036 m.

(a) Hathor head; (b) frontal Bes with flail in either arm; (c) seated lion; plant in front;

hatched area behind (? a pseudo-cartouche); (d) Horus hawk; *neb*-sign below; (e) (base) recumbent griffin, wearing double crown (Culican, 'Cubical Seals', 162–7; Gubel, 'Cubical Stamps', 215, fig. 14).

Side (a) allies the seal to the series showing frontal heads. The frontal Bes is closely paralleled by 447 side (c).

447. (Fig. 454) London 104462; black; handle; L. 0.032 m. W. 0.027 m. H. 0.042 m.

(a) Standing human figure in cut-away long dress, holding a staff with a leaf-like object at the top; (b) seated winged griffin; disc above head; (c) frontal Bes holding flail in either arm; (d) Neo-Cypriot head; (e) (base) circle; seven lines radiating outward (Gubel, 'Cubical Stamps', 206–7, fig. 9).

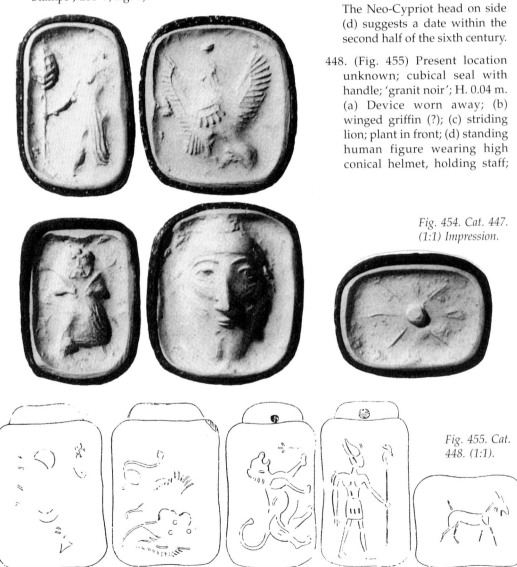

The Neo-Cypriot head on side (d) suggests a date within the second half of the sixth century.

448. (Fig. 455) Present location unknown; cubical seal with handle; 'granit noir'; H. 0.04 m. (a) Device worn away; (b) winged griffin (?); (c) striding lion; plant in front; (d) standing human figure wearing high conical helmet, holding staff;

Fig. 454. Cat. 447. (1:1) Impression.

Fig. 455. Cat. 448. (1:1).

(e) (base) striding goat (?) (known only from the drawing and description in G. Colonna-Ceccaldi, *Monuments antiques de Chypre, de Syrie et d'Égypte* (Paris, 1882), 292, no. 31; pl. 30. 31 = Gubel, 'Cubical Stamps', 203, fig. 8).

Gubel classifies this seal as belonging to the Pyrga group, but the style of 448 seems different.

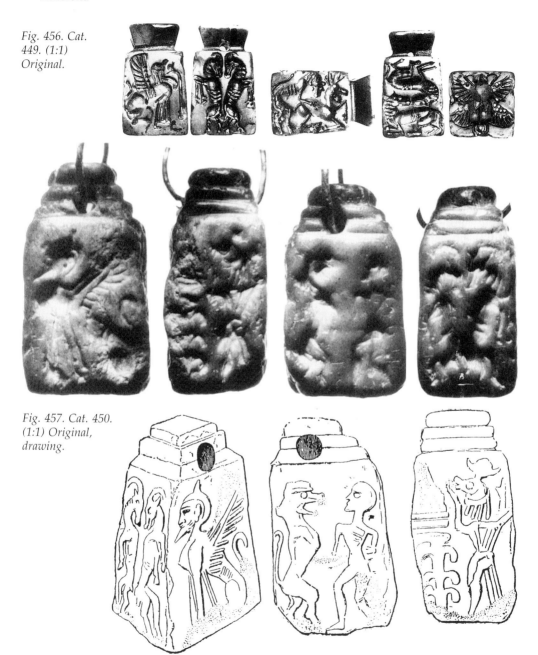

Fig. 456. Cat. 449. (1:1) Original.

Fig. 457. Cat. 450. (1:1) Original, drawing.

449. (Fig. 456) Paris, Bibl. Nat.; highly polished; black; pyramidal; knob handle; W. 0.012–0.020 m. H. 0.024 m.

   Intaglios deeply cut: (a) winged griffin; plant in front; (b) two rampant ibexes, backs to each other and heads turned back; (c) lion attacking deer from behind; (d) two horses *tête-bêche*; (e) (base) four-winged scarab; circle underneath (Gubel, 'Cubical Stamps', 219, fig. 15).

   The same hand may have cut 129.

450. (Fig. 457) Paris, Bibl. Nat.; dark-coloured; stepped handle with wire through stringhole; L. 0.030 m. W. 0.025 m. H. 0.058 m.

   Devices very worn: (a) sitting winged griffin with S-shaped tail; (b) 'a hawk-headed figure with hand raised in adoration in front of an incense burner'; (c) bearded human figure battles rampant lion; (d) two rampant ibexes, back to back, with heads turned to face each other (Ohnefalsch-Richter, *KBH*, 433, no. 7; pl. 18. 7a-c; Gubel, 'Cubical Stamps', 209, fig. 10).

451. (Fig. 458) Paris, Bibl. Nat.; lug handle; black; L. 0.029 m. W. 0.027 m. H. 0.051 m.

   (a) Standing human figure grasping a branch; (b) striding deer (?); papyri in background;

Fig. 458. Cat. 451. (1:1) Original.

cross-hatched ground; (c) two griffins (?), one on either side of tree (?); device very worn; (d) chariot with two riders; linear border; (e) (base) circle of radiating lines (?) (Gubel, 'Cubical Stamps', 202, fig. 7).
Side d allies 451 with the chariot series.

452. (Fig. 459a) Geneva 1897/P. 840; curved handle; black; L. 0.011 m. W. 0.010 m. H. 0.024 m.
(a) Standing human-figure in Egyptian double crown, arm raised in greeting; plant in front; (b) canine (?); object in front; circle above; (c) griffin (?); very worn; (d) horse and rider; (e) (base) double lattice-design (Vollenweider, *Geneva* 1, 137, no. 183; pl. 72).

453. (Fig. 459b) New York N. E. 74. 51. 4381; tabloid; black; L. 0.013 m. W. 0.010 m. H. 0.006 m.
(a) Rough triangle; two drillings inside; small, shallow drilling outside; (b) irregularly crossing lines (Myres, *HCC*, 444, no. 4381).

454. (Fig. 460) New York N. E. 74. 51. 4380; roughly tabloid; black; L. 0.016 m. W. 0.009 m.
(a) Stick-like figure holding stick in either hand; (b) similar to (a); line on either side of figure; (c) stick-like date-palm (?) framed in a rough square; (d) similar to (c); (e) groove on either side of stringhole; (f) similar to (e) (Myres, *HCC*, 444, no. 4380).

455. (Fig. 461) Berlin FG 66; tabloid; black, 'mit hellen Einsprengeln'; L. 0.030 m. W. 0.017 m. H. 0.010 m.
(a) Horse; branch above; (b) striding lion (?); object above; object in front. Other sides are less intelligible: (c) blossom (?); (d) animal (?); (e) bird (?); (f) linear design (Zwierlein-Diehl, *AGDS* 2, 62, no. 125; Taf. 30).

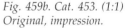

Fig. 459a. Cat. 452. (1:1) Original, impression.

Fig. 459b. Cat. 453. (1:1) Original, impression.

Fig. 460. Cat. 454. (1:1) Impression.

Fig. 461. Cat. 455. (1:1) Original.

Fig. 462. Cat. 456. (1:1) Original.

Fig. 463. Cat. 457. (1:1) Original, impression, drawing.

Fig. 464. Cat. 459. (1:1).

Fig. 465. Cat. 460. (1:1).

Fig. 466. Cat. 461. (1:1) Side e only shown.

456. (Fig. 462) Berlin FG 83; tabloid; green with brown flecks; L. 0.018 m. W. 0.014 m. H. 0.008 m.
(a) Recumbent sphinx with tail curled in an S-shape; linear border; (b) recumbent lion; one paw raised; bucranium in field; linear border (Zwierlein-Diehl, *AGDS* 2, 63, no. 126).

457. (Fig. 463) Larnaka; Pierides 1962; pyramidal; grey; groove with stringhole around top; L. 0.009–0.013 m. W. 0.009–0.010 m. H. 0.022 m.
Devices very worn: (a) recumbent lion (?); (b) standing human figure, staff in hand; (c) griffin (?) with hatched wing (?); (d) standing human figure (?); (e) (base) unintelligible (A. T. Reyes, 'Stamp-Seals in the Pierides Collection, Larnaca' *RDAC* (1991), 126, no. 20).

458. Paris, Louvre AM 1667 (A. 1182); grey; tabloid; L. 0.017 m. W. 0.015 m. H. 0.009 m.
(a) Seated figure; bird (?) overhead; hatched border; (b) quadruped; bird (?) overhead; hatched border (Delaporte, *Catalogue* 2, 211; pl. 106, no. 7a-b).

459. (Fig. 464) Nicosia 1943. viii-21. 2; pyramidal; black; H. 0.020 m.
(a) Lines, six drillings; (b) triangular shape; drilling above; (c) bird (?); (d) striding human figure; one arm raised; (e) (base) area divided into three triangular sections, a drilling in each.

460. (Fig. 465) Nicosia 1957. viii-9. 3; black; stringhole through the top; L. 0.012 m. H. 0.014 m.
(a) Striding figure holding branch; (b) striding female (?) figure in long dress, holding branch; (c) star and crescent; (d) branch.

461. (Fig. 466) Nicosia E. 45; grey; pyramidal; stringhole through top; L. 0.016 m. W. 0.013 m.
(a) Irregular line; two V-shaped incisions above; (b) irregular cross; (c) crude triangle; line through it; (d) two parallel, horizontal lines; cross-hatching in between; (e) (base) criss-cross pattern.

Fig. 467. Cat. 462. (1:1) Impression, drawing.

Fig. 468. Cat. 463. (1:1) Impression, drawing.

462. (Fig. 467) Nicosia E. 49 (once Konstantinides); grey; L. 0.008 m. W. 0.007 m. H. 0.014 m.
(a) Star pattern; (b) star pattern; (c) stick-like figure, drilling for head; arms raised; (d) similar to (c) (Ohnefalsch-Richter, *KBH*, 422; pl. 94, no. 11a-b).

463. (Fig. 468) Nicosia 1954. ix-17. 1; tabloid; black; L. 0.028 m. W. 0.020 m. H. 0.012 m.
(a) Horse standing; smaller animal below; V-shaped object in front; crescent above; (b) standing horse; object in front; drill hole above; drillwork for hooves and end of snout. The styles of the devices differ; side (a) is simply incised, without any use of the drill.

The following pendant or seal may also be noted here, since it is decorated on its different facets:

464. (Fig. 469) New York N. E. 74. 51. 4387; obelisk-shaped; black; devices on four sides and base; stringhole across top: L. 0.018 m. W. 0.015 m. H. 0.085 m.
(a) Two registers of rough concentric grooves; (b) irregular grooves; (c) two registers of roughly concentric grooves; (d) irregularly positioned diamonds and triangles; (e) (base) cross-hatching (Myres, *HCC*, 446, no. 4387).

A number of patterns are evident. These seals are especially popular along the southern coast, from Amathus to Kourion. They are also all, in a sense, 'oversize': that is, they are slightly larger in dimensions than the average scarab or scaraboid. As so often in society, greater size can imply greater importance. Is that the case here? Did these seals belong to important people, and can they be construed, in any sense, as 'official' seals? The evidence, on the whole, suggests that this is not the case. The devices are all carved in styles appropriate to the serpentine scarabs and scaraboids and stylistically appear no finer or more elaborate than any of these. There are no

Fig. 469. Cat. 464. (1:1) Original.

archaeological contexts that necessarily suggest ownership by individuals of greater social status, since the sanctuaries or graves in which these seals were recovered had no features that distinguished them from any other in which serpentine scarabs or scaraboids had been found. It is not impossible that, as oversize seals, they were simply meant to be seen and not used, another overt symbol of power and authority. But the use of serpentines and, therefore, the corresponding lack of inscribed pieces tells against the identification of these seals as official seals. Large and even flamboyant, they may have been more expensive than the standard serpentine scarab and scaraboid, but although at the top end of that particular scale, there was probably still a divide between the best of the serpentine cubical seals and the least of the seals carved from a harder stone.

12
STICKS ON STONES

The previous chapter considered cubical seals and suggested, largely on the basis of their sizes and the images on them, that they represented, in economic terms, the 'top end' on the scale of values represented by serpentine seals. This chapter considers the opposite end of that scale. The seals considered here all have devices that are summary to the extent that representations may simply be described as 'stick-figures', and there is no question of identifying, even vaguely and in general terms, the taxonomy of the animals shown. The devices may derive, at some remove, from typically Levantine or Greek motifs, but the immediate sources, if any, are no longer recoverable, and many may be of indigenous inspiration. The summariness of execution often means they are ignored in excavation reports and perhaps too much is being made of them in this chapter. But a map is no worse (and generally much better) for showing the less important routes, and these objects, simple as they are, still have something to say about popular taste. The descriptions below necessarily have to use terms such as 'quadruped' or 'animal'. The figures are presumably male, but there is no reason to think that this is invariably the case. In those instances in which a figure is seen riding an animal, it seems safe to assume that the animal is, in fact, a horse.

Fig. 470. Cat. 465. (2:1) Original.

Fig. 471. Cat. 466. (2:1).

Fig. 472. Cat. 467. (2:1).

Amathus

465. (Fig. 470) London 328 (1894. 11–1. 430, British excavations, 1894; tomb 201; lower burial; CA); scarab; black; crude markings on back; L. 0.017 m. W. 0.011 m. H. 0.008 m.

Crudely-cut standing figure with one arm raised (? or holding a stick) and confronting a horse (?) (Walters, *BM Gems*, 40, no. 328).

466. (Fig. 471) Nicosia (Amathus T. 11. 71; third burial; mid-CAII); scarab; black; legs not cut; head and prothorax unmarked; L. 0.013 m.

Striding stick-like quadruped; disc, lines above back (? crescent); line in front (*SCE* 2, 74, no. 71; pl. 18, no. 2. 71; Forgeau, *Amathonte* 3, 166, no. 72).

Arsos

467. (Fig. 472) Nicosia D. 169 (prob. Cypriot excavations, 1917; sanctuary; CA); scarab; black; rounded head; legs not cut;

Fig. 473. Cat. 468. (2:1).

Fig. 474. Cat. 469. (2:1) Original.

Fig. 475. Cat. 470. (2:1) Original.

Fig. 476. Cat. 471. (2:1) Original.

Fig. 478. Cat. 473. (2:1) Original.

Fig. 477. Cat. 472. (2:1) Impression.

Fig. 479. Cat. 474. (2:1).

pinched back; L. 0.013 m. W. 0.010 m. H. 0.006 m.
Device worn: stick-like quadruped; object above.

468. (Fig. 473) Nicosia D. 170 (prob. Cypriot excavations, 1917; sanctuary; CA); scarab; black; L. 0.013 m. W. 0.010 m. H. 0.006 m.
Device worn: standing quadruped (? goat).

Ayia Irini

469. (Fig. 474) Stockholm A. I. 2647 (period 4); scarab; black; lightly carinated spine; L. 0.012 m. W. 0.008 m. H. 0.007 m.
Striding quadruped (? lion); linear border (*SCE* 2, 770, no. 2647).

470. (Fig. 475) Stockholm A. I. 2681 (period 5); scarab; grey-green; tall beetle; worn back; L. 0.014 m. W. 0.011 m. H. 0.009 m.
Stick-like striding quadruped (*SCE* 2, 771, no. 2681).

471. (Fig. 476) Stockholm A. I. 2725 (period 6); scaraboid; mottled grey-green; L. 0.019 m. W. 0.015 m. H. 0.008 m.
Standing stick-like quadruped (*SCE* 2, 772, no. 2725).

472. (Fig. 477) Nicosia A. I. 2687 (listed as no. 2755 in *SCE* 2; context therefore uncertain); scarab; grey mottled stone; slightly chipped back; L. 0.014 m. W. 0.010 m. H. 0.006 m.
Striding, long-necked animal (*SCE* 2, 773, no. 2755; pl. 250, no. 15).

473. (Fig. 478) Stockholm A. I. (no number); scarab; grey; damaged back; large beetle; L. 0.012 m. W. 0.010 m. H. 0.007 m.
Striding quadruped, cut in outline, with rider and shield (?).

474. (Fig. 479) Nicosia A. I. 2126 (period 4); scaraboid; red stone; L. 0.019 m. W. 0.015 m. H. 0.008 m.
Device worn: three branches; linear border (*SCE* 2, 754, no. 2126).

Kition

475. (Fig. 480a) Nicosia D. 30; scarab; brown; L. 0.014 m.
Horse and rider.

Kourion

476. (Fig. 480b) New York N. E. 74. 51. 4395 (Kourion Treasure); scarab; black; legs not cut; L. 0.013 m. W. 0.011 m. H. 0.009 m.
Two stick-like human figures (? marching); circle underneath each (Myres, *HCC*, 447, no. 4395).

477. (Fig. 481) New York N. E. 74. 51. 4396; scarab; brown; summary lines at back to show beetle parts; legs not cut; L. 0.014 m. W. 0.011 m. H. 0.007 m.
Device very worn: rearing quadrupeds (?) (Myres, *HCC*, 447, no. 4396).

Pyrga

478. (Fig. 482) Larnaka (once Nicosia 1960. xi-21. 13); scarab; black; short incisions to indicate different parts of back; L. 0.018 m. W. 0.014 m. H. 0.010 m.
Device worn: human figure (?) facing quadruped (?); object in field; linear border (Charles, 'Pyrga', 30–1, no. 13, described as a king smiting an enemy).

479. Larnaka (once Nicosia 1945. i-29. 4); scarab; grey; large prothorax separated from elytra by a single line; L. 0.014 m.
Striding quadruped; papyrus brake behind.

Provenances unknown

Note also a scaraboid of grey serpentine now in the Pierides Museum, Larnaka showing a horse and rider: A. T. Reyes, 'Stamp-Seals in the Pierides Collection, Larnaca' *RDAC* (1991), 125, no. 18. (Fig. 483)

480. (Fig. 484) Nicosia D. 45; scarab; grey; L. 0.015 m.
Insect on branch (?); linear border.

Fig. 480a. Cat. 475. (2:1).

Fig. 480b. Cat. 476. (2:1) Impression.

Fig. 481. Cat. 477. (2:1) Impression.

Fig. 482. Cat. 478. (2:1).

Fig. 483. (2:1) Scaraboid of grey serpentine, with device showing a male figure, arms raised on a horse (Larnaka, Pierides Collection 1961). L. 0.020 m. W. 0.017 m. H. 0.012 m.

Fig. 484. Cat. 480. (2:1).

481. (Fig. 485) Nicosia 1956. viii-28. 3; scaraboid; black; L. 0.012 m.
Stick-like striding quadruped; linear border

482. (Fig. 486) Nicosia D. 37; scarab; black; prothorax and elytra shown by short incisions; summarily carved head; L. 0.016 m.
Device worn: striding quadruped; crescent (?) in front.

483. (Fig. 487) Nicosia D. 36; scarab; grey; head not carved; prothorax and elytra indicated by short incisions; L. 0.016 m.
Striding horned quadruped; drilling above; linear border.

484. (Fig. 488) Nicosia D. 69; scaraboid; black; L. 0.012 m.
Device worn: striding quadruped; object above.

485. (Fig. 489) Oxford 1896–1908. C. 401; scarab; black; L. 0.014 m. W. 0.010 m. H. 0.008 m.
Horse (?) and rider (Buchanan and Moorey, *Ashmolean* 3, 81, no. 540).

486. (Fig. 490) Nicosia D. 66; scaraboid; mottled grey; L. 0.015 m. W. 0.011 m. H. 0.006 m.
Stick-like horse and rider.

487. (Fig. 491) Nicosia D. 54; scaraboid; grey; L. 0.017 m.
Stick-like figure and quadruped (?); ground line.

488. (Fig. 492) Nicosia D. 44; scarab; dark grey; legs not cut; L. 0.019 m.
Device worn (some recutting?): stick-like figure above quadruped.

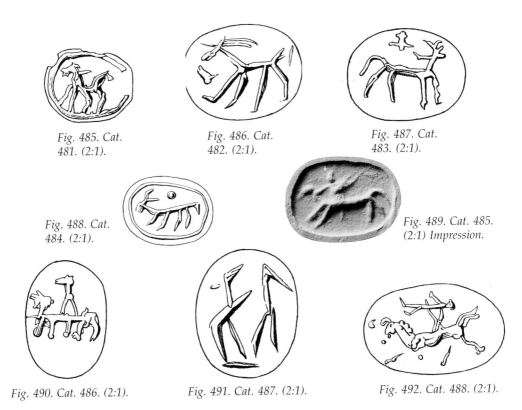

Fig. 485. Cat. 481. (2:1).

Fig. 486. Cat. 482. (2:1).

Fig. 487. Cat. 483. (2:1).

Fig. 488. Cat. 484. (2:1).

Fig. 489. Cat. 485. (2:1) Impression.

Fig. 490. Cat. 486. (2:1).

Fig. 491. Cat. 487. (2:1).

Fig. 492. Cat. 488. (2:1).

Fig. 493. Cat. 489.
(2:1) Impression.

Fig. 494. Cat.
490. (2:1).

489. (Fig. 493) Oxford 1891. 628; scaraboid; black; L. 0.016 m. W. 0.012 m. H. 0.005 m.
Device worn: two standing stick-like human figures (? marching); double ground line (Buchanan and Moorey, *Ashmolean* 3, 82, no. 563; pl. 18).

490. (Fig. 494) Nicosia D. 9; scarab; white stone; L. 0.015 m.
Three standing human figures; heads and bodies shown by drillwork.

The correspondence between shape and image needs to be noted. These are, for the most part, serpentine scaraboids or scarabs with the parts of the beetle as summarily denoted as the devices. If it is true that these are the less expensive serpentine seals, then it must also be true that scarabs and scaraboids made from hardstones and cut in this summary way reflect the lower end of the economic scale represented by the hardstone seals. Two such hardstone seals are known, with devices showing stick-animals. The example in the British Museum was chemically tested in 1966 and found to be authentically of marble.

Apostolos Varnavas (Famagusta area)
491. (Fig. 495) Nicosia 1949. vii-8. 1;
scaraboid; grey banded marble; L.
0.019 m.
Striding quadruped.

Fig. 495. Cat.
491. (2:1)
Impression.

Provenances unknown[360]
492. London 306 (1874. 3–5. 21); scaraboid; grey marble; L. 0.016 m. W. 0.012 m. H. 0.007 m.
Striding quadruped, one paw raised (Walters, *BM Gems*, 38, no. 306).
The quadruped is very close to 491, perhaps by the same hand.

It is doubtful that either one of these was regarded as a test-piece, a trial-run before the serious business of carving a hardstone seal. They are certainly not like any of the standard representations to be found on such seals, lacking the detail allowing the identification of the animal involved. Nor would a seal-cutter have used marble as a test-piece for serpentines. These two seals show once more that, in general, among the seal-wearing public, hardstones and serpentines occupied separate spheres.

In sum, then, if glyptics are classified among the 'minor' arts, these serpentine seals are among the least of the Cypriot seals. If the serpentine seals may be described as 'provincial', these are the most provincial. But they are still to be found in the same sanctuaries and cemeteries as the other finer examples. Summary as they are, they still contain all the magic and individual power of the more brilliant and better-cut examples.

13

ORIGINALS, INDIVIDUALS, SIGNS, AND SYMBOLS

The previous chapter may have given the impression that the devices of hardstone scarabs and scaraboids tend to show the art of the Cypriot seal-cutter at its finest, while the serpentines represent glyptic art at its most generic. On the whole, the best of the devices from seals cut from hardstones surpass anything on the serpentines, but there are still devices on the latter that are in every respect the stylistic equivalent of the former, and even if not, the humbler cases can often be the more interesting (as Sherlock Holmes once famously observed).[361] To complete this conspectus of the stamp-seals of Cyprus, then, this chapter presents a range of miscellaneous serpentine devices, probably locally manufactured or at least used on the island. Some devices are unique, striking, and even bold. Others clearly represent part of a glyptic fashion current within Cyprus and may be reasonably considered together, as a stylistic group.

BIRDS

Ayia Irini
493. (Fig. 496) Nicosia A. I. 2727 (period 4); scarab; grey; notched head; double curving line separating prothorax from elytra; striated front legs; tail slightly pinched; L. 0.014 m. W. 0.010 m. H. 0.010 m.

Long-necked bird with outstretched wings; crudely-incised legs (? miscut); rough ground line; linear border (*SCE* 2, 772; pl. 250, no. 9).

On the flying bird in Cypro-Phoenician iconography, see Markoe, *Bowls*, 42–3 and cf. 242, no. Cy1 from Idalion (outer register).

Provenances unknown
494. (Fig. 497) New York N. E. 74. 51. 4394; scarab; black; back worn smooth; legs not cut; L. 0.013 m. W. 0.008 m. H. 0.007 m.

Stick-like human figure confronting a bird (? ostrich); circle in between (Myres, *HCC*, 447, no. 4394, described as two human figures).

On the ostrich-motif in Middle Assyrian, Neo-Assyrian, and Palestinian art, note a ninth or eighth century B. C. cylinder seal from Arad in M. Aharoni, 'An Iron Age Cylinder Seal' *IEJ* 46 (1996), 52–4.

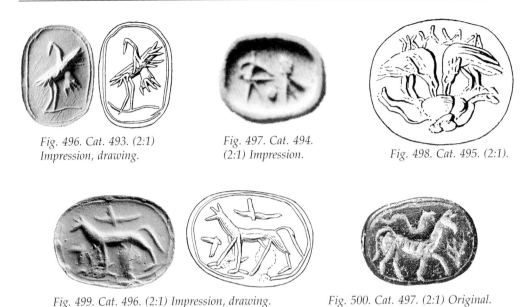

Fig. 496. Cat. 493. (2:1)
Impression, drawing.

Fig. 497. Cat. 494.
(2:1) Impression.

Fig. 498. Cat. 495. (2:1).

Fig. 499. Cat. 496. (2:1) Impression, drawing.

Fig. 500. Cat. 497. (2:1) Original.

495. (Fig. 498) once de Bellesne; conoid (?); haematite; L. 0.019 m. W. 0.017 m. H. 0.015 m.
Two birds feeding at the carcase of a calf: Cypro-syllabic inscription: *a-ru?-la-ti* (J. Boardman, 'Pyramidal Stamp-seals in the Persian Empire' *Iran* 8 (1970), 40, no. 15; fig. 6).

DOGS

A dog-like animal appears on two devices from Ayia Irini, probably cut by the same hand. The motif seems local.

Ayia Irini

496. (Fig. 499) Nicosia A. I. 2183 (period 4); scarab; black; notch at sides to indicate winglets; L. 0.017 m. W. 0.011 m. H. 0.008 m.
Striding dog (?); ears perked; bird above; floral (?) object in front; linear border (*SCE* 2, 756, no. 2183; pl. 245, no. 7).

497. (Fig. 500) Stockholm A. I. 2291 (period 4); scarab; black; small notches to indicate winglets; L. 0.016 m. W. 0.012 m. H. 0.008 m.
Striding dog (?); snake above; branch in front; linear border (*SCE* 2, 759, no. 2291; pl. 246, no. 20).

GEOMETRIC PATTERNS

These are the most basic of devices: irregular linear or circular patterns without proper stylistic comparanda.

Amathus

498. (Fig. 501) Limassol; Amathus T. 142/35 (tomb; CAI-early CAII); scarab; dark grey-green; back deeply incised; L. 0.014 m. W. 0.012 m. H. 0.008 m.
Irregular pattern of thirteen drill-holes; curved linear border to one side (Boardman, 'Seals and Amulets', 161, pl. 3).

499. (Fig. 502) Limassol; Amathus T. 142/52 (tomb; CAI-early CAII); scaraboid; black; beetle with gable spine; L. 0.008 m. W. 0.007 m. H. 0.004 m.
Circle with seven lines radiating outward (Boardman, 'Seals and Amulets', 161, pl. 3).

500. (Fig. 503) New York N. E. 74. 51. 4397; scaraboid; black; large plinth; L. 0.017 m. W. 0.011 m. H. 0.009 m.
Irregularly-cut lines (Myres, *HCC*, 447, no. 4397).

501. (Fig. 504) London 1969. 4–1. 260 (British excavations; tomb 311; context unreported); scarab; black; back damaged; notched head; L. 0.013 m. W. 0.009 m. H. 0.006 m.
Irregular lines and one drilling (? meant to represent an animal) (Forgeau, *Amathonte* 3, 58, no. 49).

Ayia Irini

502. (Fig. 505) Nicosia A. I. 2621 (sanctuary; period 4); scarab; mottled green; low back; L. 0.015 m. W. 0.011 m. H. 0.007 m.
Irregular scratches (*SCE* 2, 770, no. 2621; pl. 248, no. 28).

Idalion

503. (Fig. 506) Stockholm; Idalion (no number); scaraboid; red; L. 0.016 m. W. 0.012 m. H. 0.007 m.
Irregular lines and small holes.

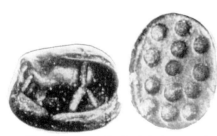

Fig. 501. Cat. 498. (2:1) Seal, original.

Fig. 502. Cat. 499. (2:1) Original, impression.

Fig. 503. Cat. 500. (2:1) Impression.

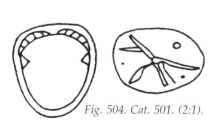

Fig. 504. Cat. 501. (2:1).

Fig. 505. Cat. 502. (2:1).

Fig. 506. Cat. 503. (2:1) Original.

Fig. 507. Cat. 504. (2:1) Seal, original.   Fig. 508. Cat. 505. (2:1).

  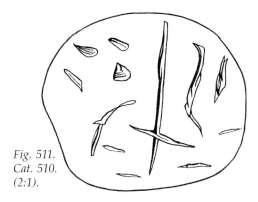

Fig. 509. Cat.   Fig. 510. Cat. 509.   Fig. 511.
508. (2:1).   (2:1) Impression.   Cat. 510.
                                                (2:1).

Kition

504. (Fig. 507) Kition 3737 (site 2; bothros 6A; 800–450); scarab; black; highly polished by wear; L. 0.016 m. W. 0.014 m. H. 0.009 m.
Circle with eleven lines curving around it, radiating outward (Clerc, *Kition* 2, 112, no. 3737).

Koupetra (Nicosia area)

505. (Fig. 508) Nicosia 1947. vii-18. 2; irregularly-shaped scaraboid; pale green; L. 0.015 m. H. 0.013 m.
Irregular pattern of lines; five interspersed drillings.

Pyrga

506. Larnaka (once Nicosia 1960. xi-21. 16); scarab; black; two short incisions to indicate prothorax; no line dividing elytra; L. 0.015 m. W. 0.012 m. H. 0.007 m.
Irregular criss-cross design (Charles, 'Pyrga', 33, no. 16).

507. Larnaka (once Nicosia 1960. xi-21. 15) scarab; grey; L. 0.020 m. W. 0.014 m. H. 0.011 m.
Irregular cuttings (Charles, 'Pyrga', 32, no. 15).

Salamis

508. (Fig. 509) Nicosia D. 77; scaraboid; back; L. 0.014 m. W. 0.009 m. H. 0.005 m.
Lattice pattern; linear border.

Fig. 512. Cat. 511.
(2:1) Original.

Fig. 513. Cat. 513.
(2:1) Original.

Fig. 514. Cat. 514.
(2:1) Impression.

Provenances unknown

509. (Fig. 510) Oxford 1891. 649; scarab; grey; markings at the top worn; L. 0.015 m. W. 0.011 m. H. 0.008 m.
Irregular curvilinear design (Buchanan and Moorey, *Ashmolean* 3, 81, no. 552; pl. 17).

510. (Fig. 511) Nicosia E. 74; scaraboid; grey; L. 0.028 m.
Irregular lines and incisions.

LOCAL IMAGERY

Ayia Irini

511. (Fig. 512) Stockholm A. I. 2663 (listed in *SCE* 2 as no. 2632; context therefore uncertain); scarab; black; legs not shown; lumpy head; L. 0.014 m. W. 0.010 m. H. 0.008 m.
Standing figure with large nose and pointed chin (? bearded); crested hairstyle; one arm raised and holding rod with sphere (?) at the bottom; ithyphallic (?); branch and floral (?) object behind (*SCE* 2, 770, no. 2632).
Gjerstad identified the type as a satyr, but there is no evidence to support the suggestion, and the figure may simply derive from local folk-lore.

Provenances unknown

512. Boston 98. 715 (impression only); reported as 'black serpentine'; L. 0.018 m.
Bearded man driving a plough drawn by a bull; whip in one hand; Cypro-syllabic inscription: *zo-wo-i-ta-u-e-mi-to-te-mi-si-ti-o* (Ζωϝοιτάν ἠμι τῶ θεμιστίω); double zigzag exergue (O. Masson, 'Quelques Intailles chypriotes inscrites' *Syria* 44 (1967), 363–8; pl. 19, no. 1; Masson, *ICS*, 391, no. 463 and 421, no. 367a).

513. (Fig. 513) Berlin FG 134; scaraboid; black; L. 0.018 m. W. 0.013 m. H. 0.010 m.
Man in congress (?) with goat (? donkey) (Zwierlein-Diehl, *AGDS* 2, 64, no. 130).

514. (Fig. 514) Oxford 1896/1908. O. 14; scaraboid; blue chalcedony; bronze pin in stringhole; L. 0.016 m. W. 0.012 m. H. 0.010 m.
A foot; Cypro-syllabic inscription: *pi-ki-re-wo* (Πίγρηϝο(ς)); hatched border (Boardman and Vollenweider, *Ashmolean Gems*, 15, no. 71; Masson, *ICS*, 348, no. 360).
For similar motifs, see Boardman, *GGFR*, pl. 513 and 524 (sandal, Classical period); J. Boardman, *Escarabeos de Piedra, Procedentes de Ibiza* (Madrid, 1984), Lam. 34. 212.

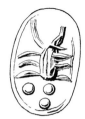

Fig. 515. Cat. 515. (2:1).

Fig. 516. Cat. 516. (2:1) Original.

Fig. 517. Cat. 517. (2:1) Original.

Fig. 518. Cat. 518. (2:1).

*Fig. 519. Cat. 519. (2:1)
Impression, drawing.*

SCORPIONS

Seals 516, 517, and 518, from Ayia Irini, were probably cut by the same hand. Each uses a scorpion as a device, its tail represented by three drillings, within a linear border. A seal with the same device and probably cut by the same hand (515) is known from Arsos and demonstrates glyptic contact between the two areas. As a motif, the scorpion is more frequently seen in Near Eastern, rather than Greek, glyptic.[362]

Arsos
515. (Fig. 515) Nicosia D. 167 (Cypriot excavations of
     1917; sanctuary; CA context); scarab; black; L.
     0.014 m. (*SCE* 3, 599i; pl. 204. 23i).

Ayia Irini
516. (Fig. 516) Stockholm A. I. 2276 (period 5); scarab;
     black; lumpy profile; slight pinching at the tail;
     notched head; L. 0.013 m. W. 0.009 m. H. 0.008 m.
     (*SCE* 2, 758, no. 2276).

517. (Fig. 517) Stockholm A. I. 2299 (period 5); scarab;
     black; lumpy profile; high beetle; L. 0.012 m. W.
     0.008 m. H. 0.007 m. (*SCE* 2, 758, no. 2299).

518. (Fig. 518) Nicosia A. I. 2706 (period 5); scarab;
     grey; two V-shaped lines separating prothorax
     from elytra; lumpy profile; L. 0.015 m. W. 0.011 m.
     H. 0.009 m. (*SCE* 2, 772, no. 2706; pl. 250, no. 1).

The following scaraboids, also with scorpions, may be noted here, although cut by different hands:

Ayia Irini
519. (Fig. 519) Nicosia A. I. 2515 (period 6); scaraboid;
     cream stone; cracked surface; L. 0.014 m. W. 0.011
     m. H. 0.005 m. (*SCE* 2, 767, no. 2515; pl. 247, no.
     11).

Maroni
520. Nicosia 1980. v-28. 1; chance find; scarab; black;
     L. 0.014 m. H. 0.009 m.
     Scorpion in very linear style.
     Scorpion (? possibly an insect); cross-hatched
     exergue.

The following device may also show a scorpion:

Soloi
521. Nicosia 1954. ix-23. 3 (west of the Roman theatre); scarab; blue; L. 0.012 m.
    Man approaching scorpion (?).

STRIATED FIGURES

A number of seals have devices with male figures
whose bodies are shown striated with horizontal
lines. They are all from Ayia Irini, perhaps by the
same hand:

Ayia Irini
522. (Fig. 520) Stockholm A. I. 2184 (period 4); scarab;
    grey-green; L. 0.014 m. W. 0.009 m. H. 0.008 m.
    Male figure standing between two branches (*SCE* 2,
    756, no. 2184).

Fig. 520. Cat. 522. (2:1) Original.

523. (Fig. 521) Stockholm A. I. 2190 (period 4); scarab;
    black; back worn; nocthed head; lumpy profile; L.
    0.014 m. W. 0.010 m. H. 0.007 m.
    Male figure standing between two branches (*SCE* 2,
    756, no. 2190).
    The seal appears to be a version of 522.

524. (Fig. 522) Stockholm A. I. 2426 (period 4); scaraboid;
    grey; legs summarily indicated; low back; L. 0.013
    m. W. 0.010 m. H. 0.006 m.
    Crude device, very worn: standing male figure with
    man bent over in front; faint traces of linear border
    (*SCE* 2, 764, no. 2426).
    For a similar scene, probably representing sex *a tergo*,
    see 24. The motif may be local.[363]

Fig. 521. Cat. 523. (2:1) Original.

525. Nicosia A. I. 2250 (period 5); scarab; dark-grey; low
    back; L. 0.015 m. W. 0.011 m. H. 0.006 m.
    Standing man bent forward; one arm raised;object
    held in other hand; horizontal branch in front (?
    ithyphallic) (*SCE* 2, 758, no. 2250; pl. 246, no. 3).
    The figure may be associated with 511.

Fig. 522. Cat. 524. (2:1) Original.

526. (Fig. 523) Stockholm A.I. 2563 (period 4); scarab;
    black; low, flat back; double line dividing elytra;
    striated front legs; L. 0.014 m. W. 0.010 m. H. 0.006
    m.
    Standing winged figure (*SCE* 2, 768, no. 2563).
    The motif may imitate Phoenician winged deities.[364]

Fig. 523. Cat. 526. (2:1) Original.

Fig. 524. Cat. 527. (2:1) Impression, drawing.

527. (Fig. 524) Nicosia A. I. 2553 (period 4); scarab; pale-grey; legs represented by short grooves above base; L. 0.018 m. W. 0.016 m. H. 0.007 m.

Human figure approaching sphinx (? bird) (*SCE* 2, 768, no. 2553; pl. 247, no. 27).

On the motif and its possibly religious significance, see Buchner and Boardman, 'Lyre-Player', 52; *cf.* R. S. Lamon and G. M. Shipton, *Megiddo* 1 (Chicago, 1939), pl. 67, no. 38 (haematite scaraboid; Iron II period).

14

PATTERNS AND HISTORIES

This final chapter will draw the disparate threads of this study together. It presents the glyptic history of the island as a whole. Characteristics peculiar to particular areas are then examined.

CHRONOLOGIES

In broad terms, a gross distinction has been set up between those seals made of hardstones and those made of serpentine, a reflection, perhaps, of different uses by people of differing social or economic status. The hardstone seals, in general, have more carefully cut devices than their counterparts in serpentine, nor are the latter found with the elaborate metal settings of the former. It is significant too that serpentine and hardstone seals are not usually found together in the same archaeological contexts. Hardstone seals more often combine inscriptions with their devices.

For the Archaic period, as with the Late Bronze Age, variety and innovation were characteristic. The majority of seals are scarabs or scaraboids, but there is still some experimenting with shapes, and a wide range of materials and motifs is apparent. A certain amount of inspiration could be drawn from the past, and certain motifs are explicable in terms of Late Bronze Age glyptic. This is not surprising, as conoids and cylinder-seals, now no longer in general use in Cyprus, have been found in Cypro-Archaic contexts at various archaeological sites.[365] Tabloids, rectangular stamp-seals, conoids, and cylinders are all known from the Archaic levels of the sanctuaries at Ayia Irini.[366] These may be considered 'survivors' – objects passed down as 'heirlooms' or else found by chance – and dated to the Bronze Age, despite their archaeological contexts, by virtue of their shapes and the styles of their devices.

After a decline in the Cypro-Geometric period, Cypriot stamp-seals proliferate again in Archaic times, a phenomenon to be associated perhaps with continued Phoenician expansion and growing Near Eastern trade. From stratigraphic evidence at Ayia Irini and the dating of tombs at Amathus, the main series of local serpentine seals seems to have been in production by roughly the second half of the seventh century. The single Horse-Group scarab of grey serpentine from Ayia Irini with a late CGIII-mid CAI context, may be an import, since the markings on its back are out of character with the less elaborately marked backs of the majority of Cypriot serpentine scarabs, and the device was widespread throughout the Levant. The Horse-Group motif would eventually be taken over in local Cypriot glyptic of the sixth century and used as a standard device for a series of serpentine head-seals, centred largely around the Kourion and Amathus areas.

The earliest of the hardstone seals are those in a clearly Phoenician style. The earliest contexts fall around the second half of the seventh century (160 from Ayia Irini, 288 from Kourion). It is at this time too, or shortly afterward, that the local serpentine series, largely imitative of a Phoenician style, begins. Excavations at the sanctuary of Ayia Irini (173, 217, 218) and the Apollo sanctuary at Kourion (443) provide the earliest archaeological evidence.

By the end of the seventh century, therefore, a local glyptic industry was well-established in Cyprus, and it is precisely at this time too that seals are first depicted on Cypriot statuary. There is no secure evidence for local manufacture in significant quantities prior to the second half of the seventh century.[367] Typical of local production are seals showing warrior-figures cut in a Sub-Geometric style. Other serpentine seals imitate Phoenician gems closely. By the second half of the sixth century, the hardstone gems with devices influenced by East Greek art appear. Similarly, serpentine seals begin to use Greek iconography, notably in the depiction of centaurs. The Pyrga workshop commences production. Throughout, hardstone seals in a purely Phoenician style may still have appeared alongside the cruder serpentine scarabs and scaraboids, but by the second half of the sixth century, they had been displaced in popularity by the production of hardstone seals in a more Hellenic style.

From the surviving Cypriot material, then, it would appear that there is no need to push the beginnings of the hardstone *Greek* glyptic back into the seventh century.[368] There is no evidence at this time for a Greek style among the hardstone seals. The hardstone gems in a Phoenician style preceded the examples based on Greek prototypes and probably served as inspiration for the Archaic Greek gems.

Unlike Island Gems, Cypriot seals do not display a chronological progression toward the appreciation of body mass, since devices in which the mass of the body is properly appreciated already occur in period four (mid-CAI-early CAII) of Ayia Irini (e.g., 168).[369] Often these bodies would have been simply gouged out, rather than drilled. More commonly, a combination of drilling and incision is used to create the effect of proper representation. In 198, bodies are created by drillings positioned closely together, a technique conventional in the contemporary glyptic of Syria and Palestine and related to the Archaic Greek Common Style.[370] There is also a gradual development of a feeling for the constraints of working within an oval frame, and as a result, the use of the exergue declines in the late sixth century.

Hardstone seals use as principal devices Phoenician and Greek deities, adorants, mythological creatures, inscriptions, human figures, and animals. Serpentine seals depict more summary, abbreviated versions of these. Motifs explicable in purely Greek terms appear less frequently on the serpentines. Minor or filling motifs include the following: linear or hatched borders, exergues with ladder patterns, cross-hatching, zigzags, or oblique hatching; birds; stars; discs and crescents; winged discs; ankhs; rearing uraei; *uzat*-eyes; papyrus brakes; irregular hatched areas; and drillings. All are attested among contemporary seals from Syria and Palestine. No firm rules can be established concerning these filling motifs, given the lack of a comparable body of material from the Phoenician coast, but certain trends may be noted. Ladder exergues tend to be early chronologically. They are found among Lyre-Player seals, green-jasper gems, and on glazed scarabs. It is likely that Cypriot seals took over these motifs from these early models.

SOME LOCAL STYLES

Currently, only the following sites provide enough material to allow for an assessment of local style: Amathus, Ayia Irini, Kition, Kourion, Marion, Pyrga, and Salamis. These will be the only sites reviewed here, but reference will be made to material from sites close to these as a way of providing a sharper focus to whatever picture emerges.

Amathus

In terms of glyptic production, Amathus, together with Kourion, seems to have been one of the most cosmopolitan sites in Cyprus. Examples of devices cut in East Greek, Phoenician, or Neo-Babylonian styles are evident, and a hybrid Graeco-Phoenician style is also attested. This same cosmopolitan atmosphere is also reflected on the finger-rings from Amathus.[371] Given the extensive number of Greek and Phoenician hardstone seals here and in Kourion, it may well be from somewhere around this area that techniques for cutting hardstone seals were transmitted to the Greek mainland during the Archaic period. The carinated spine, typical of Archaic Greek scarabs, is also characteristic of hardstone beetles from Amathus, which use double curving lines to separate the prothorax from the elytra. It does not seem accidental that one of the earliest in the sequence of Archaic Greek gems is reportedly from Amathus (353).[372]

In addition to its hardstone seals, Amathus had a large serpentine repertoire. The typically Amathusian head-pendant is carved with cross-hatched hair and a long pointed beard. Cubical seals were popular, and a striated style is found in Amathus and nearby Erimi (437, 441). Aside from Erimi, the seals of Amathus are most closely allied to those of Kourion. The number of shared motifs and styles between the two areas is striking. Head-seals are typical of both areas; the various Phoenician and Greek styles were at home here; works of the Semon Master are known from both places (as well as at Paphos and Salamis); examples of the Sub-Geometric warriors are represented. In addition, relationships are likely with Idalion and Pyrga where comparable head-seals are attested and Marion, also a centre for the production of seals cut from harder stones. Seals of lapis lazuli, a distinctive and unusual material, are known only in Amathus (216), Kition (180, 181, and 303), and Tamassos (170). In sum, from the glyptic evidence, the principal connections of Amathus are with the Kourion and Paphos areas to the south-west, the Marion area to the north-west, and the inland area around Idalion.[373]

Ayia Irini

The ancient name of Ayia Irini remains unknown. It may have been part of the territory of the Archaic kingdom of Lapethos, some twenty kilometres further east, but in the absence of epigraphical evidence, there is no certainty, and written sources concerning Lapethos in the Archaic period are poor.[374] To judge by the local coinage, the surrounding area supported a Phoenician population in the fifth and fourth centuries B.C.,[375] and a Phoenician funerary inscription from one of the tombs at Ayia Irini has been dated to the Cypro-Archaic I period on the basis of its epigraphical style.[376] Ps.-Skylax 103 records that Lapethos was Phoenician, but Strabo 14. 6. 3 (683c) reports that Praxander, a Spartan, founded the kingdom as a Laconian colony.

The Swedish Cyprus Expedition found just over 300 stamp-seals at Ayia Irini, about a quarter of which were made of serpentine or hardstones. Of these, the former predominate over the latter. The non-sculptural objects of Periods 4 through 6 were found in small groups here and there within the temenos, mainly along the west and north temenos walls. These small objects of iron and bronze, faience and glass beads, scarabs, and scaraboids were probably hung on the hurdle-fence of the temenos enclosure and on the wooden posts of the shelter along the temenos wall.[377] The presence of so many seals within a sanctuary indicates their use as cultic objects or religious votives, rather than as administrative tools. By contrast, only one seal (175) is reported from the necropolis.

Most characteristic of period four at Ayia Irini (late seventh century) is the drilled style used for the Sub-Geometric warrior, in which the bodies of the male figures are represented by two drillings and the head by a third. Arms and legs are simply incised. Seal 29, assigned by Furumark to the Late Bronze Age, probably dates to this period, and may well have been cut in Ayia Irini. Later seals use the drill only for the extremities of the figure, and the head can simply be represented by gouging (e.g., 22, 37). This early and extensive use of the drill may suggest that Cyprus played an intermediary role in reintroducing the use of the drill and cutting wheel to Greeks in the sixth century.

The seals suggest a locally-established glyptic industry working largely within a Near-Eastern iconographic tradition. Several devices derive from a specifically Phoenician iconographic tradition (14, 15, 16, 17, 20, 21, 160, 217, 218, 220, 247, 273, 526). But many devices – on both hardstone and serpentine seals – are not as carefully-executed as Phoenician examples and reflect a general association between Cypriot and Levantine glyptic. Some later seals, however, exhibit Greek influence (104, 105, 337).

Seal 328, imitative of Neo-Babylonian glyptic, need not, of course, suggest contact with Mesopotamia. Since Neo-Babylonian seals were widely disseminated throughout Syria and Palestine, as well as further east, 510 is simply indicative of the influence of the Levant. There is little explicable in terms of Greek art until the appearance of 337 with a centaur as a device in period 6. To an extent, the essentially Near Eastern nature of the glyptic material from Ayia Irini is complemented by the Phoenician-style seals of nearby Lapethos (47, 266). To judge by the seals, therefore, Ayia Irini served as a Near Eastern port-of-call along the Mediterranean. In broad terms, then, these seals roughly support the picture of Ayia Irini suggested by the ceramics from the site.[378]

There is a contrast with the essentially Greek connections of the kingdoms of Marion and Soloi to the west. Soloi, by tradition, was said to have had strong ties with Athens,[379] and Marion has provided the most extensive series of Greek ceramics from the island.[380] The distinction between Marion and Ayia Irini, however, is not entirely clear-cut, since stamp-seals exhibiting Near-Eastern influences are attested in Marion,[381] as are a few Phoenician pots.[382] Similarly, a small amount of Greek pottery is known from Ayia Irini, and a few seals reflecting Greek influences are represented there. These seals, however, appear no earlier than period 5, and seem to represent a later stage in the development of local glyptic.

The lumpy shapes and carefully modelled heads of several serpentine scarabs from Ayia Irini are reminiscent of the green-jasper scarab shapes.[383] In Cyprus, the largest number of gems made from green jasper is known from Ayia Irini. It may well be that these gems were instrumental in inspiring the local serpentine sequences.

Within Cyprus, the glyptic affiliations of Ayia Irini seem to lie within the central areas around Arsos (cf. 515 with 516, 517, and 518), the Karpass area (25, one of the Sub-Geometric warriors at home in Ayia Irini), and Pyrga (65 cut in the Pyrga-style). Only Kourion and Amathus seem to have manufactured stamp-seals as extensively as Ayia Irini. But the evidence of contact between these two areas is uncertain. Both are close to major sources of serpentine.[384] Kourion and Amathus, however, are particularly striking for the quality of the cutting on the devices of their hardstone seals. In contrast, the devices on the relatively few hardstone seals from Ayia Irini rarely approach the quality of those from the south-east of Cyprus.

In period 6 of the sanctuary, there is a decline in the number of seals dedicated at the sanctuary. In all, Gjerstad assigned 37 seals to period 6, as opposed to 129 in period 5 and 141 in period 4.[385] This decline may represent part of a wider trend within Cyprus. From the second half of the sixth century B.C., hardstone seals with Greek motifs, rather than serpentine seals with Near Eastern ones, seem to have been increasingly favoured. Since the seal-cutters of Ayia Irini tended to work in the latter, rather than the former, tradition, a decline in output may have resulted. Equally, the change may reflect a shift in votive practices during the late sixth century.

Kition and Pyrga

It is not surprising that, in a Phoenician colony, seal devices are largely Egyptianising and probably inspired by the glyptic of the mother-city. The only example of a Greek-style Cypro-Archaic gem thus far known from the site (407) may well have been imported from Amathus, Kourion, or Marion, where similar seals appear. Beetle-backs tend to be very simple.

Unfinished examples suggest that certain hardstone seals were manufactured locally. Nearby, in Pyrga, a distinctive glyptic style developed. One example of a seal in the Pyrga-style (66) is imported from Kition. The presence of unusual materials such as lapis lazuli and haematite also ally the Kition stone seals with the glyptic of Syria and Palestine, where such materials were more commonly used for seals.[386]

Kourion

An assessment of glyptic in Kourion is beset by the problem of the Kourion Treasure. Cesnola maintained that the Kourion seals were part of a hoard found in what he called a treasure chamber, but subsequent investigation at the site has been unsuccessful in locating this structure, and it now seems likely that the treasure chamber existed only in Cesnola's imagination.[387] This need not mean, however, that seals of the Kourion Treasure do not come from Kourion. An element of doubt will always hang over their provenance, but it may be provisionally assumed that, since the majority of these seals are hardstones in the same Phoenician style, they very probably came from the same area or at least from nearby Amathus.[388] The shapes are mostly scarabs, with carefully cut backs, precise markings for elytra and prothorax, often with V-winglets, and usually with carinated spines. A number of these still have their original swivel settings. When seals that do not belong to the Kourion Treasure are examined, in order to find comparable examples, with motifs and backs similar to those allegedly from Kourion, the closest examples come from either Kourion itself (288) or nearby Amathus (245). It is only in these two areas that the same carefully-cut hardstone beetle is to be found. In Kition, the hardstone seals in Phoenician style usually have simpler backs. A cornelian seal in Phoenican style (14) was excavated from a tomb in Marion, but since the Marion seals are largely Greek in character, this seal was probably imported into the area, perhaps from Kourion.

The seals of the Kourion Treasure give a strongly Phoenician flavour to Kourion, and this style permeates the serpentine seals as well. But in spite of the Phoenician character, the cosmopolitan nature of Kourion should not be neglected. Kourion and Amathus are the two sites in Cyprus in which Greek styles are well attested alongside the near Eastern ones. The same seems true for the finger-rings.[389] Like Amathus, Kourion may have had an interest in head-seals. The only provenanced Horse-Group head-seal (6) is from Kourion. Seals of rock crystal may also have been characteristic of Kourion in the Cypro-Archaic period, perhaps continuing a practice begun in the Late Cypriot period.[390] The raw material may have come from nearby Paphos. The principal glyptic connections of Kourion therefore, seem to be with Marion and Amathus.

Marion and Soloi

Unlike Kition, where seals are essentially of Phoenician inspriation, the seals of Marion are primarily Greek, and none are of serpentine. The seals largely fall within the second half of the sixth century. It appears, therefore, that the development of glyptic in Marion was due to the Greek predilection for hardstone seals, especially for cornelian. As with many Archaic Greek gems, backs are often carinated.

Three examples from Marion, however, are clearly of Phoenician inspiration and should probably be treated as imports into the area. The first (110), a green-jasper gem, is typically Phoenician in its motif and may be confidently considered intrusive. The other two, 161 and 231, are both cornelian scarabs, excavated from tombs. The heavy gold setting of 231 with its pendant attachment, is closely related to types known from Kourion, and it may be that this seal was imported from there. The carefully carved back of 231 is also consonant with the styles of the Kourion scarabs.

There is some confirmation of the essentially Greek nature of the Marion gems in the predominantly Greek styles apparent as devices on metal finger-rings from the same area. Finger-rings from Marion tend to date no earlier than the second half of the sixth century, and motifs derive either from Greek prototypes or else are locally-inspired.[391] The exception is a ring with a cartouche-bezel, whose device derives from Egyptian hieroglyphs, but even this is treated in a Greek style.[392] It seems to have been characteristic of Cypriot glyptic to isolate Egyptian hieroglyphic signs and translate these into more realistic animals (e.g., 381).

Elsewhere in north-west Cyprus, an Island Gem, allegedly from Soloi, again reflects the pattern of predominantly Greek influence. There are also two other serpentine scarabs from the north-west: 521 from Soloi and 165, from the Alakati-Galini Road. The devices of both are in essentially local styles, and they may reflect isolated glyptic activity outside Marion.

Salamis

Three hardstone seals (112, 244, and 362) and nine serpentine seals are attested (68, 141, 155, 169, 183, 233, 307, 322, and 508). Of the three hardstones, only one (362) is in a Greek style. The other two hardstones and the serpentine seals have devices which derive from Phoenician motifs. Beetle-backs are usually simple. Salamis provides an example of a seal in the Pyrga-style (68), and a gem related to the work of the Semon Master (362) associates Salamis with the glyptic of the island's southern coast.

Other regions

It is difficult to generalise about styles from other areas because of lack of evidence. The inland area around Tamassos, Lefkoniko, Golgoi, and Arsos may have acted more as intermediary between different areas, rather than as originators of particular styles. A head-pendant from Idalion (532) and a head-seal from Pyrga (7) seem more appropriate to the Kourion and Amathus areas. Seal 382 from Golgoi may have come from the same area, since the only other example of its type is from Kourion. The green-jasper seals (113, 114) from Tamassos may derive from Ayia Irini, where the majority of such gems are found. In the Karpass, Galinoporni provides an example of a Sub-Geometric warrior (25), perhaps from Ayia Irini as well.

If the fashion in the Greek world for seals made of the harder materials – quartzes, chalcedonies, crystals – was inspired by contact within Cyprus, perhaps this influential contact would have taken place in Marion, which specialised in hardstone seals in the Greek style or Amathus and Kourion, where the glyptic arts were most advanced. The consequences for the Greek world were not insignificant. The repercussions of the Orientalising Revolution of the seventh century B. C. were still being felt in Greece, and the images on the Cypriot seals contributed to the dissemination and eventual adoption of foreign motifs there. The Classical world would also acquire the habit of dedicating seals made of precious stones in their sanctuaries.[393] Cypriot glyptic no doubt also played its part in encouraging a certain desire in the Greek mainland for eastern goods and a similar desire in the Near East for Greek cargoes.[394] The consequences of that traffic still continue today.

Appendix 1
Some Unprovenanced Seals
in the Cesnola Collection

The Cesnola Collection in New York contains a small number of serpentine gable seals, a shape attested from the fourth millennium in the Near East (B. Buchanan, *Catalogue of Ancient Near Eastern Seals in the Ashmolean Museum* 2 (Oxford, 1984), 12–3 for the chronological evidence; for further bibliography, note D. Collon, 'Appendix 1: The Seals from Tille Höyük of the Late Bronze and Earlier' in G. D. Summers, *Tille Höyük* 4 (Oxford, 1993), 171–2, on no. 1). They are all unprovenanced and probably spurious additions to the corpus of Cypriot seals, since no other examples have been uncovered through excavation. The New York examples are as follows: N. E. 74. 51. 4373 (black serpentine; man and goat; hatched border; modern (?) cross-hatching on sides of gable); N. E. 74. 51. 4374 (black serpentine; two striding goats); N. E. 74. 51. 4375 (red stone; goat with branch above). A serpentine seal of the same shape, now in Paris, was also purchased in Cyprus in the nineteenth century: Louvre AM 702 (A. 1176, once Boysset; green stone; horned quadruped with bird overhead and floral motif (?) in front; see Delaporte, *Catalogue* 2, 210; pl. 106, no. 3a-b).

Two cushion-shaped seals, both unprovenanced and in the Cesnola Collection are also probably spurious: N. E. 74. 52. 4376 (green stone; two goats *tête-bêche*) and N. E. 74. 51. 4378 (brownish-white stone; standing quadruped looking back; branch above back). They may be Anatolian, dating to the second millennium (cf. H. Pittman, *Ancient Art in Miniature* (New York, 1987), 63, no. 41–2).

APPENDIX 2
SOME SEALS ATTRIBUTED
TO THE CYPRO-GEOMETRIC PERIOD

Vollenwieder, *Geneva* 3, no. 144; 155, 158–9; 160–2; 164–5; 169–70; and 179 have all been asssigned to the Cypro-Geometric period, but the art-historical criteria used to date these seals are insecure. Brandt, *ADGS* 1, 31, no. 96 has also been attributed to Geometric Cyprus on stylistic criteria; its inscription is northern Arabic, however, not Cypro-Minoan (J. Boardman, *JHS* 90 (1970), 264). Buchanan's reasons for assigning Buchanan and Moorey, *Ashmolean* 3, 80, no. 537–8 are unclear; no. 537, an ovoid, belongs to Buchanan's 'Horse-Group', the chronology of which ranges widely within the Iron Age. (Figs. 525–526)

Fig. 525. (2:1) Serpentine ovoid with a 'Horse-Group' motif (Oxford 1891. 633). L. 0.019 m. W. 0.014 m. H. 0.009 m.

Fig. 526. (2:1) Serpentine ovoid with a crude quadruped, a branch in front, as a device (Oxford 1889. 260). L. 0.035 m. W. 0.024 m. H. 0.013 m.

Albright argued that a triangular seal showing rearing goats on two faces was Cypriot and dated the object to Iron Age I, but there are no convincing parallels: see T. J. Meek, 'Ancient Oriental Seals in the Redpath Library' *BASOR* no. 93 (1944), 12–3, no. 16.

Note also M. Henig, *Classical Gems* (Cambridge, 1994), 480, no. 1065, a tabloid seal of black serpentine, assigned to the eleventh century; if Cypriot, it may simply be part of the series of tabloid seals known from the Archaic period and later.

APPENDIX 3
ADDITIONAL HEAD-PENDANTS

The list below excludes the Amathus-type of head-pendant (Fig. 28).

Amathus

528. (Fig. 527) New York 74. 51. 5010; black; negroid head; hair indicated by dots; rounded large face; flat nose; L. 0.030 m. W. 0.024 m. (V. Karageorghis, *Blacks in Ancient Cypriot Art* (Houston, 1988), 17, no. 8, assigned to the ninth or eighth cenury, but on the basis of other archaeological contexts, this is too early; catalogued in Myres, *HCC* as no. 1550).

Fig. 527. Cat. 528. (1:1)

529. (Fig. 528) Limassol; Amathus T. 542 (CCI context); negroid head; ivory; L. 0.023 m. (V. Karageorghis, 'Chronique des fouilles et découvertes archéologique à Chypre' *BCH* 113 (1989), 798, 804; fig. 43; id., *Annual Report of the Department of Antiquities for the Year 1988* (Nicosia, 1989), 61–2, no. 89).

Ayia Irini

530. Nicosia A. I. 1873 (sanctuary; period 4); black; bearded male head, wearing cap (?); stringhole through ears; L. 0.029 m. (*SCE* 2, 744–5, no. 1873; 749; pl. 242, no. 23).

The following is in a drawer at the Medelhavsmuseet, together with other seals from Ayia Irini, whence it may have come:

531. (Fig. 529a) Stockholm A. I. (? from the sanctuary); black; double head with tall headdress;

Fig. 528. Cat. 529. (2:1)

Fig. 529a. Cat. 531. (1:1)

Fig. 529b. Cat. 532. (1:1)

Fig. 530. Cat. 533. (2:1)

Fig. 531. Cat. 534. (2:1)

flat at the top; headdress splays outward toward the top; stringhole passing vertically through the head; max W. 0.012 m. H. 0.014 m.

Idalion

A number of similar pendants in the shape of human heads but of faience were said by Cesnola to have been found with the following:

532. (Fig. 529b) New York 74. 51. 1361; black; gold wire through stringhole (Cesnola and Myres suggest it was an earring); eyeballs with traces of red colouring; negroid features; L. 0.015 m. (G. H. Beardsley, *The Negro in Greek and Roman Civilization* (Baltimore, 1929), 19, no. 27; Myres, *HCC*, 380, no. 1361; Cesnola, *Atlas* 3, pl. 18. 3 with commentary).

Kourion

533. (Fig. 530) Kourion St. 871; black; negroid head; hair denoted by linear striations; stringhole across the ears; L. 0.025 m. W. 0.018 m. (V. Karageorghis, *Blacks in Ancient Cypriot Art* (Houston, 1988), 15, no. 6, assigned to the Late Bronze Age).

Salamis

534. (Fig. 531) Salamis Tomb 115. 3 (CCI context); grey; almost conoid in shape; possibly double-sided; stringhole through ears; L. 0.014 m. (Karageorghis, *Salamis* 2, 168–9; pl. 49).
For the head type, cf. larger stone masks in Ohnefalsch-Richter, *KBH*, 422; pl. 93, no. 4–6 (Larnaka) and no. 7 (Marion).

Provenance unknown

535. New York N. E. 74. 51. 4392; black; flat-topped head; clean shaven (?); smooth back; stringhole through top of head; truncated neck; H. 0.017 m. (Myres, *HCC*, 446, no. 4392, suggesting it was 'intended for the bearded head of the Egyptian god Bes').

APPENDIX 4
ADDITIONAL HEAD-SEALS

For other examples of head-seals, some of which may be Cypriot, see de Clercq, 34, no. 79; pl. 4.79; G. A. Eisen, *Ancient Oriental Cylinders and Other Seals* (Chicago, 1940), 57, no. 126; pl. 13; D. M. Robinson, 'The Robinson Collection of Greek Gems, Seals, Rings, and Earrings' in *Hesperia Supplement* 8 (1949), 310–1, no. 7; pl. 40; Kenna, *BM Cypriote Seals*, 34, no. 116; pl. 31 (Tyre, prob. incorrectly dated to the Late Bronze Age); L. Jakob-Rost, *Die Stempelsiegel im Vorderasiatischen Museum* (Berlin, 1975), 28, no. 94–5 (perhaps from Sendschirli); J. Boardman, *Intaglios and Rings* (London, 1975), 111–2, no. 210; P. Zazoff, *Die antiken Gemmen* (Munich, 1983), 69, no. 27; 75; Abb. 26k; Taf. 13.1; Vollenweider, *Geneva* 3, 57, no. 89; 113–7, no. 156, 157, 159 (all once Kenna) (Figs. 532–534); Buchanan and Moorey, *Ashmolean* 3, 24, no. 149 (purchased in Beirut) and 150 (purchased in Aleppo); C. Doumet, *Sceaux et cylindres orientaux: la collection Chiha* (Fribourg and Göttingen, 1992), 160, no. 317 and 318 (a double-head).

Fig. 532. (2:1) Head-seal of black serpentine, provenance uncertain, with a running goat, its head turned back, as a device (Geneva 20448). L. 0.018 m. W. 0.013 m. H. 0.009 m.

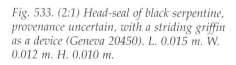

Fig. 533. (2:1) Head-seal of black serpentine, provenance uncertain, with a striding griffin as a device (Geneva 20450). L. 0.015 m. W. 0.012 m. H. 0.010 m.

Fig. 534. (2:1) Head-seal of black serpentine, provenance uncertain, with a lion as a device (Geneva 20452). L. 0.017 m. W. 0.013 m.

APPENDIX 5
SOME SEALS IMITATIVE
OF MESOPOTAMIAN DEVICES

A small number of seals in the Cesnola Collection may be imitative of styles associated with Mesopotamia and influential in Syria and Palestine during the eighth and seventh centuries. All, with the exception of 543 from the Pierides Museum in Larnaka, belong to the Cesnola Collection. Since none of these seals has a precise provenance within the island and because Cesnola and the Pierides family were friends, it is likely that these seals were brought to Cyprus as a result of the antiquities trade. They need not be Cypriot in origin. On stamp-seals in the Neo-Assyrian Empire, see, in general, S. Herbordt, *Neuassyrische Glyptik des 8.-7. Jh. v. Chr.* (Helsinki, 1992).

536. (Fig. 535) New York 74. 51. 4362; conoid; brown and white banded agate; circular base, very flat; D. 0.016 m. H. 0.025 m.
Bearded figure wearing cut-away skirt with fringed border grasps horns of rampant deer; winged disc above (Myres, *HCC*, 443, no. 4362).
Cf. Herbordt, above, 245, Taf. 6. 4 (Ninive 166).

537.(Fig. 536) New York N. E. 74. 51. 4368; circular stamp with handle; light brown; slightly convex base; D. 0.018 m. H. 0.013 m.
Tasselled crescent standard; stars; other objects in field (Myres, *HCC*, 443, no. 4368).
The device may be a copy of a Neo-Babylonian design. Cf. also Herbordt, above, 196–7, Taf. 10. 14 (Nimrud 100).

Fig. 535. Cat. 536.
(2:1) Impression.

Fig. 536. Cat. 537. (2:1) Impression.

Fig. 537. Cat. 538.
(2:1) Impression.

Fig. 538. Cat. 540. (2:1) Impression.

Fig. 539. Cat. 541. (2:1) Impression.   *Fig. 540. Cat. 542. (2:1) Impression.*

538. (Fig. 537) New York N. E. 74. 51. 4379; roughly rectangular seal with slightly convex top; black; L. 0.017 m. W. 0.015 m. H. 0.005 m.
Sphinx, with vertically striated wings and body; tree in front (Myres, *HCC*, 444, no. 4379).

539. New York N. E. 74. 51. 4365; rectangular plaque with handle; black; L. 0.023 m. W. 0.021 m. H. 0.024 m.
Scorpion (? fish-man) and seated figure with one arm raised; bodies of scorpion and figure with hatching; two crescents above (Myres, *HCC*, 443, no. 4365).

540. (Fig. 538) New York N. E. 74. 51. 4384; tabloid; brown; L. 0.019 m. W. 0.013 m. H. 0.009 m.
All bodies are cross-hatched: (a) bearded sphinx approaching plant; (b) goat; crescent above; object behind; (c) fish; (d) bird (? cock) (Myres, *HCC*, 444, no. 4384).
Myres doubted the authenticity of 540.

Both 541 and 542 may be Syrian in origin.

541. (Fig. 539) New York N. E. 74. 52. 4388; disc; black; slightly convex on one side; D. 0.020 m. H. 0.006 m.
(a) Striding horse; vertically striated body; plant in front; star above; objects in field; (b) rosette with dotted circle as centre (Myres, *HCC*, 446, no. 4388).
Boardman, *IGems*, 127–33 suggests that the disc shape and rosette pattern influenced Archaic lentoids and discs known from Crete, Argos, Corinth, and Amorgos. For the rosette, cf. Herbordt, above, 181, Taf. 11. 5 (Nimrud 40).

542. (Fig. 540) New York N. E. 74. 51. 4390; scaraboid; black; two stringholes, one transverse, the other through the top; L. 0.020 m. W. 0.017 m. H. 0.011 m.

Fig. 541. Cat. 543. (2:1) Impression, drawing.

Device worn: winged horse; one wing raised, the other lowered; star, other objects in field (Myres, *HCC*, 446, no. 4).

543. (Fig. 541) Larnaka (Pierides 1970); conoid; red stone; L. 0.015 m. H. 0.019 m.
Star; irregularly placed dots; crescent (? moon); ground line with oblique line beneath (? winged disc). (A. T. Reyes, 'Stamp-seals in the Pierides Collection, Larnaca' *RDAC* (1991), 121, no. 9).
Cf. Herbordt, above, 258, Taf. 10. 20 (Sonstige 27).

DIAGRAMS OF SHAPES

DIAGRAM A: THE SCARAB AND SCARABOID

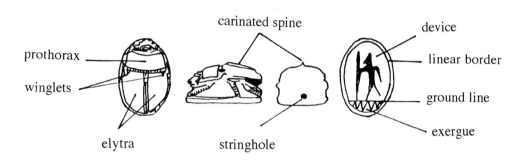

prothorax

winglets

carinated spine

elytra

stringhole

device

linear border

ground line

exergue

TOP   SIDE   BACK   BOTTOM

Scarab

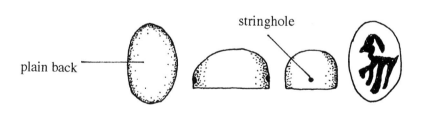

plain back

stringhole

TOP   SIDE   BACK   BOTTOM

Scaraboid

DIAGRAM B: OTHER COMMON SHAPES

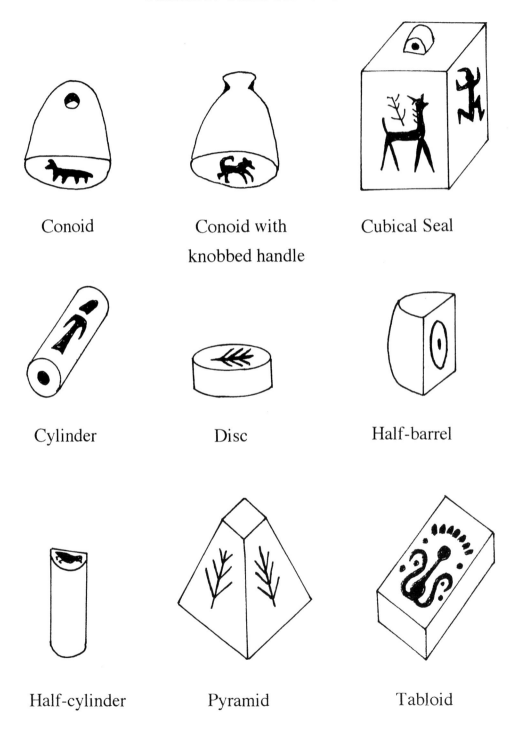

Conoid

Conoid with
knobbed handle

Cubical Seal

Cylinder

Disc

Half-barrel

Half-cylinder

Pyramid

Tabloid

GLOSSARY

This glossary lists specialist or technical words that appear with a certain frequency within the text. It is intended simply as a guide that provides basic information allowing ready elucidation of the text. It does not address controversies or complexities involving particular terms. Capitals denote cross-references within the glossary.

Agate	A banded stone, in white and brown, sometimes with a little blue.
Amethyst	A transparent QUARTZ, coloured deep purple or violet.
Azurite	A copper carbonate, distinguished by a rich blue colour.
Bes	An Egyptian protective deity associated with music, the household, and the birth of children, usually portrayed as a dwarf, often with a feathered headdress.
Bezel	A grooved ring, or that part of a ring holding a GEM.
Bloodstone	Also known as heliotrope. A dark green CHALCEDONY with small flecks of red.
Boustrophedon	Referring to inscriptions in which a line is read in one direction (e.g., left to right), with the following line read in the opposite direction.
Border	The delineation of the area at the edge of a DEVICE. The area is often shown with hatching.
Carination	A distinct ridge, used to describe the spine of a SCARAB.
Chalcedony	A type of QUARTZ, translucent and usually white or bluish grey.
Conoid	A SEAL generally resembling a cone, but tapering to a small curve, rather than to a sharp point.
Cornelian	A translucent CHALCEDONY of reddish or reddish-brown colour.
Cubical-seal	A SEAL in the shape of a box, often, but not necessarily, with all six sides carved with DEVICES. There may or may not be a handle.
Cylinder-seal	As the name indicates, a small, cylindrically-shaped stone, around which a device has been carved in intaglio so that, when the cylinder is rolled on clay or some other material, a continuous impression of the device is shown in reverse.

Cypriot syllabary	The writing system of Cyprus, in which signs, each one denoting a syllable, are used to represent the Greek language.
Device	The motif engraved on a SEAL.
Elytron	Outer hard wing-case of a beetle (*pl*. elytra).
Exergue	The part of a DEVICE below the ground line. The area is often shown with cross-hatching or a zig-zag pattern.
Faience	A composite material consisting of a body of sintered-quartz and a GLAZE.
Finger-ring	Circlet usually of metal and often set with a GEM and worn around the finger as an ornament, token, or signet, or else hung with thread, string, or twine around some other part of the body.
Frit	A sintered polycrystalline material with no GLAZE.
Gem	A stone, often precious or semi-precious, cut and polished, with an engraved design.
Gemstone	The raw material used in the manufacture of a GEM.
Glass	A material made by melting together silica and impure soda.
Glaze	A discrete layer of GLASS on the surface of crystalline or baked clay bodies.
Glyptic	Pertaining to the art of cutting engraved designs on gems or rings.
Haematite	A lustrous iron oxide, grey-black, often with a dark-red tinge.
Head-pendant	A hanging ornament, often attached to a necklace or bracelet, in the shape of a head.
Head-seal	SEAL based on the SCARAB-shape, but with a head carved on the back, rather than a beetle.
Hieroglyph	Figure of an object representing a word, syllable, or sound, as used in ancient Egyptian and other writing.
Hoop	The circular part, usually of metal, of a FINGER-RING, through which the finger passes.
Horus	Egyptian falcon-god of the sky.
Intaglio	Ornamented with a sunken or incised design, as opposed to a design in relief.
Isis	Egyptian goddess and the mother of HORUS. She is the wife of the god Osiris.
Jasper	An opaque QUARTZ, coloured, according to its impurities, red, yellow, green, or brown.
Lapis lazuli	An opaque, semiprecious stone consisting mostly of a blue mineral, a yellow mineral, a white mineral, together with small amounts of other minerals. It is the blue colour that is most often associated with lapis lazuli.
Limestone	A calcium carbonate, usually containing small proportions of other ingredients, such as silica and clay.
Maat	Egyptian goddess of order, truth, and judgement.

Marble	LIMESTONE that has metamorphosed into a harder stone, after having been subjected to high temperature and pressure.
Mount	The metal-fitting onto which a GEM is set to make a FINGER-RING.
Neb-sign	An Egyptian HIEROGLYPH intended to represent a basket. It resembles a half-oval. The EXERGUE that often appears at the bottom of a DEVICE on a SCARAB is thought to be derivative of this HIEROGLYPH. (See Egyptian sign V30 in the sign-lists of A. Gardiner, *Egyptian Grammar*, 3d ed. revised (Oxford, 1957).)
Necropolis	A cemetery.
Nefer-sign	Egyptian word meaning 'good', 'beautiful', 'complete', or perfect'; a sign of happiness and good fortune.
Onyx	A type of CHALCEDONY in which milk-white bands alternate with black ones.
Opal	Technically known as hydrous silica, the combination of water and a chalcedony-like substance. It occurs in a variety of colours.
Ovoid	GEM roughly in the shape of an egg cut in half horizontally.
Picrolite	A relatively soft stone, light green to olive green in colour belonging to the SERPENTINE group of minerals.
Plasma	A dark-green CHALCEDONY.
Prothorax	The section to the front of the body of a SCARAB.
Ptah	Egyptian patron deity of craftsmen.
Quartz	An umbrella-term for a variety of silicate minerals, occurring in a variety of colours and ranging from the opaque to the transparent.
Rock Crystal	Often simply referred to as 'crystal', it is a colourless variety of QUARTZ.
Sard	A brownish variety of CHALCEDONY.
Sardonyx	A variety of ONYX with white layers alternating with one or more strata of SARD.
Scarab	GEM cut in the form of a beetle and engraved with symbols on the flat side.
Scaraboid	GEM resembling a scarab in shape, but without the anatomical details rendered
Seal	Hard object with a carved design intended to be seen in impression. CYLINDER-SEALS are rolled onto clay or some other material to make impressions. STAMP-SEALS are simply pressed onto the material.
Sealing	Clay or other material bearing the impressed device of a SEAL.
Serpentine	A soft stone of dark green and other colours, sometimes mottled or spotted like a serpent's skin, soapy in texture and taking a high polish. In archaeological literature, the term is often used interchangeably with 'STEATITE'.

Stamp-seal	SEAL with a DEVICE carved onto its bottom face and used to leave a mark simply by impressing the engraved motif onto clay or some other material.
Steatite	A form of talc, usually white or grey in colour. Often confused with 'SERPENTINE' in the literature.
Stringhole	A piercing through which material such as string, thread or twine may have been passed to provide a means of suspension.
Tabloid	A SEAL, rectangular in section, that is small, flat, and comparatively thin; a variant of the CUBICAL SEAL.
Tête-bêche	Positioned so that one figure is reversed in relation to the other.
Terracotta	Hard, clay-baked pottery.
Thot	Egyptian deity, scribe of the gods and a patron of learning.
Uzat-eye	An Egyptian symbol for Horus; the amulet provided strength for the bearer and the protective power of the sun and the moon.
Winglet	Small wings, often represented by triangles or small notches, on the ELTYRA of a SCARAB.

BIBLIOGRAPHY

See also items cited in the list of abbreviations. The annual 'Chronique des fouilles et découvertes archéologique à Chypre' in *BCH* is an essential reference. For names inscribed on seals, see M. Egetmeyer, *Wörterbuch zu den Inschriften im Kyprischen Syllabar* (Berlin, 1992) and A. Hintze, *A Lexicon to the Cyprian Syllabic Inscriptions* (Hamburg, 1993).

Amadasi, M. G., *L'Iconografia del Carro da Guerra in Siria e Palestina* (Rome, 1965).

Amandry, P., 'Petits Objets de Delphes' *BCH* 68–9 (1944–5), 36–74.

Andrae, W., *Die Jüngeren Ischtar-Tempel in Assur* (Leipzig, 1935).

Åström, P., *Hala Sultan Tekke*, vol. 1 (Göteborg, 1976).

Åström, P., 'A Handle Stamped with the Cartouche of Seti I from Hala Sultan Tekke in Cyprus' *OpAth* 5 (1964), 115–22.

Åström, P. *et al.*, *Hala Sultan Tekke*, vol. 8 (Göteborg, 1983).

Åström, P. and Masson, E., 'Un Cachet de Hala Sultan Tekke' *RDAC* (1981), 99–100.

Arnold, R., 'The Horse-Demon in Early Greek Art and his Eastern Neighbors', Ph. D. thesis (Columbia University, New York, 1972).

Aruz, J., 'Imagery and Interconnections' *Egypt and the Levant* 5 (1995), 33–48.

Arwe, M., 'A Cypriote Cubical Stamp-Seal' in J. C. Biers and D. Soren, eds., *Studies in Cypriote Archaeology* (Los Angeles, 1981), 141–4.

Aupert, P., *Guide d'Amathonte* (Paris, 1996).

Aupert, P. and Hermary, A., 'Rapport sur les activités de la mission de l'école française et du ministère des relations extérieures à Amathonte en 1983' *BCH* 108 (1984), 967–71.

Aupert, P. *et al.*, 'Rapport sur les travaux de la mission de l'école française et du ministère des relations extérieures à Amathonte en 1979' *BCH* 104 (1980), 805–22.

Aupert, P. *et al.*,'Rapport sur les travaux de la mission de l'école française et du ministère des relations extérieures à Amathonte en 1982' *BCH* 107 (1983), 955–69.

Ball, S. H., *A Roman Book on Precious Stones* (Los Angeles, 1950).

Barnett, R. D., *Catalogue of the Nimrud Ivories*, 2d ed. (London, 1975).

Barnett, R. D. and Mendleson, C., *Tharros* (London, 1987).

Baur, P. V. C., *Centaurs in Ancient Art, The Archaic Period* (Berlin, 1912).

Baurain, C., Bonnet, C., and Krings, V., eds., *Phoinikeia Grammata: Lire et écrire en Méditerranée* (Namur, 1991).

Beardsley, G. H., *The Negro in Greek and Roman Civilization* (Baltimore, 1929).

Beazley, J. D., *The Lewes House Collection of Ancient Gems* (Oxford, 1920).

Beck, P., 'A Cypriote Cylinder Seal from Lachish' in D. Ussishkin, *Tel Aviv* 10/2 (1983), 178–81.

Beer, C., 'Economics of Cult in the Ancient Greek World' *Boreas* 21 (1992), 73–84.

Beer, C., *Temple Boys: A Study of Cypriote Votive Sculpture. Part 1. Catalogue* (Jonsered, 1994).

Beer, C., *Temple Boys: A Study of Cypriote Votive Sculpture. Part 2. Functional Analysis* (Stockholm, 1993).

Benson, J. L., 'Aegean and Near Eastern Seal Impressions from Cyprus' in S. S. Weinberg, ed., *The Aegean and the Near East: Studies Presented to Hetty Goldman* (Locust Valley, New York, 1956), 59–77.

Benson, J. L., *Bamboula at Kourion* (Philadelphia, 1972).

Benson, J. L., *The Necropolis of Kaloriziki* (Göteborg, 1973).

Betts, J. H., *Die Schweizer Sammlungen. CMS.*, vol. 10 (Berlin, 1980).

Bibliothèque Nationale, *Art antique de Chypre* (Paris, 1994).

Bielinski, P., 'A Prism-Shaped Stamp-Seal in Warsaw and Related Stamps' *Berytus* 23 (1974), 53–69.

Biers, J. C. and Soren, D., eds., *Studies in Cypriote Archaeology* (Los Angeles, 1981).

Bikai, P. M., *The Phoenician Pottery of Cyprus* (Nicosia, 1987).

Bikai, P. M., 'The Phoenicians and Cyprus' in Karageorghis, V., ed., *Cyprus in the Eleventh Century B. C.* (Nicosia, 1994), 31–7.

Bikai, P. M., *The Pottery of Tyre* (Warminster, 1978).

Biran A., 'Tell Dan, 1977' *IEJ* 27 (1977), 242–6.

Bisi, A., *Il Grifone* (Rome, 1965).

Bisi,, A. M. 'L'Iconografia del grifone a Cipro' *Oriens Antiquus* 1 (1962), 219–32.

Bloedow, E. F., 'Minoan Talismanic Goats' *Journal of Prehistoric Religion* 6 (1992), 15–23.

Boardman, J., 'Archaic Finger Rings' *Antike Kunst* 10 (1967), 3–31.

Boardman, J., 'Colour Questions' *Jewellery Studies* 5 (1991), 29–31.

Boardman, J., 'The Cypriot Contribution to Archaic Greek Glyptic' in Tatton-Brown, V., ed., *Cyprus and the East Mediterranean in the Iron Age* (London, 1989), 44–9.

Boardman, J., 'Cypriot Finger Rings' *BSA* 65 (1970), 5–15.

Boardman, J., 'The Danicourt Gems in Péronne' *RA* (1971), 195–214.

Boardman, J., *Escarabeos de Piedra, Procedentes de Ibiza* (Madrid, 1984).

Boardman, J., 'Greek Gem Engravers, Their Subjects and Style' in Porada, E., ed., *Ancient Art in Seals* (Princeton, 1980), 101–14.

Boardman, J., 'Greek Gem Engraving: Archaic to Classical' in Boulter, C. G., ed., *Greek Art, Archaic into Classical* (Leiden, 1985), 83–95.

Boardman, J., *Intaglios and Rings* (London, 1975).

Boardman, J., 'Island Gems Aftermath' *JHS* 38 (1968), 1–12.

Boardman, J., 'Near Eastern and Archaic Greek Gems in Budapest' *Bull. du Musée Hongrois des Beaux-Arts* 32–3 (1969), 7–17.

Boardman, J., 'Orientalia and Orientals in Ischia' *Annali di Archeologia e Storia Antica*, new series 1 (1994), 95–100.

Boardman, J., 'Pyramidal Stamp-Seals in the Persian Empire' *Iran* 8 (1970), 19–45.

Boardman, J., 'Scarabs and Seals: Greek, Punic, and Related Types' in Barnett, R. D. and Mendleson, C., eds., *Tharros* (London, 1987), 98–105.

Boardman, J., 'Seals and Signs. Anatolian Stamp-Seals of the Persian Period Revisited' *Iran* 36 (1998), 1–13.

Boardman, J., 'Some Syrian Glyptic' *OJA* 15 (1996), 327–40.

Boardman, J. and Moorey, R., 'The Yunus Cemetery Group: Haematite Scarabs' in Kelly-Buccellati, M., ed., *Insight through Images* (Malibu, 1986), 35–48.

Boardman, J. and Scarisbrick, D., *The Ralph Harari Collection of Finger Rings* (London, 1977).

Boehmer, R. M. and Güterbock, H. G., *Glyptik aus dem Stadtgebiet von Bogazköy* (Berlin, 1987).

Bolger, D. L., 'Engendering Cypriot Archaeology: Female Roles and Statuses Before the Bronze Age' *OpAth* 20 (1994), 9–17.

Bordreuil, P and Gubel, E., 'Bulletin d'antiquités archéologiques du Levant inédites ou méconnues IV' *Syria* 64 (1987), 309–21.

E. Borowski, 'Die Sammlung H. A. Layard', *Orientalia* 21 (1952), 168–83.

Boulter, C. G., ed., *Greek Art, Archaic into Classical* (Leiden, 1985).

Boussac, M.-F. and Invernizzi, A., *Archives et sceaux du monde hellénistique = BCH,* suppl. vol. 29 (Paris, 1996), 65–84.

Bowra, C. M., 'Homeric Words in Cyprus' *JHS* 54 (1934), 54–74.

Briend, J. and Humbert, J.-B., *Tell Keisan* (Fribourg, 1980).

Brodie, N. J., 'Chemical Characterisation of Early and Middle Iron Age Cypriot Ceramics: A Review' *RDAC* (1998), 17–28.

Brosius, M. and Kuhrt, A., *Studies in Persian History: Essays in Memory of David M. Lewis* (Leiden, 1998), 257–89.

Brown, A. and Catling, H., 'Additions in the Cypriot Collection in the Ashmolean Museum, Oxford, 1963–77' *OpAth* 13 (1980), 91–137.

Bremmer, J., ed., *Interpretations of Greek Mythology* (London and Sydney, 1987).

Briend, J. and Humbert, J.-B., *Tell Keisan* (Fribourg, 1980).

Brown, D. F., 'A Graeco-Phoenician Scarab from Byblos', *AJA* 40 (1936), 345–7.

Buchanan, B., *Catalogue of Ancient Near Eastern Seals in the Ashmolean Museum,* vol. 1 (Oxford, 1966).

Buchanan. B., *Catalogue of Ancient Near Eastern Seals in the Ashmolean Museum,* vol. 2 (Oxford, 1984).

Buitron, D., 'The Archaic Precinct at Kourion: 1981 Excavations' *RDAC* (1982), 144–7.

Burkert, W., 'Oriental and Greek Mythology: The Meeting of Parallels' in Bremmer, J., ed., *Interpretations of Greek Mythology* (London and Sydney, 1987), 10–40.

Buschor, E., 'Kentauren' *AJA* 38 (1934), 128–32

Caley, E. R. and Richards, J. F. C., eds., *Theophrastos on Stones* (Columbus, Ohio, 1956).

Carpenter, T. H., *Dionysian Imagery in Archaic Greek Art* (Oxford, 1986).

Carter, J. B., 'Egyptian Bronze Jugs from Crete and Lefkandi' *JHS* 118 (1998), 172–6.

Catling, H. W., 'A Cypriot Bronze Statuette in the Bomford Collection' in C. F. A. Schaeffer, *Alasia* 1 (Paris, 1971), 15–32.

Catling, H. W., *Cypriot Bronzework in the Mycenaean World* (Oxford, 1964).

Catling, H. W., 'The Seal of Pasitimos' *Kadmos* 11 (1972), 55–78.

Caubet, A. and Courtois, J.-C., 'Un Modèle de foie d'Enkomi' *RDAC* (1986), 72–9.

di Cesnola, A. P., *Salaminia,* 2d ed. (London, 1884).

di Cesnola, L. P., *Cyprus* (London, 1877).

Charisterion eis A. K. Orlandon, (Athens, 1966).

Charles, R.-P., 'Appendix 2: Les Scarabées égyptiens d'Enkomi' in Dikaios, P., *Enkomi,* vol. 3 (Mainz, 1971), 819–23.

Chavane, M.-J., *Salamine de Chypre,* vol. 6 (Paris, 1975).

Ciasca, A., 'Masks and Protomes' in Moscati, S., ed., *The Phoenicians* (Milan, 1988), 354–69.

Clerc, G., 'Aegyptiaca de Palaepaphos-Skales' in V. Karageorghis, *Palaepaphos-Skales* (Konstanz, 1983), 375–95.

Collon, D., *First Impressions* (London, 1987).

Collon, D., 'The Green Jasper Cylinder Seal Workshop' in Kelly-Buccellati, M., ed., *Insight through Images* (Malibu, 1986), 57–70.

Collon, D., 'A Hoard of Sealings from Ur' in Boussac, M.-F. and Invernizzi, A., *Archives et sceaux du monde hellénistique = BCH,* suppl. vol. 29 (Paris, 1996), 65–84.

Collon, D., *Near Eastern Seals* (London, 1990).

Colonna-Ceccaldi, G., 'Intaille phénicienne – Collection Péretié' *RA* 25 (1873), 30.

Colonna-Ceccaldi, G., *Monuments antiques de Chypre, de Syrie et d'Égypte* (Paris, 1882).

Connelly, J. B., *Votive Sculpture of Hellenistic Cyprus* (Nicosia,1988).

Conteneau, G., *La Glyptique Syro-Hittite* (Paris, 1922).

Cornelius, I., 'The Lion in the Art of the Ancient Near East: A Study of Selected Motifs' *Journal of Northwest Semitic Languages* 15 (1989), 53–85.

Courtois, J.-C., *Alasia* 3 (Paris, 1984).

Courtois, J.-C., Lagarce, E., and Lagarce, J., *Enkomi et le Bronze Recent a Chypre* (Nicosia, 1986).

Courtois, J.-C. and Webb, J. M., *Les Cylindres-Sceaux d'Enkomi* (Nicosia, 1987).

Culican, W., *The First Merchant Venturers* (London, 1966).

Culican, W., 'Jewellery from Sarafand and Sidon' *OpAth* 12 (1978), 133–9.

Culican, W., 'Phoenician Jewellery in New York and Copenhagen' *Berytus* 22 (1973), 31–47;

Culican, W., 'Seals in Bronze Mounts' *RSF* 5 (1977), 1–4.

Dalley, S., 'Near Eastern Patron Deities of Mining and Smelting in the Late Bronze and Early Iron Ages' *RDAC* (1987), 61–6.

Dalley, S., ed., *The Legacy of Mesopotamia* (Oxford, 1998).

Dalley, S. and J. N. Postgate, J. N., *The Tablets from Fort Shalmaneser* (Oxford, 1984).

Dalley, S. and Reyes, A. T., 'Mesopotamian Contact and Influence in the Greek World 1: To the Persian Conquest' in Dalley, S., ed., *The Legacy of Mesopotamia* (Oxford, 1998).

Danthine, H., *Le Palmier-Dattier et les arbres sacrés dans l'iconographie de l'Asie Occidentale ancienne* (Paris, 1937).

Davies, G. I., *Megiddo* (Cambridge, 1986).

Demisch, H., *Die Sphinx* (Stuttgart, 1977).

Desborough, V., Nicholls, R. V., and Popham, M., 'A Euboean Centaur' *BSA* 65 (1970), 21–30.

Destrooper, A. and Symeonides, A., 'Classical Coins in the Symeonides Collection: The Coin Circulation in Marion During the Vth and IVth Centuries' *RDAC* (1998), 111–23.

Diakonoff, I. M., 'The Naval Power and Trade of Tyre' *IEJ* 42 (1992), 168–93.

Dikaios, P., *Enkomi* (Mainz, 1971).

Dikaios, P., *Khirokitia* (London, 1953).

Dikaios, P., 'Principal Acquisitions of the Cyprus Museum, 1937–1939' *RDAC* 1937–9 (1951), 199–202.

Dothan, T., *The Philistines and their Material Culture* (Jerusalem, 1982).

Dothan, T. and A. Ben-Tor, A., *Excavations at Athienou, Cyprus. Qedem* 16 (Jerusalem, 1983).

Doumet, C., *Sceaux et chlindres orientaux: la collection Chiha* (Fribourg and Göttingen, 1992).

Dunand, M., *Fouilles de Byblos*, vol. 1 (Paris, 1939).

Dunand, M., *Fouilles de Byblos*, vol. 2 (Paris, 1954).

DuPlat Taylor, J., 'A Late Bronze Age Settlement at Apliki, Cyprus' *AJ* 32 (1952), 133–67.

DuPlat Taylor, J., *Myrtou-Pigadhes* (Oxford, 1957).

Eichholz, D. E., ed., *Theophrastus, De Lapidibus* (Oxford, 1965).

Eisen, G. A., *Ancient Oriental Cylinders and Other Seals* (Chicago, 1940).

Elayi, J. and Lemiare, A., 'Graffiti monétaires ouest-sémitiques' *Studia Phoenicia* 9 = Hackens, T. and Moncharte, G., *Numismatique et histoire économique phéniciennes et puniques* (Louvain, 1992), 59–76.

Farkas, A. E. *et al.*, eds., *Monsters and Demons in the Ancient and Medieval Worlds* (Mainz, 1987).

Ferioli, P. and Fiandra, E., 'The Use of Clay Sealings in Administrative Functions from the Fifth to First Millennium B. C. in the Orient, Nubia, Egypt, and the Aegean: Similarities and Differences' in Palaima, T. G., ed., *Aegaeum 5: Aegean Seals, Sealings and Administration: Proceedings of the NEH-Dickson Conference of the Program in Aegean Scripts and Prehistory of the Department of Classics, University of Texas at Austin, January 11-13, 1989* (Liège, 1990), 221–9.

Fittschen, K., *Untersuchungen zur Beginn der Sagendarstellungen bei den Griechen* (Berlin, 1969).

Flourentzos, P., *Excavations in the Kouris Valley* 1: *The Tombs* (Nicosia, 1991).

Forbes, B. A., 'Catalogue of Engraved Gems in the Art Museum, Princeton University', Ph.D. thesis (Berkeley, 1978).

de Foville, J., 'Études de numismatique et de glyptique: Pierres gravées inédites du Cabinet de France' *Rev. Num.* 9 (1905), 277–308.

Frankel, D. and Webb, J. M., *Marki Alonia: An Early and Middle Bronze Age Town in Cyprus: Excavations 1990-1994* (Jonsered, 1996).

Frankfort, H., *Cylinder Seals* (London, 1939).

Furtwängler, A., *Die antiken Gemmen* (Leipzig and Berlin, 1900).

Furumark, A., 'A Scarab from Cyprus', *OpAth* 1 (1953), 47–65.

Gadd, C. J., 'An Old Babylonian Frog-Amulet' *British Museum Quarterly* 10 (1935–36), 7–9.

Gal, Z., 'A Phoenician Bronze Seal from Hurbat Rosh Zayit' *JNES* 53 (1994), 27–31.

Garrison, M. B., 'A Persepolis Fortification Seal on the Tablet MDP 11 308 (Louvre Sb 13078)' *JNES* 55 (1996), 15–35.

Given, M. J. M., 'Symbols, Power, and the Construction of Identity in the City-Kingdoms of Ancient Cyprus c. 750–312 BC' Ph.D. thesis (Cambridge, 1991).

Giveon, R., *Egyptian Scarabs from Western Asia Minor from the Collection of the British Museum* (Göttingen, 1985).

Gjerstad, E., *Greek Geometric and Archaic Pottery Found in Cyprus* (Stockholm, 1977).

Gorelick, L. and Gwinnett, A. J., 'Innovative Methods in the Manufacture of Sassanian Seals' *Iran* 34 (1996), 79–84.

Gorelick, L. and Gwinnett, A. J., 'Minoan versus Mesopotamian Seals: Comparative Methods of Manufacture' *Iraq* 54 (1992), 57–64.

Goring, E., *A Mischievous Pastime* (Edinburgh, 1988).

Gorton, A. F., *Egyptian and Egyptianizing Scarabs* (Oxford, 1996).

Goyon, J.-C., 'Un Scarabée de Salamine' in *Salamine de Chypre, histoire et archeologie* (Paris, 1980), 137–9.

Gubel, E., 'Cinq Bulles inédites des archives Tyriennes de l'époque achéménide' *Semitica* 47 (1997), 53–64.

Gubel, E., 'La Glyptique et la genèse de l'iconographie monétaire phénicienne I' in *Studia Phoenicia* 9 = Hackens, T. and Moncharte, G., eds., *Numismatique et histoire économique phéniciennes et puniques* (Louvain, 1992), 1–11.

Gubel, E., 'Notes on a Phoenician Seal in the Royal Museum for Art and History, Brussels (CGPH.1)' *OLP* 16 (1985), 91–110.

Gubel, E., *Les Phéniciens et le monde méditerranean* (Brussels, 1986).

Gubel, E., 'Phoenician Seals in the Allard Pierson Museum, Amsterdam' *RSF* 16 (1988), 145–63.

Gubel, E. and Cauet, S., 'Un Nouveau Type de coupe phénicienne' *Syria* 64 (1987), 193–204.

Güterbock, H., 'The Hittite Conquest of Cyprus Reconsidered' *JNES* 26 (1967), 73–81.

Gutzwiller, K. J., 'Cleopatra's Ring' *GRBS* 36 (1995), 383–98.

Guzzo, P. G., 'La Gemme a Scarabeo nel Museo Nazionale di Napoli' *MEFRA* 3 (1971), 325–66.

Gwinnett, A. J. and Gorelick, L., 'Beads, Scarabs, and Amulets: Methods of Manufacture in Ancient Egypt' *Journal of the American Research Center in Egypt* 30 (1993), 125–32.

Hackens, T. and Moncharte, G., eds., *Numismatique et histoire économique phéniciennes et puniques* (Louvain, 1992) = *Studia Phoenicia* 9.

Harris, D., *The Treasures of the Parthenon and Erechtheion* (Oxford, 1995).

Henig, M., *Classical Gems* (Cambridge, 1994).

Herbordt, S., *Neuassyrische Glyptik des 8.-7. Jh. v. Chr.* (Helsinki, 1992).

Hermary, A., *Amathonte*, vol. 2 (Paris, 1981).

Hermary, A., 'Un nouveau Chapiteau hathorique trouvé à Amathonte' *BCH* 109 (1985), 657–99.

Hermary, A., 'Une Tête de Bes chypriote au Musée de Cannes' *Cahiers: Centre d'études chypriotes* 23, no. 1 (1995), 23–7.

Herrmann, G., 'Lapis Lazuli: The Early Phases of its Trade' *Iraq* 30 (1968), 21–57.

Herrmann, G. and Curtis, J. E., 'Reflections on the Four-Winged Genie: A Pottery Jar and an Ivory Panel from Nimrud' *Iranica Antiqua* 33 (1998), 107–34.

Hestrin, R. and Dayagi-Mendels, M., *Inscribed Seals* (Jerusalem, 1979).

Hill, G. F., *Catalogue of the Greek Coins of Cyprus* (London, 1904).

Hill, G. F., *Catalogue of the Greek Coins of Phoenicia* (London, 1910).

Höcker, C., *Antike Gemmen* (Kassel, 1987/8).

Hölbl, G., 'Die Aegyptiaca von Kition' *Orientalia* 51 (1982), 259–64.

Hölbl, G., *Ägyptisches Kulturgut im phönikischen und punischen Sardinien* 1 (Leiden, 1986).

Hölbl, G., *Beziehung der agyptischen Kultur zu Altitalien* 1(Leiden, 1979).

Hogarth, D. G., *Hittite Seals* (Oxford, 1920).

Holmes, Y. L., 'The Foreign Trade of Cyprus during the Late Bronze Age', in N. Robertson, ed., *The Archaeology of Cyprus: Recent Developments* (New Jersey, 1975), 90–110.

Hornung, E. and Staehlin, E., *Skarabäen und anderen Siegelamulette* (Mainz, 1976).

Jacobsson, I., *Aegyptiaca from Late Bronze Age Cyprus* (Jonsered, 1994).

Jakob-Rost, L., *Die Stempelsiegel im Vorderasiatischen Museum* (Berlin, 1975).

Johnson, J., *Maroni de Chypre* (Göteborg, 1980).

Kahil, L., Augé, C., and Linant de Bellefonds, P., eds., *L'Iconographie classique et identités régionales* (Athens, 1986).

Karageorghis, J., *La grande Déesse de Chypre et son culte* (Lyon, 1977).

Karageorghis, J. and Masson, O., ed., *The History of the Greek Language in Cyprus* (Nicosia, 1988).

Karageorghis, V., *Blacks in Ancient Cypriot Art* (Houston, 1988).

Karageorghis, V., *The Coroplastic Art of Ancient Cyprus IV. The Cypro-Archaic Period: Small Male Figurines* (Nicosia, 1995).

Karageorghis, V., *The Coroplastic Art of Ancient Cyprus VI. The Cypro-Archaic Period: Monsters, Animals, and Miscellanea* (Nicosia, 1996).

Karageorghis, V., 'A Cypro-Archaic I Tomb at Palaepaphos-Skales' *RDAC* (1987), 85–96.

Karageorghis, V., *Excavations at Kition*, vol. 1 (London, 1974).

Karageorghis, V., 'Fouilles de Kition 1959' *BCH* 84 (1960), 504–88.

Karageorghis, V., *Greek Gods and Heroes in Ancient Cyprus* (Athens, 1998).

Karageorghis, V., *Kition* (London, 1976).

Karageorghis, V., 'Monkeys and Bears in Cypriote Art' *OpAth* 20 (1994), 63–9.

Karageorghis, V., 'Notes on Some Centaurs from Cyprus' in *Charisterion eis A. K. Orlandon*, vol. 2 (Athens, 1966), 160–9.

Karageorghis, V., *Palaepaphos-Skales* (Konstanz, 1983).

Karageorghis, V., 'Some Aspects of the Maritime Trade of Cyprus During the Late Bronze Age' in Karageorghis, V., and Michaelides, D., eds., *The Development of the Cypriot Economy from the Prehistoric Period to the Present Day* (Nicosia, 1996), 61–70.

Karageorghis, V., ed., *The Civilizations of the Aegean and their Diffusion in Cyprus and the Eastern Mediterranean, 2000-600 BC* (Larnaca, 1991),

Karageorghis, V., *Excavations at Kition* 1 (London, 1974).

Karageorghis, V. and Demas, M., *Excavations at Maa-Palaeokastro* (Nicosia, 1988).

Karageorghis, V. and Demas, M., *Kition*, vol. 5.2 (Nicosia, 1985).

Karageorghis, V. and des Gagniers, J., *La Céramique chypriote de style figuré* (Rome, 1974).

Karageorghis, V., ed., *Cyprus in the Eleventh Century B. C.* (Nicosia, 1994).

Karageorghis, V. and Michaelides, D., eds., *The Development of the Cypriot Economy from the Prehistoric Period to the Present Day* (Nicosia, 1996).

Karageorghis, V. and Muhly. J. D., eds., *Cyprus at the Close of the Late Bronze Age* (Nicosia, 1984).

Karageorghis, V. et al., eds., *La Nécropole d'Amathonte, tombes 113-367* (Paris, 1987).

Karageorghis, V., Picard, O., and Tytgat, C., *La Nécropole d'Amathonte: Tombes 113-367 VI: Bijoux, armes, verre, astragales, et coquillages, squelettes* (Nicosia, 1992).

Kearsley, R., 'The Greek Geometric Ares from Al Mina Levels 10–8 and Associated Pottery' *Mediterranean Archaeology* 8 (1995), 7–81.

Keel, O., *Das Böcklein in der Milch Seiner Mutter und Verwandtes im Lichte eines altorientalischen Bildmotive* (Freiburg, 1980)

Keel, O., *Corpus der Stempelsiegel-Amulette aus Palästina/Israel* (Göttingen, 1995, 1997).

Keel, O., 'Die Jaspis-Skarabäen-Gruppe. Eine vorderasiatische Skarabaen Werkstatt des 17. Jahrhunderts v. Chr.' in Keel, O., Keel-Leu, H., and Schroer, S., eds., *Studien zu den Stempelsiegeln aus Palastina/ Israel*, vol. 2 (Freiburg and Gottingen, 1989), 209–42.

Keel, O., *Studien zu den Stempelsiegeln aus Palästina/Israel*, vol. 4 (Göttingen, 1997).

Keel, O., Keel-Leu, H., and Schroer, S., eds., *Studien zu den Stempelsiegeln aus Palästina/Israel*, vol. 2 (Freiburg and Gottingen, 1989).

Keel, O., Shuval, M., and Uehlinger, C., eds., *Studien zu den Stempelsiegeln aus Palästina/Israel*, vol. 3 (Freiburg and Gottingen, 1990).

Keel-Leu, H., 'Die Herkunft der Konoïde in Palästina/Israel' in Keel, O., Shuval, M., and Uehlinger, C., eds., *Studien zu den Stempelsiegeln aus Palästina/Israel*, vol. 3 (Freiburg and Gottingen, 1990), 378–9.

Keel-Leu, H., *Vorderasiatische Stempelsiegel* (Göttingen, 1991).

Kelly-Buccellati, M., ed., *Insight through Images* (Malibu, 1986).

Kenna, V. E. G., *The Cretan Talismanic Stone in the Late Minoan Age* (Lund, 1969).

Kenna, V. E. G., 'Cyprus and the Aegean World: The Evidence of Seals', in *The Mycenaeans in the Eastern Mediterranean* (Nicosia, 1973), 290–4.

Kenna, V. E. G., 'Appendix V: A Marble Seal from Kazaphani T. 2' in Nicolaou, I. and Nicolaou, K., *Kazaphani: A Middle/Late Cypriot Tomb at Kazaphani in Ayios Andronikos: T. 2A, B* (Nicosia, 1989).

Kenna, V. E. G., 'The Seal Use of Cyprus in the Bronze Age' *BCH* 91 (1967), 255–68.

Kenna, V. E. G., 'The Seal Use of Cyprus in the Bronze Age III', *BCH* 92 (1968), 142–56.

Kenna, V. E. G., 'Seals and Sealstones from the Tombs of Perati' in *Charisterion eis A. K. Orlandon*, vol. 2 (Athens, 1966), 320–6.

Kenna, V. E. G., 'Studies of Birds on Seals of the Aegean and Eastern Mediterranean in the Bronze Age' *OpAth* 8 (1964), 23–38.

Kepinski, C., *L'Arbre stylisé en Asie Occidentale au 2e millénnaire avant J.-C.* (Paris, 1982).

Klingbeil, M. G., 'Syro-Palestinian Stamp-Seals from the Persian Period: The Iconographic Evidence' *Journal of Northwest Semitic Languages* 18 (1992), 95–124.

Kozloff, A. P., ed., *Animals in Ancient Art* (Cleveland, 1981).

Kraay, C. M., *Archaic and Classical Greeek Coins* (London, 1976).

Kunz, G. F., *The Curious Lore of Precious Stones* (New York, 1913).

Kyrieleis, H., 'New Cypriot Finds from the Heraion of Samos' in V. Tatton-Brown, ed., *Cyprus and the East Mediterranean in the Iron Age* (London, 1989), 52–64

Kyrieleis, H., 'The Relations between Samos and the Eastern Mediterranean: Some Aspects' in V. Karageorghis, ed., *The Civilizations of the Aegean and their Diffusion in Cyprus and the Eastern Mediterranean, 2000-600 BC* (Larnaca, 1991), 129–32.

Lacroix, L., *Études d'archéologie numismatique* (Paris, 1974).

Laffineur, R., 'Bijoux et orfèvrerie' in Karageorghis, V., Picard, O., and Tytgat, C., *La Nécropole d'Amathonte: Tombes 113-367 VI: Bijoux, armes, verre, astragales, et coquillages, squelettes* (Nicosia, 1992), 1–32.

Lagarce, E., 'Remarques sur l'utilisation des scarabées, scaraboïdes, amulettes, et figurines de type égyptien à Chypre' in Clerc, *Kition* 2, 167–82.

Lambert, W. G., 'Gilgamesh in Literature and Art: The Second and First Millennia' in Farkas, A. E. *et al.*, eds., *Monsters and Demons in the Ancient and Medieval Worlds* (Mainz, 1987), 37–52.

Lamon, R. S. and Shipton, G. M., *Megiddo*, vol. 1 (Chicago, 1939).

Leclant, J., 'Appendix 3: Les Scarabées de la tombe 9' in Karageorghis. V., *Excavations at Kition*, vol. 1 (London, 1974), 148–50.

Lemaire, A., 'Milkiram, nouveau roi phénicien de Tyr?' *Syria* 53 (1976), 83–93.

Lemaire, A., 'Nouveau Sceau nord-ouest sémitique avec un lion rugissant' *Semitica* 29 (1979), 67–9.

Lemaire, A., 'Sept Nouveaux Sceaux nord-ouest sémitiques inscrits' *Semitica* 41–2 (1991–2), 63–80.

Lemaire, A. and Sass, B., 'Sigillographie ouest-sémitique: Nouvelles Lectures' *Semitica* 45 (1996), 27–35.

Lewe. B., *Studien zur archaischen kyprischen Plastik* (Frankfurt, 1975).

Littauer, M. and J. Crouwel, J., *Wheeled Vehicles and Ridden Animals in the Ancient Near East* (Leiden, 1979).

Loud, G., *Megiddo*, vol. 2 (Chicago, 1948).

Lubsen-Admiraal, S. M. and Crouwel, J., *Cyprus and Aphrodite* ('s-Gravenhage, 1989).

Lurker, M., *The Gods and Symbols of Ancient Egypt* (London, 1974).

Maaskant-Kleibrink, M., *Catalogue of the Engraved Gems in the Royal Coin Cabinet, The Hague* (The Hague, 1978).

MacAlister, R. A. S., *Excavations of Gezer* vol. 3 (London, 1912).

McCown, C. C., *Tell en-Nasbeh*, vol. 1 (Berkeley and New Haven, 1947).

Magness-Gardiner, B., 'The Function of Cylinder Seals in Syrian Palace Archives' in Palaima, T. G., ed., *Aegaeum 5: Aegean Seals, Selaings and Administration: Proceedings of the NEH-Dickson Conference of the Program in Aegean Scripts and Prehistory of the Department of Classics, University of Texas at Austin, January 11-13, 1989* (Liège, 1990), 61–76.

Maier, F. G., *Alt-Paphos auf Cypern: Ausgrabungen zur Geschichte von Stadt und Heiligtum 1966-1984* (Mainz, 1985).

Maier, F. G. and Karageorghis, V., *Paphos* (Nicosia, 1984).

Marcus, E. and Artzy, M., 'A Loom Weight from Tel Nami with a Scarab Seal Impression' *IEJ* 45 (1995), 136–49.

Markoe, G. E., 'A Terracotta Warrior from Kazaphani, Cyprus, with Stamped Decoration in the Cypro-Phoenician Tradition' *RSF* 16 (1988), 15–9.

Masson, O., 'Cesnola et le trésor de Curium' *Cahiers: Centre d'études chypriotes* 1 (1984), 16–25.

Masson, O., 'Cesnola et le trésor de Curium' *Cahiers: Centre d'études chypriotes* 2 (1984), 3–15.

Masson, O., 'Cylindres et cachets chypriotes portant des caractères chypro-minoens' *BCH* 81 (1957), 6–37.

Masson, O., 'Une Inscription chypriote syllabique de Dora (Tel Dor) et les avatars des noms grecs en Aristo-' *Kadmos* 33 (1994), 87–92.

Masson, O., 'Kypriaka' *BCH* 86 (1964), 199–238.

Masson, O., 'Nouvelles Variétés chypriotes' *Cahiers: Centre d'études chypriotes* 24, no. 2 (1995), 7–18.

Masson, O., 'Pélérins chypriotes en Phénicie (Sarepta et Sidon)' *Semitica* 32 (1982), 45–9.

Masson, O., 'Quelques Intailles chypriotes inscrites' *Syria* 44 (1967), 363–74.

Masson, O., 'Un Scarabée de Cambridge à inscription chypriote syllabique' *Kadmos* 25 (1986), 162–3.

Masson, O. and Sznycer, M., *Recherches sur les phéniciens à Chypre* (Paris, 1972).

Matthews, D., 'The Random Pegasus: Loss of Meaning in Middle Assyrian Seals' *Cambridge Archaeological Journal* 2 (1992), 191–201.

Maxwell-Hyslop, K. R., *Western Asiatic Jewellery* (London, 1971).

Meek, T. J., 'Ancient Oriental Seals in the Redpath Library' *BASOR* no. 93 (1944), 2–13.

Meekers, M., 'The Sacred Tree on Cypriote Cylinder Seals' *RDAC* (1987) 67–76.

Meiggs, R., *The Athenian Empire* (Oxford, 1972).

Merrillees, P. H., *Cylinder and Stamp-Seals in Australian Collections = Victoria College, Archaeological Research Unit, Occasional Paper*, no. 3 (Victoria, 1990).

Michaelidou-Nicolaou, I., 'Nouveaux Documents pour le syllabaire chypriote' *BCH* 117 (1993), 343–7.

Mitford, T. B., *The Inscriptions of Kourion* (Philadelphia, 1971).

Moscati, S., ed., *The Phoenicians* (Milan, 1988).

Moseley, C. W. R. D., ed., *The Travels of John Mandeville* (Harmondsworth, 1983).

Moorey, P. R. S., *Ancient Mesopotamian Materials and Industries* (Oxford, 1994).

Muhly, J. D., 'The Role of the Sea Peoples in Cyprus during the LCIII Period' in Karageorghis, V. and Muhly. J. D., eds., *Cyprus at the Close of the Late Bronze Age* (Nicosia, 1984), 39–56.

Muhly, J., Madden, R., and Karageorghis, V., eds., *Early Metallurgy in Cyprus 4000-50 BC* (Nicosia, 1982).

Munro, J. A. R. and Tubbs, H. A., 'Excavations in Cyprus, 1889' *JHS* 11 (1890), 1–99.

Nagy, G., *Pindar's Homer* (Baltimore and London, 1990).

Negbi, O., 'The "Libyan Landscape" from Thera: A Review of Aegean EnterprisesOverseas in the Late Minoan Iron Age Period' *JMA* 7 (1994), 73–112.

Nicolaou, I., 'The Jewellery of Cyprus from Neolithic to Roman Times' *Archaeologia Cypria* 2 (1990), 117–20.

Nicolaou, I. and Nicolaou, K., *Kazaphani: A Middle/Late Cypriot Tomb at Kazaphani in Ayios Andronikos: T. 2A, B* (Nicosia, 1989).

Nicolaou, K., 'A Late Cypriote Necropolis at Yeroskipou, Paphos' *RDAC* (1983), 142–52.

Nicolaou, K.,'Anaskaphe Taphon eis Marion' *RDAC* (1964), 131–85.

Oddy, W. A., Meeks, N. D., and Ogden, J. M., 'A Phoenician Earring: A Scientific Examination' *Jewellery Studies* 1 (1983–4), 3–13.

Ogden, J., *Ancient Jewellery* (London, 1992).

Ogden, J., *Jewellery of the Ancient World* (London, 1982).

Onassoglu, A., *Die 'Talismanischen' Siegel* (Berlin, 1985).

von Oppenheim, M. F., *Tell Halaf* 1 (Berlin, 1943).

Orthmann, W., *Der alte Orient* (Berlin, 1975).

von der Osten, H. H., *The Alishar Hüyük*, vol. 2 (Chicago, 1937).

von der Osten, H. H., *The Alishar Hüyük*, vol. 3 (Chicago, 1937).

von der Osten, H. H., 'Altorientalische Siegelsteine' *Med. Bull.* 1 (1961), 20–41.

von der Osten, H. H., *Altorientalische Siegelsteine der Sammlung Hans Silvius von Aulock* (Uppsala, 1957).

von der Osten, H. H., *Ancient Oriental Seals in the Collection of Mr. Edward T. Newell* (Chicago, 1934).

Palaima, T. G., ed., *Aegaeum 5: Aegean Seals, Sealings and Administration: Proceedings of the NEH-Dickson Conference of the Program in Aegean Scripts and Prehistory of the Department of Classics, University of Texas at Austin, January 11-13, 1989* (Liège, 1990).

Pannuti, U., *La Collezione Glittica* 2 (Rome, 1994).

Papadopoulos, J. K., 'Early Iron Age Potters' Marks in the Aegean' *Hesperia* 63 (1994), 437–507.

Parker, B., 'Seals and Seal Impressions from the Nimrud Excavations, 1955–58' *Iraq* 24 (1962), 26–40.

Peltenburg, E. J., 'From Isolation to State Formation, c. 3500–1500 B. C.' in Karageorghis, V., and Michaelides, D., eds., *The Development of the Cypriot Economy from the Prehistoric Period to the Present Day* (Nicosia, 1996), 17–44.

Peltenburg, E. J., 'Kissonerga-Mosphilia: A Major Chalcolithic Site in Cyprus' *BASOR* 282/283 (1991), 17–35.

Peltenburg, E. J., *Lemba Archaeological Project I: Excavations at Lemba Lakkous, 1976-1983* (Göteborg, 1985).

Peltenburg, E. J., *Lemba Archaeological Project II.1A: Excavations at Kissonerga-Mosphilia, 1979-1992* (Jonsered, 1998).

Peltenburg, E. J., 'Lemba Archaeological Project, Cyprus, 1976–77' *Levant* 11 (1979), 9–45.

Peltenburg, E. J., 'Lemba Archaeological Project, Cyprus, 1985' *Levant* 19 (1987), 221–4.

Peltenburg, E. J., 'Local Exchange in Prehistoric Cyprus: An Initial Assessment of Picrolite' *BASOR* 282/283 (1991), 107–26.

Petit, T., 'Syllabaire et alphabet au "palais" d'Amathonte de Chypre vers 300 avant notre ère' in Baurain, C., Bonnet, C., and Krings, V., eds., *Phoinikeia Grammata: Lire et écrire en Méditerranée* (Namur, 1991), 481–90.

Petrie, W. M. F., *Ancient Gaza*, vol. 2 (London, 1932).

Petrie, W. M. F., *Ancient Gaza*, vol. 4 (London, 1934).

Petrie, W. M. F., *Scarabs and Cylinders with Names* (London, 1917).

Philip, G., 'Cypriot Bronzework in the Levantine World: Conservatism, Innovation, and Social Change' *JMA* 4 (1991), 59–107.

Phokaides, P. N., *Lapethos: Istoria kai Paradosis* (Nicosia, 1982).

Pierides, D., 'Notes on Cypriote Palaeography' *Transactions of the Society of Biblical Archaeology* 5 (1876), 88–96.

Pini, I., 'Kypro-Ägäische Rollsiegel' *JdAI* 95 (1980), 77–108.

Pisano, G. Q., 'Dieci Scarabei da Tharros' *RSF* 6 (1978), 37–56.

Pisano, G., 'Jewellery' in R. D. Barnett and C. Mendleson, *Tharros* (London, 1987), 78–95.

Pittman, H., *Ancient Art in Miniature* (New York, 1987).

Popham, M. R. *et al.*, 'Further Excavations at the Toumba Cemetery at Lefkandi, 1984 and 1986, a Preliminary Report' *Archaeological Reports for 1988-1989* (1989), 117–29.

Popham, M. R. and Sackett, L. H., *Lefkandi*, vol. 1 (London, 1979/1980).

Poppa, R., *Kamid-el-Loz* (Bonn, 1978).

Porada, E., ed., *Ancient Art in Seals* (Princeton, 1980).

Porada, E., 'Appendix 1: Relief Friezes and Seals from Maa-Palaeokastro' in Karageorghis, V. and Demas, M., *Excavations at Maa-Palaeokastro* (Nicosia, 1988), 301–13.

Porada, E., 'Appendix 1: Seals' in Dikaios, P., *Enkomi*, vol. 3 (Mainz, 1971), 783–810.

Porada, E., *The Collection of the Pierpont Morgan Library* (Washington, D.C., 1948).

Porada, E., 'Cylinder and Stamp-Seals' in I. A. Todd, ed, *Kalavassos-Ayios Dhimitrios* 2 (Göteborg, 1989), 33–7.

Porada, E., 'Cylinder and Stamp-Seals from Kition' in Karageorghis, V. and Demas. M., *Excavations at Kition*, vol. 5.2 (Nicosia, 1985), 250–4.

Porada, E., 'The Cylinder Seals Found at Thebes in Boeotia' *AfO* 28 (1981–2), 1–70.

Porada, E., 'The Cylinder Seals of the Late Cypriote Bronze Age' *AJA* 52 (1948), 178–98.

Porada, E., 'Glyptics' in J. L. Benson, *Bamboula at Kourion* (Philadelphia, 1972), 141–7.

Porada, E., 'A Lyre-Player from Tarsus and his Relations' in Weinberg, S. S., ed., *The Aegean and the Near East: Studies Presented to Hetty Goldman* (Locust Valley, New York, 1956), 185–211.

Porada, E., 'A Seal Ring and Two Cylinder Seals from Hala Sultan Tekke' in Åström, P. *et al.*, *Hala Sultan Tekke* 8 (Göteborg, 1983), 219–20.

Porada, E., 'Seals from the Tombs of Maroni' in J. Johnson, *Maroni de Chypre* (Göteborg, 1980), 68–72.

Postgate, N., 'Mesopotamian Petrology: Stages in the Classification of the Material World' *Cambridge Archaeological Journal* 7 (1997), 205–24.

Procopé-Walter, A., 'Zum Fortleben hethitischer Tradition in der späteren Glyptik' *AfO* 5 (1928–9), 164–8.

Rahmani, L. Y., 'Two Syrian Seals' *IEJ* 14 (1964), 180–4.

Reyes, A. T., *Archaic Cyprus* (Oxford, 1994).

Reyes, A. T., 'A Group of Cypro-Geometric Stamp-Seals' *Levant* 25 (1993), 194–205.

Reyes, A. T., 'Stamp-Seals in the Pierides Collection, Larnaca' *RDAC* (1991), 117–28.

Richter, G. M. A., *Catalogue of the Engraved Gems* (New York, 1956).

Robertson, N., ed., *The Archaeology of Cyprus: Recent Developments* (New Jersey, 1975).

Robinson, D. M., 'The Robinson Collection of Greek Gems, Seals, Rings, and Earrings' in *Hesperia Supplement* 8 (1949), 305–23.

Rocchetti, L., *Le Tombe dei Periodi Geometrico ed Arcaico Della Necropoli A Mare di Ayia Irini 'Paleokastro'* (Rome, 1978).

Root, M., 'Pyramidal Stamp-Seals – The Persepolis Connection' in Brosius, M. and Kuhrt, A., *Studies in Persian History: Essays in Memory of David M. Lewis* (Leiden, 1998), 257–89.

Sakellariou, M., 'Achéens et Arcadiens' in Karageorghis, J. and Masson, O., ed., *The History of the Greek Language in Cyprus* (Nicosia, 1988), 9–17.

Sakellariou, A., *Die minoischen und mykenischen Siegel des Nationalmuseums in Athens. CMS*, vol. 1 (Berlin, 1964).

Salamine de Chypre, histoire et archeologie (Paris, 1980).

Sansone, D., 'The Survival of the Bronze Age Demon' *Illinois Classical Studies* 13 (1988), 1–17.

Sax, M., 'Innovative Techniques Used to Decorate the Perforations of Some Akkadian Rock Crystal Cylinder Seals' *Iraq* 53 (1991), 91–5.

Sax, M., 'Recognition and Nomenclature of Quartz Materials with Specific Reference to Engraved Gemstones' *Jewellery Studies* 7 (1996), 63–72.

Sax, M., Collon, D., and Leese, M. N., 'The Availability of Raw Materials for Near Eastern Cylinder Seals During the Akkadian, Post-Akkadian, and Ur III Periods' *Iraq* 55 (1993), 77–90.

Sax, M., McNabb, J., and Meeks, N. D., 'Methods of Engraving Mesopotamian Cylinder Seals: Experimental Confirmation' *Archaeometry* 40 (1998), 1–21.

Sax, M. and Meeks, N. D., 'The Introduction of Wheel Cutting as a Technique for Engraving Cylinder Seals: Its Distinction from Filing' *Iraq* 56 (1994), 153–66.

Sax, M. and Meeks, N. D., 'Methods of Engraving Mesopotamian Quartz Cylinder Seals' *Archaeometry* 37 (1995), 25–36.

Sax, M. and Middleton, A. P., 'A System of Nomenclature for Quartz and Its Application to the Material of Cylinder Seals' *Archaeometry* 34 (1992), 11–20.

Schaeffer, C. F. A., *Alasia* 1 (Paris, 1971).

Schaeffer, C. F. A., *Enkomi-Alasia* vol. 1 (Paris, 1952).

Schaeffer, C. F. A., 'Fouilles d'Enkomi-Alasia' *Syria* 45 (1968), 263–74.

Schaeffer, C. F. A., 'Les Fouilles de Ras-Shamra' *Syria* 15 (1934), 105–36.

Shaw, I. and Jameson, R., 'Amethyst Mining in the Eastern Desert: A Preliminary Survey at Wadi el-Hudi' *JEA* 79 (1993), 81–97.

Shear, T. L., 'A Terra-Cotta Relief from Sardes' *AJA* 27 (1923), 131–50.

Schefold, K., 'Die Grabungen in Eretria im Herbst 1964 und 1965' *Antike Kunst* 9 (1966), 106–24.

Shuval, M., 'A Catalogue of Early Iron Stamp-Seals from Israel' in Keel, O., Shuval, M., and Uehlinger, C., *Studien zu den Stempelsiegeln aus Palästina/ Israel*, vol. 3 (Freiburg and Gottingen, 1990), 67–161.

Smith, J. S., 'Cylinder Seals in the Aegean: Contextual and Spatial Analyses of Exchange' MA thesis (Bryn Mawr College, Pennsylvania, 1989).

Smith, J. S., 'Seals for Sealing in the Late Cypriot Period' Ph. D. thesis (Bryn Mawr College, Pennsylvania, 1994).

Sophocleous, S., *Atlas des représentations chypro-archaïques des divinités* (Göteborg, 1985).

Soren, D. and J. James, J., *Kourion* (New York, 1988).

Spier, J., 'Emblems in Archaic Greece' *BICS* 37 (1990), 107–29.

Stern, E., 'Assyrian and Babylonian Elements in the Material Culture of Palestine in the Persian Period' *Transeuphratène* 7 (1994), 51–62.

Stern, E., 'A Cypro-Phoenician Dedicatory Offering from Tel Dor Depicting a Maritime Scene' *Qadmoniot* 27 (1994), 34–7.

Stern, E., 'A Phoenician-Cypriote Votive Scapula from Tel Dor: A Maritime Scene' *IEJ* 44 (1994), 1–12.

Tatton-Brown, V., ed., *Cyprus and the East Mediterranean in the Iron Age* (London, 1989).

Tatton-Brown, V., 'Le Sarcophage d'Amathonte' in Hermary, A., *Amathonte*, vol. 2 (Paris, 1981), 74–83.

Teissier, B., *Ancient Near Eastern Cylinder Seals from the Marcopoli Collection* (Berkeley, 1984).

Teissier, B., *Egyptian Iconography on Syro-Palestinian Cylinder Seals of the Middle Bronze Age* (Fribourg and Göttingen, 1996).

Teissier, B., 'Glyptic Evidence for a Connection between Iran, Syro-Palestine, and Egypt in the Fourth and Third Millennium' *Iran* 25 (1987), 27–53.

Todd, I. A., ed., *Kalavassos-Ayios Dhimitrios* 2 (Göteborg, 1989).

Tufnell, O., *Lachish*, vol. 3 (London, 1953).

Tufnell, O., 'Some Scarabs with Decorated Backs' *Levant* 2 (1967), 95–99.

Tytgat, C., *Les Nécropoles sud-ouest et sud-est d'Amathonte 1. Les Tombes 110-385* (Nicosia, 1989).

Vagnetti, L., 'Stone Sculpture in Chalcolithic Cyprus' *BASOR* 282/3 (1991), 139–51.

Vattioni, F., 'I Sigilli Fenici' *AION* 41 (1981), 177f.

Vercoutter, J., *Les Objets égyptiens et égyptisants du mobilier carthaginois* (Paris, 1945).

Vermeule, E., *Toumba tou Skourou* (Boston, 1974).

Vermeule, E. and F. Wolsky, F., 'The Bone and Ivory of Toumba tou Skourou' *RDAC* (1977), 80–96.

Voyatzis, M., 'Arcadia and Cyprus: Aspects of their Interrelationship between the Twelfth and Eighth Centuries BC' *RDAC* (1985), 155–63.

Walters, H. B., 'On Some Acquisitions of the Mycenaean Age Recently Acquired by the British Museum' *JHS* 17 (1897), 63–77.

Webb, J. M., *Corpus of Cypriote Antiquities 12: Cypriote Antiquities in the Abbey Museum, Queensland, Australia* (Gothenburg, 1986).

Weinberg, S. S., ed., *The Aegean and the Near East: Studies Presented to Hetty Goldman* (Locust Valley, New York, 1956).

Weingarten, J., 'The Multiple Sealing System of Minoan Crete and Its Possible Antecedents in Anatolia' *OJA* 11 (1992), 25–37.

Weingarten, J., 'Three Upheavals in Minoan Sealing Administration: Evidence for Radical Change' in Palaima, T. G., *Aegaeum 5: Aegean Seals, Sealings and Administration. Proceedings of the NEH-Dickson Conference of the Program in Aegean Scripts and Prehistory of the Department of Classics, University of Texas at Austin January 11-13, 1989* (Liège, 1990), 105–14.

Wilkinson, R. H., *Reading Egyptian Art* (London, 1992).

Wilson, V., 'The Iconography of Bes in Cyprus and the Levant' *Levant* 7 (1975), 77–103.

Winter, I. J., 'Phoenician and North Syrian Ivory Carving in Historical Context: Questions of Style and Distribution' *Iraq* 38 (1976), 1–22.

Xenophontos, C., 'Environment and Resources' in Frankel, D. and Webb, J. M., *Marki Alonia: An Early and Middle Bronze Age Town in Cyprus: Excavations 1990-1994* (Jonsered, 1996), 16–8.

Xenophontos, C., 'Picrolite, Its Nature, Provenance, and Possible Distribution Patterns in the Chalcolithic Period of Cyprus' *BASOR* 282/283 (1991), 127–38.

Xenophontos, C., 'Steatite vs. Picrolite' in Muhly, J., Madden, R., and Karageorghis, V., eds., *Early Metallurgy in Cyprus 4000-50 BC* (Nicosia, 1982), 59.

Yadin, Y. *et al.*, *Hazor* , vols. 3–4 (Jerusalem, 1961).

Yon, M., 'A propos de l'Heraklès à Chypre' in Kahil, L., Augé, C., and Linant de Bellefonds, P., eds., *L'Iconographie classique et identités régionales* (Athens, 1986), 287–97.

Younger, J. G., *The Iconography of Late Minoan and Mycenaean Sealstones and Finger-Rings* (Bristol, 1988).

Zazoff, P., *Die antiken Gemmen* (Munich, 1983).

Zwierlein-Diehl, E., *Die antiken Gemmen des Kunsthistorischen Museums in Wien*, vol. 1 (Munich, 1973).

SOURCES OF ILLUSTRATION

Fig. 18. (a) M.-J. Chavane, *Salamine de Chypre* 6 (1975), 151–2, no. 436.
          (b) M.-J. Chavane, *Salamine de Chypre* 6 (1975), 151–2, no. 437.
Fig. 19. (a) V. E. G. Kenna, *BCH* 91 (1967), 262–5, no. 6, fig. 4.6.
          (b) V. E. G. Kenna, *BCH* 91 (1967), 262–3, no. 4; fig. 3.4.
Fig. 20. (a) J. Boardman and R. L. Wilkins.
          (b) V. E. G. Kenna, *BCH* 91 (1967), 261, no. 3; 263, fig. 3.
Fig. 21. J. Boardman and R. L. Wilkins; Marion Cox.
Fig. 22. K. Nicolaou, *RDAC* (1964), 148, no. 1; fig. 5.
Fig. 23. Masson, *ICS*, 350–1, no. 367.
Fig. 24. Cat. 1.   Boardman and Vollenweider, *Ashmolean Gems*, 15, no. 72; pl. 13.
Fig. 25. Cat. 2.   Masson, *ICS*, 347, no. 358; Marion Cox.
Fig. 26. Cat. 3.   Masson, *ICS*, 349, no. 361.
Fig. 27. (a) Clerc, *Kition* 2, 115–6, no. 516.
          (b) Clerc, *Kition* 2, 116, no. 1072.
Fig. 28. (a) V. Karageorghis, *BCH* 97 (1973), 622; fig. 145.
          (b) V. Karageorghis, *BCH* 113 (1989), 801, fig. 42.
          (c) Boardman, 'Seals and Amulets', pl. 5, no. 4–7.
Fig. 29. Cat. 4.   V. Karageorghis, *Blacks in Ancient Cypriot Art* (1988), 19, no. 11; Clerc, 'Aegyptiaca, 25, no. T. 242/76.
Fig. 30. Cat. 5.   V. Karageorghis, *Blacks in Ancient Cypriot Art* (1988), 18–9, no. 10; Clerc, 'Aegyptiaca', 19–21, no. T. 236/60.
Fig. 31. Cat. 6.   V. Karageorghis, *Blacks in Ancient Cypriot Art* (1988), 17, no. 7.
Fig. 32. (a) Ashmolean Museum, Oxford.
          (b) Vollenweider, *Geneva* 3, 57–8, no. 89.
Fig. 33. Cat. 8.   Ashmolean Museum, Oxford.
Fig. 34. Cat. 9.   V. Karageorghis, *Blacks in Ancient Cypriot Art* (1988), 39–40, no. 31.
Fig. 35. Cat. 10. Vollenweider, *Geneva* 3, 116, no. 158.
Fig. 36. Cat. 11. V. Karageorghis, *Blacks in Ancient Cypriot Art* (1988), 18, no. 9.
Fig. 37. Cat. 13. Boardman, 'Seals and Amulets', pl. 4, no. 1.
Fig. 38. Cat. 14. J. Boardman and R. Wilkins.
Fig. 39. Cat. 15. J. Boardman and R. L. Wilkins.
Fig. 40. Cat. 16. Author.
Fig. 41. Cat. 18. Author.
Fig. 42. Cat. 19. J. Boardman and R. L. Wilkins.
Fig. 43. Cat. 20. J. Boardman and R. L. Wilkins.
Fig. 44. Cat. 21. Marion Cox.
Fig. 45. Cat. 22. J. Boardman and R. L. Wilkins; Marion Cox.
Fig. 46. Cat. 23. Marion Cox.
Fig. 47. Cat. 24. J. Boardman and R. L. Wilkins.
Fig. 48. Cat. 25. Masson, *ICS* 328, no. 328; Marion Cox.
Fig. 49. Cat. 26. J. Boardman and R. L. Wilkins; Marion Cox.
Fig. 50. Cat. 27. J. Boardman and R. L. Wilkins; Marion Cox.
Fig. 51. Cat. 28. The Metropolitan Museum of Art, The Cesnola Collection, purchased by subscription, 1874–76. (74. 51. 4399). Negative number 93291.
Fig. 52. Cat. 29. P. Zazoff, *Die antiken Gemmen* (1983), 71; Taf. 14.3.
Fig. 53. Cat. 30. Marion Cox.
Fig. 54. Cat. 31. M. Maaskant-Kleibrink, *Catalogue of the Engraved Gems in the Royal Coin Cabinet, the Hague* (1978), 74, no. 6.
Fig. 55. Cat. 32. H. H. von der Osten, *Med. Bull.* 1 (1961), 35, no. 27.
Fig. 56. Cat. 33. Vollenweider, *Geneva* 1, 138, no. 185; pl. 72.

Fig. 57.   Cat. 34.   Vollenweider, *Geneva* 1, 139, no. 186; pl. 72.
Fig. 58.   Cat. 35.   Marion Cox.
Fig. 59.   Cat. 36.   Ashmolean Museum, Oxford.
Fig. 60.   Cat. 37.   Ashmolean Museum, Oxford.
Fig. 61.   Cat. 38.   Zwierlein-Diehl, *AGDS* 2, 61, no. 120; Taf. 29.
Fig. 62.   Cat. 39.   Vollenweider, *Geneva* 1, 139, no. 86; pl. 72.
Fig. 63.   Cat. 40.   Author.
Fig. 64.   Cat. 41.   J. Boardman, *Intaglios and Rings* (1975), 112, no. 211.
Fig. 65.   Cat. 42.   Author.
Fig. 66.   Cat. 43.   Author.
Fig. 67.   Cat. 44.   Author.
Fig. 68.   Cat. 45.   M. Henig, *Classical Gems* (1994), 23, no. 29.
Fig. 69.   Cat. 46.   P. Zazoff, *Die antiken Gemmen* (1983), Taf. 14, no. 5.
Fig. 70.   Cat. 47.   M. G. Amadasi, *L'Iconografia del Carro da Guerra in Sirie e Palestina* (1965),
                      fig. 25.1.
Fig. 71.   Cat. 48.   Ashmolean Museum, Oxford.
Fig. 72.   Cat. 49.   Marion Cox.
Fig. 73.   Cat. 50.   Marion Cox.
Fig. 74.   Cat. 51.   Zwierlein-Diehl, *AGDS* 2, 63, no. 128; Taf. 128.
Fig. 75.   Cat. 53.   J. Boardman, *AGGems*, 162, no. 591; pl . 38.
Fig. 76.   Cat. 54.   Zwierlein-Diehl, *AGDS* 2, 50–1, no. 85; Taf. 22.
Fig. 77.   Cat. 55.   J. Boardman and R. L. Wilkins; Marion Cox.
Fig. 78.   Cat. 56.   J. Boardman and R. L. Wilkins; Marion Cox.
Fig. 79.   Cat. 57.   J. Boardman and R. L. Wilkins; Marion Cox.
Fig. 80.   Cat. 58.   J. Boardman and R. L. Wilkins; Marion Cox.
Fig. 81.   Cat. 60.   J. Boardman and R. L. Wilkins; Marion Cox.
Fig. 82.   Cat. 61.   J. Boardman and R. L. Wilkins; Marion Cox.
Fig. 83.   Cat. 62.   E. Gubel, *Studia Phoenicia* 5 (1987), 198; fig. 2; Marion Cox.
Fig. 84.   Cat. 63.   E. Gubel, *Studia Phoenicia* 5 (1987), 199; fig. 3; Marion Cox.
Fig. 85.   Cat. 64.   J. Boardman and R. L. Wilkins; Marion Cox.
Fig. 86.   Cat. 65.   J. Boardman and R. L. Wilkins; Marion Cox.
Fig. 87.   Cat. 66.   J. Boardman and R. L. Wilkins; Marion Cox.
Fig. 88.   Cat. 67.   J. Boardman and R. L. Wilkins; Marion Cox.
Fig. 89.   Cat. 68.   E. Gubel, *Studia Phoenicia* 5 (1987), 200; fig. 5.
Fig. 90.   Cat. 69.   E. Gubel, *Studia Phoenicia* 5 (1987), 200; fig. 4.
Fig. 91.   Cat. 70.   Vollenweider, *Geneva* 3, 129–30, no. 175.
Fig. 92.   Cat. 71.   Vollenweider, *Geneva* 3, 133, no. 177.
Fig. 93.   Cat. 72.   Author.
Fig. 94.   Author.
Fig. 95.   E. Zwierlein-Diehl, *Die antiken Gemmen des Kunsthistorischen Mueums in Wien* (1973),
           35, no. 13.
Fig. 96.   Cat. 73.   Author; Buchner and Boardman, 'Lyre-Player', 36, no. 132.
Fig. 97.   Cat. 74.   Marion Cox.
Fig. 98.   Cat. 75.   Buchner and Boardman, 'Lyre-Player', 35, no. 126, fig. 45; Marion Cox.
Fig. 99.   Cat. 76.   Buchner and Boardman, 'Lyre-Player', 36, no. 130; Marion Cox.
Fig. 100. Cat. 77.   Marion Cox.
Fig. 101. Cat. 78.   Marion Cox.
Fig. 102. Cat. 79.   Author.
Fig. 103. Cat. 80.   Author.
Fig. 104. Cat. 81.   Author; Boardman and Buchner, 'Lyre-Player', 36, no. 131.

Fig. 105. Cat. 82. Marion Cox.
Fig. 106. Marion Cox.
Fig. 107. Cat. 83. Marion Cox.
Fig. 108. Cat. 84. Marion Cox.
Fig. 109. Cat. 85. Marion Cox.
Fig. 110. Cat. 86. Marion Cox.
Fig. 111. Cat. 87. Author.
Fig. 112. Cat. 88. The Metropolitan Museum of Art, The Cesnola Collection, purchased by subscription, 1874–76. (74. 51. 4386). Negative number 62573.
Fig. 113. Cat. 89. V. Karageorghis, *BCH* 113 (1989), 811, 814; fig. 85.
Fig. 114. Cat. 90. Delaporte, *Catalogue* 2, 210; pl. 106, no. 1a.
Fig. 115. Cat. 91. Marion Cox.
Fig. 116. Cat. 92. J. Boardman and R. L. Wilkins; Marion Cox.
Fig. 117. Cat. 93. J. DuPlat Taylor, *Myrtou-Pighades* (0xford, 1957), 94, no. 405.
Fig. 118. Cat. 94. Marion Cox.
Fig. 119. Cat. 95. Marion Cox.
Fig. 120. Cat. 96. Marion Cox.
Fig. 121. Cat. 97. Marion Cox.
Fig. 122. Cat. 98. Marion Cox.
Fig. 123. Cat. 99. Author.
Fig. 124. Cat. 100. Author.
Fig. 125. Cat. 101. V. Karageorghis, *BCH* 111 (1987), 713; fig. 127.
Fig. 126. Cat. 102. V. Karageorghis, *RDAC* (1987), 90; pl. 32.
Fig. 127. Cat. 103. Author; Marion Cox.
Fig. 128. Cat. 104. Marion Cox.
Fig. 129. Cat. 105. J. Boardman and R. L. Wilkins; Marion Cox.
Fig. 130. Cat. 106. J. Boardman and R. L. Wilkins.
Fig. 131. Cat. 107. J. Boardman and R. L. Wilkins; Marion Cox.
Fig. 132. Cat. 108. J. Boardman and R. L. Wilkins; Marion Cox.
Fig. 133. Cat. 109. O. Masson, *Cahiers: Centre d'études chypriotes* 24, no. 2 (1995), 14–5; pl. 2, no. 1 and 3.
Fig. 134. Cat. 110. J. Boardman and R. L. Wilkins; Marion Cox.
Fig. 135. Cat. 111. V. Karageorghis, *RDAC* (1987), 89–90; pl. 32.
Fig. 136. Cat. 112. J. Boardman and R. L. Wilkins.
Fig. 137. Cat. 113. Zwierlein-Diehl, *AGDS* 2, 66, no. 136; Taf. 32.
Fig. 138. Cat. 114. Zwierlein-Diehl, *AGDS* 2, 65, no. 135; Tas. 32.
Fig. 139. Cat. 115. Ashmolean Museum, Oxford.
Fig. 140. Cat. 116. Ashmolean Museum, Oxford.
Fig. 141. Cat. 118. Marion Cox.
Fig. 142. Cat. 119. Marion Cox.
Fig. 143. Cat. 120. Marion Cox.
Fig. 144. Cat. 122. K. Galling, *ZPDV* 64 (1941), 174, no. 13; Taf. 5.
Fig. 145. Cat. 123. U. Pannuti, *La Collezione Glittica* 2 (1994), 21.
Fig. 146. Cat. 124. Ashmolean Museum, Oxford.
Fig. 147. Cat. 125. Marion Cox.
Fig. 148. Boardman, *AGGems*, 23, no. 24.
Fig. 149. Cat. 126. Boardman, 'Seals and Amulets', pl. 4, no. 3.
Fig. 150. Cat. 127. J. Boardman and R. L. Wilkins.
Fig. 151. Cat. 128. E. Zwierlein-Diehl, *Die antiken Gemmen des Kunsthistorisches Museums in Wien* 1 (1973), 36, no. 16; Taf. 4.

Fig. 152.   Cat. 129.   V. Karageorghis, *BCH* 88 (1964), 292–3; fig. 5; Marion Cox.
Fig. 153.   Cat. 131.   V. Karageorghis, *BCH* 87 (1963), 327–8, fig. 3a-c.
Fig. 154.   Cat. 132.   G. M. A. Richter, *Engraved Gems of the Greeks and the Etruscans* (1968), 33,
            no. 14.
Fig. 155.   Author.
Fig. 156.   Cat. 133.   G. M. A. Richter, *Engraved Gems of the Greeks and the Etruscans* (1968), 33,
            no. 13.
Fig. 157.   Cat. 134.   Marion Cox.
Fig. 158.   Cat. 135.   J. Boardman and R. L. Wilkins; Marion Cox.
Fig. 159.   Cat. 136.   Masson, *ICS*, 389, no. 46.
Fig. 160.   Cat. 137.   G. M. A. Richter, *Engraved Gems of the Greeks and the Etruscans* (1968), 35,
            no. 30; Marion Cox.
Fig. 161.   Cat. 138.   Walters, *BM Gems*, 42; pl. 6, no. 348.
Fig. 162.   Cat. 139.   O. Masson, *Cahiers: Centre d'études chypriotes* 24, no. 2 (1995), 7–8; pl. 1, no.
            1–2.
Fig. 163.   Cat. 140.   Author.
Fig. 164.   Cat. 141.   Marion Cox.
Fig. 165.   Cat. 142.   *Southesk*, 207, no. O. 21; pl. 17.
Fig. 166.   Cat. 143.   Ashmolean Museum, Oxford.
Fig. 167.   Cat. 144.   Ashmolean Museum, Oxford.
Fig. 168.   Cat. 145.   Marion Cox.
Fig. 169.   Cat. 146.   Marion Cox.
Fig. 170.   Cat. 147.   Marion Cox.
Fig. 171.   Cat. 148.   Marion Cox.
Fig. 172.   Cat. 149.   Author.
Fig. 173.   Cat. 150.   Author.
Fig. 174.   Cat. 151.   The Metropolitan Museum of Art, The Cesnola Collection, purchased by
            subscription, 1874–76. (74. 51. 4405). Negative number 62572.
Fig. 175.   Cat. 152.   The Metropolitan Museum of Art, The Cesnola Collection, purchased by
            subscription, 1874–76. (74. 51. 4398). Negative number 62572.
Fig. 176.   Cat. 153.   J. Boardman and R. L. Wilkins.
Fig. 177.   Cat. 154.   J. Boardman and R. L. Wilkins; Marion Cox.
Fig. 178.   Cat. 155.   J. Boardman and R. L. Wilkins; Marion Cox.
Fig. 179.   Cat. 156.   Ashmolean Museum, Oxford.
Fig. 180.   Cat. 157.   Ashmolean Museum, Oxford.
Fig. 181.   Cat. 158.   Ashmolean Museum, Oxford.
Fig. 182.   Cat. 159.   Author.
Fig. 183.   Marion Cox.
Fig. 184.   Cat. 160.   J. Boardman and R. L. Wilkins; Marion Cox.
Fig. 185.   Cat. 161.   Myres and Ohnefalsch-Richter, *CMM*, 136, no. 4582; Marion Cox.
Fig. 186.   Cat. 162.   Masson, *ICS*, 346–7, no. 357.
Fig. 187.   Cat. 163.   The Metropolitan Museum of Art, The Cesnola Collection, purchased by
            subscription, 1874–76. (74. 51. 4193). Negative number 135327.
Fig. 188.   Cat. 164.   Bibliothèque Nationale, Paris.
Fig. 189.   Cat. 165.   J. Boardman and R. L. Wilkins; Marion Cox.
Fig. 190.   Cat. 166.   Boardman, 'Seals and Amulets', pl. 4, no. 4.
Fig. 191.   Cat. 167.   Walters, *BM Gems*, 41, no. 338.
Fig. 192.   Cat. 168.   J. Boardman and R. L. Wilkins; Marion Cox.
Fig. 193.   Cat. 169.   V. Karageorghis, *Excavations in the Necropolis of Salamis* 2 (1970), 51, no. 53;
            pl. 105.

Fig. 194. Cat. 170. Zwierlein-Diehl, *AGDS* 2, 62, no. 122.
Fig. 195. Cat. 171. Boardman, 'Seals and Amulets', pl. 4, no. 6.
Fig. 196. Cat. 172. Author.
Fig. 197. Cat. 173. Author.
Fig. 198. Cat. 174. Author.
Fig. 199. Cat. 175. G. S. Matthiae in L. Rocchetti, *Le Tombe dei Periodi Geometrico ed Archaico della Necropoli a Mare di Ayia Irini* 'Palaeokastro' (1978), 117–20.
Fig. 200. Cat. 176. Marion Cox.
Fig. 201. Cat. 177. Author; Marion Cox.
Fig. 202. Cat. 178. Marion Cox.
Fig. 203. Cat. 179. Author.
Fig. 204. Cat. 180. Clerc, *Kition* 2, 53–4.
Fig. 205. Cat. 181. Clerc, *Kition* 2, 70, no. 801.
Fig. 206. Cat. 184. Marion Cox.
Fig. 207. Cat. 185. Ashmolean Museum, Oxford.
Fig. 208. Cat. 186. Marion Cox.
Fig. 209. Cat. 187. Marion Cox.
Fig. 210. Cat. 188. Marion Cox.
Fig. 211. Cat. 190. G. Colonna-Ceccaldi, *RA* 25 (1873), 30.
Fig. 212a. Cat. 191. Marion Cox.
Fig. 212b. Cat. 192. The Metropolitan Museum of Art, The Cesnola Collection, purchased by subscription, 1874–76. (74. 51. 4147). Negative number 246991tf.
Fig. 213. Cat. 193. Marion Cox.
Fig. 214. Cat. 194. V. Karageorghis, *BCH* 87 (1963), 325–8; fig. 2; Marion Cox.
Fig. 215. Cat. 195. Boardman, 'Seals and Amulets', pl. 3, no. 10.
Fig. 216. Cat. 196. Boardman, 'Seals and Amulets', pl. 4, no. 5.
Fig. 217. Cat. 197. Vollenweider, *Geneva* 1, 136, no. 82; pl. 38.
Fig. 218. Cat. 198. J. Boardman and R. L. Wilkins; Marion Cox.
Fig. 219. Cat. 199. Forgeau, *Amathonte* 3, 157, no. 46.
Fig. 220. Cat. 200. Boardman, 'Seals and Amulets', pl. 4, no. 8.
Fig. 221. Cat. 201. Author.
Fig. 222. Cat. 202. J. Boardman and R. L. Wilkins; Marion Cox.
Fig. 223. Cat. 203. Author.
Fig. 224. Cat. 204. Marion Cox.
Fig. 225. Cat. 205. Clerc, *Kition* 2, 62, no. 766.
Fig. 226. Cat. 206. Author.
Fig. 227. Cat. 207. J. Boardman and R. L. Wilkins; Marion Cox.
Fig. 228. Cat. 208. The Metropolitan Museum of Art, The Cesnola Collection, purchased by subscription, 1874–76. (74. 51. 4172). Negative number 247146tf.
Fig. 229. Cat. 209. Zwierlein-Diehl, *AGDS* 2, 62, no. 123; Taf. 129.
Fig. 230. Cat. 210. Author.
Fig. 231. Cat. 211. Marion Cox.
Fig. 232. Cat. 212. Ashmolean Museum, Oxford.
Fig. 233. Cat. 213. Marion Cox.
Fig. 234. Cat. 215. The Metropolitan Museum of Art, The Cesnola Collection, purchased by subscription, 1874–76. (74. 51. 4401). Negative number 62572.
Fig. 235. Cat. 216. P. Aupert *et al.*, *BCH* 107 (1983), 967.
Fig. 236. Cat. 218. Author.
Fig. 237. Cat. 219. Author.
Fig. 238. Cat. 220. J. Boardman and R. L. Wilkins; Marion Cox.

Fig. 239. Cat. 221. Marion Cox.
Fig. 240. Cat. 222. J. Boardman and R. L. Wilkins (left); author (right).
Fig. 241. Cat. 224. Marion Cox.
Fig. 242. Cat. 225. The Metropolitan Museum of Art, The Cesnola Collection, purchased by subscription, 1874–76. (74. 51. 4168). Negative number 247018tf.
Fig. 243. Cat. 226. The Metropolitan Museum of Art, The Cesnola Collection, purchased by subscription, 1874–76. (74. 51. 4188). Negative number 247042tf.
Fig. 244. Cat. 227. The Metropolitan Museum of Art, The Cesnola Collection, purchased by subscription, 1874–76. (74. 51. 4189). Negative number 247045tf.
Fig. 245. Cat. 228. The Metropolitan Museum of Art, The Cesnola Collection, purchased by subscription, 1874–76. (74. 51. 4191). Negative number 247051tf.
Fig. 246a. Cat. 229. The Metropolitan Museum of Art, The Cesnola Collection, purchased by subscription, 1874–76. (74. 51. 4187). Negative number 247039tf.
Fig. 246b. Cat. 230. The Metropolitan Museum of Art, The Cesnola Collection, purchased by subscription, 1874–76. (74. 51. 4143). Negative number 62574.
Fig. 247. Cat. 232. V. Karageorghis, *BCH* 85 (1961), 263; fig. 6.
Fig. 248. Cat. 233. V. Karageorghis, *BCH* 95 (1971), 361–2; fig. 56.
Fig. 249. Cat. 235. Ashmolean Museum, Oxford.
Fig. 250. Cat. 236. Ashmolean Museum, Oxford.
Fig. 251. Cat. 237. Ashmolean Museum, Oxford.
Fig. 252. Cat. 238. The Metropolitan Museum of Art, The Cesnola Collection, purchased by subscription, 1874–76. (74. 51. 4400). Negative number 62572.
Fig. 253. Clerc, 'Aegyptiaca', 18–9, no. T. 236/59.1.
Fig. 254. Cat. 239. Murray *et al.*, *Excavations*, 98, 126; fig. 3
Fig. 255. Cat. 240. Author.
Fig. 256. Cat. 241. Markoe, *Bowls*, 371, no. 18.
Fig. 257. Cat. 242. The Metropolitan Museum of Art, The Cesnola Collection, purchased by subscription, 1874–76. (74. 51. 4149). Negative number 62574.
Fig. 258. Cat. 243. The Metropolitan Museum of Art, The Cesnola Collection, purchased by subscription, 1874–76. (74. 51. 4150). Negative number 62574.
Fig. 259. Cat. 244. Walters, *BM Gems*, 33, no. 274; pl. 5.
Fig. 260. Cat. 245. Walters, *BM Gems*, 35, no. 286; pl. 6.
Fig. 261. Cat. 246. Forgeau, *Amathonte* 3, 158, no. 50.
Fig. 262. Cat. 247. Author.
Fig. 263. Cat. 248. The Metropolitan Museum of Art, The Cesnola Collection, purchased by subscription, 1874–76. (74. 51. 4164). Negative number 247008tf.
Fig. 264. Cat. 249. Marion Cox.
Fig. 265. Cat. 250. Marion Cox.
Fig. 266. Cat. 251. V. Karageorghis, *BCH* 103 (1979), 678–81; fig. 32.
Fig. 267. Cat. 252. Boardman, 'Seals and Amulets', pl. 4, no. 7.
Fig. 268. Cat. 253. Author.
Fig. 269. Cat. 254. Marion Cox.
Fig. 270. Cat. 255. Author; Marion Cox.
Fig. 271. Cat. 258. G. M. A. Richter, *Engraved Gems of the Greeks and the Etruscans* (1968) 33, no. 12.
Fig. 272. Cat. 259. Vollenweider, *Geneva* 1, 117, no. 148; pl. 61.
Fig. 273. Cat. 260. Boardman, *AGGems*, 22, no. 27; pl. 1.
Fig. 274. Cat. 261. Brandt, *AGDS* 1, 33, no. 109; Taf. 13.
Fig. 275a. Cat. 262. Zwierlein-Diehl, *AGDS* 2, 62, no. 124; Taf. 30.

Fig. 275b. Cat. 263. The Metropolitan Museum of Art, The Cesnola Collection, purchased by subscription, 1874–76. (74. 51. 4377). Negative number 62573.

Fig. 276. Cat. 264. Marion Cox.

Fig. 277. Cat. 265. Markoe, *Bowls*, 371, no. 19.

Fig. 278. Cat. 266. Zwierlein-Diehl, *AGDS* 2, 65, no. 133; Taf. 32.

Fig. 279. Cat. 269. Murray *et al.*, *Excavations* 126; pl. 4; Amathus, no. 2.

Fig. 280. Cat. 270. Marion Cox.

Fig. 281. Cat. 271. Vollenweider, *Geneva* 1, 119, no. 151; pl. 61.

Fig. 282. Cat. 273. Marion Cox.

Fig. 283. Cat. 275. J. Boardman and R. L. Wilkins; Marion Cox.

Fig. 284. Cat. 276. Ashmolean Museum, Oxford.

Fig. 285. Cat. 277. The Metropolitan Museum of Art, The Cesnola Collection, purchased by subscription, 1874–76. (74. 51. 4139). Negative number 246978tf.

Fig. 286. Cat. 279. Vollenweider, *Geneva* 1, 137–8, no. 184; pl. 72.

Fig. 287. Cat. 280. The Metropolitan Museum of Art, The Cesnola Collection, purchased by subscription, 1874–76. (74. 51. 4402). Negative number 92854tf; 62572.

Fig. 288. Cat. 281. Boardman, *AGGems*, 23, no. 30; pl. 1; Marion Cox.

Fig. 289. Cat. 282. Zwierlein-Diehl, *AGDS* 2, 64, no. 131; Taf. 31.

Fig. 290. Cat. 283. G. M. A. Richter, *Engraved Gems of the Greeks and the Etruscans* (1968), 65, no. 168.

Fig. 291. Cat. 284. Boardman, 'Seals and Amulets', pl. 6, no. 2.

Fig. 292. Cat. 285. Boardman, 'Seals and Amulets', pl. 3, no. 5.

Fig. 293. Cat. 286. Boardman, 'Seals and Amulets', pl. 3, no. 7.

Fig. 294. Cat. 287. P. Aupert, *BCH* 104 (1980), 814; fig. 20.

Fig. 295. Cat. 288. D. Buitron-Oliver, *The Sanctuary of Apollo-Hylates at Kourion* (1996), 163–4, no. 2; V. Karageorghis, *BCH* 106 (1982), 727–8; fig. 96.

Fig. 296. Cat. 289. The Metropolitan Museum of Art, The Cesnola Collection, purchased by subscription, 1874–76. (74. 51. 4166). Negative number 247012tf.

Fig. 297a. Cat. 290. The Metropolitan Museum of Art, The Cesnola Collection, purchased by subscription, 1874–76. (74. 51. 4192). Negative number 247054tf.

Fig. 297b. Cat. 291. The Metropolitan Museum of Art, The Cesnola Collection, purchased by subscription, 1874–76. (74. 51. 4151). Negative number 247002tf.

Fig. 298. Cat. 292. The Metropolitan Museum of Art, The Cesnola Collection, purchased by subscription, 1874–76. (74. 51. 4190). Negative number 247048tf.

Fig. 299. Cat. 293. Ashmolean Museum, Oxford.

Fig. 300. Cat. 294. The Metropolitan Museum of Art, The Cesnola Collection, purchased by subscription, 1874–76. (74. 51. 4140). Negative number 62574.

Fig. 301. Clerc, 'Aegyptiaca', 35–6, no. T. 297/21.

Fig. 302. Cat. 295. Walters, *BM Gems*, 20–1, no. 151; pl. 4.

Fig. 303. Cat. 296. Walters, *BM Gems*, 21, no. 154; pl. 4.

Fig. 304. Cat. 297. Ashmolean Museum, Oxford.

Fig. 305. Cat. 298. Clerc, *Kition* 2, 82, no. 92.

Fig. 306. Cat. 299. Marion Cox.

Fig. 307. Cat. 300. The Metropolitan Museum of Art, The Cesnola Collection, purchased by subscription, 1874–76. (74. 51. 4145). Negative number 62574.

Fig. 308. Cat. 301. The Metropolitan Museum of Art, The Cesnola Collection, purchased by subscription, 1874–76. (74. 51. 4167). Negative number 247014tf.

Fig. 309. Cat. 302. The Metropolitan Museum of Art, The Cesnola Collection, purchased by subscription, 1874–76. (74. 51. 4217). Negative number 247060tf.

Fig. 310. Cat. 303. Clerc, *Kition* 2, 62, no. 755.

Fig. 311. Cat. 304. The Metropolitan Museum of Art, The Cesnola Collection, purchased by subscription, 1874–76. (74. 51. 4197). Negative number 88927tf.
Fig. 312. Cat. 306. Walters, *BM Gems*, 34–5, no. 281; pl. 5.
Fig. 313. Cat. 307. Author.
Fig. 314. Cat. 308. O. Masson, *Kadmos* 25 (1986), 162–3.
Fig. 315. Author.
Fig. 316. Cat. 309. Boardman, 'Seals and Amulets', pl. 3, no. 6.
Fig. 317. Cat. 310. Author.
Fig. 318. Cat. 311. J. Boardman and R. L. Wilkins; Marion Cox.
Fig. 319. Cat. 312. J. Boardman and R. L. Wilkins; Marion Cox.
Fig. 320. Cat. 313. Clerc, *Kition* 2, 107, no. 2021.
Fig. 321. Cat. 314. Ashmolean Museum, Oxford.
Fig. 322. Cat. 315. Boardman, 'Seals and Amulets', pl. 3, no. 2.
Fig. 323. Cat. 316. Boardman, 'Seals and Amulets', pl. 3, no. 9.
Fig. 324. Cat. 317. Boardman, 'Seals and Amulets', pl. 4, no. 2.
Fig. 325. Cat. 318. *SCE* 3, pl. 204. 23.b; Marion Cox.
Fig. 326. Cat. 319. *SCE* 3, pl. 204. 23.l; Marion Cox.
Fig. 327. Cat. 320. Author; Marion Cox.
Fig. 328. Cat. 321. J. Boardman and R. L. Wilkins; Marion Cox.
Fig. 329. Cat. 322. V. Karageorghis, *Excavations in the Necropolis of Salamis* 2 (1970), 139; pl. 170, no. 32.
Fig. 330. Cat. 323. Marion Cox.
Fig. 331. Cat. 324. Marion Cox.
Fig. 332. P. Zazoff, *Die antiken Gemmen* (1983), 71; Taf. 14. 2.
Fig. 333. Cat. 327. The Metropolitan Museum of Art, The Cesnola Collection, purchased by subscription, 1874–76. (74. 51. 4404). Negative number 62572.
Fig. 334. Cat. 328. J. Boardman and R. L. Wilkins; Marion Cox.
Fig. 335. Cat. 329. Ashmolean Museum, Oxford.
Fig. 336. Cat. 330. V. Karageorghis, *BCH* 112 (1988), 805; fig. 24.
Fig. 337. Cat. 331. J. Boardman and R. L. Wilkins.
Fig. 338. Cat. 332. Ashmolean Museum, Oxford.
Fig. 339. Cat. 333. Ashmolean Museum, Oxford.
Fig. 340. Cat. 334. Masson, *ICS*, 344, no. 353.
Fig. 341. Cat. 335. Vollenweider, *Geneva* 1, 74, no. 81; pl. 37.
Fig. 342. Cat. 336. Boardman, 'Seals and Amulets', pl. 3, no. 8.
Fig. 343. Cat. 337. J. Boardman and R. L. Wilkins; Marion Cox.
Fig. 344. Zwierlein-Diehl, *AGDS* 2, no. 129.
Fig. 345. Cat. 338. Author.
Fig. 346. Cat. 339. Author.
Fig. 347. Cat. 342. Marion Cox.
Fig. 348. Cat. 343. V. Karageorghis in *Charisterion eis A. K. Orlandon* 2 (1966), 108; fig. 11.
Fig. 349. Zwierlein-Diehl, *AGDS* 2, no. 88.
Fig. 350. Cat. 344. Boardman, *AGGems*, 94, no. 258; pl. 17.
Fig. 351. Cat. 345. Boardman, *GGFR*, 184; pl. 363.
Fig. 352. Cat. 346. Boardman, *AGGems*, 94, no. 257; pl. 17.
Fig. 353. Cat. 347. Boardman, *AGGems*, 94, no. 254; pl. 17.
Fig. 354. Cat. 348. Boardman, *AGGems*, 94, no. 255; pl. 17.
Fig. 355. Cat. 349. The Metropolitan Museum of Art, The Cesnola Collection, purchased by subscription, 1874–76. (74. 51. 4223). Negative number 135432.
Fig. 356. Cat. 350. Boardman, *AGGems*, 97, no. 274; pl. 18.

Fig. 357. Cat. 351. Boardman, *AGGems*, 97, no. 265; pl. 18.
Fig. 358. Cat. 352. Boardman, 'Seals and Amulets', pl. 6, no. 3.
Fig. 359. Cat. 353. Boardman, *AGGems*, 31, no. 41; pl. 3.
Fig. 360. Cat. 354. Boardman, *GGFR*, colour pl., after p. 148; Boardman, *AGGems*, 90.
Fig. 361. Cat. 355. Boardman, *AGGems*, 104, no. 299; pl. 20.
Fig. 362. Cat. 356. J. Boardman and R. L. Wilkins; The Metropolitan Museum of Art, The Cesnola Collection, purchased by subscription, 1874–76. (74. 51. 4152). Negative number 247264tf; 62574.
Fig. 363. Cat. 357. Boardman, *AGGems*, 104, no. 301; pl. 20.
Fig. 364. Cat. 358. Boardman, *AGGems*, 45, no. 71; pl. 5.
Fig. 365. Cat. 359. Boardman, *AGGems*, 46, no. 72; pl. 5.
Fig. 366. Cat. 360. Boardman, *AGGems*, 81, no. 206; pl. 13.
Fig. 367. Cat. 361. Boardman, *AGGems*, 98, no. 274; pl. 19.
Fig. 368. Vollenweider, *Geneva* 3, no. 181.
Fig. 369. Cat. 362. V. Karageorghis, *Excavations in the Necropolis of Salamis* 2 (1970), 114; 116.
Fig. 370. Cat. 363. Boardman, *AGGems*, 104, no. 295; pl. 20.
Fig. 371. Cat. 364. Boardman, *AGGems*, 46, no. 70; pl. 5.
Fig. 372. Boardman, *AGGems*, 36, no. 65.
Fig. 373. Cat. 366. J. Boardman, *Iran* 8 (1970), 26; 40, no. 12.
Fig. 374. Cat. 367. H. W. Catling, *Kadmos* 11 (1972), 62, no. 5 (Marion Cox).
Fig. 375. Cat. 368. Boardman, *AGGems*, 106, no. 307; pl. 21.
Fig. 376. Cat. 369. Boardman, *AGGems*, 31, no. 40; pl. 3.
Fig. 377. Boardman, *AGGems*, 36, no. 63; pl. 4.
Fig. 378. Cat. 370. Zwierlein-Diehl, *AGDS* 2, 47, no. 77; Taf. 21.
Fig. 379. Cat. 371. Boardman, *AGGems*, 104, no. 292; pl. 20.
Fig. 380. Cat. 372. The Metropolitan Museum of Art, The Cesnola Collection, purchased by subscription, 1874–76. (74. 51. 4194). Negative number 135859tf.
Fig. 381. Cat. 373. Boardman, *AGGems*, 91, no. 281; pl. 15.
Fig. 382. Cat. 374. Zwierlein-Diehl, *AGDS* 2, 68, no. 145.
Fig. 383. Cat. 375. The Metropolitan Museum of Art, The Cesnola Collection, purchased by subscription, 1874–76. (74. 51. 4224). Negative number 135188tf.
Fig. 384. Cat. 376. Boardman, *AGGems*, 106, no. 305; pl. 20.
Fig. 385. Cat. 377. W. Culican, *AJBA* 1 (1968), 97–100.
Fig. 386. Cat. 378. Murray *et al.*, *Excavations*, 98; pl. 4; fig. 6.
Fig. 387. Cat. 379. Author.
Fig. 388. Cat. 380. Marion Cox.
Fig. 389. Cat. 381. Boardman, *GGFR*, 185, pl. 385.
Fig. 390. Cat. 382. Boardman, *AGGems*, 132, no. 428; pl. 31.
Fig. 391. Cat. 383. Boardman, *GGFR*, 185; pl. 389.
Fig. 392a. Cat. 384. Boardman, *AGGems*, 154, no. 585; pl. 37.
Fig. 392b. Cat. 385. The Metropolitan Museum of Art, The Cesnola Collection, purchased by subscription, 1874–76. (74. 51. 4209). Negative number 247057tf.
Fig. 393. Cat. 386. Masson, *ICS*, 161, no. 121.
Fig. 394. Cat. 387. Boardman, *AGGems*, 148, no. 529; pl. 35.
Fig. 395. Cat. 388. Myres and Ohnefalsch-Richter, *CCM*, 81, no. 4584.
Fig. 396. Cat. 389. Ohnefalsch-Richter, *KBH*, 367; pl. 32.32.
Fig. 397. Cat. 390. Boardman, *AGGems*, 130, no. 421; pl. 30.
Fig. 398. Cat. 391. Boardman, *GGFR*, 185, pl. 384.
Fig. 399. Cat. 393. Boardman, *GGFR*, 185, pl. 386.
Fig. 400. Cat. 394. Boardman, *GGFR*, 186, pl. 391.

Fig. 401.   Cat. 395.   Boardman, *AGGems*, 133, no. 443; pl. 31.
Fig. 402.   Cat. 396.   Boardman, *AGGems*, 144, no. 476; pl. 33.
Fig. 403.   Cat. 397.   Boardman, *AGGems*, 144, no. 489; pl. 33.
Fig. 404.   Cat. 398.   Boardman, *AGGems*, 154, no. 583; pl. 37.
Fig. 405.   Cat. 399.   Boardman, *AGGems*, 145, no. 503; pl. 33.
Fig. 406.   Cat. 400.   The Metropolitan Museum of Art, The Cesnola Collection, purchased by
            subscription, 1874–76. (74. 51. 4195). Negative number 135179tf.
Fig. 407.   Cat. 401.   Boardman, *AGGems*, 148, no. 523; pl. 35.
Fig. 408.   Cat. 402.   Boardman, *AGGems*, 150, no. 651; pl. 36.
Fig. 409.   Cat. 403.   J. Boardman, *The Ralph Harari Collection of Finger Rings* (1977), no. 3.
Fig. 410.   Cat. 404.   Boardman, *AGGems*, 147, no. 520; pl. 34.
Fig. 411.   Cat. 405.   Boardman, *GGFR*, 183; pl. 341 (left); Boardman, *AGGems*, pl. 37, no. 589
            (right).
Fig. 412.   Cat. 406.   Boardman, *GGFR*, 183; pl. 336.
Fig. 413.   Cat. 407.   Boardman and Vollenweider, *Ashmolean Gems*, 14, no. 68.
Fig. 414.   Cat. 408.   G. M. A. Richter, *Engraved Gems of the Greeks and Etruscans* (1968), no. 109.
Fig. 415.   Cat. 410.   Boardman, *AGGems*, 99, no. 281; pl. 19.
Fig. 416.   Cat. 411.   Boardman, *AGGems*, 105, no. 304; pl. 20.
Fig. 417.   Cat. 412.   Boardman, *AGGems*, 96, no. 260; pl. 17.
Fig. 418.   Cat. 413.   The Metropolitan Museum of Art, The Cesnola Collection, purchased by
            subscription, 1874–76. (74. 51. 4225). Negative number 135186tf.
Fig. 419.   Cat. 414.   Boardman, *AGGems*, 78, no. 181; pl. 32.
Fig. 420.   Cat. 415.   The Metropolitan Museum of Art, The Cesnola Collection, purchased by
            subscription, 1874–76. (74. 51. 4221). Negative number 135185tf.
Fig. 421.   Cat. 416.   The Metropolitan Museum of Art, The Cesnola Collection, purchased by
            subscription, 1874–76. (74. 51. 4173). Negative number 135183tf.
Fig. 422.   Cat. 418.   Boardman, *AGGems*, 97, no. 267; pl. 18.
Fig. 423.   Cat. 419.   The Metropolitan Museum of Art, The Cesnola Collection, purchased by
            subscription, 1874–76. (74. 51. 4201). Negative number 135182tf.
Fig. 424.   Cat. 420.   Boardman, *AGGems*, 99, no. 286; pl. 19.
Fig. 425.   Cat. 421.   Walters, *BM Gems*, 86, no. 692; pl. 12.
Fig. 426.   Cat. 422.   Boardman, *AGGems*, 60, no. 111; pl. 8.
Fig. 427.   Cat. 423.   Marion Cox.
Fig. 428.   Cat. 424.   Boardman, *AGGems*, 78, no. 184; pl. 12.
Fig. 429.   Cat. 425.   Boardman, *GGFR*, 287; pl. 457.
Fig. 430.   Cat. 426.   The Metropolitan Museum of Art, The Cesnola Collection, purchased by
            subscription, 1874–76. (74. 51. 4146). Negative number 88949tf; 62574.
Fig. 431.   Cat. 427.   Boardman, *AGGems*, 83–4, no. 226; pl. 14.
Fig. 432.   Cat. 428.   D. M. Robinson, *AJA* 57 (1953), pl. 24. 47
Fig. 433.   Cat. 429.   Boardman, *AGGems*, 83, no. 224; pl. 14.
Fig. 434.   Cat. 430.   The Metropolitan Museum of Art, The Cesnola Collection, purchased by
            subscription, 1874–76. (74. 51. 4210). Negative number 135192LS.
Fig. 435.   Cat. 431.   Boardman, *GGFR*, 351–2; pl. 847.
Fig. 436.   Cat. 432.   Ashmolean Museum, Oxford.
Fig. 437.   E. Gubel, *Studia Phoenicia* 5 (1987), 213, fig. 12.
Fig. 438.   E. Gubel, *Studia Phoenicia* 5 (1987), 213, fig. 11.
Fig. 439.   P. Bielinski, *Berytus* 23 (1974), 53–69.
Fig. 440.   Cat. 433.   J. Boardman and R. L. Wilkins; Marion Cox.
Fig. 441.   Cat. 434.   Boardman, 'Seals and Amulets', pl. 1, no. 3.
Fig. 442.   Cat. 435.   Boardman, 'Seals and Amulets', pl. 2, no. 2.

Fig. 443. Cat. 436. Boardman, 'Seals and Amulets', pl. 1, no. 2.
Fig. 444. Cat. 437. Boardman, 'Seals and Amulets', pl. 2, no. 4.
Fig. 445. Cat. 438. Murray *et al.*, *Excavations*, 99, fig. 147, no. 40.
Fig. 446. Cat. 439. Boardman, 'Seals and Amulets', p. 2, no. 1.
Fig. 447. Cat. 440. Author.
Fig. 448. Cat. 441. J. Boardman and R. L. Wilkins; Marion Cox.
Fig. 449. Cat. 442. V. Karageorghis, *BCH* 94 (1970), 210; fig. 34.
Fig. 450. Cat. 443. E. Gubel, *Studia Phoenicia* 5 (1987), 201.
Fig. 451. Cat. 444. M. Arwe in J. C. Biers and D. Soren, eds., *Studies in Cypriote Archaeology* (1981), 144.
Fig. 452. Cat. 445. Buchanan and Moorey, *Ashmolean* 3, 83, no. 569; pl. 18.
Fig. 453. Cat. 446. E. Gubel, *Studia Phoenicia* 5 (1987), 215; fig. 14.
Fig. 454. Cat. 447. E. Gubel, *Studia Phoenicia* 5 (1987), 206–7; fig. 9.
Fig. 455. Cat. 448. E. Gubel, *Studia Phoenicia* 5 (1987), 203, fig. 8.
Fig. 456. Cat. 449. E. Gubel, *Studia Phoenicia* 5 (1987), 219; fig. 15.
Fig. 457. Cat. 450. E. Gubel, *Studia Phoenicia* 5 (1987), 209; fig. 10 (top); Ohnefalsch-Richter, *KBH*, pl. 118, no. 7 (bottom).
Fig. 458. Cat. 451. E. Gubel, *Studia Phoenicia* 5 (1987), 202; fig. 7.
Fig. 459a. Cat. 452. Vollenweider, *Geneva* 1, 137, no. 183; pl. 72.
Fig. 459b. Cat. 453. The Metropolitan Museum of Art, The Cesnola Collection, purchased by subscription, 1874–76. (74. 51. 4381). Negative number 182388tf.
Fig. 460. Cat. 454. The Metropolitan Museum of Art, The Cesnola Collection, purchased by subscription, 1874–76. (74. 51. 4380). Negative number 62573.
Fig. 461. Cat. 455. Zwierlein-Diehl, *AGDS* 2, 62, no. 125; Taf. 30.
Fig. 462. Cat. 456. Zwierlein-Diehl, *AGDS* 2, 63, no. 126; Taf. 30.
Fig. 463. Cat. 457. Author.
Fig. 464. Cat. 459. Marion Cox.
Fig. 465. Cat. 460. Marion Cox.
Fig. 466. Cat. 461. Marion Cox.
Fig. 467. Cat. 462. J. Boardman and R. L. Wilkins; Marion Cox.
Fig. 468. Cat. 463. J. Boardman and R. L. Wilkins; Marion Cox.
Fig. 469. Cat. 464. The Metropolitan Museum of Art, The Cesnola Collection, purchased by subscription, 1874–76. (74. 51. 4387). Negative number 142376–7tf.
Fig. 470. Cat. 465. Author.
Fig. 471. Cat. 466. Marion Cox.
Fig. 472. Cat. 467. Marion Cox.
Fig. 473. Cat. 468. Marion Cox.
Fig. 474. Cat. 469. Author.
Fig. 475. Cat. 470. Author.
Fig. 476. Cat. 471. Author.
Fig. 477. Cat. 472. J. Boardman and R. L. Wilkins.
Fig. 478. Cat. 473. Author.
Fig. 479. Cat. 474. Marion Cox.
Fig. 480a. Cat. 475. Marion Cox.
Fig. 480b. Cat. 476. The Metropolitan Museum of Art, The Cesnola Collection, purchased by subscription, 1874–76. (74. 51. 4395). Negative number 62572.
Fig. 481. Cat. 477. The Metropolitan Museum of Art, The Cesnola Collection, purchased by subscription, 1874–76. (74. 51. 4396). Negative number 62572.
Fig. 482. Cat. 478. Marion Cox.
Fig. 483. Author.

Fig. 484. Cat. 480. Marion Cox.
Fig. 485. Cat. 481. Marion Cox.
Fig. 486. Cat. 482. Marion Cox.
Fig. 487. Cat. 483. Marion Cox.
Fig. 488. Cat. 484. Marion Cox.
Fig. 489. Cat. 485. Ashmolean Museum, Oxford.
Fig. 490. Cat. 486. Marion Cox.
Fig. 491. Cat. 487. Marion Cox.
Fig. 492. Cat. 488. Marion Cox.
Fig. 493. Cat. 489. Ashmolean Museum, Oxford.
Fig. 494. Cat. 490. Marion Cox.
Fig. 495. Cat. 491. J. Boardman and R. L. Wilkins.
Fig. 496. Cat. 493. J. Boardman and R. L. Wilkins; Marion Cox.
Fig. 497. Cat. 494. The Metropolitan Museum of Art, The Cesnola Collection, purchased by subscription, 1874–76. (74. 51. 4394). Negative number 62572.
Fig. 498. Cat. 495. J. Boardman, *Iran* 8 (1970) 40, no. 15; fig. 6; Marion Cox.
Fig. 499. Cat. 496. J. Boardman and R. L. Wilkins; Marion Cox.
Fig. 500. Cat. 497. J. Boardman and R. L. Wilkins.
Fig. 501. Cat. 498. Boardman, 'Seals and Amulets', pl. 3, no. 1.
Fig. 502. Cat. 499. Boardman, 'Seals and Amulets', pl. 3, no. 3.
Fig. 503. Cat. 500. The Metropolitan Museum of Art, The Cesnola Collection, purchased by subscription, 1874–76. (74. 51. 4397). Negative number 62572.
Fig. 504. Cat. 501. Forgeau, *Amathonte* 3, 58, no. 49.
Fig. 505. Cat. 502. Author; Marion Cox.
Fig. 506. Cat. 503. Author.
Fig. 507. Cat. 504. Clerc, *Kition* 2, 112, no. 3737.
Fig. 508. Cat. 505. Marion Cox.
Fig. 509. Cat. 508. Marion Cox.
Fig. 510. Cat. 509. Ashmolean Museum, Oxford.
Fig. 511. Cat. 510. Marion Cox.
Fig. 512. Cat. 511. Author.
Fig. 513. Cat. 513. Zwierlein-Diehl, *AGDS* 2, 64, no. 130.
Fig. 514. Cat. 514. Boardman, *GGFR*, 183; pl. 344.
Fig. 515. Cat. 515. Marion Cox.
Fig. 516. Cat. 516. Author.
Fig. 517. Cat. 517. Author.
Fig. 518. Cat. 518. Marion Cox.
Fig. 519. Cat. 519. Author; Marion Cox.
Fig. 520. Cat. 522. Author.
Fig. 521. Cat. 523. Author.
Fig. 522. Cat. 524. Author.
Fig. 523. Cat. 526. Author.
Fig. 524. Cat. 527. J. Boardman and R. L. Wilkins; Marion Cox.
Fig. 525. Ashmolean Museum, Oxford.
Fig. 526. Ashmolean Museum, Oxford.
Fig. 527. Cat. 528. The Metropolitan Museum of Art, The Cesnola Collection, purchased by subscription, 1874–76. (74. 51. 5010). Negative number 233496tf.
Fig. 528. Cat. 529. V. Karageorghis, *BCH* 113 (1989), 798, 804; fig. 43.
Fig. 529a. Cat. 531. Author.

Fig. 529b. Cat. 532. The Metropolitan Museum of Art, The Cesnola Collection, purchased by subscription, 1874–76. (74. 51. 1361). Negative number 84704ff.

Fig. 530. Cat. 533. V. Karageorghis, *Blacks in Ancient Cypriot Art* (1988), 15, no. 6.

Fig. 531. Cat. 534. V. Karageorghis, *Excavations in the Necropolis of Salamis* 2 (1970), 168–9; pl. 49.

Fig. 532. Vollenweider, *Geneva* 3, 113–5, no. 156.

Fig. 533. Vollenweider, *Geneva* 3, 115–6. no. 157.

Fig. 534. Vollenweider, *Geneva* 3, 117, no. 159.

Fig. 535. Cat. 536. The Metropolitan Museum of Art, The Cesnola Collection, purchased by subscription, 1874–76. (74. 51. 4362). Negative number 93291.

Fig. 536. Cat. 537. The Metropolitan Museum of Art, The Cesnola Collection, purchased by subscription, 1874–76. (74. 51. 4368). Negative number 93291.

Fig. 537. Cat. 538. The Metropolitan Museum of Art, The Cesnola Collection, purchased by subscription, 1874–76. (74. 51. 4379). Negative number 62573.

Fig. 538. Cat. 540. The Metropolitan Museum of Art, The Cesnola Collection, purchased by subscription, 1874–76. (74. 51. 4384). Negative number 62574.

Fig. 539. Cat. 541. The Metropolitan Museum of Art, The Cesnola Collection, purchased by subscription, 1874–76. (74. 51. 4388). Negative number 62573.

Fig. 540. Cat. 542. The Metropolitan Museum of Art, The Cesnola Collection, purchased by subscription, 1874–76. (74. 51. 4390). Negative number 62573.

Fig. 541. Cat. 543. Author.

NOTES

1   Athen. 689b = B. Snell, ed., *Tragicorum Graecorum Fragmenta* 1(Göttingen, 1971), 117 (20F5).

2   Below, chapter 4.

3   Pliny, *HN* 37. 3. 6.

4   E. Porada, 'The Cylinder Seals of the Late Cypriote Bronze Age', *AJA* 52 (1948), 178–98. Cf. B. Teissier, *Ancient Near Eastern Cylinder Seals from the Marcopoli Collection* (Berkeley, 1984), 99; D. Collon, *First Impressions* (London, 1987), 73–4.

5   As a recent editorialist for the *New York Times* put it, commenting on the still-prevalent significance of Professor Porada's work on the understanding of ancient and modern society: '... to awaken the past by one's commitment to it, to become the matrix where past and present converge, that was Porada's culture' (V. Klinkenborg, 'One Scholar and the Matrix of the Past', *New York Times* (1 March 1998), 14).

6   On the need for such a study: Boardman, *AGGems*, 25, n. 17; P. Zazoff, *Die antiken Gemmen* (Munich, 1983), 69 and n. 26; H. W. Catling, 'The Seal of Pasitimos' *Kadmos* 11 (1972), 73; Buchanan and Moorey, *Ashmolean* 3, 79.

7   Myres, *HCC*, 45–53; for Kenna's extensive work on Cypriot glyptic of the Late Bronze Age, see the bibliography.

8   A. Furtwängler, *Die antiken Gemmen* (Leipzig and Berlin, 1900), 18.

9   See, e.g., V. E. G. Kenna, 'The Seal Use of Cyprus in the Bronze Age', *BCH* 92 (1968), 142–56; id., 'Cyprus and the Aegean World: The Evidence of Seals III', in *The Mycenaeans in the Eastern Mediterranean* (Nicosia, 1973), 290–1; Myres *HCC*, 434, and note the term 'Cypro-Mycenaean'. Myres, however, was more apt to recognise the Near Eastern characteristics of Cypriot glyptic than Kenna supposed: cf. V. E. G. Kenna in *SCE* 4. 1D, 623, n. 1.

10   E.g., Zazoff (n. 6), 65–75; cf. Y. L. Holmes, 'The Foreign Trade of Cyprus during the Late Bronze Age', in N. Robertson, ed., *The Archaeology of Cyprus: Recent Developments* (New Jersey, 1975), 106, n. 88 ('...examples from Cyprus, beginning before LCIIC, contained no discernible Near Eastern motifs.').

11   E.g., Myres and Ohnefalsch-Richter, *CCM*, 135–6; Walters, *BM Gems*, 31f.

12   Myres, *HCC*, 442–53.

13   Ibid., xxi–xxii; 442.

14   Furtwängler (n. 8), 67: '...Cyperns Kunst hatte immer nur eine lokale Bedeutung.'

15   The terminology for glazed materials is confusing, since archaeologists have traditionally used definitions which need bear no relation to scientific reality; see P. R. S. Moorey, *Ancient Mesopotamian Materials and Industries* (Oxford, 1994), 166–68. I have used the terms 'glazed material' and 'glazed stone' to describe objects of faience or glazed white steatite and have also assumed that when, in older literature, 'paste' or 'porcelain' is used, glass, faience, or some sort of glazed stone is indicated. For 'frit', see Moorey, above, 167: 'sintered polycrystalline bodies and no glaze'.

16   Rings: J. Boardman, 'Cypriot Finger Rings' *BSA* 65 (1970), 5–15, and for further examples, see also E. Porada, 'A Seal Ring and Two Cylinder Seals from Hala Sultan Tekke' in P. Åström *et al.*, *Hala Sultan Tekke* 8 (Göteborg, 1983), 218–9, fig. 54; Karageorghis, *Salamis* 2, 20, no. 84; 23, pl. 5, no. 84; 114, no. 10; 116; pl. 153, no. 10; id., *Kition* (London, 1976), colour pl. V, opp. p. 82; id., *Palaepaphos-Skales* (Konstanz, 1983), 379–83, pl. 125, no. 40. Glazed materials, glass, and frit: A. Gorton, *Egyptian and Egyptianizing Scarabs* (Oxford, 1996); G. Hölbl, *Beziehungen der agyptischen Kultur zu Altitalien* 1(Leiden, 1979); id., *Agyptisches Kulturgut im phönikischen und punischen Sardinien* 1 (Leiden, 1986); id., 'Die Aegyptiaca von Kition' *Orientalia* 51 (1982), 259–64; G. Pisano, 'Jewellery' in R. D. Barnett and C.

Mendleson, *Tharros* (London, 1987), 78–95. See also J. Boardman, 'Orientalia and Orientals in Ischia' *Annali di Archeologia e Storia Antica*, new series 1 (1994), 95–100.

17　　Amathus: Forgeau, *Amathonte* 3, 135–76; Ayia Irini: *SCE* 2, 826–30; 833–44; Kition: Charles, 'Pyrga', 1–21 ; Clerc, *Kition* 2. An important cultural relationship seems thereby indicated between these three areas, but isolated finds of frit or glazed scarabs are known from elsewhere around Cyprus: e.g., Marion (*SCE* 2, 826); Idalion (*SCE* 2, 826, 833); Salamis (J.-C. Goyon, 'Un Scarabée de Salamine' in *Salamine de Chypre, histoire et archeologie* (Paris, 1980), 137–9).

18　　Hölbl, *Beziehungen* (n. 16), 220–1 with 372; Gorton (n. 16), 103, and see also 41–2 on Egyptian scarabs, particularly from Naukratis, imported into Cyprus; 62–3 on Levantine imports; and 125–6 on imports from the Greek islands, especially Rhodes.

19　　L. P. di Cesnola, *Cyprus* (London, 1877), 302–37 and 353–89 for comments by C. W. King. For recent assessments, see D. Soren and J. James, *Kourion* (New York, 1988), 176–7; Markoe, *Bowls*, 176–7, n. 19 with references; O. Masson, 'Cesnola et le trésor de Curium' *Cahiers: Centre d'études chypriotes* 1 (1984), 16–25; id., 'Cesnola et le trésor de Curium' *Cahiers: Centre d'études chypriotes* 2 (1984), 3–15. Note also Collon, *BM Cat* 3, 125, no. 255, where it is established that at least one of the cylinder seals which Cesnola claimed was in the Kourion Treasure had actually been in the British Museum since 1825 and had previously been in the Rich Collection.

20　　V. Karageorghis, 'Chronique des fouilles et découvertes archéologiques à Chypre en 1961' *BCH* 86 (1962), 365–72.

21　　L. Rocchetti, *Le Tombe dei Periodi Geometrice ed Arcaico della Necropoli a Mare di Ayia Irini 'Palaeokastro'* (Rome, 1978).

22　　*SCE* 2, 810–20.

23　　Following *SCE* 2, 818; at 219, Gjerstad wrote that period 4 defines 'the later part of CAI and the beginning of CAII.'

24　　B. Lewe, *Studien zur archaischen kyprischen Plastik* (Frankfurt, 1975), 64–92.

25　　Note H. Kyrieleis, 'New Cypriot Finds from the Heraion of Samos' in V. Tatton-Brown, ed., *Cyprus and the East Mediterranean in the Iron Age* (London, 1989), 52–64; id., 'The Relations between Samos and the Eastern Mediterranean: Some Aspects' in V. Karageorghis, ed., *The Civilizations of the Aegean and their Diffusion in Cyprus and the Eastern Mediterranean, 2000-600 BC* (Larnaca, 1991), 129–32.

26　　For a history of research on the site, see P. Aupert, *Guide d'Amathonte* (Paris, 1996).

27　　C. Tytgat, *Les Nécropoles sud-ouest et sud-est d'Amathonte: 1. Les Tombes 110-385* (Nicosia, 1989).

28　　V. E. G. Kenna, 'The Seal Use of Cyprus in the Bronze Age' *BCH* 91 (1967), 255–68; Kenna, *BM Cypriote Seals*, 7–10.

29　　*SCE* 4. 1D, 622–74.

30　　Khirokitia: P. Dikaios, *Khirokitia* (London, 1953), 287–98. Paphos: E. J. Peltenburg, 'Lemba Archaeological Project, Cyprus, 1976–77' *Levant* 11 (1979), 29–30 (cf. E. Goring *A Mischievous Pastime* (Edinburgh, 1988), 53, no. 35); id., 'Lemba Archaeological Project, Cyprus, 1985' *Levant* 19 (1987), 221; id., *Lemba Archaeological Project I: Excavations at Lemba Lakkous, 1976-1983* (Göteborg, 1985), 289; pl. 47.11; fig. 85.5; id., 'Kissonerga-Mosphilia: A Major Chalcolithic Site in Cyprus' *BASOR* 282/283 (1991), 17–35; id., *Lemba Archaeological Project II.1A: Excavations at Kissonerga-Mosphilia, 1979-1992* (Jonsered, 1998), 196, 200; pl. 37.12, 13; fig. 102.6, 7.

31　　P. Flourentzos, *Excavations in the Kouris Valley 1: The Tombs* (Nicosia, 1991), 15, pl. 14, no. 1.

32　　An alleged sealing also from Mosphilia may, in fact, be part of a figurine: Peltenburg, *Lemba Archaeological Project II. 1A* (n. 30), 200. Vollenweider, *Geneva* 3, 101–2, no. 141, a rectangular plaque without a stringhole from Paphos, identified as a stamp-seal of the third millennium, may not be a seal at all.

33　　Peltenburg, *Lemba Archaeological Project II. 1A* (n. 30), 196.

34　　H. W. Catling in *CAH*[3] 2.1, 173; for some early seals that are probably spurious additions to the Cypriot corpus, see Appendix 1.

35　　Kenna (n. 28), 255–68; Kenna's no. 11 and 12 are properly dated to the end of the Late Bronze Age. Of other items cited by Kenna, no. 1 was found in a Cypro-Archaic tomb and may date to that time; no. 2 has a Late Bronze Age context; no. 5, 9, and 10 find parallels for both shape and style in Late Bronze Age seals excavated at Enkomi; no. 3 and 7 are typical Late Bronze Age conoids; no. 4 and 6 are limestone seals, on which, see further below; no. 8 may be compared to R. S. Lamon and G. M. Shipton, *Megiddo* 1 (Chicago, 1939), pl. 73, no. 6.

36 E. Peltenburg, 'From Isolation to State Formation in Cyprus, c. 3500–1500 B. C.' in V. Karageorghis and D. Michaelides, eds., *The Development of the Cypriot Economy from the Prehistoric Period to the Present Day* (Nicosia, 1996), 22–3.

37 For examples of Cypriot cylinders which have been scientifically tested, see J. Johnson, *Maroni de Chypre* (Göteborg, 1980), 34, no. 250; 70–1, pl. IXL (after pl. 48); Vollenweider, *Geneva* 3, 111, no. 153; pl. 153.

38 On sources for serpentine, see C. Xenophontos, 'Picrolite, Its Nature, Provenance, and Possible Distribution Patterns in the Chalcolithic Period of Cyprus', *BASOR* 282/283 (1991), 127–38.

39 Rock crystal: e.g., J. L. Benson, *Bamboula at Kourion* (Philadelphia, 1972), 145–7, pl. 38; Johnson (n. 37), 35; pl. IXL (after pl. 48), no. 254. Haematite: e.g., T. Dothan and A. Ben-Tor, *Excavations at Athienou, Cyprus*. Qedem 16 (Jerusalem, 1983), 118–9; pl. 381–2; C. F. A. Schaeffer, *Enkomi-Alasia* 1 (Paris, 1952), 77–8.

40 J. DuPlat Taylor, 'A Late Bronze Age Settlement at Apliki, Cyprus' *AJ* 32 (1952), 163, pl. 26b; 166, no. 6; O. Masson, 'Cylindres et cachets chypriotes portant des caractères chypro-minoens' *BCH* 81 (1957), 19–20, fig. 14; K. Nicolaou, 'A Late Cypriote Necropolis at Yeroskipou, Paphos' *RDAC* (1983), 144, pl. 20.5; E. Porada, 'Cylinder and Stamp-Seals' in A. South, P. Russell, and P. S. Kewsani, *Kalavassos-Ayios-Dhimitrios* 2 (Göteborg, 1989), 35–7. Two conoids and an additional scarab, all of serpentine, are reported from Yeroskipou, from a tomb dated generally to the Late Bronze Age: A. Papageorghiou, *Annual Report of the Department of Antiquities for the Year 1990* (Nicosia, 1991), 68.

41 Apliki and Yeroskipou: n. 40; Kalavassos: e. g., D. Christou, 'Chronique des fouilles et découvertes archéologiques à Chypre en 1995', *BCH* 120 (1996) 1076–7.

42 J. Leclant, 'Appendix 3: Les Scarabées de la tombe 9' in V. Karageorghis, *Excavations at Kition* 1 (London, 1974), 148–50; R.-P. Charles, 'Appendix 2: Les Scarabées égyptiens d'Enkomi' in P. Dikaios, *Enkomi* 3 (Mainz, 1971), 819–23. See also I. Jacobsson, *Aegyptiaca from Late Bronze Age Cyprus* (Jonsered, 1994), 47–55.

43 E. Vermeule, *Toumba tou Skourou* (Boston, 1974), fig. 61; E. Vermeule and F. Wolsky, 'The Bone and Ivory of Toumba tou Skourou' *RDAC* (1977), 86–7, pl. 18.

44 Vermeule and Wolsky (n. 43), 87.

45 E. Hornung and E. Staehlin, *Skarabäen und anderen Siegelamulette* (Mainz, 1976), 23; bone is not listed as a scarab material in W. M. F. Petrie, *Scarabs and Cylinders with Names* (London, 1917), 8–9.

46 *SCE* 4. 1D, 607–8.

47 Rowe, *Scarabs*, 222, no. SO 5; SO 8; O. Tufnell, *Lachish* 3 (London, 1953), 370, no. 62–7, 71, and 76.

48 Schaeffer (n. 39), 87–9.

49 Dikaios (n. 42), pl. 95.3; 183–4; 197, no. 19, and frontispiece; J. D. Muhly, 'The Role of the Sea Peoples in Cyprus during the LCIII Period' in V. Karageorghis and J. D. Muhly, eds., *Cyprus at the Close of the Late Bronze Age* (Nicosia, 1984), 45–6; cf. T. Dothan, *The Philistines and their Material Culture* (Jerusalem, 1982), 274.

50 Cf. H. Keel-Leu, 'Die Herkunft der Konoide in Palästina/Israel' in O. Keel, M. Shuval, and C. Uehlinger, *Studien zu den Stempelsiegeln aus Palästina/Israel* 3 (Göttingen, 1996), 378–9.

51 E. Porada, 'Appendix 1: Seals' in Dikaios (n. 42), 801; ead., 'Glyptics' in J. L. Benson, *Bamboula at Kourion* (Philadelphia, 1972), 145.

52 For an example of a tabloid with a Late Bronze Age archaeological context (c. 1230 B.C.), see V. E. G. Kenna, 'Appendix V: A Marble Seal from Kazaphani T. 2' in I. Nicolaou and K. Nicolaou, *Kazaphani: A Middle/Late Cypriot Tomb at Kazaphani in Ayios Andronikos: T. 2A, B* (Nicosia, 1989), 115; pl. 39, no. 540.

53 Cf. E. Porada, 'Cylinder and Stamp-Seals' in V. Karageorghis and M. Demas, *Excavations at Kition* 5.2 (Nicosia, 1985), 253. For the shape, see J.-C. Courtois, E. Lagarce, and J. Lagarce, *Enkomi et le Bronze Recent à Chypre* (Nicosia, 1986), pl. 32, no. 30 and A. Caubet and J.-C. Courtois, 'Un Modèle de foie d'Enkomi' *RDAC* (1986), 74.

54 Cf. Caubet and Courtois (n. 53), 74–5, fig. 7; pl. 19.5 with B. Buchanan, *Catalogue of Ancient Near Eastern Seals in the Ashmolean Museum* 1 (Oxford, 1966), 253.

55 Head-seals: e.g., Dikaios (n. 30), 803, no. 19a; pl. 184; 188; 197. 19a; cf. also Vollenweider, *Geneva* 3, 115, no. 157; pl. 157 (unprovenanced) with Karageorghis and Demas (n. 53), 253; pl. B (LC context). Tabloids: e.g., *SCE* 2, 564–5, pl. 185 (LCIIIA context); Vollenweider, *Geneva* 3, 105, no. 145; 130, no. 149; pl. 68.169; Kenna (n. 28), 259, no. 11 (cf. 265, no. 11, incorrectly drawn); Buchanan and Moorey, *Ashmolean* 3, 78, no. 530; pl. 17. The above are made of dark serpentine. For a tabloid of pale green

serpentine, see F. G. Maier and V. Karageorghis, *Paphos* (Nicosia, 1984), 66–7, fig. 47–8. Note also Ohnefalsch-Richter, *KBH*, pl. 121, no. 10–1; E. Porada, 'Appendix 1: Relief Friezes and Seals from Maa-Palaeokastro' in V. Karageorghis and M. Demas, *Excavations at Maa-Palaeokastro* (Nicosia, 1988), 306; pl. G, no. 8 (from Maa). P. Åström, *Hala Sultan Tekke* 1 (Göteborg, 1976), 103–4, fig. 81 (blue faience) is probably imported.

56   Dikaios (n. 42), 809–10, no. 33. Cf. M. F. von Oppenheim, *Tell Halaf* 1 (Berlin, 1943), Taf. 38. 15; M. Dunand, *Fouilles de Byblos* 1 (Paris, 1939), pl. 134. 5217a.

57   Buchanan and Moorey, *Ashmolean* 3, 79, no. 536; pl. 17.

58   Dikaios (n. 42), 804, no. 20; pl. 183–4; 187.20; cf. J. H. Betts, *Die Schweizer Sammlungen. CMS* 10 (Berlin, 1980), 168, no. 174, 175; 170, no. 178, 179.

59   Porada (n. 51), 145.

60   P. Åström and E. Masson, 'Un Cachet de Hala Sultan Tekke' *RDAC* (1981), 99–100.

61   E.g., Masson (n. 40), 23, no. 17.

62   E. Porada, 'Appendix 1: Seals', in Dikaios (n. 42), 806, no. 23.

63   Ead. (n. 62), 801, no. 19. On the complex, see, e. g., A. B. Knapp, 'The Bronze Age Economy of Cyprus', in V. Karageorghis and D. Michaelides, eds., *The Development of the Cypriot Economy* (Nicosia, 1996), 78. On the findspots of the Enkomi cylinder-seals, see, in general, J.-C. Courtois and J. M. Webb, *Les Cylindres-Sceaux d'Enkomi* (Nicosia, 1987), 4–21.

64   Idalion: *SCE* 2, 591–2; Bamboula: Porada (n. 51), 145–7.

65   *SCE* 1, 356, 359, 361.

66   For a gold setting, see, e.g., Johnson (n. 37), pl. IXL (after pl. 48); for bronze, note Courtois *et al.* (n. 53), pl. 32, no. 7. On the identification of talismanic gems in the Aegean, see V. E. G. Kenna, The Cretan Talismanic Stone in the Late Minoan Age (Lund, 1969); A. Onassoglu, *Die 'Talismanischen' Siegel* (Berlin, 1985); E. F. Bloedow, 'Minoan Talismanic Goats' *Journal of Prehistoric Religion* 6 (1992), 15–23.

67   E. Lagarce, 'Remarques sur l'utilisation des scarabées, scaraboïdes, amulettes, et figurines de type égyptien à Chypre' in Clerc, *Kition* 2, 170; cf. J. Karageorghis, *La grande Déesse de Chypre et son culte* (Lyon, 1977), 104; H. W. Catling, 'A Cypriot Bronze Statuette in the Bomford Collection' in C. F. A. Schaeffer, *Alasia* 1 (Paris, 1971), 20.

68   *SCE* 2, 562, no. 1217; pl. 186, no. 3.

69   E.g., J. L. Benson, 'Aegean and Near Eastern Seal Impressions from Cyprus' in S. S. Weinberg, ed., *The Aegean and the Near East: Studies Presented to Hetty Goldman* (Locust Valley, New York, 1956), 59–77; Porada (n. 55), 301f. Note also Ohnefalsch-Richter, *KBH*, pl. 127.5; Maier and Karageorghis (n. 55), 95–6, fig. 80; C. F. A. Schaeffer, 'Les Fouilles de Ras-Shamra' *Syria* 15 (1934), 118, 123, fig. 8 (right) for an impression found at Ugarit, made by a Cypriot cylinder.

70   But note, at Hala Sultan Tekke, an imported Canaanite jar with a stamped handle: P. Åström, 'A Handle Stamped with the Cartouche of Seti I from Hala Sultan Tekke in Cyprus' *OpAth* 5 (1964), 115–22. An LCII/III pithos from Paphos is stamped with a circular seal, but its device is difficult to construe from the photograph alone: V. Karageorghis, 'Chronique des fouilles et découvertes archéologiques à Chypre', *BCH* 101 (1977), 760–1, fig. 89.

71   P. Ferioli and E. Fiandra, 'The Use of Clay Sealings in Administrative Functions from the Fifth to First Millennium B. C. in the Orient, Nubia, Egypt, and the Aegean: Similarities and Differences' in T. G. Palaima, *Aegaeum 5: Aegean Seals, Sealings, and Administration: Proceedings of the NEH-Dickson Conference of the Program in Aegean Scripts and Prehistory of the Department of Classics, University of Texas at Austin, January 11-13, 1989* (Liège, 1990), 221–29.

72   V. E. G. Kenna, 'The Seal Use of Cyprus in the Bronze Age III' *BCH* 92 (1968), 143.

73   Id., 'Studies of Birds on Seals of the Aegean and Eastern Mediterranean in the Bronze Age' *OpAth* 8 (1964), 23–38.

74   For Mycenaean sphinxes, cf. J. G. Younger, *The Iconography of Late Minoan and Mycenaean Sealstones and Finger-Rings* (Bristol, 1988), 213; H. Demisch, *Die Sphinx* (Stuttgart, 1977), 64–74; on the Berlin conoid: Zwierlein-Diehl, *AGDS* 2, 40, no. 63; Taf. 16.64; cf. I. Pini, 'Kypro-Ägäische Rollsiegel' *JdAI* 95 (1980), 106; Abb. 19; H. W. Catling, *Cypriot Bronzework in the Mycenaean World* (Oxford, 1964), pl. 23b-c. On the Minoan genius, see D. Sansone, 'The Survival of the Bronze Age Demon' *Illinois Classical Studies* 13 (1988), 1–17.

75   A. M. Bisi, 'L'Iconografia del grifone a Cipro' *Oriens Antiquus* 1 (1962), 219–32.

76 V. Karageorghis, 'Some Aspects of the Maritime Trade of Cyprus During the Late Bronze Age' in V. Karageorghis and D. Michaelides, eds., *The Development of the Cypriot Economy from the Prehistoric Period to the Present Day* (Nicosia, 1996), 61–70. Note also, for a possible Middle Minoan glyptic import into Cyprus, J. M. Webb, *Corpus of Cypriote Antiquities 12: Cypriote Antiquities in the Abbey Museum, Queensland, Australia* (Gothenburg, 1986), 40. On Minoan influences on Near Eastern glyptic, see J. Aruz, 'Imagery and Interconnections' *Egypt and the Levant* 5 (1995), 33–48.

77 From Enkomi, note Dikaios (n. 42), 807, no. 25–7; pl. 183–4; 187, no. 25–7, perhaps from a single workshop.

78 Kenna, *BM Cypriote Seals*, 34, no. 110; pl. 29 with bibliography; Schaeffer (n. 39), 75, fig. 25.4.

79 B. Teissier, 'Glyptic Evidence for a Connection between Iran, Syro-Palestine, and Egypt in the Fourth and Third Millennia' *Iran* 25 (1987), 27–53.

80 Included are Dikaios (n. 42), 801, no. 19; Schaeffer (n. 39) 73–4; pl. 5.4; Boardman, *GGFR*, 106, pl. 203.

81 A pyramidal stone found at Bamboula, interpreted by the excavators as an unfinished seal, may suggest the existence of a workshop: Porada (n. 51), 145–6 and n. 22. Note also ead., *Excavations at Kition* 5.2 (n. 53), 253 from Kition and ead., *Excavations at Maa-Paleokastro* (n. 55), 306, no. 5 from Maa; Courtois and Webb, (n. 63), 7.

82 Courtois and Webb, (n. 63), 74–84.

83 Cylinder-seals: Courtois and Webb, above, 74 and W. M. F. Petrie, *Ancient Gaza* 4 (London, 1934), pl. 12, no. 4 for examples. Stamp-seals: Dikaios (n. 42), 809, no. 31a; pl. 183–4, no. 31a; *SCE* 2, 564–5; pl. 185d; Benson (n. 51), 145, 147; pl. 38; Vollenweider, *Geneva* 3, 105–7, no. 145 (unknown provenance). Note also the following conoids, both lost: *SCE* 2, 556, no. 935 (Idalion); A. P. di Cesnola, *Salaminia*, 2d ed. (London, 1884), 131, fig. 144.

84 M. Meekers, 'The Sacred Tree on Cypriote Cylinder Seals' *RDAC* (1987), 72, no. 3–11. See also R. S. Lamon and G. M. Shipton, *Megiddo* 1 (Chicago, 1939), pl. 66, no. 12 and commentary. On the iconography of the date-palm in Cypriot cylinders in general, see Meekers, above, 67–76; G. Conteneau, *La Glyptique Syro-Hittite* (Paris, 1922), 154; pl. 32, no. 214; H. Danthine, *Le Palmier-Dattier et les arbres sacrés dans l'iconographie de l'Asie Occidentale ancienne* (Paris, 1937), 195–209.

85 Ohnefalsch-Richter, *KBH*, 435, no. 10–11; pl. 221; cf. 420, no. 4, 5, 7, 8; pl. 87.

86 Vollenweider, *Geneva* 1, 130, no. 169; pl. 68. 169, no. 3–5. Note also the following unprovenanced, black serpentine tabloids: Kenna (n. 28), 259, no. 11; Buchanan and Moorey, *Ashmolean* 3, 78, no. 530; pl. 17 (bought in Nicosia).

87 J. DuPlat Taylor, *Myrtou-Pigadhes* (Oxford, 1957), 92–3, no. 328.

88 C. Kepinski, *L'Arbre stylisé en Asie Occidentale au 2e millénnaire avant J.-C.* 3 (Paris, 1982), no. 787; 788; 790–1; 802; 822; 830–1; 833; 838; 839. For an unprovenanced example, note H. Keel-Leu, *Vorderasiatische Stempelsiegel* (Göttingen, 1991), 141, no. 172.

89 On the style, note Collon (n. 4), 73; Buchanan and Moorey, *Ashmolean* 3, 78.

90 Idalion: *SCE* 2, 550, no. 643; pl. 186.2; 555, no. 891. Kourion: Kenna, *BM Cypriote Seals*, 21, no. 19; pl. 5; 26, no. 56; pl. 13; Benson (n. 51) 146–7; pl. 38. Ayios Dhimitrios: E. Porada, 'Cylinder and Stamp-Seals' in I. A. Todd, ed, *Kalavassos-Ayios Dhimitrios* 2 (Göteborg, 1989), 33–7.

91 Enkomi: Courtois *et al.* (n. 53), pl. 32, no. 24–5. Apliki: J. DuPlat Taylor, 'A Late Bronze Age Settlement at Apliki, Cyprus' *AJ* 32 (1952), 163; pl. 26b; 166, no. 6 = Masson (n. 40), 19–20; fig. 14.

92 Karageorghis and Demas (n. 53), 253, no. 754; cf. Courtois *et al.* (n. 53), pl. 32.

93 Courtois *et al.* (n. 40), pl. 32, no. 25; Benson (n. 51), pl. 38, no. B 1634.

94 Enkomi: Dikaios (n. 42), 805, no. 21; pl. 183–4, no. 21 (conoid); C. F. A. Schaeffer, 'Fouilles d'Enkomi-Alasia' Syria 45 (1968), 264, fig. 1 = J.-C. Courtois, *Alasia* 3 (Paris, 1984), 149, no. 1257; pl. 23.2; fig. 45.29 (rectangular stamp); cf. Vollenweider, *Geneva* 1, 132, no. 172; pl. 69 (Nicosia); Porada (n. 4), pl. 9, no. 24 (Amathus) and pl. 10, no. 40 (Kourion).

95 V. E. G. Kenna, 'Seals and Sealstones from the Tombs of Perati' in *Charisterion eis A. K. Orlandon* 2 (Athens, 1966), 320–6; A. Sakellariou, *Die minoischen und mykenischen Siegel des Nationalmuseums in Athens. CMS* 1 (Berlin, 1964), 407, no. 396; cf. Dikaios (n. 42), pl. 184, no. 26–7. For a Cypriot cylinder seal found at Perati, see Collon (n. 4), 72–3, no. 319. On glyptic contact between Cyprus and Thebes at the end of the Late Bronze Age, see E. Porada, 'The Cylinder Seals Found at Thebes in Boeotia' *AfO* 28 (1981–2), 1–70.

96 Above, n. 83.

97 Cylinder-seal: R. A. S. MacAlister, *Excavations of Gezer* 3 (London, 1912), pl. 214, no. 14. Conoid: Masson (n. 40), 23–4, no. 18, fig. 16. H. Frankfort, *Cylinder Seals* (London, 1939), 290 mentions that several cylinders in 'the third Syrian group' may have been cut in Cyprus.

98 P. Beck, 'A Cypriote Cylinder Seal from Lachish' in D. Ussishkin, *Tel Aviv* 10/2 (1983), 178–81.

99 Collon (n. 4), 73.

100 Tripod-seal: D. G. Hogarth, *Hittite Seals* (Oxford, 1920), 37; 72, no. 191; pl. 7; O. Masson, 'Kypriaka' *BCH* 86 (1964), 204–5. Disc: Åström and Masson (n. 60), 99–100. Stalk-handled seal: Porada (n. 55), 306; pl. G, no. 6–7 (Late Bronze Age context, but possibly Early Bronze Age in date).

101 Rectangular stamp-seals with handles: e. g., Courtois *et al.* (n. 53, pl. 32, no. 24–5, 27, 30–2; cf. Porada (n. 51), 810. Documentary evidence: H. Güterbock, 'The Hittite Conquest of Cyprus Reconsidered' *JNES* 26 (1967), 73–81.

102 Conoids: V. Karageorghis, *Palaepaphos-Skales* (Konstanz, 1983), 165–6; 410; pl. 115 (Paphos); *SCE* 2, 129, no. 78; pl. 250, no. 32 (Amathus). Tabloid: Karageorghis, above, 301, 409–10; pl. 179 (Paphos); Kenna (n. 28), 262–3, no. 4; fig. 3.4 (Kyrenia). Flat-topped cones: M.-J. Chavane, *Salamine de Chypre* 6 (Paris, 1975), 151–2, no. 436–7 (Salamis). Pyramid: Kenna (n. 28), 262–5, no. 6; fig. 4.6 (Kition). It is sometimes implied that the conoid was entirely a phenomenon of the Late Bronze Age, but its appearance in Syria and Palestine in archaeological levels dated after the end of the Bronze Age suggests otherwise. See, e.g., Megiddo Level 5 (following the chronology summarised in G. I. Davies, *Megiddo* (Cambridge, 1986), viii-ix): G. Loud, *Megiddo* 2 (Chicago, 1948), pl. 164.20; Lamon and Shipton (n. 84), pl. 67–8, no. 41–2, 55; Lachish, Iron I-II: O. Tufnell, *Lachish* 3 (London, 1953), 372; pl. 45.143–5.

103 For a cylinder seal in a purely Geometric context, note *SCE* 2, 93, no. 59; pl. 23.2 (Amathus).

104 See Appendix 2 for some Cypriot stamp-seals thought to date to the Cypro-Geometric period.

105 A. T. Reyes, 'A Group of Cypro-Geometric Stamp-Seals' *Levant* 25 (1993), 194–205. Note also Clerc, 'Aegyptiaca', 21–2 (T. 240/71, CAI context); 24–5 (T. 242/73, CAI-early CAII context, possible example); 47 (T. 380/27, CGIII-CAI context); H. Keel-Leu, *Vorderasiatische Stempelsiegel* (Göttingen, 1991), 53–5, no. 62–4; O. Keel, *Corpus der Stempelsiegel-Amulette aus Palästina/Israel* (Göttingen, 1995), 102, section 252; O. Keel, *Studien zu den Stempelsiegeln aus Palästina/Israel* 4 (Göttingen, 1997), 26–8.

106 On blue frit as a material in the ancient world, see Moorey (n. 15), 186–9; F. L. Vergès, *Bleus égyptiens* (Louvain and Paris, 1992).

107 Boardman, *GGFR*, 109.

108 Chavane (n. 102), 151–2, no. 436–7. Cf. V. Karageorghis, 'Fouilles de Kition 1959' *BCH* 84 (1960), 535–6, fig. 47–8; Kenna (n. 28), 260–1, no. 2–3.

109 Kenna (n. 28), 262–5, no. 4 and 6; fig. 3.4 and 4.6.

110 On characteristics of typical Phoenician seals, see, e. g., E. Gubel, 'Cinq Bulles inédites des archives Tyriennes de l'époque achéménide' *Semitica* 47 (1997), 53–64.

111 P. Bikai, 'The Phoenicians and Cyprus' in V. Karageorghis, ed., *Cyprus in the Eleventh Century B. C.* (Nicosia, 1994), 31–7.

112 Note, however, Ohnefalsch-Richter, *KBH*, 365; pl. 31, no. 8 allegedly from Ayia Paraskevi (drawing only), showing a seated youth with one arm raised in front of a tree, and a deer springing toward the tree from the other side: cf. Boardman, *AGGems*, no. 178, 181–2; Walters, *BM Gems*, no. 300.

113 See, in general, R. Hestrin and M. Dayagi-Mendels, *Inscribed Seals* (Jerusalem, 1979).

114 Mari: B. Magness-Gardiner, 'The Function of Cylinder Seals in Syrian Palace Archives' in Palaima, (n. 71), 63; Persepolis: M. B. Garrison, 'A Persepolis Fortification Seal on the Tablet MDP 11 308 (Louvre Sb 13078)' *JNES* 55 (1996), 29–30.

115 Below, p. 33.

116 Brandt, *AGDS* 1, 31, no. 95 is identified as an unfinished Cypriot stamp of black serpentine, in the shape of a lion. There are Greek nonsense inscriptions at the top and bottom of the seal. Since the inscriptions are Greek and not Cypro-syllabic, and the shape is unattested in Cyprus, the attribution to the island is insecure.

117 K. Nicolaou,'Anaskaphe Taphon eis Marion' *RDAC* (1964), 148, no. 1; fig. 5.

118 Masson, *ICS*, 350–1, no. 367.

119 J. Boardman, 'Archaic Finger Rings' *Antike Kunst* 10 (1967), 6.

120 Masson, *ICS*, 183–4, no. 170.

121 See, in general, R. Hestrin and M. Dayagi-Mendels, *Inscriptions Reveal* (Jerusalem, 1979).

122 See E. Porada, 'A Lyre-Player from Tarsus and his Relations' in S. S. Weinberg, ed., *The Aegean and the Near East: Studies Presented to Hetty Goldman* (Locust Valley, New York, 1956), 185–211.

123 See, e. g., J. Weingarten, 'The Multiple Sealing System of Minoan Crete and its Possible Antecedents in Anatolia' *OJA* 11 (1992), 25–37.

124 Clerc, *Kition* 2, 115–6, no. 516, 116, no. 1072.

125 T. Petit, 'Syllabaire et alphabet au "palais" d'Amathonte de Chypre vers 300 avant notre ère' in C. Baurain, C. Bonnet, and V. Krings, eds., *Phoinikeia Grammata: Lire et écrire en Méditerranée* (Namur, 1991), 485, no. 11; fig. 12; P. Aupert and P. Leriche, 'La Muraille médiane de l'acropole' in P. Aupert, ed., *Guide d'Amathonte* (Paris, 1996), 103.

126 I. Michaelidou-Nicolaou, 'Nouveaux Documents pour le syllabaire chypriote' *BCH* 117 (1993), 393–7.

127 F. G. Maier, *Alt-Paphos auf Cypern: Ausgrabungen zur Geschichte von Stadt und Heiligtum 1966-1984* (Mainz, 1985), 19, pl. 8. 6a-b.

128 On this practice, see E. Marcus and M. Artzy, 'A Loom Weight from Tel Nami with a Scarab Seal Impression' *IEJ* 45 (1995), 136–49; J. K. Papadopoulos, 'Early Iron Age Potters' Marks in the Aegean' *Hesperia* 63 (1994), 437–507. For the practice in Cyprus during the Late Bronze Age, see J. S. Smith, 'Seals for Sealing in the Late Cypriot Period' Ph.D thesis (Bryn Mawr, 1994), 212–32.

129 On superstitions attached to the different stones, see G. F. Kunz, *The Curious Lore of Precious Stones* (New York, 1913).

130 *SCE* 2, 809.

131 Clerc, *Kition* 2, 15–6.

132 E. Gubel, 'The Seals' in D. Buitron-Oliver, ed., *The Sanctuary of Apollo Hylates at Kourion: Excavations in the Archaic Precinct* (Jonsered, 1996), 163.

133 Charles, 'Pyrga', 3–4.

134 On the evidence, see, in general, Smith (n. 128).

135 E. Lagarce, 'Remarques sur l'utilisation des scarabées, scaraboïdes, amulettes, et figurines de type égyptien à Chypre' in Clerc *Kition* 2, 167–82; W. Culican, *The First Merchant Venturers* (London, 1966), 96; 103.

136 E. Lagarce, 'Remarques sur l'utilisation des scarabées, scaraboïdes, amulettes et figurines de type égyptien à Chypre' in Clerc, *Kition* 2, 167–82; C. Beer, *Temple-Boys* 1 (Jonsered, 1994), pl. 48–9; ead., *Temple-Boys* 2 (Stockholm, 1993), 26–7; ead., 'Economies of Cult in the Ancient Greek World' *Boreas* 21 (1992), 83.

137 Volume 2, Chapter 2.

138 For an exception, see 269 in Geneva. See also Clerc, 'Aegyptiaca', 42–3 (T. 321/114, CGIII-CA), a serpentine scarab from Amathus with the remains of a silver setting.

139 For scarabs of glazed materials with metal settings, see, e.g., W. Culican, 'Seals in Bronze Mounts' *RSF* 5 (1977), Tab. 1a-b. A black serpentine seal from Tharros, with a metal setting and showing Bes battling a rampant lion, has been thought to be Cypriot on the basis of its material and device: G. Q. Pisano, 'Dieci Scarabei da Tharros' *RSF* 6 (1978), 38–40, Tab. 5. 1; E. Gubel, 'Phoenician Seals in the Allard Pearson Museum, Amsterdam' *RSF* 16 (1988), 157 and n. 53. But the type of setting, a length of wire thickened towards the middle, inserted into the stringhole and twisted is uncommon in the island; cf. however 405 in London. The cutting of the beetle also seems too precise for a Cypriot serpentine scarab.

140 V. Karageorghis, 'Chronique des fouilles et découvertes archéologique à Chypre' *BCH* 113 (1989), 846–7; fig. 143a-b.

141 It is not possible to account for differences in settings on the basis of chronology, as Myres, *HCC*, 410–26.

142 See, e.g., Myres, *HCC*, 413, no. 4146.

143 For a similar mount on a Greek gem with an Orientalising motif, note J. Boardman, *Intaglios and Rings* (London, 1975), 10, no. 7.

144 E.g., Myres, *HCC*, 413, no. 4140.

145 Ibid., no. 4150.

146 E.g., Lagarce (n. 135), 169, no. 7A-C.

147 Cf. for Anatolia, K. R. Maxwell-Hyslop, *Western Asiatic Jewellery* (London, 1971), 234; for Phoenicia, W. Culican, 'Phoenician Jewellery in New York and Copenhagen' *Berytus* 22 (1973), 31–47; id., 'Seals in Bronze Mounts' *RSF* 5 (1977), 1–4; id., 'Jewellery from Sarafand and Sidon' *OpAth* 12 (1978), 133–9.

148   E.g., E. Gubel, *Les Phéniciens et le monde méditerranéen* (Brussels, 1986), 244, no. 280–2.

149   Boardman, 'Seals and Amulets', 162, pl. 5; Murray *et al.*, *Excavations*, 99i; fig. 147, no. 32.

150   E.g., A. Ciasca, 'Masks and Protomes' in S. Moscati, ed., *The Phoenicians* (Milan, 1988), 356.

151   Boardman, 'Seals and Amulets', 162, on 297/810. 4–7.

152   Buchanan and Moorey, *Ashmolean* 3, 23–4; for glazed head-seals, probably Archaic, from Kameiros in Rhodes, note Walters, *BM Gems*, 22, no. 260–1 (no. 261 = Kenna, *BM Cypriote Seals*, 35, no. 118, assigned to the Late Bronze Age).

153   Note also New York N. E. 74. 51. 1551, described as 'a human headed pendant of steatite representing … a bearded man of Assyrian type: Myres, *HCC*, 271, no. 1551.

154   Porada (n. 51), 803–4, n. 624.

155   Dikaios (n. 42), 803, no. 19a; pl. 187–8 (LCIIIB context).

156   M. R. Popham *et al.*, 'Further Excavations at the Toumba Cemetery at Lefkandi, 1984 and 1986, a Preliminary Report' *Archaeological Reports for 1988-1989* (1989), 119, 124, fig. 9a.

157   V. Karageorghis, 'Chronique des fouilles et découvertes archéologique à Chypre' *BCH* 113 (1989), 798–804; fig. 42–3.

158   Above, p. 22–40.

159   Pyrga: 7. Idalion: 532.

160   For head-pendants, other than the Amathus-head type, see Appendix 3.

161   For additional head-seals possibly Cypriot, see Appendix 4.

162   On this motif, see further below, Chapter 6.

163   Volume 2, chapter 5.

164   For what follows, I am grateful to Dr. C. Xenophontos of the Geological Survey Department in Nicosia for a brief discussion of Cypriot raw material.

165   J. Boardman, 'Colour Questions' *Jewellery Studies* 5 (1991), 29–31; M. Sax and A. P. Middleton, 'A System of Nomenclature for Quartz and Its Application to the Material of Cylinder Seals' *Archaeometry* 34 (1992), 11–20; Moorey (n. 15), 74–7; N. Postgate, 'Mesopotamian: Petrology: Stages in the Classification of the Material World' *Cambridge Archaeological Journal* 7 (1997), 207–8.

166   For indications of what might be done, see Moorey (n. 15), 74–7; J. Ogden, *Ancient Jewellery* (London, 1992), 18–26; W. A. Oddy, N. D. Meeks and J. M. Ogden, 'A Phoenician Earring: A Scientific Examination' *Jewellery Studies* 1 (1983–84), 3–13.

167   On identifying gemstones scientifically, see M. Sax, 'Recognition and Nomenclature of Quartz Materials with Specific Reference to Engraved Gemstones' *Jewellery Studies* 7 (1996), 63–72; Moorey (n. 15), 79–103. See also the chapters on materials in Collon, *BM Cat* 3.

168   On the techniques for manufacturing seals, see, e. g., P. H. Merrillees, *Cylinder and Stamp-Seals in Australian Collections = Victoria College, Archaeology Research Unit, Occasional Paper, no. 3* (Victoria, 1990), 23–43; M. Sax, 'Innovative Techniques Used to Decorate the Perforations of Some Akkadian Rock Crystal Cylinder Seals' *Iraq* 53 (1991), 91–5; L. Gorelick and A. J. Gwinnett, 'Minoan versus Mesopotamian Seals: Comparative Methods of Manufacture' *Iraq* 54 (1992), 57–64; M. Sax and N. D. Meeks, 'The Introduction of Wheel Cutting as a Technique for Engraving Cylinder Seals: Its Distinction from Filing' *Iraq* 56 (1994), 153–66; eid., 'Methods of Engraving Mesopotamian Quartz Cylinder Seals' *Archaeometry* 37 (1995), 25–36; L. Gorelick and A. J. Gwinnett, 'Innovative Methods in the Manufacture of Sassanian Seals' *Iran* 34 (1996), 79–84; M. Sax, J. McNabb, and N. D. Meeks, 'Methods of Engraving Mesopotamian Cylinder Seals: Experimental Confirmation' *Archaeometry* 40 (1998), 1–21; Moorey (n. 15), 74–7.

169   On the use of the drill in ancient glyptic, see, e. g., J. Boardman, 'Some Syrian Glyptic' *OJA* 15 (1996), 327–40; Moorey (n. 15), 74–7; A. J. Gwinnett and L. Gorelick, 'Beads, Scarabs, and Amulets: Methods of Manufacture in Ancient Egypt' *Journal of the American Research Center in Egypt* 30 (1993), 125–32.

170   Collon (n. 4), 73.

171   On the uses of picrolite in the prehistoric periods, see E.J. Peltenburg, 'Local Exchange in Prehistoric Cyprus: An Initial Assessment of Picrolite' *BASOR* 282/283 (1991), 107–26; L. Vagnetti, 'Stone Sculpture in Chalcolithic Cyprus' *BASOR*, cited above, 139–51.

172   What follows is based on Xenophontos (n. 38), 127–38. See also C. Xenophontos, 'Steatite vs. Picrolite' in Muhly, J., Madden, R., and Karageorghis, V., eds., *Early Metallurgy in Cyprus 4000–50 BC* (Nicosia, 1982), 59.

173 C. Xenophontos, 'Environment and Resources' in D. Frankel and J. M. Webb, *Marki Alonia: An Early and Middle Bronze Age Town in Cyprus: Excavations 1990–1994* (Jonsered, 1996), 89; D. L. Bolger, 'Engendering Cypriot Archaeology: Female Roles and Statuses Before the Bronze Age' *OpAth* 20 (1994), 9–17; E. Peltenburg, 'Local Exchange in Prehistoric Cyprus: An Initial Assessment of Picrolite' *BASOR* 282/283 (1991), 107–26.

174 For examples of dark-coloured serpentine seals in Syria and Palestine, note, e.g., C. C. McCown, *Tell en-Nasbeh* 1 (Berkeley and New Haven, 1947), pl. 54, no. 7, 8, 17, 18; J. Briend and J.-B. Humbert, *Tell Keisan* (Fribourg, 1980), pl. 136, no. 14–6; R. Poppa, *Kamid-el-Loz* (Bonn, 1978), Taf. 22, no. 20.

175 The correlation of ancient geological terms with modern ones is difficult. In general, I have relied with slight modifications on equivalents suggested in S. H. Ball, *A Roman Book on Precious Stones* (Los Angeles, 1950); E. R. Caley and J. F. C. Richards, eds., *Theophrastos on Stones* (Columbus, Ohio, 1956); D. E. Eichholz, ed., *Theophrastus, De Lapidibus* (Oxford, 1965); Boardman, *GGFR*, 447–8.

176 Ball (n. 175), 138 on Cypriot '*adamas*' translates this as 'rock crystal'; *adamas* may refer to diamonds, but Pliny's meaning remains uncertain: see J. Ogden, *Jewellery of the Ancient World* (London, 1982), 95–6. Diamond, although thought to exist in Cyprus (cf. C. W. R. D. Moseley, ed., *The Travels of John Mandeville* (Harmondsworth, 1983), 118) was not valued as a gemstone until Roman times.

177 Κύανος also refers to frit, which, Theophrastos implies, was produced in Cyprus; this seems to be Pliny's *caeruleum* (*NH* 33. 57. 161, based on Theophrastos).

178 Cf. Ogden (n. 176), 107.

179 Ball (n. 175), 162 translates this as 'green jasper', but that is impossible, since Pliny describes the stone as translucent.

180 Ball (n. 175), 142 translates as 'malachite' crystals; but these are rare in ancient jewellery (Ogden (n. 176), 101). From Pliny's description, it is clear that *smaragdus* must be a green stone that flashes in bright light.

181 *NH* 37. 204; Ogden (n. 176), 106.

182 Cf. Catling (n. 6), 78 on his no. 16.

183 On Egypt as a source of amethyst, see I. Shaw and R. Jameson, 'Amethyst Mining in the Eastern Desert: A Preliminary Survey at Wadi el-Hudi' *JEA* 79 (1993), 81–97. See also Moorey (n. 15), 94–5.

184 Haematite cylinder-seals: e.g., B. Teissier, *Ancient Near Eastern Cylinder Seals from the Marcopoli Collection* (Berkeley, 1984), 98.

185 Collon, *BM Cat* 3 (London, 1986), 11; J. Boardman and R. Moorey, 'The Yunus Cemetery Group: Haematite Scarabs' in M. Kelly-Buccellati, ed., *Insight through Images* (Malibu, 1986), 42–3; Ogden (n. 176), 99; M. Sax, D. Collon, M. N. Leese, 'The Availability of Raw Materials for Near Eastern Cylinder Seals during the Akkadian, Post Akkadian and Ur III Periods' *Iraq* 55 (1993), 77–90; Boardman (n. 169); Moorey (n. 15), 84.

186 Ogden (n. 176), 99.

187 Ibid., 109.

188 Ogden (n. 176), 108; Moorey (n. 15), 97.

189 Note Xenophontos (n. 173), 18.

190 For the sources of lapis lazuli, see Ogden (n. 176), 100–1; G. Herrmann, 'Lapis Lazuli: The Early Phases of its Trade' *Iraq* 30 (1968), 21–57; Moorey (n. 15), 85–7; for marble, note J. B. Connelly, *Votive Sculpture of Hellenistic Cyprus* (Nicosia, 1988), 3; Ogden (n. 176), 93; otherwise, little work has been done on sources of marble for Cyprus; for green jasper and its sources, note D. Collon in Kelly-Buccellati, ed. (n. 185), 62–3 with n. 14; J. Boardman, 'Scarabs and Seals: Greek, Punic, and Related Types' in R. D. Barnett and C. Mendleson, eds., *Tharros* (London, 1987), 100 with references.

191 It is doubtful that the Indian trade in gems would have begun by this time.

192 Ezekiel 27: 16. For a discussion of this passage, see I. M. Diakonoff, 'The Naval Power and Trade of Tyre' *IEJ* 42 (1992), 168–93.

193 Ezekiel 18: 13 (Revised Standard Version).

194 On the different shapes of scarab backs, see Boardman, *AGGems*, 15. Myres in *HCC*, 418 had already noted that carination, which he called a 'keel', was a distinctively Cypriot trait.

195 Boardman, *AGGems*, 16.

196 Boardman, 'Seals and Amulets', 161–2 on 237/72.

197 E.g., Young and Young, *Terracotta Figurines*, pl. 19.

198 *SCE* 2, 797–810.

199 E.g., A. Biran, 'Tell Dan, 1977' *IEJ* 27 (1977), 244, pl. 37c (eighth century); Y. Yadin *et al.*, *Hazor* 3–4 (Jerusalem, 1961), pl. 196, no. 27 (Iron II period).
200 V. Karageorghis, *Excavations at Kition* 1 (London, 1974), 149, fig. 2.
201 E. Porada, 'Seals from the Tombs of Maroni' in J. Johnson, *Maroni de Chypre* (Göteborg, 1980), 71, no. 246.
202 Markoe, *Bowls*, 49–51. For vases and sculpture, see, e.g., M. Littauer and J. Crouwel, *Wheeled Vehicles and Ridden Animals in the Ancient Near East* (Leiden, 1979), 101–2; Young and Young, *Terracotta Figurines*, 216; V. Karageorghis and J. des Gagniers, *La Céramique chypriote de style figuré*, text vol. (Rome, 1974), 15–7; V. Tatton-Brown, 'Le Sarcophage d'Amathonte' in A. Hermary, *Amathonte* 2 (Paris, 1981), 79.
203 Markoe, *Bowls*, 50; *cf.* Tatton-Brown (n. 202), 79.
204 Cf. Boardman and Vollenweider, *Ashmolean Gems*, 16, no. 74; pl. 14; Boardman, *IGems*, 80, no. 345.
205 E. Gubel, 'Phoenician Seals in the Allard Pierson Museum, Amsterdam' *RSF* 16 (1988), 160–3.
206 G. E. Markoe, 'A Terracotta Warrior from Kazaphani, Cyprus with Stamped Decoration in the Cypro-Phoenician Tradition' *RSF* 16 (1988), 15–9; Markoe, *Bowls*, 52–4.
207 The tomb contained a Phoenician pot dated to roughly the seventh century: V. Karageorghis *et al.*, eds., *La Necropole d'Amathonte, tombes 113-367* (Nicosia, 1987), 12, with 5 and 16.
208 Boardman, 'Seals and Amulets', 161–2.
209 Collon, *BM Cat.* 3, 165–80.
210 Note, possibly, also M. Henig, *Classical Gems* (Cambridge, 1994), 6, no. 12 (warrior fighting animal).
211 E. g., Littauer and Crouwel (n. 202), 101–2; Young and Young, *Terracotta Figurines*, 216; Karageorghis and des Gagniers (n. 202), 15–7; Tatton-Brown (n. 202), 74–83.
212 For examples, see V. Karageorghis, *The Coroplastic Art of Ancient Cyprus* 4 (Nicosia, 1995), 61–128.
213 For a Cypriot seal of frit (?) with the chariot motif, see Zwierlein-Diehl, *AGDS* 2, 50–1, no. 85.
214 For the context, see Murray *et al.*, *Excavations*, 124.
215 The almost circular proportions of the Hermitage scaraboid in A. Procopé-Walter, 'Zum Fortleben hethitischer Tradition in der späteren Glyptik' *AfO* 5 (1928–9), 164–8 make it unlikely to be Cypriot.
216 E.g., 428 and Ohnefalsch-Richter, *KBH*, pl. 93. 3 (aryballos).
217 Charles, 'Pyrga', 1–34. On the style, see also Gubel, 'Cubical Stamps', 195–224; cf. A. T. Reyes, 'The Stamp-Seals in the Pierides Collection, Larnaca' *RDAC* (1991), 124 on no. 13.
218 Contrast Gubel, 'Cubical Stamps', 199–200; Culican, 'Cubical Seals', 165.
219 Culican, 'Cubical Seals', 165, noting, in particular, the lion on side (c) of 63.
220 Note also the following with devices close to the Pyrga-style: *SCE* 2, 136, no. 1; pl. 29, no. 6 from Amathus (scarab; black; L. 0.013 m.; striding figure with high conical helmet, carrying branch with circle at the top; linear border); Nicosia D. 29 (scarab; black summary incisions at the back; L. 0.023 m.; three stems with knobbed tops; lines radiating from the knob of the middle stem; linear border); Nicosia D. 43 (scarab; black; L. 0.014 m.; schematic tree; object with rounded top on either side; linear border).
221 See p. 85 below.
222 Add too seal 154. Cf. also *Hotel Drouot, Collection de cachets et cylindres orientaux: 20 avril 1964*, no. 96; pl. 6 = ibid.: 10–11 mars 1969, no. 122 (classified as Anatolian): 'cachet rectangulaire de stéatite noir avec anneau de suspension', showing a striding deer, drillings beneath the feet, branch behind, a plant with a rectangular top, an object above, and a linear border.
223 Stockholm A. I. 2760; L. 0.015 m. W. 0.012 m. H. 0.007 m.: *SCE* 2, 773, no. 2760.
224 Buchanan and Moorey, *Ashmolean* 3, 23–5.
225 Above, on 6.
226 Vienna ix. 1977 (E. Zwierlein-Diehl, *Die antiken Gemmen des Kunsthistorisches Museums in Wien* 1 (Munich, 1973), 35, no. 13 = J. Boardman, 'Island Gems Aftermath' *JHS* 38 (1968), 8–9, no. J6; Zazoff, *AGDS* 3, 191, no. 9; Taf. 87; C. Höcker, *Antike Gemmen* (Kassel, 1987/8), 55–6). On Island Gems in general, see Boardman, *IGems*.
227 Boardman, *IGems*, 18 and 89–91.
228 Cf. Zwierlein-Diehl, *AGDS* 2, 61.
229 On Lyre-Player seals, see, in general, Buchner and Boardman, 'Lyre-Player', 1–62; Boardman, 'Encore', 1–17.
230 Porada, (n. 122), 192.

231 Boardman, 'Seals and Amulets', 162: Limassol; Amathus T. 354/115; L. 0.013 m. W. 0011 m. H. 0.011 m. For the shape, cf. Buchanan and Moorey, *Ashmolean* 3, pl. 5, no. 155 and 162, both probably from the Syrian coast.

232 Nicosia E. 34; grey; L. 0.019 m. H. 0.013 m. (circular base; irregularly arranged branches ?; circular border); Nicosia E. 35; grey; L. 0.021 m. H. 0.012 m. (triangular base: striding deer; object beneath; another animal above). On the stud-shape and its chronology, see Buchanan and Moorey, *Ashmolean* 3, 29.

233 P. Bielinski, 'A Prism-Shaped Stamp-Seal in Warsaw and Related Stamps' *Berytus* 23 (1974), 59.

234 Ibid.

235 L. Y. Rahmani, 'Two Syrian Seals' *IEJ* 14 (1964), 180–4; cf. Gubel, ' Cubical Stamps', 221–3.

236 P. Dikaios, *Enkomi* (Mainz, 1971), 809–10, no. 33; pl. 183. For the shape, cf. also Buchanan and Moorey, *Ashmolean* 3, pl.l 4, no. 110, 112 (probably from Syro-Palestine); R. M. Boehmer and H. G. Güterbock, *Glyptik aus dem Stadtgebiet von Bogazköy* (Berlin, 1987), Taf. 34, no. 276–8. The shapes of M. Dunand, *Fouilles de Byblos* 1 (Paris, 1937), pl. 134, no. 4046 (a) and 5217 (a) also seem related. Some similarity to Archaic seals known from the East Greek islands is also evident; cf. Boardman, *IGems*, 122–3.

237 Note also M. Louloupis, *Annual Report of the Department of Antiquities for the Year* 1991 (Nicosia, 1992), 70, no. 9. The device is indistinct on the photograph.

238 Information from the inventory of the Louvre Museum.

239 For the motif, cf. the shield emblem of a warrior on the device of a Graeco-Phoenician green jasper gem from Byblos: D. F. Brown, 'A Graeco-Phoenician Scarab from Byblos', *AJA* 40 (1936), 345–7.

240 On Cyprus and Al Mina, see, e. g., R. Kearsley, 'The Greek Geometric Wares from Al Mina Levels 10–8 and Associated Pottery' *Mediterranean Archaeology* 8 (1995), 7–81.

241 On the term 'green jasper,' Near Eastern and Classical seals made of green jasper, the sources of the stone and its use in the Levant and the Mediterranean, see Buchanan and Moorey, *Ashmolean* 3, 71–2; D. Collon, 'The Green Jasper Cylinder Seal Workshop' in M. Kelly-Buccellati, ed., *Insight through Images* (Malibu, 1986), 57–70; J. Boardman, 'Scarabs and Seals: Greek, Punic, and Related Types' in R. D. Barnett and C. Mendleson, eds., *Tharros* (London, 1987), 99–103; O. Keel, 'Die Jaspis-Skarabaen-Gruppe. Eine vorderasiatische Skarabaen Werkstatt des 17. Jahrhunderts v. Chr.' in O. Keel *et al.*, *Studien zu den Stempelsiegeln aus Palastina/Israel*, vol. 2 (Freiburg and Gottingen, 1989), 209–42; D. Collon, *Near Eastern Seals* (London, 1990), 36–7; J. Boardman, 'Colour Questions' *Jewellery Studies* 5 (1991), 29–31.

242 On the chronological problems, see Buchanan and Moorey, *Ashmolean* 3, 70–4; Boardman in Barnett and Mendleson (n. 241), 99–103.

243 A 'greenish-black' jasper scarab from Tyre Stratum VIII (? late ninth century) is reported: P. M. Bikai, *The Pottery of Tyre* (Warminster, 1978), 85; pl. 21, no. 4; pl. 85, no. 15.

244 Cf. W. Orthmann, *Der alte Orient* (Berlin, 1975), pl. 131b, g.

245 E. Gubel, *Les Phéniciens et le monde méditerranéen* (Brussels, 1986), 224, no. 256. Cf. also representations on what seem to be the fourth-century B.C. coinage of Tyre: G. F. Hill, *Catalogue of the Greek Coins of Phoenicia* (London, 1910), 230, no. 23–9; pl. 29, no. 7.

246 As defined in Boardman, *AGGems*, 147–53.

247 Ibid., 16.

248 Boardman, *IGems*, 64–5 and n. 1 for bibliography.

249 Cf. Boardman, *AGGems*, pl. 31, no. 433; pl. 32, no. 451.

250 Note their use on 74 and 217, and see V. Karageorghis, 'A Cypro-Archaic I Tomb at Palaephos-Skales' *RDAC* (1987), 85–96.

251 Note also Kassel gem Ge20 (C. Höcker, *Antike Gemmen* (Kassel, 1987/8), 55–6 = Zazoff, *AGDS* 3, 196, no. 20, Taf. 89); J. Boardman, *Intaglios and Rings* (London, 1975), 101, no. 112; Ohnefalsch-Richter, *KBH*, 324, fig. 836–9. There is some confusion over whether the Kassel seal or 110 is the seal discovered by the British at Marion (J. A. R. Munro and H. A. Tubbs, 'Excavations in Cyprus, 1899' *JHS* 11 (1890), 54, fig. 1).

252 Cf. H. Pittman, *Ancient Art in Miniature* (New York, 1987), 76, no. 86; A. Bisi, *Il Grifone* (Rome, 1965), fig. 7, no. 60–1; V. Karageorghis, 'A Cypro-Archaic I Tomb at Palaepaphos-Skales' *RDAC* (1987), 90 with n. 48.

253 Cf. Boardman, *AGGems*, no. 108, pl. 7.

254 For a historical account of this period, see A. T. Reyes, *Archaic Cyprus* (Oxford, 1994), 49–68.

255 On the use of stamp-seals in the Assyrian Empire, see B. Parker, 'Seals and Seal Impressions from the Nimrud Excavations, 1955–58' *Iraq* 24 (1962), 27; Buchanan and Moorey, *Ashmolean* 3, 53; S. Dalley and J. N. Postgate, *The Tablets from Fort Shalmaneser* (Oxford, 1984), 3–4; E. Porada, *The Collection of the Pierpont Morgan Library* (Washington, D.C., 1948), 72.

256 The majority of stone seals from Kition were found in bothros 1, the contents of which span the late seventh and mid-fifth centuries (c. 600–450 B.C.): Clerc, *Kition* 2, 11.

257 The same was true of Ayia Irini even in the Bronze Age; note, e. g., G. Philip, 'Cypriot Bronzework in the Levantine World: Conservatism, Innovation, and Social Change' *Journal of Mediterranean Archaeology* 4 (1991), 59–107; O. Negbi, 'The "Libyan Landscape" from Thera: A Review of Aegean Enterprises Overseas in the Late Minoan IA Period' *Journal of Mediterranean Archaeology* 7 (1994), 86.

258 For a Phoenician bronze seal of the tenth or ninth century B. C., see Z. Gal, 'A Phoenician Bronze Seal from Hurbat Rosh Zayit' *JNES* 53 (1994), 27–31.

259 E.g., Buchanan and Moorey, *Ashmolean* 3, pl. 10, no. 289.

260 Boardman, *AGGems*, 41, n. 22; E. Gubel, 'Phoenician Seals in the Allard Pearson Museum, Amsterdam' *RSF* 16 (1988), 153, n. 36; Culican, 'Cubical Seals', 164 and n. 28.

261 On seals in Phoenician style across the Levant, see, e. g., A. Lemaire and B. Sass, 'Sigillographie ouest-sémitique: Nouvelles Lectures' *Semitica* 45 (1996), 27–35; A. Lemaire, 'Sept Nouveaux Sceaux nord-ouest sémitiques inscrits' *Semitica* 41–2 (1991–2), 63–80. On travel between Cyprus and Phoenicia, see, e. g., E. Stern, 'A Cypro-Phoenician Dedicatory Offering from Tel Dor Depicting a Maritime Scene' *Qadmoniot* 27 (1994), 34–7; id., 'A Phoenician-Cypriote Votive Scapula from Tel Dor: A Maritime Scene' *IEJ* 44 (1994), 1–12; O. Masson, 'Pélérins chypriotes en Phénicie (Sarepta et Sidon)' *Semitica* 32 (1982), 45–9; id., 'Une Inscription chypriote syllabique de Dora (Tel Dor) et les avatars des noms grecs en Aristo-' *Kadmos* 33 (1994), 87–92.

262 This is possibly the same seal as the one identified in E. Gubel, 'Phoenician Seals in the Allard Pierson Museum, Amsterdam' *RSF* 16 (1988), 157–8, n. 58 as Dublin University College, 1. x. 1978 ('formerly in the Collection of M. Ohnefalsch-Richter, Vienna').

263 A. Hermary, 'Une Tête de Bès chypriote au Musée de Cannes', *Centre d'études chypriotes: cahier* 23 (1995, no. 1), 23–7.

264 On contact between Cyprus and Cyrene, see Reyes, (n. 254), 75–6.

265 Cf. E. Gubel, 'Phoenician Seals in the Allard Pearson Museum, Amsterdam' *RSF* 16 (1988), 151–5.

266 C. J. Gadd, 'An Old Babylonian Frog-Amulet' *British Museum Quarterly* 10 (1935–36), 7–9; A. P. Kozloff, ed., *Animals in Ancient Art* (Cleveland, 1981), 20–1, no. 4–5; 6, no. 47.

267 Cf. Markoe, *Bowls*, 256, no. Cy8, middle register.

268 D. Pierides, 'Notes on Cypriote Palaeography' *Transactions of the Society of Biblical Archaeology* 5 (1876), 92, no. 7; L. P. di Cesnola, *Cyprus* (London, 1877), pl. 26.

269 Cesnola, *Atlas* 3, pl. 32. 2; cf. Myres, *HCC*, 419, no. 4193.

270 For the context, see Murray *et al.*, *Excavations*, 123.

271 Cf. O. Tufnell, 'Some Scarabs with Decorated Backs' *Levant* 2 (1967), 99, fig. 2, no. 1–4.

272 A. P. di Cesnola, *Salaminia*, 2d ed. (London, 1884), 134, with reference to 139, no. 29.

273 For a simlar motif on another black serpentine seal, found in Athens and possibly Cypriot, see Brandt, *AGDS* 1, 32, no. 104; Taf. 13. Note also Brandt, *AGDS* 1, no. 108.

274 E.g., Buchanan and Moorey, *Ashmolean* 3, 50–1, no. 330–7, pl. 11.

275 Markoe, *Bowls*, 54–5. See also E. Gubel and S. Cauet, 'Un Nouveau Type de coupe phénicienne', *Syria* 64 (1987), 193–204.

276 P. Amandry, 'Petits Objets de Delphes' *BCH* 68–9 (1944–5), 50–1 suggests a Cypriot origin for a scarab from Delphi ('pierre dure, de couleur gris-blanc') showing an animal file consisting of a goat followed by a bull in the middle of a papyrus brake, within a linear border, above a ladder exergue. The motif is certainly Phoenician-inspired, but the shape of the beetle and the markings on its back (hatched borders to distinguish elytra and prothorax with V-winglets carefully incised) are not common to serpentine seals from Cyprus. The cross-hatching on the forepart of the bull and the light, horizontal striations used to mark out the goat's horns are also unusual.

277 Possibly Cypriot as well is *Southesk*, 199, no. O. 5; pl. 16 (sard scarab showing a seated hawk-headed figure, one hand raised, the other with a sceptre; incense burner in front; disc and crescent above; zigzag exergue).

278 Markoe, *Bowls*, 248–9, no. Cy4.

279 For the context, see Murray *et al.*, *Excavations*, 123.

280 On the context, see further P. Aupert and A. Hermary, 'Rapport sur les activités de la mission de l'école française et du ministère des relations extérieures à Amathonte en 1983' *BCH* 108 (1984), 967–71; fig. 1–4; A. Hermary, 'Un nouveau Chapiteau hathorique trouvé à Amathonte' *BCH* 109 (1985), 657 with reference to 699, fig. 42.

281 G. F. Hill, *Catalogue of the Greek Coins of Cyprus* (London, 1904), 24; pl. 5; C. M. Kraay, *Archaic and Classical Greeek Coins* (London, 1976), 304; pl. 64, no. 1096–7.

282 Boardman, *AGGems*, 23, no. 24; pl. 1 showing two sphinxes at a date-palm above a cross-hatched exergue may also be Cypriot; cf. Markoe, *Bowls*, 259, no. Cy8. Note also Brandt, *AGDS* 1, 46, no. 201; Taf. 22: black serpentine cut scaraboid showing a sphinx with a sharply curved wing and a short Greek hairstyle (Munich A. 1367).

283 J. L. Benson, *The Necropolis of Kaloriziki* (Göteborg, 1973), 127–9; pl. 41.

284 *SCE* 3, pl. 112; 119, no. 4 (Mersinaki); Young and Young, *Terracotta Figurines*, 202, type A.

285 Juvenal 1. 26–30:

cum pars Niliacae plebis, cum verna Canopi
Crispinus Tyrias umero revocante lacernas
ventilet aestivum digitis sudantibus aurum
nec sufferre queat maioris pondera gemmae,
difficile est saturam non scribere.

The translation is by P. Green (London, Penguin, 3d ed., 1998). Like the Tyrian purple, might the gems be Phoenician as well? Nisbet argues that line 29 is an interpolation, but even if that is the case, the interpolation would already have appeared in antiquity, since the line is attested in the fifth century A. D.: R. G. M. Nisbet, 'Notes on the Text and Interpretation of Juvenal' in N. Horsfall, *Vir Bonus Discendi Peritus: Studies in Celebration of Otto Skutsch's Eightieth Birthday*, BICS, suppl. vol. 51 (London, 1988), 86–7 = id., *Collected Papers on Latin Literature* (Oxford, 1995), 227–9.

286 For superstitions regarding stones in the Classical world, see, e. g., K. J. Gutzwiller, 'Cleopatra's Ring' *GRBS* (1995), 383–98.

287 On the glyptic use of 'look-alikes', see, e. g., J. Weingarten, 'Three Upheavals in Minoan Sealing Administration: Evidence for Radical Change' in Palaima, (n. 71), 111.

288 On the possibility that seal emblems are simply decorative and drawn from a stock repertoire, see J. Spier, Emblems in Archaic Greece' *BICS* 37 (1990), 107–29.

289 Cf. Bordreuil, *Sceaux ouest-sémitiques*, 33, no. 22.

290 Boardman, *AGGems*, no. 513, pl. 34.

291 Walters, *BM Gems*, 21, describes the context as a 'homogeneous tomb of the Mycenaean period' and the selection of pottery from the tomb published in Murray *et al.*, *Excavations*, 72, fig. 124 and 74, fig. 129 is certainly of this date. But the material is not otherwise attested among Late Cypriot gems, and the device seems more appropriate to the Cypro-Archaic period.

292 *Cf.* Markoe, *Bowls*, 55.

293 For the context, see V. Karageorghis, 'Chronique des fouilles et découvertes archéologiques à Chypre' *BCH* 108 (1984), 915.

294 E.g., J. Boardman, 'Scarabs and Seals: Greek, Punic, and Related Types' in R. D. Barnett and C. Mendleson, eds., *Tharros* (London, 1987), 100; J. Boardman, *Escarabeos de Piedra, Procedentes de Ibiza* (Madrid, 1984), Lam. 15, no. 87.

295 Stud-seals from Anatolia and North Syria provide very rough parallels, but these are not always carved on both sides and are often more rectangular (e.g., Buchanan and Moorey, *Ashmolean* 3, pl. 6, no. 197). Irregularly-shaped tabloids pinched-in at the centre and with devices cut on both ends are also known from the first half of the seventh century in the Greek world (e.g., Boardman, *IGems*, 139, no. M. 12).

296 London 245 (1889. 11–10. 2) = P. Zazoff, *Die antiken Gemmen* (Munich, 1983), 71, Taf. 14. 2. Cf. the goat in W. M. F. Petrie, *Ancient Gaza* 2 (London, 1932), pl. 6 (lower left quadrant; third row from the bottom, last scarab). For the shape of the beetle and its markings, cf. R. Giveon, *Egyptian Scarabs from Western Asia from the Collections of the British Museum* (Göttingen, 1985), 116–7, no. 22.

297 On the early use of Egyptian iconography in Syrian and Palestinian glyptic, see, in general, B. Teissier, *Egyptian Iconography on Syro-Palestinian Cylinder Seals of the Middle Bronze Age* (Fribourg and Göttingen, 1996).

298   On the western Mediterranean, note, e. g., Hölbl, *Beziehungen* (n. 16), 181–2; id., *Ägyptisches Kulturgut* (n. 16), 172; Gorton (n. 16), 158–62.

299   Note, e. g., Gorton (n. 16), 40–2; 175–6. See also Boardman, 'Orientalia' (n. 16), 95–100.

300   See Gorton (n. 16), 9–12 (Types 1 and 2) for geometric patterns on faience and steatite scarabs; 31–42 (Types 11–14) for the use of registers, with Maat- and Ptah- figures appearing in the middle register; 93–103 (Type 28) for animals with discs above them; 123 (Type 34) for examples of head-seals.

301   Hölbl, *Beziehungen* (n. 16), 370–2 on the date of Cypriot glazed scarabs in Italy.

302   E. g., Gorton (n. 16), 121–7.

303   Hdt. 2. 182. 2; Boardman, *AGGems*, 24. For a historical account and a full argument on the nature of the relationship between Egypt and Cyprus in the sixth century, see A. T. Reyes, *Archaic Cyprus* (Oxford, 1994), 77–8. Herodotos' language may also have been prejudiced by his views on Athenian tyranny in the fifth century and thus need not be taken as historically accurate; see G. Nagy, *Pindar's Homer* (Baltimore and London, 1990), 309–10.

304   See also Appendix 5.

305   See, in general, Buchanan and Moorey, *Ashmolean 3*, 56–7.

306   Myres, *HCC*, 444, no. 4382 (New York N. E. 74. 51. 4382) may also be noted, since its devices (scorpion, worshipper, quadruped, and bull) seem to derive from the Neo-Babylonian style, and it is reported as having been found in Cyprus. But its shape, a quarter-cylinder, is not readily parallelled, and it lacks a precise provenance within the island.

307   Note also Ohnefalsch-Richter, *KBH*, pl. 79, no. 13 and Nicosia E. 1, E. 2, and E. 3.

308   See, e. g., S. Dalley and A. T. Reyes, 'Mesopotamian Contact and Influence in the Greek World 1: To the Persian Conquest' in S. Dalley, ed., *The Legacy of Mesopotamia* (Oxford, 1998), 85–106.

309   Cf. E. Stern, 'Assyrian and Babylonian Elements in the Material Culture of Palestine in the Persian Period' *Transeuphratène* 7 (1994), 51–62.

310   *Anthologia Palatina* 11. 146.

311   Cf. Boardman, *AGGems*, pl. 27, no. 377. Boardman, *AGGems*, 162, no. 592 (pseudo-scarab from Etruria showing a dolphin) and no. 593 (pseudo-scarab showing a lion) have been attributed to Cypriot manufacture on the basis of the distinctively pale green serpentine out of which they are made.

312   P. V. C. Baur, *Centaurs in Ancient Art, The Archaic Period* (Berlin, 1912); T. H. Carpenter, *Dionysian Imagery in Archaic Greek Art* (Oxford, 1986), 7, n. 24.

313   S. Sophocleous, *Atlas des répresentations chypro-archaïques des divinités* (Göteborg, 1985) 20f., s. v. 'hommes-taureaux'. V. Karageorghis, *The Coroplastic Art of Ancient Cyprus VI. The Cypro-Archaic Period: Monsters, Animals, and Miscellanea* (Nicosia, 1996), 1–4. Note also the figure of Nessos on 359 and 365.

314   For a conspectus of numismatic devices from Cyprus and a summary of recent numismatic work identifying coin types, see, e. g., A. Destrooper and A. Simeonides, 'Classical Coins in the Symeonides Collection: The Coin Circulation in Marion During the VIth and IVth Centuries' *RDAC* (1998), 111–23; pl. 9–11. For a summary of the problems involved in assessing what is Cypriot and what is Greek among Archaic gems, see J. Boardman, 'The Cypriot Contribution to Archaic Greek Glyptic' in V. Tatton-Brown, ed., *Cyprus and the East Mediterranean in the Iron Age* (London, 1989), 44–9.

315   M.-L. Vollenweider in V. Karageorghis, 'Chronique des fouilles et découvertes archéologiques à Chypre' *BCH* 89 (1965), 237; J. Boardman, 'Greek Gem Engravers, Their Subjects and Style' in E. Porada, ed., *Ancient Art in Seals* (Princeton, 1980), 112.

316   For a full list of gems, see Boardman, *AGGems*, 94, no. 249–58; id., *Intaglios and Rings* (London, 1975), 13, 113; Zwierlein-Diehl, *AGDS 2*, 52.

317   Zwierlein-DIehl, *AGDS 2*, 52, denies the attribution of 344 to the Semon Master.

318   T. B. Mitford, *The Inscriptions of Kourion* (Philadelphia, 1971), 60, no. 25 (4th c. B.C.); 128–9, no. 65–6 (3d c. B.C.); 165, no. 89 (2d/3d c. A.D.); 195, no. 104 (2d. c. A.D.).

319   Myres, *HCC*, 229, no. 1354B.

320   Boardman, *AGGems*, 27–30.

321   Masson, *ICS*, 193–4, no. 178; cf. ibid., 235–44, no. 217 for the same name, clearly not royal.

322   See J. D. Beazley, *The Lewes House Collection of Ancient Gems* (Oxford, 1920), 28, no. 33; Vollenweider, *Geneva 3*, 135, no. 181 (? Cypriot); Boardman, *AGGems*, 98–9, no. 272–7.

323   J. Boardman, 'Cypriot Finger Rings' *BSA* 65 (1970), 12, no. 38–40. Note also Vollenweider, *Geneva 3*, no. 181, possibly Cypriot.

324   Vollenweider, *Geneva 3*, no. 181, perhaps with a Cypro-syllabic inscription.

325 Note also Berlin VA 2145, a limestone cylinder seal with Perseus, face averted, holding the Gorgon by the wrist, a sickle in hand. There is an object behind Perseus (W. Burkert, 'Oriental and Greek Mythology: The Meeting of Parallels' in J. Bremmer, ed., *Interpretations of Greek Mythology* (London and Sydney, 1987), 31; fig. 2. 3 and 39 n. 75; W. G. Lambert, 'Gilgamesh in Literature and Art: The Second and First Millennia' in A. E. Farkas *et al.*, eds., *Monsters and Demons in the Ancient and Medieval Worlds* (Mainz, 1987), 48, pl. 9. 22). Dr. E. Klengel of Berlin, who has looked at the seal, thinks it may have been recut and need not be authentic (I owe this information to Dr. D. Collon.).

326 Note also a scaraboid in black serpentine reported in E. Borowski, 'Die Sammlung H. A. Layard', *Orientalia* 21 (1952), 183, no. 18; pl. 25: running four-winged demon; Egyptian hairstyle; hatched wings; linear border.

327 On the winged horse in the Near East, note, e.g., D. Matthews, 'The Random Pegasus: Loss of Meaning in Middle Assyrian Seals' *Cambridge Archaeological Journal* 2 (1992), 191.

328 E.g., O. Masson and M. Sznycer, *Recherches sur les phéniciens à Chypre* (Paris, 1972), 108–10.

329 G. F. Hill, *Catalogue of the Greek Coins of Cyprus* (London, 1904), 70; pl. 13, no. 9–10.

330 *LIMC* 4–5, s. v., 'Herakles; S. Dalley, 'Near Eastern Patron Deities of Mining and Smelting in the Late Bronze and Early Iron Ages' *RDAC* (1987), 65; M. Yon, 'A propos de l'Héraklès à Chypre' in L. Kahil *et al.*, eds., *L'Iconographie classique et identités régionales* (Athens, 1986), 287–97.

331 T. B. Mitford, *The Inscription of Kourion* (Philadelphia, 1971), 60, no. 25 (fourth century B.C.); 128–9, no. 65–6 (third century B.C.); 165, no. 89 (second/third century A.D.); 195, no. 104 (second century A.D.).

332 On the connections between Arcadia and Cyprus, cf. M. Voyatzis, 'Arcadia and Cyprus: Aspects of their Interrelationship between the Twelfth and Eighth Centuries BC' *RDAC* (1985), 155–63; C. M. Bowra, 'Homeric Words in Cyprus' *JHS* 54 (1934), 54–74; cf. M. Sakellariou, 'Achéens et Arcadiens' in J. Karageorghis and O. Masson, ed., *The History of the Greek Language in Cyprus* (Nicosia, 1988), 9–17. Nearby Argos, tradition recounted, provided the settlers who founded Kourion (Hdt. 5. 113; Str. 14. 683).

333 The myth is preserved in Nonnos 5. 609–15; 14. 193–202.

334 V. Desborough, R. V. Nicholls, and M. Popham, 'A Euboean Centaur' *BSA* 65 (1970), 30 and n. 40; V. Karageorghis, 'Notes on Some Centaurs from Cyprus' in *Charisterion eis Anastasiou K. Orlandon* 2 (Athens, 1966), 167.

335 Cf. K. Fittschen, *Untersuchungen zur Beginn der Sagendarstellungen bei den Griechen* (Berlin, 1969), 91 and n. 467.

336 On this subject, see P. V. C. Baur, *Centaurs in Ancient Art, The Archaic Period* (1912); E. Buschor, 'Kentauren' *AJA* 38 (1934), 128–32; note also R. Arnold, 'The Horse-Demon in Early Greek Art and his Eastern Neighbors', Ph.D thesis (Columbia University, New York, 1972).

337 It is a curious coincidence that a number of black-figure pots by the Centaur Painter have been found in Cyprus: e.g., Beazley, *ABV*, 189, no. 3, 5; 190, no. 19, l.

338 Beazley (n. 322), 29, no. 34.

339 C. M. Kraay, *Archaic and Classical Greek Coins* (London, 1976), 309.

340 Cf. G. F. Hill, *Catalogue of the Greek Coins of Cyprus* (London, 1904), xliv–xlvii.

341 Kraay (n. 339), 299f. does not identify a particular series as coinage from Golgoi.

342 Ibid., 301.

343 Ibid., 301; pl. 63. 1078–1082.

344 L. Lacroix, *Études d'archéologie numismatique* (Paris, 1974) 53f.; for the legend, Apollod. 1. 9. 1.

345 See, e.g., Boardman, *AGGems*, 121–2.

346 E.g., Beazley (n. 322), 25, no. 30; Boardman, *AGGems*, 82, no. 220; 99, no. 279 and 280; pl. 19; 100, no. 288 and 289.

347 Boardman and Vollenweider, *Ashmolean Gems*, 70, no. 69 reports Cyprus as the provenance of *Münzen und Medaillen*, Sonderliste K, no. 111, showing a youth picking up a discus. Note also J. Boardman, 'The Danicourt Gems in Péronne' *RA* (1971), 198–9, fig. a–c.

348 Cf. M. G. Klingbeil, 'Syro-Palestinian Stamp-Seals from the Persian Period: The Iconographic Evidence' *Journal of Northwest Semitic Languages* 18 (1992), 95–124.

349 Ohnefalsch-Richter suspected that *KBH*, 32, no. 7 and 11 (= J. Boardman, 'Pyramidal Stamp-Seals in the Persian Empire' *Iran* 8 (1970), pl. 3, no. 36); and 12 (octagonal pyramids showing various animals and mythological creatures in heraldic pose) were Cypriot.

350 Cf. the reading in Catling (n.6), 69, no. 25.

351 On this style in general, see Buchanan and Moorey, *Ashmolean* 3, 66–8. For examples reported from Cyprus, note, for example, J. Boardman, 'Pyramidal Stamp-seals in the Persian Empire' *Iran* 8 (1970), 44, no. 168; pl. 7 (crouching sphinx with goat's head), and Buchanan and Moorey, *Ashmolean* 3, 82, no. 567 (seated lion (?) with horns and curving wing).

352 For other possible Cypriot seals of the Persian period, see also J. Boardman, 'Seals and Signs. Anatolian Stamp-Seals of the Persian Period Revisited' *Iran* 36 (1998), 3. On stamp-seals in this period in general, see also M. C. Root, 'Pyramidal Stamp-Seals – The Persepolis Connection' in M. Brosius and A. Kuhrt, eds., *Studies in Persian History: Essays in Memory of David M. Lewis* (Leiden, 1998), 257–89.

353 For other possibly Cypriot cubical seals, note H. H. von der Osten, *Ancient Oriental Seals in the Collection of Mr. Edward T. Newell* (Chicago, 1934), pl. 33, no. 540–3; 546–7 (cf. comments in Culican, 'Cubical Seals', 165); Vollenweider, *Geneva* 3, 130–1, no. 176; Delaporte, *Catalogue* 1, pl. 54, no. 33 (D. 137); 2, pl. 105, no. 1–2; Brandt, *AGDS* 1, Taf. 11, no. 99; 100; and Taf. 15, no. 125; Bielinski (n. 233), 53–69 (= Culican, 'Cubical Seals', 167; Gubel, 'Cubical Stamps', 195–7; 201 n. 18); Gubel, above, 213, fig. 11–2.

354 On Anatolia and Cyprus, see above, Chapter 1.

355 Some of the motifs are clearly Orientalising; note the winged man on F. 28, side C and the sphinx on side D; the rampant goats on either side of a branch on F. 28, side D in Boardman, *IGems*, 127, pl. 15. The love-making scene on Boardman, *IGems*, 127, no. F. 29, side A recalls the similar devices on 24 and 524 from Ayia Irini.

356 The following may also be noted, although reported as 'grey faience':
Amathus T. 25. 21 (Swedish excavations; tomb; CAII); tabloid; L. 0.016 m.
(a) Cypro-syllabic inscription: *pa*-sign (? vertical line with two short, horizontal lines across); (b) device worn: horse and rider (?) (*SCE* 2, 135, no. 21; pl. 29, no. 4).

357 E.g., S. Sophocleous, *Atlas des représentations chypro-archaiques des divinités* (Göteborg, 1985), pl. 3. 8, 4. 1–3.

358 Cf. the boar with bristing mane to Boardman, *AGGems*, pl. 36, no. 537; 540; 546; 554.

359 H. H. von der Osten, 'Altorientalische Siegelsteine', *Med. Bull.* 1 (1961), 35, no. 28 (tabloid with lion and bucranium) may be Bronze Age in date.

360 Possibly Cypriot also is Brandt, *AGDS* 1, no. 109 (Munich A. 1301; agate scarab; two seated figures facing each other, each with one arm raised, in front of an incense burner).

361 A. Conan Doyle, 'The Adventure of the Noble Bachelor'.

362 For Near Eastern examples, see, e.g., M. Shuval, 'A Catalogue of Early Iron Stamp-Seals from Israel' in O. Keel *et al.*, *Studien zu den Stempelsiegeln aus Palastina/ Israel* 3 (Freiburg and Gottingen, 1990), 103. On the rare appearance of scorpions in Greek glyptic art, see Boardman, *IGems*, 47.

363 But cf. from Mesopotamia W. Andrae, *Die Jüngeren Ischtar-Tempel in Assur* (Leipzig, 1935), Taf. 45.

364 *Cf.* Culican, 'Iconography', 98–100 = *id.*, *Opera*, 259–61; *id.*, 'Seals in Bronze Mounts' *RSF* 5 (1977) = *id.*, *Opera*, 529; Buchanan and Moorey, *Ashmolean* 3, 40 with references.

365 For conoids, note, e.g., *SCE* 2, 771, no. 2689 (Ayia Irini); 550, no. 643; no. 645 (Idalion). Zwierlein-Diehl, *AGDS* 2, 61, no. 121, a haematite conoid purchased in Beirut but classified as Cypriot of the eighth or seventh century is probably earlier in date. For cylinder seals, see, e.g., two serpentine cylinder-seals of the late second millennium from Ayia Irini period 4: *SCE* 2, 730, no. 1550; 773, no. 2752; pl. 243, no.20–1. Note also *SCE* 2, 542, no. 369; 540, no. 390 (Idalion); *SCE* 3, 98–9, no. 160 (Vouni).

366 Tabloid: *SCE* 2, 771, no. 2661; pl. 243, no. 12 (period 6, black serpentine; L. 0.010 m. W. 0.005 m. H. 0.012 m.; (a) seated figure in long robe; linear border; (b) bucranium; circle above; three drillings; linear border; (c) and (d) circled dot; line on either side). Rectangular stamp: ibid., 710, no. 1119; pl. 243, no. 11 (period 4; black serpentine; L. 0.019 m. W. 0.018 m. H. 0.018 m.; bucranium; disc above with two drillings on the side; animal below; double linear border); cf. a stamp said to be from Erimi: Nicosia 1935. v-22. 5 (mottled green serpentine; L. 0.013 m. W. 0.013 m. H. 0.013 m.; heraldic bird; linear border). Note also Ohnefalsch-Richter, *KBH*, 422; pl. 94, no. 12a (tabloid with a striding ox on one side and a bucranium with a disc between its horns on the other) and Walters, *BM Gems*, 42, no. 340; pl. 6 (London 340 = 1900. 5–23. 1; haematite scarab with back marked by central line, traversed by two horizontal ones; legs not cut; L. 0.015 m. W. 0.011 m. H. 0.008 m.; four bucrania arranged in a circle; linear border).

367 On the appearance of seals on Cypriot statuary, see Lagarce (n. 135). For an argument that presupposes a flowering of the Cypriot glyptic industry in the eighth century, if not earlier, see Gubel, 'Cubical Stamps', 195–224; cf. id., 'Phoenician Seals in the Allard Pearson Museum, Amsterdam' *RSF* 16 (1988), 162–3. It has long been seen that glyptics in Cyprus were related to the production of the Cypro-Phoenician metal bowls: Markoe, *Bowls*, 87–9; J. Boardman, 'Cypriot Finger Rings' *BSA* 65 (1970), 8. Markoe has now dated the earliest Cypro-Phoenician bowl to the late ninth or early eighth century (his bowl Cy3) with the sequence ending by the third quarter of the seventh century (Markoe, *Bowls*, 156).

368 On this problem and its bibliography, see J. Boardman, 'Greek Gem Engraving: Archaic to Classical' in C. G. Boulter, ed., *Greek Art, Archaic into Classical* (Leiden, 1985), 84.

369 Boardman, *IGems*, 18–9, 89.

370 Note, e.g., Bordreuil, *Sceaux ouest-sémitiques*, 66, no. 74; 67, no. 75. This seems to be what M. A. Murray called the 'drilled' or 'blob' style in her publication of the seals from Lachish; cf. O. Tufnell, *Lachish* 3 (London, 1953), 370, no. 70–5 (Iron II); 371, no. 96. She also compared 77, a Lyre-Player seal, to her no. 73 from Lachish: Tufnell, above, 363–4; 372; pl. 44.

371 Note, e.g., J. Boardman, 'Cypriot Finger Rings' *BSA* 65 (1970), 8, no. 1, 5–6 for rings with Phoenician devices; 9, no. 11 for a Greek device from nearby Maroni; 12, no. 28 and 41 for local Cypriot versions of Greek models.

372 On the date, see Boardman, *AGGems*, 31, no. 41.

373 Cf. this distribution with the distribution around Cyprus of pottery from Amathus in N. J. Brodie, 'Chemical Characterisation of Early and Middle Iron Age Cypriot Ceramics: A Review' *RDAC* (1998), 20–1.

374 Ayia Irini may possibly have fallen within the territory of Soloi, some twenty-two kilometres further west. See M. J. M. Given, 'Symbols, Power, and the Construction of Identity in the City-Kingdoms of Ancient Cyprus c. 750–312 BC' Ph.D. thesis (Cambridge, 1991), 120. For a history of Lapethos, see Ph. N. Phokaides, *Lapethos: Istoria kai Paradosis* (Nicosia, 1987).

375 O. Masson and M. Sznycer, *Recherches sur les phéniciens à Chypre* (Paris, 1972), 98.

376 Rocchetti (n. 21), 114–6.

377 *SCE* 2, 809.

378 Phoenician pottery: P. M. Bikai, *The Phoenician Pottery of Cyprus* (Nicosia, 1987), 75; Greek pottery: E. Gjerstad, *Greek Geometric and Archaic Pottery Found in Cyprus* (Stockholm, 1977), 29, no. 87; 30, no. 93–102; Rocchetti (n. 21), 109.

379 Str. 14. 6. 3 (683c); Plu. *Sol.* 26; Hdt. 7. 3.

380 R. Meiggs, *The Athenian Empire* (Oxford, 1972), 480; cf. also Ps.-Skyl. 103 on the Greek character of Marion.

381 See below on Marion.

382 Bikai (n. 378), 75, s.v., 'Marion' and 'Ayios Demetrios'.

383 Cf. also above, Chapter 6.

384 See also above, Chapter 4.

385 *SCE* 2, 812.

386 Analysis of haematite cylinder seals at the British Museum suggests that the haematite from Anatolia and North Syria is from a different source to that from Cyprus (information from Dr. D. Collon).

387 L. P. di Cesnola, *Cyprus* (London, 1877), 302–37, and comments by C. W. King in ibid., 353–89; cf. D. Soren and J. James, *Kourion* (New York, 1988), 176–7.

388 Markoe, *Bowls*, 176–7, n. 19; O. Masson, *Cahiers: Centre d'études chypriotes* 1 (1984), 16–25. For other problems connected with the provenance of the Kourion Treasure, note Collon, *BM Cat.* 3, 125.

389 E.g., J. Boardman, 'Cypriot Finger Rings' *BSA* 65 (1970), 8–9, no. 7 (with a Phoenicianising device); no. 9 (with a Greek device); and 12, no. 26 (with a local Cypriot version of a Phoenician motif, treated in a Greek style).

390 E.g., J. L. Benson, *Bamboula at Kourion* (Philadelphia, 1972), 147, no. B1635; note, however, that a rock-crystal conoid is also reported from Moni (Limassol area) in the Late Cypriot period: J. Johnson, *Maroni de Chypre* (Göteborg, 1980), pl. IXL (after pl. 49), no. 254 (? possibly an import from the Kourion area). There is some uncertainty over its actual provenance and the means of its recovery; cf. H. B. Walters, 'On Some Acquisitions of the Mycenaean Age Recently Acquired by the British Museum' *JHS* 17 (1897), 65–6.

391 Greek: e.g., J. Boardman, 'Cypriot Finger Rings' *BSA* 65 (1970), 9, no. 11–3; 12, no. 380–40. Local: ibid., 12–3, no. 31–4, 42, 45, 47, 49.
392 Ibid., 8–9, no. 3.
393 E.g., D. Harris, *The Treasures of the Parthenon and Erechtheion* (Oxford, 1995), 45, no. 6; 51, no. 36–7; 53–6, no. 44–46, 49, 53, 56–8, 61; 94, no. 32–3; 142–3, no. 157–8, 160–4.
394 On a collection of Greek impressions kept by a Near Eastern seal-cutter presumably for reference, see D. Collon, 'A Hoard of Sealings from Ur' in M.-F. Boussac and A. Invernizzi, *Archives et sceaux du monde hellénistique* (Paris, 1996), 65–84.

INDEXES AND CONCORDANCES

Numbers refer to catalogue entries.

INSCRIBED SEALS

MATERIALS

MUSEUMS

Paris
    Bibliothèque Nationale   11, 136, 164, 189, 363, 390, 424, 427, 429, 449–451.
    Louvre   3, 90, 458.
Princeton   52.
Private collection   29, 41, 139.
Stockholm   16, 18–20, 24, 32, 73, 79–81, 149, 150, 173, 179, 201, 203, 218, 219, 222, 231, 247, 310,
    338, 339, 440, 469, 470, 471, 473, 497, 503, 511, 516, 517, 522–524, 526, 531.
Vienna   128.

PROVENANCES

Alakati-Galini Road (northwest Cyprus)   165.
Aleppo (Syria)   412.
Amargeti (Paphos area)   194.
Amathus   4, 5, 13, 46, 89, 101, 126, 140, 166, 167, 171, 172, 195–200, 214, 215, 216, 239, 240, 245,
    246, 251–253, 269, 272, 284–287, 309, 311, 315–317, 326, 327, 336, 344, 345, 352–355, 378–
    380, 406, 425, 433–439, 465, 466, 498–501, 528, 529.
Apostolos Varnavos (Famagusta area)   491.
Arsos   102, 127, 221, 318, 319, 467, 468, 515.
Ayia Irini   14–24, 65, 73–82, 103–108, 135, 148–150, 160, 168, 173–178, 201–204, 217–220, 247,
    254, 255, 273, 310, 312, 320, 321, 328, 337–339, 440 (?), 469–474, 493, 496, 497, 502, 511, 516–
    519, 522–527, 530, 531.
Ayios Dhimitrios (Limassol area)   264.
Beirut   381.
Cyrenaica   136.
Erimi (Limassol area)   274, 275, 441.
Galinoporni (Karpass area)   25.
Golgoi   382.
Idalion   26, 179, 222, 223, 325, 503, 532.
Kalavassos (between Limassol and Larnaka)   442.
Karpass region   90.
Kition   27, 66, 128 (?), 180, 181, 205, 224, 276, 293, 297, 298, 303, 313, 329, 407, 475, 504.
Koupetra (Limassol area)   505.
Kourion   6, 28, 83, 88, 91, 92, 109, 129, 130, 151, 152, 206, 225–230, 241–243, 248, 256, 257, 265,
    277–280, 288–292, 294–296, 300–302, 304, 305, 356, 357, 383–385, 408, 426, 430, 443, 444,
    476, 477, 533.
Lapethos   47, 266.
Lefkoniko   153.
Lysi (Famagusta area)   131.
Mari   132.
Marion   110, 161, 231, 346, 358–360, 386–405, 409–411.
Myrtou-Pigadhes   93.
Paphos   111, 182, 207, 270, 330, 340, 361 (?).
Pera (near Tamassos)   67, 249.
Provenances unknown   1–3, 8–12, 29–45, 48–54, 69–72, 84–87, 94–100, 115–125, 133, 134, 137–
    139, 142–147, 156–159, 162–164, 184–193, 208–213, 234–238, 250, 258–263, 267, 271, 281–
    283, 299, 306, 308, 314, 323, 324, 332–335, 342–343, 347–351, 364–377, 413–424, 428, 429,
    431, 432, 445–464, 480–490, 492, 494, 495, 509, 510, 512–514, 535, 536–543.
Pyrga   7, 55–64, 154, 232, 341, 478, 479, 506, 507.

SHAPES

General Index

Numbers refer to pages.